SEEING ENGLAND

SEEING ENGLAND

Antiquaries, Travellers & Naturalists

Charles Lancaster

NONSUCH

To Rosemary

First published 2008

Nonsuch Publishing
Cirencester Road, Chalford, Stroud, Gloucestershire, GL6 8PE
www.nonsuch-publishing.com

Nonsuch Publishing is an imprint of NPI Media Group

British Library Cataloguing in Publication Data:
A catalogue record for this book is available from the British Library

ISBN 978 1 84588 611 0

Typesetting and origination by NPI Media Group
Printed in Great Britain

Contents

Acknowledgements

I would like to express my gratitude to the scholars who inspired and supported me during my mature-age studies at the University of Western Australia and the University of Notre Dame Australia: Patricia Crawford, Philippa Maddern, Iain Brash, and Catherine Kovesi. I would like to thank certain scholars in England who, in 1998, invited me to call on them and discuss my PhD thesis: Graham Parry of the University of York, Richard Cust of the University of Birmingham, and Jan Broadway, now of Queen Mary University of London. I would like particularly to thank Simon Hamlet, of Nonsuch Publishing, for his advice and assistance in the preparation of this work for publication.

I have acknowledged organisations which have allowed me to use images from works in their care in the captions to the illustrations. I am grateful for the generous and ready assistance offered by the staff of the libraries from which I have obtained these images: the Chatsworth Photo Library, the Wiltshire County Library, the Cornwall County Library, the Warwickshire County Library, the Hertfordshire County Library, the Cumbria County Library, the Oxfordshire County Library, the Hereford Cathedral Library and the Guildhall Library, London.

Most of all I am grateful to my wife Rosemary, my companion in everything, for her encouragement, criticism, and love.

Editorial Note

In transcribing the texts of these readings, I have tried to retain the early modern conventions and vagaries of spelling, punctuation, and usage of fonts. In the interests of giving the reader a slightly more familiar experience, however, I have modernised the use of 'i' and 'j' and of 'u' and 'v', I have used 'the' in place of 'ye', 'that' in place of 'yt', and have expanded such abbreviations as 'wch'. I have not used blackletter, usually replacing it with italics, although in the case of those authors, such as Dugdale, who consistently used italics for personal names and blackletter for place names, I have used italics and bold respectively.

Introduction

Concerning the Soyle: It is for the most part, chalkie, though the upper cruste in the South and West parts, be for the most part of redde earth mixed with gravell, which yet by reason of the white marle under it, yeeldeth good wheat and oates: But of it owne nature most enclined to wood, and coupisses, affording also faire wayes. In the North part of the Shire, as in the hundreds of *Hitche*, and *Oddesey*, the soyle is very apt to yeeld corne, and dertie wayes, especially that part which is accompted parcell of a vayle called of the countrie men the *vayle* of *Ring-tayle* or *Wring-tayle* or rather *Ringdale*, which extendeth it selfe also into *Cambridg-shire*. And affordeth no small store of wheat and malte towards the provision of *London*.

John Norden, 1598, describing Hertfordshire

This parish hath severall lands belonging thereunto, to be imployed to pious uses, *viz. Henry Parson*, and *William* his sonne, 13°. *Junii* 22°. *Edw*. 4. conveyed (to their use for ever) a messuage and acre of land (which messuage was of late times called the *Church house*, and adjoyneth to the Church-yard) the rent thereof, and of the land thereunto, is imployed towards reparation of the Church, and upon part of the land was erected an Almeshouse (which is imployed for the use of the poore of this Parish) and in the close of the said messuage, is another house, usually called the *Sexton's house*, the same having been, for about sixty years past, used for the habitation of the Sexton of this Parish, and these messuages and lands are enjoyed accordingly.

Richard Kilburne, 1659, describing Hawkhurst, Kent

But 'tis more remarkable still, how great a Part of these Downs comes, by a new Method of Husbandry, not only to be made arable, but to bear plentiful Crops of Wheat, tho' never known to our Ancestors to be capable of such a Thing; nay, they would probably have laughed at any one that had gone about to plough up the wild Downs and Hills, which they thought only fit for Sheep-walks; but Experience has made the present Age wiser, and more skilful in Husbandry; for only by folding the Sheep upon those Lands, after they are turn'd up with the Plough, (which generally goes within Three or Four Inches of solid Rock of Chalk) they become abundantly fruitful, and bear very good Wheat, as well as Rye and Barley.

Daniel Defoe, 1722, describing Salisbury Plain

Among the singularities of this place the two rocky hollow lanes, the one to *Alton*, and the other to the forest, deserve our attention. These roads, running through the malm lands, are, by the traffic of ages, and the fretting of water, worn down through the first stratum of our freestone, and partly through the second; so that they look more like water-courses than roads; and are bedded with naked *rag* for furlongs together. In many places they are reduced sixteen or eighteen feet beneath the level of the fields; and after floods, and in frosts, exhibit very grotesque and wild appearances, from the tangled roots that are twisted among the strata, and from the torrents rushing down their broken sides; and especially when those cascades are frozen into icicles, hanging in all the fanciful shapes of frost-work. These rugged gloomy scenes affright the ladies when they peep down into them from the paths above, and make timid horsemen shudder while they ride along them; but delight the naturalist with their various botany, and particularly with their curious *filices* with which they abound.

Gilbert White, 1789, describing Selborne, Hampshire

We see in different ways. We see by looking, but we also see without consciously looking. On returning to a place inhabited earlier in life, for example, we recognise not only the landmarks and features, but also the background landscape, the part of the scene which we never really noticed. When seventeenth-century writers described places in England, they gave details about whatever they deemed most significant about the place, and this did not usually include the background scenery. But they were not unaware of this background, and occasionally it emerged in their writing: a glimpse, an impression, perhaps something more. A writer reports consciously that which has been observed, and in an incidental way that of which he or she is aware by familiarity. In this collection, extracts containing remarks which, to a greater or lesser degree, describe scenes—either the landscapes of places or features of the landscape—have been taken from the works of certain seventeenth- and eighteenth-century antiquaries, travellers, and naturalists whose purpose was place description.

Over the course of the two hundred years in which these writers were active, the English landscape was seen and described in very different ways. The four passages quoted above, each describing a place in England, might serve to illustrate this statement. Yet it could justifiably be asked whether the authors were attempting to describe landscape at all, or, indeed, at least for the first two, whether they had a concept which would correspond to the idea of landscape as we understand it now.[1] The first, written by John Norden, is from a topographical county survey and concentrates only on salient features, without any close detail. The passage by Richard Kilburne is from a county survey whose chief concerns are tenancy and genealogy: the county is seen only as consisting of properties. Six decades later, Defoe is writing an immediate and personal account, based on his own travels, in which the county is a lively society. Instead of boundaries, names, and dates drawn from documents, we are amongst the opinions and talk of people and learning something of their lives. Another sixty-odd years and we find, in Gilbert White's description of Selborne, images of the landscape so vivid that we are conscious of the writer in the act of seeing; as well, we become aware of his lively interest in people and society, and the varied responses people may have to the landscape—and all this in an account of his investigations into the natural world as he found it in his parish.

In spite of the differences, each of these accounts may be read as a landscape of a type, whether rural, urban, or social. The early modern passages offered in this book are mainly from works which were written with the express purpose of describing places in England, including early topographical or, more correctly, chorographical county and town surveys,[2] some other types of seventeenth-century antiquarian literature, and finally, looking ahead, descriptions which were not specifically antiquarian, like Gilbert White's, and with which readers in the twenty-first century may feel more familiar. As well as illustrating the different ways town and country England might be seen, they describe country estates, streets, markets, churches, games, megalithic monuments, and scenery wild and gentle. But to begin, some remarks should be made about antiquarian writing, and for this purpose we will consider one of the most celebrated examples of its time.

The Antiquities of Warwickshire, which appeared in 1656, was a description written by William Dugdale of the county in which he was born, lived, and had his estate. Dugdale had searched for and collected detailed information over a period of about twenty years, and the resulting work was a daunting volume of some 800 folio pages of close printing. That it was an undertaking of such industry and dedication suggests that his feelings for his county were both proud and affectionate, and that his descriptive words and phrases should betray these feelings. And no more than a cursory scan of his text is sufficient not only to show this to be the case, but also to reveal the special direction of his admiration. But in the whole of his detailed textual traversal of Warwickshire, Dugdale scarcely used the adjective 'beautiful'.[3] Adjectives which he used much more frequently included 'noble', 'ancient', and 'honourable', consistent with the point of view of a gentleman writing for the class of people who owned land and who belonged to families of long and noteworthy standing. Therefore we may expect, instead of reading about hills and valleys, forests and fields, villages and farms, and of the buildings and views in which they consist, to encounter family lineages and histories of tenancies; instead of the architecture and decoration of church buildings and monastic remains, we read of charters and bequests, of the patrons and incumbents of livings, of obits and funeral monuments. The Warwickshire scene which Dugdale saw was indeed quite particular, and was different from that which other observers, in different times and with different attitudes, might have seen when they looked upon the same set of objects. The word 'antiquities' in the title of his book suggests immediately the selectiveness of his view: he sees that which is honourable and praiseworthy, that which can be perceived to be comparable with the remains of classical times. It was in these terms that he framed his description.[4]

Such county surveys were written primarily for readers who were themselves members of the families that were the subject-matter of the books. They were the subscribers who funded the printing, they contributed plates depicting their country houses or family tombs, they gave the authors access to their 'evidences'—arms, charters, seals—and it was their ancestors whose exploits and titles were the matter of the historical narratives. The resulting book was a celebration of the gentry and an assertion of the place of gentry families in society. Amid the political uncertainties of the mid-seventeenth century, the county survey became moreover a means of preserving the fragile memorials of ancestors, for printed books, unlike stained-glass windows and marble gravestones, could not be smashed or defaced, and enjoyed the security of existing in numerous copies. And for the same reason they could better serve as evidence in future litigation when title to arms or land was contested.

The writing of place descriptions, whether historical or topographical, or with regard to sovereignty and tenancy of lands, was one of the main endeavours in which antiquaries were engaged. The modern counterparts of their works would perhaps be travel books, visitors' guides, municipal directories, year books; all of which, to a greater or lesser extent and in one way or another, tell what a place looks like. Depending on purpose and intended readership, some such books will give prominence to the beauty of the place being described, others will give mainly factual data and statistics. The antiquaries, however, might be expected to provide both of these aspects of a place description, because as well as giving factual details, they were also, usually, extolling the superior resources, achievements, and desirability of the place. And amongst the attributes to be praised one would expect some account to be given of the landscape: its highlights and its unique features. But, in most cases, this is not so. For it is a very particular attribute of a place which predominates the antiquarian scene: this quality most earnestly sought is *antiquity*, whether in the place, in its name, in its buildings, or in the people and events of its past.

The dates of the antiquarian extracts in this book range from 1576, when the first early modern county survey was published, to 1777. Most are taken from works whose stated purpose was to describe a county, a town, or a parish, or, in the case of William Camden, who could also be described as a traveller, the nation as a whole. Some of the antiquarian authors, such as John Aubrey and Robert Plot, could also be described as natural historians, encompassing a broader range of interests than the more prevalent gentry-oriented subject-matter of which Dugdale's book is an example. Surveying the works of this genre through the seventeenth century, it is possible to see a development from one decade to the next, but that development is neither consistent nor chronological. Of course, this is not at all surprising: a review of so many years of observing and writing should indeed produce a variety of ways of seeing England. Every writer has individual notions of the goals of the writing, the expected readership, and the purposes for which readers will read. But in antiquarian writing about England the constant reference to the *past* is ubiquitous: descriptions of places begin with their histories; families and estates are traced back, preferably to Domesday Book, or, failing that, as far as possible; placenames are analysed etymologically to determine their origins; earlier authorities are called upon in examining natural phenomena.

While this historical predilection is evident in all the antiquaries' works, it may not be immediately apparent in every one of the scenes presented in this collection. This is an editorial consequence of the chosen extracts having been selected primarily for their descriptive content, so that they are not always typical of the whole works from which they were drawn. But the historical element is usually present to some degree, and, in many cases, especially in the type of writing of which Dugdale's survey of Warwickshire is typical, it is not possible to find a single descriptive passage which does not primarily offer an historical point of view. It must also be said that much of what antiquarian works contain, while once of intense interest to certain contemporary readers, is now of value only to historical researchers. The present-day reader must hunt through pages of data to find those more lively interludes which give some glimpse of the background against which the transactions are made, the successions realised, the battles fought, the laws enacted. And it is in such interludes that we might see what the writer saw, and his words might betray his feelings as he wrote. But, if we are to judge by these extracts, the evocation of sensibilities on seeing the landscape is not readily discernible in descriptive writing during the seventeenth century, and it is the somewhat erratic emergence of the personal response that will be one of the more interesting features of the sequence of documents covered in this survey. In the latter section of the book are presented a few contrasting extracts of genres which emerged out of the antiquarian tradition: also descriptions of places in England, they have more focussed views and more specific purposes. Antiquarian research was their precursor, and in it their beginnings may be discerned.

The seventeenth-century antiquarian authors of county surveys were members of a scholarly profession which has no corresponding counterpart in our own times, the nearest approach to it being in the use of the adjective 'antiquarian' applied to old or rare books which are collected, bought, or sold. The obsolescence of a profession is intriguing, for it casts some light on our understanding of the needs of a past society and its differences from our own. Antiquarianism was, in the sixteenth and seventeenth centuries, a sophisticated and arcane field of learning which found application in dealing with any of a wide range of interests. In general, antiquaries sought origins: of institutions, of laws, of names, of families, of estates. Their source materials were manuscripts, seals, coins, monuments, epitaphs, representations of arms in stained-glass windows and on tombs. Many had studied or were practising law, or else were gentlemen writing genealogical records of their ancestry, and therefore antiquaries were able to offer a very pertinent service to a particular sector of the population: those who owned land. They were frequently called upon in support of litigation, and their services were especially in demand after the dissolution of the monasteries in the later years of the reign of King Henry VIII: a far-reaching redistribution of property had taken place, and many landowners found it necessary to seek evidence of their title to lands which were held on the basis of ancestry.

The type of antiquarian research which developed in the sixteenth and seventeenth centuries in England is generally thought to have begun in Renaissance Italy with the work of Flavio Biondo.[5] It is well known that one of the characteristics of early humanist thought was the admiration of classical civilization, with an associated concern to recover its remains from ruin. Biondo documented the remains in a geographical framework, producing early examples of what came to be known as chorography.[6] Essentially this referred to the description of either or both of the natural and civil history of a particular place by following through the various locations in some systematic manner. By this means, local features which provided evidence of natural or past phenomena or events could be discussed. Some writers classified chorography according to the nature of the place being surveyed, so as to distinguish it from other methodologies such as cosmography, geography and topography.[7] Although the chorographical form came to prominence at this time, it was not new, and moreover it was adopted into humanist scholarship, not invented by it. Medieval examples which were known in England included the works of Gerald of Wales, William of Worcester, and John Rous.[8]

The pursuit of antiquarian knowledge, like so many other types of learning, spread from Italy to other parts of Europe in the fifteenth and sixteenth centuries. In England this development coincided with the somewhat reluctant debate, which began in the first half of the sixteenth century, about the veracity of the traditional account of the history of Britain, the 'Brut', which had originally been written comprehensively four hundred years earlier by Geoffrey of Monmouth.[9] It was becoming evident to scholars who were reading literature by Continental authors that this ancient history was discordant with those being written in Italy and France. Indeed it was an expatriate Italian scholar, Polydore Vergil, whose more detached and critical view of English history precipitated its re-examination.[10] The growing consciousness of England as a prominent identity in the world, under the Tudor regime, stimulated the desire to discover anew the remains of England's past, both in documents and in artefacts. The first major attempt to undertake such a work in the sixteenth century was an ambitious one whose author endeavoured to embrace the nation as a whole. He was John Leland, who had been commissioned in 1533 by Henry VIII to search monastic libraries for ancient documents, although the motives which prompted this task are not entirely clear.[11] His vast project, which was to have included a detailed topographical description and maps of England and Wales, was never brought to completion, although his notes, compiled during years of travel through the country, served as valuable source material for antiquaries in decades to come.

Leland's view was conservative: he was fervently patriotic, so that his work was to have been a celebration of the Tudor state, so much the better for an heroic history. Kendrick said of him that he had 'in spite of his Renaissance upbringing, a medieval mind'[12], suggesting that there were anomalies in his critical evaluation of sources, such that certain legendary figures were accorded historical status. It is, nevertheless, evident that Leland's work was the beginning of a new approach in English scholarship, for he initiated, in his own age, the chorographical methodology for antiquarianism, he used observation as a tool for research, and he highlighted the wealth of manuscripts that could be used as historical sources. His name occurs frequently in the footnotes of authors of the seventeenth century. Above all, his work was the inspiration for a plan by Elizabethan antiquaries to develop a description of all the counties. William Lambarde was the author of the first of these, devoted to Kent.

It was not until fifty years after his death that the goal to which Leland had aspired was attained. William Camden's *Britannia*, printed in 1586, was the first comprehensive description of the whole country; it became a model for antiquarian research, both in terms of its subject-matter and its methods. It was also the first historical study of England in which the country's classical past was examined. Camden was in touch with European humanist scholarship, and he was aware of new approaches which had been taken to the historical and geographical framing of nationhood. His project was the investigation of the remains of the past in order to understand British origins—of places, customs, institutions, names. His chorographical methodology was inspired not only by Leland, whose notes he used, but also by the Flemish cartographer Abraham Ortelius.[13] The particular past to which his attention was directed was the Roman past, the era before which he did not believe it was possible to go with any certainty.[14] Camden's work became so well known that it was a precedent which all succeeding antiquaries would have had in mind. Indeed, their footnotes show that they used it frequently as a source, thus according it significant scholarly standing.

Britannia was not, however, Camden's only contribution to the development of English antiquarianism; he was one of the founders of the Elizabethan Society of Antiquaries, at about the same time as his great book first appeared.[15] This group of up to twenty-four scholars, lawyers and administrative officials met regularly to exchange ideas on topics relevant to the English past. Their activities continued until early in the reign of King James I, when they suddenly ceased. This was possibly a result of royal disapproval, since the topical emphasis had moved from topography, titles and institutions to religion, law and parliament, and the flavour of the discussions had drifted from antiquity to politics.[16] One of the most important contributors to the society's proceedings was Robert Cotton, one of Camden's pupils.[17] He also made available to his fellow antiquaries his extensive library, which became one of the most valuable English antiquarian resources of the seventeenth century.[18] The growth of libraries and the development of antiquarian research went hand in hand, for collections of manuscripts were the most necessary resource. Other significant collections were those of John Selden and of Corpus Christi College, Cambridge, home of the manuscripts which were collected in the sixteenth century by Matthew Parker, Queen Elizabeth's first Archbishop of Canterbury.[19]

Genealogical county surveys and histories of families and estates constituted only a small segment of the range of works that English antiquarian scholars were producing in the seventeenth century. With the benefit of the accumulation of manuscripts and books begun by John Leland and continued with great industry by Matthew Parker and others, editions of ancient documents, as well as surveys and investigations of pre-Conquest inhabitants and institutions, derived primarily from the study of such documents, were now being printed.[20] Some idea of the variety of antiquarian investigation is indicated by a small sample of titles from the period: John Selden's *Jani Anglorum Facies Altera* (1610), on the history of English law; his *Titles of Honour* (1614); his *De Diis Syriis* (1617), a study of Middle Eastern deities in biblical times; his *History of Tithes* (1618); James Ussher's history of the British church, *Britannicarum Ecclesiarum Antiquitates* (1639) and his *Annales Veteris et Novi Testamenti* (1650–54), an historical commentary on the Bible; Henry Spelman's history of church councils, *Concilia, Decreta, Leges, Constitutiones in Re Ecclesarium Orbis Britannici* (1639); Thomas Fuller's *Church History of Britain* (1655); William Burton's *Commentary on Antoninus his Itinerary* (1658); and William Somner's Anglo-Saxon dictionary (1659).

The business of collecting, classifying, and interpreting the remains of the past was not the same as that of the historian, who was also concerned with the past but who had different goals in dealing with it. Through the Middle Ages there had been numerous chroniclers, whose narratives simply recounted reigns and events as they happened, year by year, and these compilations of data were indeed somewhat akin to antiquarian collections, in that their authors had not sought to understand the underlying causes and effects. The writing of real history demanded analysis of the past, enabling the writer to develop a narrative informed by some sort of understanding of the motives for and outcomes of the words and actions of the people whose lives and deeds it recounted. Its value was primarily didactic: history offered an extension, back into the past, of living human experience, from which we might learn and benefit. This was relevant especially for leaders, for history was made by the heads of nations, of churches, of armies, of monasteries. It is not surprising, then, that history was primarily written as material for the moral instruction of those who would become princes and generals, and that most histories dealt with the reigns of particular monarchs. Writers of history often sought to maximise the moral significance of events by having the historical protagonists deliver speeches which would seemingly have been appropriate, or by modifying details such as numbers of soldiers in armies.

Over the course of the sixteenth century, intellectual change in England was to a considerable extent precipitated by the introduction of the ideas which are now referred to as Renaissance humanism. In particular, historical methodology was influenced by the model of the classical historian Thucydides, demanding a new paradigm of accuracy and truth, to the extent that the only reliable source of data was the eyewitness. Such a position would have impossible consequences, not the least of which was that history about the more distant past could not be written. Here, then, was a part for antiquaries to play, for they could support history-writing by providing, from their collected remains of the past, sources of information comparable in their veracity with eyewitness accounts. The knowledge discovered by the antiquaries was the raw material for the revelation of wisdom by the historians. It was inevitable that antiquarian scholarship would come to be thought of as inferior, as Thomas Blundeville remarked in 1574 in his treatise on history-writing: '… I can not tell whyther I may deryde, or rather pittie the great follie of those which having consumed all theyr lyfe tyme in hystories, doe know nothing in the ende, but the discents, genealoges, and petygrees, of noble men, and when such a King or Emperour raigned, & such lyke stuffe …'[21]

While histories were narrations, an antiquary had less need for eloquence and rhetoric, and could present his information in such basic forms as lists, tables, and transcripts of documents. Fortunately few confined their treatises to so bald a presentation, and sought instead a more engaging and readable style. The first work from which we present an extract is *A Perambulation of Kent*, by William Lambarde, and this is an excellent example of the approach which antiquaries were to take in describing places in England: Lambarde's was the first topographical survey for a very long time, and it was taken as a model for humanist county surveys for years to come. Apart from the fact that his work was the first of its type, Lambarde was influential because it was his stated desire that books should be written about all the counties, so that *A Perambulation of Kent* would be the beginning of an illustrious description of the whole of England. At the time, Lambarde's friend William Camden was working on his description of the whole nation, *Britannia*, which was finished in 1586, ten years after the appearance of the survey of Kent.

Following the chorographical methodology, the reader of one of these works is taken from place to place and is given an historical account at each of the stops. The information provided might include any or all of the origins of the placename, the earliest establishment of the manor or whatever other seat of power that might be or have been there, references to relevant Domesday Book records, the lineal descent of the successive occupying families, patrons and beneficiaries of the living of the local parish church, and accounts of great events which occurred either at the place or which involved members of the families of the local lords. Prior to all this, the book would usually offer some more general data applicable to the county as a whole, such as important physical attributes, as well as administrative details: lists of members of parliament, sheriffs, mayors of cities, incumbents of bishoprics, and divisions into hundreds and parishes. It can readily be seen that such a scheme does not leave much room for describing the landscape, but elements of this may be found in the outlines of physical attributes or even in the passages on particular places. In Lambarde's general description of Kent, where the features of the county are treated in turn with concision and purpose, the language is impersonal and rhetorical:

> In fertile and fruitfull woodes and trees, this Country is most florishing also, whether you respect the mast of Oke, Beeche and Chesten for cattaile: or the fruit of Apples, Peares, Cherries, and Plums for men: for besides great store of oke and beeche, it hath whole woodes that beare Chestnutt, a mast (if I may so call it, and not rather a fruite, whereof even delicate persons disdaine not to feede) not commonly seene in other countries: But as for Ortchards of Apples, and Gardeins of Cheries, and those of the most delicious and exquisite kindes that can be, no part of the Realme (that I know) hath them, either in such quantitie and number, or with such arte and industrie, set and planted.[22]

This is descriptive in a very limited way: it does not in fact describe any particular place, but gives only a general impression of a type of landscape one might expect to encounter in Kent. Yet William Lambarde himself is not entirely absent from this text, which faintly betrays his contentment and pride in his own part of England.

Lambarde's hope that his study of Kent would be an example for others to write about their own counties was the beginning of an engagement, by several chorographical antiquaries, in the daunting task of describing their nation. Camden's *Britannia* was an attempt to embrace all of the country, John Norden took up Lambarde's challenge, himself writing about a number of counties, and, early in the seventeenth century, John Speed was the author of an ambitious cartographical project, presenting the nation and all its counties in maps.[23] It was a period of national awareness, promoted by the emergence of England under the Tudor monarchy as a power in Europe, but searching for an identity which could be anchored to a heritage in antiquity.

By the end of the reign of Elizabeth I, the sense of nationhood in England was reinforced both in the light of having resisted the threats of the Catholic Church and of Spain, and with the advent of the Stuart monarchy and the concomitant union with Scotland. But a generation later, a new menace began to develop with the growing antagonism between Crown and Parliament. Even before the outbreak of civil war in 1642, there were tensions at many levels: between institutions of government, between classes of citizens, between adherents of differing religious practices. It was a time of iconoclasm and 'levelling', of political engagement and social change, its violent end being a world 'turned upside down'.[24] Those most threatened were the nobility and gentry, the traditional holders of political and social power and of wealth and influence. The writers of descriptions and histories of places in the nation were of this group, and in these works the dominant concern became the documentation of title and heritage. This is why books such as Dugdale's study of Warwickshire are almost wholly genealogical, creating a permanent record, in the form of a published book, of the marble epitaphs and glass depictions of family coats-of-arms whose future preservation had become so precarious. As well, such texts, resolutely located in another, better time, nostalgically recaptured for their readers what Dugdale called 'those flourishing Ages past'.[25] *The Antiquities of Warwickshire* was not the first book of its type, but it was the culmination of a development and the most perfectly realised example. Its predecessors were Samson Erdeswicke's *Survey of Staffordshire* (1593–1603), which was not published during its author's lifetime, an early edition of it being produced by Dugdale himself; John Stow's *Survay of London* (1598), a vivid description of the late Elizabethan city; William Burton's *Description of Leicester Shire* (1632); and another town survey, William Somner's *Antiquities of Canterbury* (1640).

In the middle years of the seventeenth century, another type of observation of England became apparent. This had an investigative agenda which was part of a revival of scientific thinking and was consistent with the methodology of Francis Bacon.[26] At the heart of the Baconian system was a principle which has been accepted without question ever since: that to find out about the world, it was necessary to observe it, and to know the truth of conjecture, it was necessary to experiment. Moreover, it came to be inherent in scientific methodology that knowledge did not have to be certain, as given by divine revelation or deduced by logic, but could be developed with increasing degrees of probability, by collecting numerous instances of confirmation and inducing a conclusion. Using such intellectual tools, antiquarian research could address natural history as well as civic history, and new fields of knowledge could be explored. Robert Plot, author of *The Natural History of Oxfordshire* (1677) and *The Natural History of Staffordshire* (1686) was a pioneer of studies which would now be classified as botany, zoology, geology, meteorology, and agronomy; John Aubrey, who wrote much but published little (his most interesting work, *Monumenta Britannica,* was not in print till 1982), was an early systematic investigator of archaeology and anthropology. In both cases, however, the maturity of their work does not really warrant the application of these names, belonging as they do to disciplines of a later age. But it was a major advance: when Dugdale investigated the origin of barrows, he relied for his evidence on the writings of previous, even Roman, observers; Aubrey, doing the same thing, went out and made measurements.

The second half of the seventeenth century was the time of a proliferation of intellectual endeavours: mathematics, astronomy, physics, chemistry, anatomy, medicine; it was the time of the Royal Society and of a growing fascination with scientific experimentation. Part of this was 'natural history', the term used to describe the study of all that which is to be found in the world around us, but which could not readily be attributed to people. Its objects were soils, rivers, rocks, plants, animals, meteorological phenomena, and the more inexplicable phenomena, such as fossils and megalithic monuments. With this last item we are again investigating the past, for it was understood that dolmens, standing stones and barrows were ancient, but that their history was apparently unwritten. In the observation and speculation on the origins of such ancient monuments, natural history and history merged, and knowledge of the world could be driven further and further back into the past. This was mysterious territory indeed, for it was understood that, as Bishop Ussher had demonstrated in 1650, the Creation had taken place in 4004 BC,[27] so that exploration so far back in time made a significant approach to that awesome event.

The urge to discover more about the world naturally led to keener observation of the landscape, and this is evident in the texts of the time. But in the works of the exemplars included here (Robert Plot, John Aubrey and Thomas Browne), the landscape remains in the background, it is certain particulars within it which are being seen, and there is little more recognition of its qualities than there was in the genealogical studies of honour and tenure. At the same time as scholars were examining parts of the country to learn about nature, many continued to produce studies of estates and landed families, although in the early eighteenth century there was a perceptible change of emphasis from the manor to the parish. Robert

Thoroton's *Antiquities of Nottinghamshire* (1677), James Wright's *History and Antiquities of the County of Rutland* (1684), and Henry Chauncy's *Historical Antiquities of Hertfordshire* (1700) are all modelled on William Dugdale's survey of Warwickshire. With Robert Atkyns's *Ancient and Present State of Glostershire* (1712) the subject is, as the title suggests, as much the present as the past, and the more extensive examination of parishes broadens the scope from the gentry to the wider community.

Of these several surveys, the present collection includes, besides an extract from Dugdale's *Warwickshire*, only one other, an example from Chauncy's *Hertfordshire*, these two being offered as representatives of the genealogical approach.[28] The second, updated, edition of Dugdale's description of Warwickshire, produced in 1730 by William Thomas, was a financial failure, suggesting that there was a declining demand for folio tomes enumerating county estates and families. The selected eighteenth-century antiquarian descriptions include readings from Francis Drake's magisterial *Eboracum*, a study of York, which appeared in 1736, and a very different piece, describing Yorkshire scenery, which is from a travel guide written by the antiquary William Bray in 1777. The former is a detailed and scholarly examination of the city as municipality, archdiocese and site of Roman remains, while the other, taken from the *Sketch of a Tour in Derbyshire and Yorkshire*, is a new genre and an example of a later direction in antiquarian writing.

This book is about written description, but in considering landscape scenes, it is pictorial art which comes firstly to mind, and some mention should be made of its part. Prior to the end of the Tudor period, the depiction of landscape is scarcely encountered in English painting, except when it constitutes a background in a portrait. The work usually credited to be the first English landscape is that known as *Wedding at Bermondsey*,[29] and the genre did not develop until the seventeenth century, and then only in the hands of certain visiting Dutch artists, especially Anthony Van Dyck. Another continental artist, who stayed in England and did considerable work for antiquaries, including William Dugdale, Thomas Fuller, Inigo Jones, and Elias Ashmole, was the etcher Wenceslaus Hollar, who came from Prague in 1636 in the service of Thomas Howard, Earl of Arundel. Hollar's best-known works now are his spectacular views of London from the south bank of the Thames, executed at various times both before and after the Great Fire of 1666. These are valuable historically, as are his views of the interior and exterior of St Paul's Cathedral before it was destroyed in that same disaster: his images are the only record of the great building. His etchings of scenes at Albury, the Earl of Arundel's seat in Surrey, are tranquil, nostalgic images which are utterly unlike contemporaneous antiquarian descriptions, recording neither events nor dates nor names, but only the perception of beauty in still waters, reflections of trees, and clouds above. These were perhaps more personal works, intended not as records and not undertaken for commission. If we are to judge by the remarks made variously by John Aubrey and Elias Ashmole when they had viewed collections of paintings, it would seem that the main function of pictorial art was deemed to be portraiture—the creating of likenesses of famous and powerful people—and the illustration of stories from classical mythology.[30]

As from the first half of the eighteenth century, there was huge diversification in the writing of the landscape, and the second group of selections given here is intended to do no more than show some of the directions to which antiquarian scholarship eventually led. The authors are the solitary traveller Celia Fiennes, the novelist and social commentator Daniel Defoe, the archaeologist William Borlase, the aesthetic tourist William Gilpin, and the naturalist Gilbert White. In their several ways, these observers attend specifically to the landscape so that it becomes a subject of enquiry itself: the background to which writers a hundred or so years before had been indifferent becomes the predominant component of what is seen. These are manifestations of the tandem cultivation of scientific research, which has been remarked upon above, and of sensibility to natural beauty, which were almost contiguous in the time-frame of their development.

Certainly there was at this time a consciousness of the landscape which led people to become aware, when seeing it, of such qualities as fecundity, beauty, mystery, power or desolateness. This is a sensibility which is familiar, for it has remained with us ever since, and there is no reason to suppose that it had not been a normal part of people's perception of the world in earlier times, but prior to the eighteenth century it seems not to have been given expression in everyday descriptive accounts of places. Even when feelings evoked by nature are evident in earlier poetry and paintings, it is not as the subject of the work but as the backdrop. By the mid-eighteenth century this had changed: landscape scenes were becoming subjects for painting, they were being celebrated in poetry, and people were travelling away from their homes to seek them out. And moreover these scenic qualities, which are not empirical but are apprehended by human sentiment, came to be evident in descriptions which were written not to be poetical, but just to be informative. The response to nature became spontaneous instead of cerebral.

There were two important influences in the genesis of this development. The classical emphasis in literary education had made people familiar with the works of Horace and Virgil, both of whose poetry included pastoral episodes which invoked an idyllic Golden Age in which everyone enjoyed a peaceful existence in harmony with the natural world. In response to this came a tendency to associate real scenery with poetic imagery and a wistful contemplation of achieving the pleasures of a pastoral life by escaping into the countryside. As well, the eighteenth-century institution of the Grand Tour afforded those who were fortunate enough to participate in this indulgence the chance to enjoy the classical landscapes in reality, as they visited Italy, France, and the Alps. Travellers who desired to return to England with tangible memories of the evocative scenes they had experienced could purchase paintings by such artists as Claude Lorrain, Gaspard Dughet, and Salvator Rosa.[31] Naturally the influx of this art had an influence, and landscape painting in England began to be valued more highly. At the same time there was a growing desire to seek such scenery at home, and travel to the more promising parts, such as the mountains of Wales, the highlands of Scotland, and the Lake District of northern England, began to become more popular.

There came, then, to be a new awareness of country scenery in which it was associated firstly with classical art and subsequently with vernacular art as painters increasingly produced local landscapes—especially in Gothic and Celtic traditions—comparable with those of the Italian masters. The aesthetic pursuit in this art was to capture the feelings termed the 'Beautiful' and the 'Sublime', which could not be apprehended by reason but by the imagination. Beauty was attractive and reassuring, while the Sublime was terrifying and powerful; Beauty was evoked by green meadows, calm waters and country cottages, the Sublime by towering mountains, waterfalls, and ruined castles. This was art which refrained from making moral or social statements, hence the relative unimportance of figures in the landscape. It was also art which invited travel into the countryside in order to experience the source of the art and to enjoy the comforting pleasure of the Beautiful and the 'pleasing melancholy' and 'agreeable horror' of the Sublime. This striking focus on seeing the landscape is in marked contrast to the general indifference with which it had usually been treated in earlier times. It was analysed, sketched, described, and extolled in poetry as people 'discovered' it and made it one of the most significant objects of their travels and leisure. William Gilpin developed an aesthetic system, the *picturesque*, for seeing the country and painting landscapes. Using picturesque guidelines, the artist could even improve the scenery encountered in nature. Scenes could be viewed with a 'Claude glass', a framed mirror which allowed the prospective picture to be visualised and the best angle chosen, the glass could be tinted to give the picture the mellow tones so common in the works of the Italian masters (possibly caused by over-zealous varnishing), and extra objects could be inserted in order to create more pleasing foregrounds or 'off-skips', framing of the landscape at the sides.

In the mid-eighteenth century, with the diminishing danger of highwaymen, improved roads, and better accommodation, travel became an activity in which more people participated, and this was a development which was supported by a burgeoning trade in travel guidebooks. As might be expected, these were to a considerable extent associated with the aesthetic interest in the countryside, and those locations which offered wild and undeveloped scenery became the most favoured. It was after the battle of Culloden in 1746 that the Highlands of Scotland became accessible to tourists, who could now be free from fear of Jacobite rebels.[32] The attraction of this part of the country was enhanced by an interest in Celtic culture, especially after the publication in 1760 of James Macpherson's *Fragments of Ancient Poetry, Collected in the Highlands of Scotland*, which was the first of several purported works of a third-century Caledonian bard called Ossian and his father Fingal.[33] The wild and rugged landscapes of the Highlands were quite unlike the gentle scenes encountered in Italy, but they corresponded to the sentiments of Romanticism, an aesthetic attitude remote from the neoclassical influence of the destinations in the Grand Tour. A new kind of tourism developed, its destinations being Scotland, Wales, and the more remote parts of northern England, especially the Lake District.

Thomas West was a native of Cumberland, and his *Guide to the Lakes* did much to popularise the spectacular mountain and lake scenery which he described.[34] He specified 'stations' around each lake, to which the artist-traveller was directed in order to obtain the ideal sketches. William Gilpin, who was from Westmorland, wrote a lengthy description of the Lakes in one of his 'tour journals', each of which describes a region of Britain and analyses the scenes in the countryside according to picturesque guidelines. Many were drawn to this region, the most famous being William Wordsworth, his sister Dorothy, and their friend Samuel Taylor Coleridge. Wordsworth himself wrote a *Guide to the Lakes* and the gentle beauty of the surroundings of Grasmere, where he lived when he first came to the district, pervades much of his earlier poetry. These last writers are not included in this collection, for it cannot be argued that they are descendants of the antiquaries of the seventeenth century: they represent a break from that tradition and set out on the declaration of a new apprehension of the landscape.

With William Borlase, the pioneering archaeologist, there can be no hesitation in recognising his literary ancestry: he was, indeed, an antiquary in the full sense of the word, but, like the remarkable John Aubrey, he went a step further in his methodology. For Borlase, observation and measurement were the main sources of knowledge, more than the authority of predecessors. Finally, in the work of Gilbert White little more remains of the antiquarian tradition than its essential framework. His survey embraces all that is in the parish of Selborne, the people, their properties, animals, and plants; he is an observant, thorough, and systematic naturalist; he is a scholar of the classics; he is a poet of the world around him.

1. John Norden was a topographer who embarked on a project to write descriptions of all the counties of England, collectively to be called *Speculum Britanniae*. Richard Kilburne wrote two studies of Kent; Defoe and White are discussed in later chapters of this book. The extracts are taken from: John Norden, *1598 Speculi Britanniae pars the description of Hartfordshire*, 1598, pp.1–2; Richard Kilburne, *A Topographie or Survey of the County of Kent*, 1659, p.134; Daniel Defoe, *A Tour thro' the Whole Island of Great Britain*, vol I, pp.272-273, Gilbert White, *The Natural History of Selborne*, p.11.
2. A chorographical survey is one in which the reader is given historical accounts of places arranged according to their geographical locations.
3. Three rare instances are when Dugdale is writing about the church of St Michael at Coventry, pp.92, 96, and 105.
4. The full title was *The Antiquities of Warwickshire Illustrated; From Records, Leiger-Books, Manuscripts, Charters, Evidences, Tombes, and Armes: Beautified With Maps, Prospects, and Portraictures.* The word 'illustrated' was not an indication that the book contained pictures (although it did), but in this context meant 'made famous'.
5. See, for example, Joseph M. Levine, *Humanism and History: Origins of Modern English Historiography*, Ithaca and London: Cornell University Press, 1987, p.77; Barbara Shapiro, *Probability and Certainty in Seventeenth-Century England*, Princeton University Press, 1983, p.121.
6. The first of these was the *Roma instaurata* of 1453, a survey of Rome's ancient monuments.
7. Wilhelm Bedwell explained types of geography thus: '*Cosmography* importeth a description of the world, the whole world, consisting of the Heav'nly spheares and Earthly globe: *Geography*, of the Earth alone, and the Sea invironing it: *Chorography*, of some particular kingdome or province of the Earth: So is *Topography*, nothing els but a description of some one particular place, village, or towne in some kingdome, province, country or other.' (Wilhelm Bedwell: *A Brief Description of The Town of Tottenham High Crosse, in Middlesex*, London, 1631, reprinted in 1818 as Appendix II of William Robinson: *The History and Antiquities of the Parish of Tottenham High Cross, in the County of Middlesex*, Middlesex, 1818, Book I, Ch. I, 'Of the Definition, or Forme of the Village'.)
8. Gerard of Wales wrote accounts of journeys through Wales; John Rous studied arms, armour, clothing and seals in Warwickshire; and William Worcester wrote an account of a journey from Norwich to St Michael's Mount and a survey of Bristol.
9. The date of Geoffrey of Monmouth's book, now known as *The History of the Kings of Britain*, has been put at between 1130 and 1138. Little is known of his life (*c.*1100–1154) except for the last years, when he was Bishop of St Asaph. He was Welsh, but spent most of his life in England, probably at Oxford. See, for example, the Introduction in the edition by Lewis Thorpe, Penguin Books, 1966, pp.9 and 38.
10. Polydore Vergil (*c.*1470–1555) worked initially at Urbino, where he wrote his *De inventoribus rerum*, a learned study of origins, which quickly became widely celebrated. Joining the service of the Pope, Polydore was sent to England as sub-collector of Peter's Pence in 1502, and was enthusiastically received both by Henry VII and by the leading English scholars. His major work was his history of England, *Anglica historia*, for which he used many sources which he treated critically and comparatively, following the rigorous precepts of humanist historiography. His research led him to repudiate the traditional history of Geoffrey of Monmouth, a matter which caused considerable controversy amongst English historical writers for decades to come. The development of doubt about the 'Brut' is discussed by Thomas Kendrick, *British Antiquity*, London: Methuen, 1950, chapters III, V, and VI, and May McKisack, *Medieval History in the Tudor Age*, Oxford: Clarendon Press, 1971, chapter V. Kendrick in his chapter VI, 'The Battle over the British History', gives a number of the arguments that were used to

defend the traditional account. Camden's cautious approach is discussed by Graham Parry, *The Trophies of Time: English Antiquarians of the Seventeenth Century*, Oxford University Press, 1995, pp.27–8.

11. John Leland (*c*.1503–1552), poet and antiquary, studied at Cambridge, Oxford and Paris. On his return to England he was given a commission by Henry VIII to survey monastic libraries. Subsequently he travelled extensively in England, making his topographical observations. Kendrick, *British Antiquity*, pp.50–51; McKisack, *Medieval History in the Tudor Age*, pp.2–5. Kendrick's fourth chapter is a useful account of Leland's career.
12. *British Antiquity*, p.49. Kendrick was using the word 'medieval' pejoratively to suggest credulity. His assessment of Leland's achievement was ambivalent.
13. Abraham Ortelius (1527–1598), map-maker of Antwerp, travelled widely and had many contacts in England. He corresponded extensively with intellectuals from all parts of Europe and accumulated a large library and a considerable collection of coins.
14. *Britannia* was first published in Latin in 1586, with an English edition appearing in 1610. A revised edition appeared in 1695. For a discussion of Camden's *Britannia*, see Parry, *Trophies of Time*, pp.23-43.
15. McKisack, *Medieval History in the Tudor Age*, p.153; Kevin Sharpe, *Sir Robert Cotton, 1586–1631: History and Politics in Early Modern England*, Oxford University Press, 1979 pp.17–18.
16. Sharpe, *Sir Robert Cotton*, pp.30–32; Parry, *Trophies of Time*, p.44.
17. *Ibid.*, pp.19–22. Robert Cotton (1571–1631) was both antiquary and member of parliament.
18. *Ibid.*, pp.48–83.
19 *Ibid.*, p.73. Matthew Parker (1504–1575) was a reforming clergyman who became the first Archbishop of Canterbury of the reign of Queen Elizabeth I. He was a patron of scholars and himself collected and edited medieval manuscripts, some not very sympathetically (his editing often involved correcting material with which he, as a Protestant, did not agree). See McKisack, *Medieval History in the Tudor Age*, pp.26–49.
20. See Parry, *Trophies of Time*, chapters 1–6, for a review of the work of the major antiquaries of the first half of the seventeenth century: Camden, Verstegan, Cotton, Selden, Ussher, Spelman, and Somner.
21. Blundeville, Thomas, *The True Order and Method of Wryting and Reading Hystories*, Amsterdam: Theatrum Orbis Terrarum, 1979. (1st edn, London, 1574)
22. *A Perambulation of Kent*, p.10.
23. John Norden (*c*.1547–1625), was himself a cartographer, but also the author of *Speculum Britanniae*, a set of county descriptions, of which he completed Northamptonshire, Middlesex, Surrey, Essex, Sussex, Hampshire, the Isle of Wight, Jersey, Guernsey, Hertfordshire, and Cornwall, each including a map. Some were published in his life-time, some later. The maps were incorporated into a later edition of Camden's *Britannia*. John Speed (1552–1629) produced more detailed county maps in his *Theatre of the Empire of Great Britain*, with brief county descriptions which were, in turn, borrowed from Camden. The English 'father of map-making', however, was Christopher Saxton (*c*.1543–1610), creator, for Elizabeth I, of the first national atlas (although he did not use that term).
24. A contemporary phrase, used in recent times by Christopher Hill in the title of one of his studies of the English Revolution.
25. From the dedicatory epistle 'To my Honoured Friends the Gentry of Warwickshire', unpaginated. (In the second edition this is placed at the beginning of Volume II.)
26. Francis Bacon (1561–1657), of London and St Albans, pursued a legal and political career under Elizabeth I and James I, culminating in his appointment as Lord Chancellor and his being created Viscount St Alban, although this career ended abruptly in

impeachment after he fell out of favour with the king and his favourite, the Duke of Buckingham. Of more lasting influence was his philosophical career: he wrote on politics and ethics and, most importantly, on natural philosophy.

27. The two completed parts of James Ussher's *Annales Veteris et Novi Testamenti* appeared in 1650 and 1654 respectively. An English translation, *The Annals of the Old and New Testament or The Annals of the World deduced from the origin of Time*, was published in 1658, two years after Ussher's death.
28. The inclusion of these titles here serves to show how few county surveys actually came to publication between 1656 and 1712. To those given must be added two studies of Kent, which would substantially have been written before Dugdale's *Antiquities of Warwickshire* became available: *A Topographie, or Survey of the County of Kent* by Richard Kilburne and *Villare Cantianum, or, Kent Surveyed and Illustrated,* by John Philipot (both 1659). The paucity of these books is doubtless due to the enormous amounts of intricate research which they demanded: many were projected, but few authors were able to see the task through to completion. Dugdale commented critically on what he saw as inaccuracies and inadequacies in Thoroton's *Nottinghamshire*, resulting from that author's inability to do all his research himself and consequently having relied on work undertaken by others.
29. *Wedding at Bermondsey*, by Joris Hoefnagel, 1570, also known as *Wedding at Horsleydown in Bermondsey*, and as *Fete at Bermondsey*, is the result of a visitor seeing England. Hoefnagel was a Belgian artist who visited England for a few years, and his vision of a rural English festive occasion is Flemish in appearance. Sometimes described as the earliest English landscape painting, it is a valuable source of information about English dress and social customs of its time. Jan Siberechts (1627–1703) was another Flemish visitor of the late seventeenth century. He painted some scenes of country houses, one of which was Chatsworth, and it was from this painting that Richard Wilson's *View of Elizabethan Chatsworth* was copied.
30. See extracts from these authors, below.
31. Claude Lorrain (1602–1682), also known as Claude Gellée, or simply as 'Claude', and Gaspard Dughet (1615–1675), were French artists who worked mainly in the vicinity of Rome, producing landscapes whose distinctive style was characterised by the choice of Arcadian scenery, presented in golden afternoon or morning light, with foregrounds of dark trees or rocks, backgrounds of serene mountains, and small pastoral figures to one side. Landscapes by the Italian Salvator Rosa (1615–1673) offered a different kind of Romance, with stormy skies, dark forests, waterfalls, and forbidding mountains.
32. It was the last battle fought on mainland Britain. The Jacobite Rising of 1745, in support of Charles Edward Stuart ('Bonnie Prince Charlie') as a claimant of the British throne, finished with the decisive defeat of the rebels by the British Army at Culloden.
33. James Macpherson (1736–1796), of the Scottish highlands, brought out other works of 'Ossian': *Fingal: an Ancient Epic Poem* in 1762 and *Temora* in 1763.
34. Thomas West (1720–1779), antiquary and Jesuit priest, was the author of *The Antiquities of Furness* as well as the *Guide to the Lakes.*

THE SOUTH-EAST

I

Kent: William Lambarde (1536–1601)

Amongst the antiquarian writers of early modern descriptions of English counties, William Lambarde holds a special place as the author of the first such work to be published, *A Perambulation of Kent*. It was an immediate success, and for more than a century after its publication it was referred to by subsequent antiquaries as a model of its genre. It established a method for topological description and, combining this with historical accounts of places, was a clear example of the chorographical approach, which was the basis of antiquarian surveys for the next hundred and fifty years. While Lambarde's abiding interest was Anglo-Saxon history and culture, he was by profession a lawyer, and, as might be expected, his view of the county was to some extent administrative, and to a more considerable extent historical.

Lambarde was born in London in October, 1536, and died in August, 1601, at his manor, Westcombe, in Greenwich, Kent, which he had inherited from his father in 1554.[1] He was admitted to Lincoln's Inn in 1556, but was not called to the bar until 1567. This lengthy career development was no doubt due to his pursuit of Anglo-Saxon studies, which research he undertook with Laurence Nowell until the latter's departure for France in 1567.[2] Lambarde's first published work was *Archaionomia*, a collection of paraphrased Anglo-Saxon laws, in 1568. The idea for this work was probably Nowell's originally, but it was Lambarde who did the bulk of the translating and writing. His next antiquarian work, not published in his lifetime, was entitled *Alphabetical Description of the Chief Places of England and Wales*. It was a collection of personal observations on places, together with transcripts taken from chronicles and ancient documents.

The first draft of *A Perambulation of Kent* was completed in 1570, but before submitting his work to print, Lambarde sought the services of a former sheriff of Kent, Thomas Wotton, as a first reader. While this suggests that he wanted to check the accuracy of his data, perhaps also he felt that his work would benefit from the support of a native of the county. As was the practice of the time, Lambarde circulated his manuscript amongst certain friends, one of whom was Matthew Parker, then Archbishop of Canterbury, who in 1573 brought it to the attention of Lord Burghley, the Lord Treasurer and chief adviser to Queen Elizabeth.[3] Whatever encouragement Lambarde may have had, publication was nevertheless delayed further till 1576, perhaps because of personal circumstances during that time: Lambarde's first wife died, and he founded an almshouse. But when the book appeared, it was well received, so much so that he brought out an expanded version in 1596, and, later, there were subsequent editions in the seventeenth century, and the second edition was reprinted, with a biography of the author, in 1826.

His subsequent antiquarian research was confined to legal topics. In 1581 he published *Eirenarcha, or of the Office of Justices of the Peace*, which was reprinted seven times between 1582 and 1610, the last three with additions. *Archeion; or, a Commentary upon the High Courts of Justice in England*, appeared in 1591. The official posts held and responsibilities taken on by Lambarde in the course of his career included: 1579, bencher of Lincoln's Inn; 1579, Justice of the Peace for Kent; 1592, Master in Chancery; 1597, Keeper of the Records at the Rolls Chapel; 1597, trustee to Lord Cobham for the establishment of a college for the poor; and 1601, Keeper of the Records in the Tower. In this last capacity he had a private audience with Queen Elizabeth on 4 August, to present her with his new catalogue of the documents. It was in this meeting that Elizabeth famously referred to the recent conspiracy of the Earl of Essex with the remark, 'I am Richard II, know ye not that?'[4] The meeting was a high point of the antiquary's career, the queen praising him as 'good and Honest Lambarde'. It was just two weeks before his death.

Lambarde's antiquarian interest is the first of many cases in which we will see a close association with a legal career. The collection of details about the past, especially with respect to the land and its administration, is of a forensic nature, and clearly leads to the development of resources invaluable for the pursuits both of litigation and constitutional interpretation. Moreover, Lambarde was a member of a circle of scholarly Elizabethan men with a Renaissance outlook. Together with Lawrence Nowell, and under the patronage of William Cecil, he planned the writing of descriptions of all the counties of the nation. Indeed, his original intention had been to write a topography of the whole of Great Britain, but, as he stated in his closing remarks at the end of the book, the composition of a survey of his own county had made him realise that a collaborative effort would be more realistic:

> As touching the *description* of the residue of this Realme, finding by this one, how harde it will be for any one (and much more for my selfe) to accomplish it for all, I can but wish in like sort, that some one in each *Shyre* woulde make the

> enterprise for his owne Countrie, to the end that by joyning our Pennes, and conferring our labours (as it were, *ex symbolo*) we might at the last by the union of many partes and papers compact one whole and perfect bodie and booke of our English *Topographie*.[5]

By the time his book was to be published, he added to this remark, taking account of the fact that his friend William Camden was indeed proceeding on a such a project as he had envisaged.

> Here left I (good Reader) when I first set foorth this Woorke: Since which time I finde my desire not a little served by Master *Camdens Britannia*: wherein, as he hath not onely farre exceeded whatsoever hath been formerly attempted in that kynd, but hath also passed the expectation of other men & even his own hope: So do I acknowledge it written to the great Honour of the realme with men abroad & to the singular delight of us all at home, having for mine own particular found my self thereby to have learned much even in that Shyre wherein I had endevoured to know most. Neverthelesse, being assured that the *Inwardes* of each place may best be knowen by such as reside therein, I can not but still encourage some one able man in each Shyre to undertake his owne, whereby both many good particularities will come to discoverie every where, and Master *Camden* him selfe may yet have greater choice wherewith to amplifie and enlarge the whole.

Thus Lambarde's *Perambulation of Kent* and Camden's *Britannia* could complement each other: the former, a model for a series of county studies written by dwellers in each county; the latter, a comprehensive view of the whole realm.

The emergence of such projects in Elizabethan England is not surprising. Italian and French humanists had long been writing chorographically about their countries' historical monuments and the investigations of John Leland in England had shown that, even if it was no longer possible to believe that the founder of the nation was Brutus of Troy, there was nevertheless evidence of a distant and glorious past. A description of the country would be an affirmation of national identity based on the continuation of governance and laws, on the identification of antique origins and on the discovery of associations with the classical world. While Camden chose to give emphasis to Britain's period as a Roman province, Lambarde was concerned with both Anglo-Saxon heritage and the present. The earlier work, *Archaionomia*, was a pioneering essay into Anglo-Saxon research, the significance of which was the affirmation of the antiquity and continuity of institutions since pre-conquest times. In particular, the English church could be shown to have preceded the Roman church in the nation.

The characterisation of his book as a *Perambulation* was apt, for it is a true chorography, in that description and history are called upon as the county is traversed topologically. The principal framework is place, and the *ad hoc* historical passages are incidental. This is not to say that the history is of secondary importance, but rather that it is called up in the narrative as a subsequence of location. Little of Lambarde's history is specifically concerned with county families, so that genealogy and lineage are not prominent in this first of the county surveys in the manner which they assume in the mid-seventeenth century. Dealing firstly with the county as a whole, Lambarde gives a general description and history, with certain facts regarding administration, markets, and notable houses and institutions. He then begins his 'perambulation', taking the two sees of Canterbury and Rochester in turn and describing each of their important localities individually. In each of these descriptions, the main features of the place are outlined, together with relevant significant historical events or developments. Frequently these points are concerned with religious foundations, great houses, important historical figures or noteworthy royal charters, but they may also provide information about produce, for example that the Isle of Sheppey's name derives from its abundance of sheep. Finally, in a section headed 'The Customes of Kent', is a discussion of the county's unique system of land tenure, gavelkind, a topic of which the author had specialist knowledge.

In the text as a whole, Lambarde seems to have pursued as his main purpose the identification, mainly through historical accounts, of Kent as an individual county, and as a significant constituent part of the nation. It emerges principally as an administrative entity with a noble history. As for scenery and the ordinary people, there are only fleeting glimpses, yet it is nevertheless possible to sense that the author belongs this county, and has a love for it. The absence of landscape as a feature of the county suggests not that it was not noticed, nor even that it was not loved, but that it was, to sixteenth-century eyes, unremarkable. Unlike the crops, the churches, the traditions, it had no impact on the life of the people; it was simply there.

The first of the following extracts is from the general description of the county, which clearly provided guidance to later chorographical writers. He begins with a specification of the county's location and size and a discussion of the etymology of its name. After stating how it is divided administratively, Lambarde then comments on the 'air' (we would now think of this more as the weather) and the 'soil', and then crops, stock, and other produce, and the rivers and the sea. Following this, but not included here, comes a discussion on the classes of people. These several headings under which a county could be characterised came to be used in many subsequent county descriptions. Lambarde had, of course, himself become a man of Kent, and there is a certain degree of pleasure evident as he undertakes the task of relating its features. The details of the various towns and parishes were based on the chorographical template which also became a model for county descriptions for decades to come. The extract dealing with Tenham is, however, a little different, and is offered as an example of the author *describing* the countryside. It was the special beauty of this part of the county, he explained, which provoked a departure from his usual approach.

The Estate of Kent

From *A Perambulation of Kent*, 1596, pp.8–12

Kent..., lying in the southeast region of this realme, hath on the North the river of *Thamise*, on the East the Sea, on the South the Sea and *Sussex*, and on the West *Sussex* and *Surrey*. It extendeth in length, from the West of the landes in *Beckenham*, called (I will not say, purposely hereof) *Langley*, where is the stile, as it were, over into *Surrey*, to the *Ramsgate* in the Isle of *Thanet*, about fiftie and three Myles: and reacheth in breadthe from the River *Rother* on the South of *Newendene* next *Sussex*, to the river of *Thamise*, at *Nowrheade* in the Isle of *Greane*, twentie sixe Miles, and somewhat more; And hath in circuit 160. Miles, or thereabouts.

It is called by *Cæsar*, and other auncient writers, *Cancium,* and *Cancia* in Latin; which name (as I make conjecture) was framed either out of *Cainc*, a woord that (in the language of the *Britaines*, whom *Cæsar* at his arrivall founde inhabiting there) signifieth, *Bowghes*, or woods, and was imposed, by reason that this countrie, both at that time, and also long after, was in manner wholy overgrowne with *woode*, as it shall hereafter in fit place more plainly appeare: or else, of *Cant*, or *Canton*, which denoteth an *Angle*, or *Corner* of land, (so this and sundry others bee) as Master *Camden* the most lightsome Antiquarie of this age hath observed.[6]

The whole Shyre hath long been, and is at this day, divided into five partes, communly called Lathes, not altogither equall: which also be broken into Hundrethes, and they againe parted into townes and borowes, most aptly for assemblie and administration of Justice.

The Aire in *Kent*, by reason that the Countrye is on sundry partes bordered with water, is somewhat thicke: for which cause (as also for that it is scituate neerest to the Sunne risinge and furthest from the *North pole* of any part of the realme) it is temperate, not so colde by a great deale as *Northumberland*, and yet in maner as warme as *Cornwall*. It hath also the better side of the river of *Thamise*, from whence by the benefit of the South and Southwest windes, (most common in this region) the fog and mist is carried from it.

The *Soile* is for the most parte bountifull, consisting indifferently of arable, pasture, meadow and woodland: howbeit of these, wood occupieth the greatest portion even till this day, except it be towards the East, which coast is more champaigne[7] than the residue.

It hath Corne and Graine, common with other Shyres of the Realme; as Wheat, Rye, Barly, and Oats, in good plenty, save onely, that in the *Wealdish*,[8] or wooddy places, where of late daies they used much *Pomage*,[9] or Cider for want of Barley, now that lacke is more commonly supplied with Oates.

Neither wanteth *Kent* such sorts of pulce, as the rest of the Realme yeeldeth, namely beanes, peason, and tares,[10] which some (reteining the sounde of the Latine woord *Vicia*) call vetches, and which *Polydor*[11] supposed not to be found in Ingland.

The pasture and meadowe, is not onely sufficient in proportion to the quantitie of the country itselfe for breeding, but is comparable in fertilitie also to any other that is neare it, in so much that it gayneth by feeding.

In fertile and fruitfull woodes and trees, this Country is most florishing also, whether you respect the mast[12] of Oke, Beeche and Chesten for cattaile: or the fruit of Apples, Peares, Cherries, and Plums for men: for besides great store of oke and beeche, it hath whole woodes that beare Chestnut, a mast (if I may so call it, and not rather a fruite, whereof even delicate persons disdaine not to feede) not commonly seene in other countries: But as for Ortchards of Apples, and Gardeins of Cheries, and those of the most delicious and exquisite kindes that can be, no part of the Realme (that I knowe) hath them, either in such quantitie and number, or with such arte and industrie, set and planted. So that the Kentish man, most truely of all, may say with him in Vergil,

Sunt nobis mitia poma,
Castaneæ molles, &c.[13]

Touching domestical cattel, as horses, mares, oxen, kine, and sheepe, *Kent* differeth not muche from others: onely this it challengeth as singular, that it bringeth forth the largest of stature in ech kinde of them: The like whereof also *Polydore* (in his historie) confesseth of the *Kentish* poultrie.

Parkes of fallow Deere, and games of graie Conies,[14] it maintaineth many, the one for pleasure, & the other for profit, as it may well appeere by this, that within memorie almost the one halfe of the first sort be disparked,[15] & the number of warreins continueth, if it do not increase daily.

As for red Deere, and blacke Conies, it nourisheth them not, as having no forests, or great walks of waste ground for the one, & not tarying the time to raise the gaine by the other: for, blacke conyes are kept partly for their skins, which have their season in Winter: and *Kent* by the neernesse to London, hath so quicke market of yoong Rabbets, that it killeth this game chiefely in summer.

There is no *Mineral*, or other profit digged out of the belly of the earth heere, save only that in certeine places they have Mines of *Iron*, quarreys of *Paving stone*, and pits of fat *Marle*.

Besides diverse pieres, jetties, and creekes, that bee upon the coastes of the *Thamys* and the *Sea*, *Kent* hath also sundrie fresh rivers and pleasaunt streames, especially *Derent*, *Medwey*, and *Stowre*, of the which, *Medwey* is more navigable then the rest, for which cause, and (for that it crosseth the Shyre almost in the midst) it is the most beneficiall also.

The *Sea*, and these *Waters*, yeeld good & wholesome fishes competently, but yet neither so muche in quantitie, nor suche in varietie, as some other coastes of the Realme do afoorde …

Tenham

From *A Perambulation of Kent*, 1596, pp.246–248

I Woulde begin with the *Antiquities* of this place, as commonly I doe in others, were it not that the latter and present estate thereof far passeth any that hath beene tofore it. For heere have wee, not onely the most dainty piece of all our *Shyre*, but such a *Singularitie* as the whole British *Iland* is not able to patterne.[16] The Ile of *Thanet*, and those Easterne parts, are the *Grayner*: the *Weald* was the *Wood*: *Rumney* Marsh, is the *Medow plot*: the *Northdownes* towards the *Thamyse*, be the *Cony garthe*, or Warreine: and this *Tenham* with thirty other parishes (lying on each side this porte way, and extending from *Raynham* to *Blean Wood*) bee the *Cherrie* gardein, and *Apple* orcharde of *Kent*.

But, as this at *Tenham* is the parent of all the rest, and from whome they have drawen the good juice of all their pleasant fruite: So is it also the most large, delightsome, and beautifull of them. In which respect you may phantasie that you now see *Hesperidum Hortos*,[17] if not where *Hercules* founde the golden apples, (which is reckoned for one of his *Heroical* labours) yet where our honest patriote *Richard Harrys* (Fruiterer to King *Henrie* the 8.) planted by his great coste and rare industrie, the sweet *Cherry*, the temperate *Pipyn*, and the golden *Renate*. For this man, seeing that this Realme (which wanted neither the favour of the Sunne, nor the fat of the Soile, meete for the making of good apples) was neverthelesse served chiefly with that Fruit from forrein Regions abroad, by reason that (as *Vergil* saide)

Pomaq degenerant, succos oblita priores:[18]

and those plantes which our ancestors had brought hither out of *Normandie* had lost their native verdour, whether you did eate their substance, or drink their juice, which we call *Cyder*, he (I say) about the yeere of our Lord *Christ* 1533. obtained 105. acres of good ground in *Tenham*, then called the *Brennet*, which he divided into ten parcels, and with great care, good choise, and no small labour and cost, brought plantes from beyonde the *Seas*, and furnished this ground with them, so beautifully, as they not onely stand in most right line, but seeme to be of one sorte, shape, and fashion, as if they had beene drawen thorow one Mould, or wrought by one and the same patterne.

Within *Tenham* there was long since some Mansion perteining to the *See* of *Canterburie*: For, in the time of King *Henrie* the Seconde, there was a great dispute (before the Archbishop, then sojourning at *Tenham*) betweene the *Prior* of *Canterburie*, and the *Prior* of *Rochester*, not for the *Crosse* (for that is the *Archbishops* warre) but for the *Crosier* of the Bishop of *Rochester*, then lately dead, which (as they of *Canterbury* claymed) ought to lye upon the *Altar* with them, to be delivered to the next Bishop, but was contradicted by them of *Rochester*. This pointe of *Prioritie* was to and fro mainteined with such pertinacitie, that neither would yeelde to other, but in the end they of *Rochester* put the *Crosier* into the hands of *Baldwyne* the *Archbishop*, who foorthwith delivered it to the *Prior* of *Canterburie*, of whom *Gilbert Glanvile* the next successor tooke it. And at this house in the time of King *John*, *Hubert* the Archbishop departed this life, as *Mathew Parise* reporteth: who addeth also, that when the King had intelligence of his death, he brast foorth into great joy, & said, that he was never King (in deede) before that houre.

It seemeth, that he thought himselfe delivered of a shrewe, but little forsawe he that a shrewder should succeede in the roome; for if he had, he would rather have praied for the continuaunce of his life, than joyed in the understanding of his death.

For after this *Hubert*, followeth *Stephan Langton*, who brought upon King *John* such a tempesteous sea of sorrowfull trouble, that it caused him to make shipwrack, both of his honour, crowne, and life also: The storie hath appeered at large in *Dover*, and therefore needeth not now eftsoones[19] to bee repeated. Touching the sickly situation of this towne, and the region thereabout, you may be admonished by the common *Rythme* of the countrie, singing thus,

He that will not live long,
Let him dwell at Muston, Tenham, or Tong.

1. A detailed study is by Retha M. Warnicke, *William Lambarde: Elizabethan Antiquary 1536-1601,* London and Chichester: Phillimore, 1973.
2. Laurence Nowell (1530–1570), antiquary and friend of Lambarde and William Cecil. He worked in collaboration with Lambarde in his initial surveying of Kent.
3. On Parker, see Note 19 in the *Introduction*, above. William Cecil (1520–1598), later Lord Burghley, was a statesman who served as Secretary of State for Elizabeth from the beginning of her reign till his old age.
4. The subject was called to mind as the queen's perusal of the catalogue came to the documents from the reign of Richard II, who was the victim of a conspiracy, led by Bolingbroke, which led to his being deposed. Shakespeare's play *King Richard II* had also been playing recently in London.
5. *A Perambulation of Kent*, p.526.
6. 'Kent' is from the Latin name 'Cantium', given by Julius Caesar, from the Brythonic word 'cantus', meaning a border or rim.
7. *Champaigne*, level and open.
8. *Wealdish*, wooded.
9. *Pomage*, cider.
10. *Tares*, or *vetches*, are leguminous plants, usually cultivated for forage.
11. On Polydore Vergil see the *Introduction*, above, Note 10.
12. *Mast*, the fruit of forest trees, usually used to feed swine.
13. From Virgil, *Eclogue* I:

    'I can offer you ripe fruit,
    'And mealy chestnuts and abundance of milk cheese'

    (*Virgil's Eclogues*, edited and translated by Guy Lee, Liverpool Latin Texts 1, Liverpool: Francis Cairns, 1980, p.11)
14. *Conies*, rabbits.
15. That is, half of the deer parks have been put to other uses.
16. *Pattern*, emulate.
17. An orchard, from *Hesperidum*, a fruit, usually citrus, and *hortos*, garden.
18. From Virgil, *Georgics* II:

    'its fruit
    'degenerates, forgetting its old flavour'

    (Virgil, *The Georgics*, translated with an introduction by L. P. Wilkinson, Penguin Books, 1982, p.79)
19. *Eftsoons*, soon afterwards.

II

Canterbury: William Somner (1606–1669)

William Somner's great achievement was the compilation of the *Dictionarium Saxonico-Latino-Anglicum*, published in 1659, a pioneering work of scholarship which responded to a need which had developed with the growing awareness of England's Anglo-Saxon history.[1] He was born in 1606 and lived all of his life in Canterbury, indeed in the same house, and his career, like that of his father, was associated with the see and parishes of that place. At an early age he was apprenticed to his father in the business of ecclesiastical law and proceeded to admission in 1623 as a Notary Public. The demands of his career would have been such as to necessitate his antiquarian scholarship to be pursued in his spare time. He married in 1634, and was admitted as Proctor of the Consistory Court in 1638, this being the period in which he would have been working on his *Antiquities of Canterbury*, which was published in 1640. He was recognised by his peers as a scholar of great distinction, and was invited by Roger Twysden to contribute to *Scriptores X*, a collection of ancient historians, and by William Dugdale, who referred to him as 'my singular friend', to contribute to the *Monasticon Anglicanum*, the great collection of monastic histories and documents.

The Antiquities of Canterbury, true to its title,[2] deals with 'antiquities': it is concerned only with that which is the work of civilization, and, its subject being Canterbury, it is not a county description, but an urban description. We should not, therefore, expect to find descriptions of rural landscapes, but we may anticipate some attention to either the built landscape or some of the particular buildings of which it is constituted. But such an expectation is met only to a degree, for while Somner takes some basic notice of architecture, he does so in order to help determine age rather than to appreciate the impression a building might make on a visitor or resident. It is only in describing his beloved cathedral that there is some betrayal of such sentiments, and the following passage is part of the lengthy section devoted to the great edifice with which he was so closely associated. Somner takes his readers on a veritable guided tour of Canterbury Cathedral, and we may imagine that he was, in his text, rehearsing an itinerary which he had often followed in reality, while showing the great church to visitors.

In touring the building, Somner endeavours to inform his readers of the period of construction of each of the component sections, the benefactor or builder, and changes which may have transpired in the form or utilization. While he seems almost oblivious to the feelings the visit might evoke, he is not entirely so, remarking, for example, at the outset, that the cathedral building 'raiseth it self aloft with so great a Majesty and Stateliness, that it striketh a sensible Impression of Religion in their minds that behold it afar off'.[3] It must not be supposed from the pragmatic tone of his account that he had no sensitivity to the cathedral's size, symmetry, decoration, and venerableness, but rather that he would probably not have thought the admission of personal feelings to be appropriate in his book. In his *Preface* Somner refers with conviction, albeit in the rhetoric of scholarly humility, to his love and affection both for 'Antiquities' and 'the place of his birth, education, and present abode'.

The spaciousness and numerous features of Somner's subject are complemented by his extension of the temporality of awareness of the cathedral into both the past and the future, in the first case by quoting words written by Erasmus of his visit to the same place in pre-Reformation times; and in the other—ironically, as it was to turn out just two years after the publication of the book—by intimating the assured continuity of the state of the cathedral with its treasures into the years to come. The library, for example, is now, says Somner, being replenished by the 'piety of the present Churchmen' and 'may it have (what it well deserves) many Benefactors'.[4] The wonderful decoration of the altars witnessed by Erasmus in 1512 has been restored and is 'very rich and becoming such days of blessed peace as our Church (by God's mercy) now enjoys'.

The Antiquities of Canterbury was published at an unfortunate time: the eve of the outbreak of civil war, the time of a zealous campaign of puritan iconoclasm. One day in 1642, the cathedral was visited by the fanatical Reverend Richard Culmer, together with the mayor and recorder of Canterbury, bearing a copy, as he later reported, of 'the *Proctors* book', which included 'a *register* of the *Cathedrall Idolls*'.[5] It may be imagined that it was the very copy which Somner had proudly presented to the mayor of the town two years earlier, a terrible irony indeed, were it so. For the purpose of the visit of Culmer and his accompanying hoodlums was destruction, and Somner's loving account of his cathedral's treasures served them as

> ... a card and compasse to sail by, in that *Cathedrall Ocean of Images*: by it many a Popish picture was discovered and demolished. It's sure working by the

> booke: But here is the wonder, that this booke should be a means to pull down Idols, which so much advaunceth Idolatry.[6]

The iconoclast could hardly contain his delight; the gentle and scholarly proctor's grief must have been devastating.

The following extract is the description of the interior of the church at the levels of the nave and choir. As will be seen in Thomas Westcote's description of Devonshire, there is the sense that we are reading an early travel-guide. The tour continues with the crypt, chapter-house, cloister, and, finally, as Somner comments with palpable relish, 'to make my Survey compleat, I must another while play the *Mystagogus*, and shew you the Monuments ...' While he was an assured guide, he nevertheless referred frequently to the earlier description by Erasmus, as if to confirm the veracity of his account. A more likely purpose of this device was to couple the cathedral's present and its past; as we read of the present state of the edifice, we are simultaneously reminded of its glory when it was still the shrine of its great saint, Thomas Becket. It is a striking example of the antiquarian reach into the past, to the extent that Erasmus's experience almost merges with the present experience which Somner is offering.

It may be surmised that Somner admired Erasmus and agreed with his theological position, but the great scholar's narrative has an ironic edge which sits a little uncomfortably with Somner's ingenuous adoration of the cathedral. The dedication of his book to William Laud, the then Archbishop of Canterbury, is also incongruent with the evangelical humanism of Erasmus, but may have been a formality which Somner could not avoid. Laud's ecclesiastical reforms, which were so unpopular that they contributed to the forces which motivated rebellion against the English Church and the monarchy, nevertheless facilitated the restoration of much of the church ornamentation which Somner so admired. And just as these modifications to the church's contents could remind observers of the glorious medieval past, they also signalled a return to the 'popish regime' that had come to be so widely feared since the 'bloody' reign of Queen Mary. Apparently innocent of this dilemma, Somner seems able to indulge in the outward beauties of his church and remain oblivious to the underlying sinister implications which so disturbed the faithful.

The description of the cathedral interior[7]

From *The Antiquities of Canterbury*, pp.90-96[8]

Now we enter the Body of the Church; a right noble Structure. *And as soon as we are entred, a spacious and stately Fabrick presents it self to our view*, saith ... *Erasmus*.[9] This questionless is the identical nave or Body; of whose Age and

Authors you so lately heard.[10] There are two fair and great Steeples, namely, at the West end of the Church, furnished with very large Bells, saith *Erasmus.* Now that Steeple which you see at the West-end and South-side of the Church, is the *Oxford*-tower, or *Dunstan*-Steeple I so lately spake of, and one of them. And the opposite one with the lofty Spire or Shaft covered with Lead is the other, and the same that is said to be of Archbishop *Arundel*'s building, and at this day called by his name. But under correction, without warrant of truth, as I conceive, induced thereunto partly from the work of the Steeple, which I hold elder than *Arundel*'s time by comparing it with other pieces of that age, and partly by this Note in the Records of the Church, seeming to me by the Character almost as ancient as the time of *Arundel. The Weight of the Five Bells in* Angel-*Steeple, newly given by the most Reverend* Thomas Arundel, Anno 1408.[11]

This Note, you see, calls it *Angel*, not *Arundel*-Steeple, as I suppose it would have done, or at the least have mentioned him the Founder, had he indeed erected it. Besides I meet with the *Angel*-Steeple in the Church-Records long before *Arundel*'s time, *i.e.* in the days of *Henry* of *Eastry*, the Prior; and by the same name this very Steeple I find to be called in divers dead mens Wills since *Arundel*'s time. Let me but add, that *Harpsfield* in the life of Archbishop *Arundel*, mentions not this Steeple amongst the rest of his Acts of Note, and I proceed.

This Nave or Body of the Church admits all Comers, (saith *Erasmus*) but at the upper end, for the better security of the upper part of the Church, where the Shrine was and other Treasure, was of old parted off from the Quire by certain Iron Grates or Bars; the Doors whereof for the same reason doubtless, Archbishop *Winchelsey* by his Statutes, commanded to be kept always close shut, unless in time of Divine Service, or at other time of necessary Ingress and Egress. Without offence to the Injunction let us enter. At or near which place of entrance, sometime stood a great Cross, in the head whereof was kept and inclosed that Golden Crown (as is shewed before) King *Knute* gave to the Church; and under it an Altar, which was known by the name of *The Altar of the Holy Cross, between the Quire and the Nave*; and, *The Altar under the great Cross of the Church.*

Next observe we the first Cross-Isles (Wings, some call them) of the Church, those (I mean) between the Nave and the Quire; which by the work, seem of like age with the Body, saving that the North-Isle (the goodly and glorious Window at the head whereof, a piece in its kind beyond compare, was the Gift of *Edward* IV. as may be seen upon it) with the lofty Tower or Steeple in the midst or meeting of the Crosier, by these Capital Letters *T. G. P.* with the three Gold Stones, the Mitre also and the Pastoral Staff in them both, and Archbishop *Warham*'s Coat of Arms beside, in the roof of the latter (the Steeple,) I conceive of somewhat a later building, and perfected, as in the time, so chiefly at the cost of Prior *Goldstone*, in *Henry* VIII. days.[12]

In this North-Isle, between the Cloyster-door and the Lady-Chapel, is a place inclosed and set apart, called to this day the *Martyrdom*. Archbishop *Becket* (as tradition hath it) being here or hard by (at or upon the third or fourth griece[13] or step of the *Pulpitum*,[14] or ascent to the Presbytery or Quire, as some will) murdered, martyred they call it; whence those Verses, on each leaf of the door one, yet legible in part, importing, that *St* Thomas *was martyred within this place* ...,[15]

I pass hence to the Chapel contiguous, commonly called a Lady-Chapel, a piece not old; by the work it should be much what about the age of *Dunstan*-steeple. *In Anno Domini* 1452. I find it called *The New Chapel of the Blessed* Mary.

I confess I read of the Lady-Chapel long before. Archbishop *Richard*, *Becket*'s immediate Successor, was buried in it. But that Chapel stood within the old body of the Church, and was parcel of it. I have it from the Church records verified by the leaden Inscription and pontifical Relicks, to wit, his Cope, Crosier, and Chalice lately found in digging Dr. *Anian*'s Grave by Sir *John Boys* his Monument on the North side of the Body, toward the upper end. That old Chapel was not heard of since the present body of the Church was built.

By the entry or *testudo*,[16] under the grieces or steps (the *pulpitum* as wont to be called) leading up to the Quire, from the body, I proceed and come to St *Michael*'s Chapel, standing on the other (the South) side of the Quire. A Chapel indeed in name old. For Archbishop *Langton* in *Henry* III. days is storied to be there intombed. But the work of the building of the modern Chapel will not bear that age. I am therefore persuaded that the old one was fain to be taken down, whilest the body and cross Isles of the Church were in building, to give better way to that work, and that that being finished, this was new built as now it is.

Ascend we now by the steps or *Pulpitum* to the Quire (Chancel or Presbytery.) *And these steps are many*, saith *Erasmus*: which whole work of the Quire, from end to end, I mean, from the Western door thereof unto the Archiepiscopal throne or marble Chair behind the high Altar, with the side-isles, cross-isles and other buildings on both sides of the Quire (the Quire's curious[17] Western door-case only excepted, built, I take it, about the time that the body was) together with the under-croft (or vaults) to them (except the Princes Chapel there) are much of an age; there is that harmonious symmetry and agreement between the parts. But certainly of what age I cannot define; only confessing it far elder than the Nave; I dare constantly and confidently deny it to be elder than the *Norman* Conquest; because of it upon Arches, a form of Architecture though in use with and among the *Romans* long before, yet after their departure not used here in *England* till the *Normans* brought it over with them (as I told you) from *France*. So that (I say) elder than the Conquest this piece cannot be, and I dare not pronounce it, the roof of it at least-wise to be so old, because of the many combustions betiding the Fabrick since the Conquest.[18] But by many inducements I am thoroughly perswaded that it is (for the main) the upper part of the new Church which *Lanfranc* first built, whereof I have treated sufficiently before. And so I have shortly done with the antiquity of this Fabrick, the Quire.

Now a word or two of the Ornaments, and what else in it may worthily call for our speculation. To begin with the Hangings setting forth the whole story both of our Saviour's Life and Death. They were given, one part of them by Prior *Goldstone*, and the other by *Richard Dering* the Church-Cellerar, in *Henry* VIII. days. Witness these several Memorials legible in the bordure of the Hangings.[19]

In the Church Records I meet with Inferior and Superior *chorus*; and one *Thomas Ingram* of *Canterbury*, by his will in the office gives *To every Monk in the Superior Quire* xii. *d. to every Monk in the Inferior Quire* viii. *d.* Now as we see there are two rows of Stalls (an Upper and a Lower) on either side of the Quire: so I conceive the Seniors and Superiors of the Monks used to sit in the upper, as the Juniors or Inferiors in the lower row; and that thence sprang the distinction of the superior and inferior Chorus.

Above these Stalls on the South-side of the Quire stands the Archbishop's wooden Seat or Chair, sometime richly guilt and otherwise well set forth, but now nothing specious[20] through age and late neglect. It is a close seat made after the old fashion of such Stalls, called thence *Faldistoria*: Only in this they differ, that they were Moveable, this is Fixt.[21]

A little higher up, on the other side of the Quire, between *Chichlie*'s, and *Bourgchier*'s Tombs was provision made heretofore for the storing and treasuring up of Saints Relicks. This Repository was shewed to *Erasmus*, who spends these words upon it. *On the North-side (of the Presbytery) were kept close under Lock and Key, such precious Rarities as were not to be seen by every body: You would wonder, if I should tell you, what a number of Bones were brought forth, Skulls, Jaw-bones, Teeth, Hands, Fingers, whole Arms, all which out of devotion we kissed*, &c. Hence *Erasmus* then beheld, as we may now, the Altars, Table, and Ornaments; indeed (thanks to the piety of the times) very rich and becoming such days of blessed peace as our Church (by God's mercy) now enjoys, but not comparable surely to those that *Erasmus* saw, or else he much hyperboliseth, where he saith: *You should think the richest Monarchs mere Beggars in comparison of the abundance of Silver and Gold, which did belong to the Furniture of this Altar*. This Altar is and was called the high Altar, more properly so, heretofore, than now, because it was the chief one in the whole Church, Christ's Altar, and to distinguish it from the Saints Altars, whereof the Church had many, 25 in number, one in the midst of the Crosier between the Nave and the Quire, a second in the Martyrdom, a third in the Lady-chapel, a fourth in St *Michael*'s Chapel, two in either wing of the Quire, *viz.* in each semicircle there one, one in the Vestry, one in St *Anselm*'s Chapel on the other side of the Quire, three near unto the high Altar it self, whereof one was St *Dunstan*'s, a second St *Elphege*'s, a third (and that standing behind the high Altar) St *Blase*'s, two at least in *Becket*'s Chapel, whereof one in the little side Chapel against *Henry* IV. Monument, and the other behind the shrine, in the place called *Becket*'s Crown, besides seven other in the undercroft, and two in the body of the Church which I had almost forgotten, whereof one was belonging to *Arundel*'s, and the other to *Brenchlye*'s Chantery there. One more there was, and that in the now *Dean*'s-Chapel.

But leaving these things and the Quire too, let us now ascend. *From behind the high Altar we go up as it were into another Church by several steps*, saith *Erasmus*. To this I proceed, the upper part of the Church (I mean) from the Grate between the Archiepiscopal Throne or marble Chair, by the Mosaick or Musaick-work, upwards, called (from the standing of this Shrine there) *Becket*'s Chapel: which with the *vertex* of the work, called *Becket*'s Crown (intended by *Erasmus*, where he saith, *There in a certain Chapel is to be seen the whole Face of the Blessed Martyr set in Gold and adorn'd with many Jewels*, &c.) the either side-Isles, (except the Chapel on the North-side, and the Undercroft of it) I hold to be somewhat less ancient than the Quire and its Undercroft: The ocular and peeked or pointed form of the Arch, the round marble Pillars or Columns both above and below (to pass by other disagreements easily observable) showing a manifest discrepancy and difference one from the other. For truth is, about the place where the Quire ends and that Chapel begins (observe but the works above and underneath, and you will easily perceive it) the Church once ended, and extended no further, the Pillars and work coming in and closing there.

The certain age of this part neither can I find, but from great probability do conceive it to be that new work (whereof *Edmerus* speaks[22]) begun and furthered by his Patron, Archbishop *Anselm*, but continued and consummated by *Ernulph* the Prior with the help of his Monks in *Henry* I. time. A work that (as I told you erewhile) was so envied by some about that King, and on the other side so much applauded and extolled by *William* the Monk of *Malmesbury*, who for the Windows, Pavement, and other Ornaments of it prefers it to any other in the whole Kingdom.[23] *The like*, says he, *was not to be seen in* England, *&c.* as before. Properties wherein it justly deserves the comparison.

Some haply may here ask me, why *Becket*'s Crown, if it be a piece so ancient, is so imperfect on the top? For Answer unto them, I say, that time was, when that piece was to the mind of the first Founders compleat; being built not altogether as high at first, as now it is. The Monks (saith Tradition) at the time of the Dissolution, were in hand (in honour of *Becket*) to have advanc'd the Building to a higher pitch; but their fall prevented that's rise. So that whereas before it had a handsome compleat Battlement, it is now a great blemish to the Church, and an Eye-sore to Spectators, by the ragged and imperfect ruins of it. This is that *Crown of* St Thomas, in beautifying whereof the Church-Records tell me, and I have before told you 115 *l.* 12 *s.* was expended in *Henry* the Prior's time.

Now retreating, let us take a view of the Vestry. A place, of the *Greeks* called *Diaconion*, and *Diaconicon*; but of the *Latins*, *Sacrarium*, *Secretarium*, and *Vestiarium*. This Vestry stands (like as Vestries generally do) on the North-side of the Quire. The words which *Erasmus* spends upon it, are to this effect. *We are led into the Vestry. What an incredible number of rich embroidered Vestments of Silk and Velvet, was to be seen there? How many Candlesticks of Gold? There we saw the pastoral Staff of St* Thomas. *It seem'd to be a Cane, cover'd over with a thin plate of Silver; very light, plain, and no longer than to reach from the ground to the girdle*, &c. …[24]

There is a Room next Wall to this, having had a door leading into it from hence, wherein partly, and partly in the Loft over this Vestry, the Church-Records are kept. The Treasury, we call it, but it was known to former times by the name either of *Armarium* or *Armariolum*, and properly, since it was the Church-Arcenal, yielding them weapons or Muniments wherewith to secure unto the Monks their Possessions and Privileges; whence also the Curator thereof was called *Armarius.*

Now a word or two of the Dean's Chapel, and my Survey of the Fabrick's upper part is at an end. This Chapel, with a Closet to it newer than the Chapel, fell to the then Dean's share, upon the division of Houses and Buildings, made anon after the change of the Foundation by *Henry* VIII. By what name it was formerly called, is a thing uncertain, and wherefore built. That division calls it only the Chapel next the *Dorter*. But …[25] I am assured that this was St *Thomas*'s Chapel, otherwise, *Anno* 16. *Edward* II. called *The Chapel of the blessed* Mary, *and the blessed* Thomas *the Martyr, near the gate of the Priory*; our Lady pictured in many of the Windows, sharing (it seems) with him in the dedication.

Over this Chapel is the Church-Library; not the same to the repair whereof Archbishop *Hubert* gave the Church of *Halstow*, this being built (as erewhile I told you,) by Archbishop *Chicheley*, and borrowed from the Chapel, or superadded to it; the juniority of the work, and the passage to it, plainly intimate so much. It was by the Founder and others once well stored with Books, but in man's memory shamefully robbed and spoiled of them all; an act much prejudicial and very injurious both to Posterity and the Commonwealth of Letters. The piety of the present Churchmen hath begun to replenish it, and may it have (what it well deserves) many Benefactors, to the perfecting of the fair beginning; with which wish I leave both it and the Chapel.

And now I desire you should take notice of the Windows, especially in the Church's upper part, which both for the Glass and Iron-work thereof are well worthy your observation. This part of the Church was highly commended by *Malmesbury* in his time, amongst other things, for this Ornament. *No such thing could be seen elsewhere in* England, *&c.* saith he. And I think his words hold true still. And I believe as much may be said of the Iron-work about them, apparently various in every Window. Besides, these Windows afford and offer to our view certain Verses containing a Parallel of the Old and New Testament. They are many, and therefore to avoid too great an Interruption here, you may find them in my *Appendix*, Numb. XXX.[26]

1. On William Somner, see the introduction by William Urry in the 1977 reprint of *The Antiquities of Canterbury*, listed in the bibliography.
2. The full title is: *The Antiquities of Canterbury or, A Survey of that Ancient City, with the Suburbs and Cathedral.*
3. *The Antiquities of Canterbury*, p.90.
4. *Ibid.*, p.96.
5. Richard Culmer, *Cathedrall Newes from Canterbury, shewing the Canterburian Cathedrall to bee in an Abbey-like, Corrupt, and rotten condition, which cals for a speedy Reformation, or Dissolution*, London, 1644, p.22.
6. *Ibid.*
7. For a modern essay on the cathedral's architecture, see Francis Woodman, *The Architectural History of Canterbury Cathedral*, London & Boston: Routledge & Kegan Paul, 1981.
8. The 1703 edition has been used for easier reading: the numerous quotations from Erasmus are all given in Latin in the first edition.
9. Desiderius Erasmus (*c.*1467-1536) visited the cathedral in 1512 with John Colet, while the shrine of St Thomas was still intact and a place of pilgrimage, and described it in his colloquium *Peregrinatio Religionis Ergo.* The Dutch scholar Erasmus was perhaps the most celebrated of the humanists, applying plain thinking and common sense to the questions of his time. He exposed abuses of the Church and attacked the pedantries of scholasticism, and did much to prepare the way for the revival of learning and the reformation of religious practice. He made several visits to England, staying for five years from 1509 at the invitation of Henry VIII.
10. These matters were presented in Somner's preceding section, 'The History of the Church's Fabrick'.
11. Thomas Arundel (1353-1414) was Archbishop of Canterbury in 1397 and from 1399 till his death. Somner, as is to be expected of an antiquary, was constantly seeking to determine the ages and origins of the cathedral buildings. He mainly took account of

comparative architectural styles and information from archives. Here he continues, in the following paragraph, to explore archival evidence.

12. T(homas) G(oldstone) P(rioris). On Goldstone, see Woodman, p.209.
13. *Griece*, stairway.
14. *Pultipum*, the screen, with a loft, separating the choir from the nave.
15 There follows a paragraph on the former altar at the place of the Martyrdom and the relics kept there. Thomas Becket was archbishop from 1162 to 29 December 1070, when he was murdered in the cathedral.
16. *Testudo*, probably used figuratively here, a *testudo* was a Roman besieging engine on wheels, having a protective screen and a heavy arched frame.
17. *Curious*, carefully detailed.
18. The preceding history of the church recounts the several occasions on which it was damaged by fire.
19. Somner here quotes, in a footnote, the texts of the two memorials.
20. *Specious*, outwardly beautiful and honourable.
21. *Faldistorium*, a medieval folding-stool; it was the basis for the design of a bishop's seat in the chancel.
22. Edmerus, or Eadmer, was a Canterbury historian whose writing covered the period from 1066 to 1122.
23. William of Malmesbury (*c.*1090–*c.*1143) was a major English historian whose work is one of the most valuable records of the kings of the early twelfth century.
24 There follow two paragraphs speculating on the roles of the various officers associated with the vestry.
25. Somner here discusses archival evidence for the original endowment of this chapel, whose function was changed in the Henrician Reformation.
26. The appendix indicated gives the verses in twelve windows.

III

Berkshire: Elias Ashmole (1617–1692)

Elias Ashmole addressed so many fields of enquiry that he was described by contemporaries as 'the greatest *virtuoso* and *curioso* that ever was known or read of in England'. Beginning his career as a lawyer and Royalist servant of the king in several capacities during the Civil War, he was, after the Restoration, appointed Comptroller of the Excise of the City of London and, in 1668, Accountant General of Excise. He also became a herald, antiquary, and avid collector of curiosities; but the interests to which he devoted most enthusiasm were astrology, alchemy, and magical sigils. Although for a time he studied mathematics and physics at Brasenose College, Oxford, he did not pursue scientific activities, preferring methodologies more ancient and more arcane for the discovery of knowledge. He became a founding, but non-active, member of the Royal Society. The achievement for which he is best remembered is the establishment of the first public museum in Britain, the Ashmolean in Oxford.

Ashmole was born in 1617 at Lichfield, Staffordshire, where his father was a saddler. His mother had connections with an influential London family and through them he was able to enter the legal profession. In the Civil War Ashmole's sympathies were strongly royalist, and while he had no real involvement in the fighting, he held posts as Excise Commissioner in Lichfield and Worcester successively, then as Gentleman of the Ordnance in Oxford. While in Oxford he found time to study and especially to pursue his interest in astrology, which had been encouraged by his friend George Wharton, the leading royalist practitioner of the time, and in 1646 he began a lifelong friendship with the even more prominent astrologer William Lilly.[1] In the same period he was developing complementary interests in alchemy and the study of magical sigils.[2] Alchemy became his main interest around 1650, although as a researcher rather than practitioner. He learned much from the alchemical adept William Backhouse[3] who, near death in 1653, passed on to him the secret of the philosopher's stone, which he in turn passed on to Robert Plot, of whose work an extract is offered in the following chapter.

(Neither passed on documentation of the secret for posterity.) In 1652 Ashmole published his *Theatrum Chemicum Britannicum*, a collection of annotated ancient alchemical verse treatises, probably the most significant alchemical work ever written in English. He followed this in 1658 with *The Way of Bliss*, another treatise on the same subject.

Ashmole was an avid collector of curiosities and had especially accumulated significant numbers of coins, medals, seals, and historical documents including medieval illuminated manuscripts. Having made acquaintance with the Tradescant family,[4] he undertook in 1652 to work with John Tradescant the Younger and the physician Thomas Wharton to catalogue the collection at their home in Lambeth. As well, he personally funded the resulting publication, *Musæum Tradescantianum*, so earning the family's confidence to the extent that, in 1659, they decided to bequeath to him the collection, their son and heir having died ten years earlier. Ashmole moved to Lambeth at about this time and in fact lived next to the Tradescants. On the death of John Tradescant, in 1662, his widow Hester regretted the transaction and contested the deed, but Ashmole's legal expertise ensured that she was pursuing an unwinnable cause. The validity of the deed was upheld by the courts and relations between Ashmole and Hester Tradescant were strained until her mysterious death by drowning in a pond in her garden in 1678. It was now easy for Ashmole to make whatever arrangements he chose for the collection and he had already been negotiating a bequest to the University of Oxford and for the provision by them of a building in which the collection could be exhibited. And so the Ashmolean Museum was founded: the intention was that it should be a resource for scientific research. The first keeper to be appointed was Robert Plot.

During the 1650s Ashmole became involved in antiquarian and heraldic research, probably encouraged by William Dugdale, with whom he had formed a friendship. Indeed, Dugdale became Ashmole's father-in-law in 1668, when the latter took Elizabeth, Dugdale's daughter, as his third wife.[5] In 1658 he undertook to catalogue the Bodleian Library's collection of Roman coins. His major antiquarian work was a comprehensive study of the Order of the Garter, perhaps as an affirmation of his monarchist beliefs during the period of the interregnum. The resulting work, lavishly illustrated by Wenceslaus Hollar, appeared in 1672: *The Institution, Laws and Ceremonies of the Most Noble Order of the Garter*. He helped with the planning of the restored king's coronation and did much to revive the Garter; in 1660 he was appointed Windsor Herald in the College of Arms, although in later life he relinquished this position.

Overall, it would hardly be accurate to say that Ashmole was a describer of landscapes: he observed the ordering of society, especially that close to the monarch; the remains of the past; objects of scientific interest; curiosities and mysteries; the occult. The extract which follows, from his *Antiquities of Berkshire*,[6] is a description of an interior, and it is one which would have been well known to him and close to his heart: Windsor Castle. The main object of his interest was the paintings, and, as shall be seen with Aubrey on his visit to Wilton House, it was by their representation and nothing else that he appraised them. Such an example of his writing is appropriate, for Elias Ashmole was a man of books and institutions, of which he especially favoured monarchy, which the paintings in Windsor Castle lavishly celebrated; and he was a servant of Charles II, a monarch closely associated with the castle. His description captures the sumptuousness and ostentation of the reign of the restored king.

Windsor Castle: the interior

From *The Antiquities of Berkshire*, 1719, vol 3, pp.114-119

This Castle [Windsor] consists of two square Courts, with a Tower betwixt them, which are also called three Wards. The higher Ward is call'd the *inner Square* or Court, the middle Ward the *Tower*, and the lower Ward the *outer Square*. In the inner Square, toward the *East*, is the Royal Palace, and in the Middle of the Square is a very fine Statue of King *Charles* II. on Horseback, erected in the Year 1680. On the Park-side of the Square, to the *North*, are the Royal Apartments, with those of the Officers of the Household. The rest of the Square composes the Apartments of the Officers of the Crown. The Entrance to the Royal Apartment is through a *Vestibulo*, supported by Pillars, with some antick Bustoes in the Niches; from whence you ascend the great Stairs to these Apartments on one Side; and on the Right Side of the *Vestibulo*, through a little Court, up another Pair of Stairs to St *George's Hall* on the other Side. The Domes of these Stair-Cases are painted. From each of these Stairs you pass into a Guard-Hall, which is finely embellished with several Sorts of Arms, artfully disposed into Figures, as at the Tower of *London*. In the Cieling is *Britannia* on a Globe, the *Indies* offering her Riches, and *Europe* a Crown; all surrounded with a Circle in Form of a Snake. Above the Chimney of one of these Halls is the picture of Prince *George* of *Denmark* on Horseback, excellently done by Mr. *Dahl*; and that of the late King of *Sweden* over that of the other. In the *Preference Chamber*, over the Chimney, is *Judith* and *Holofernes*, an admirable Piece; and over the Door St *Mary Magdalen*, masterly done. There is another *Magdalen*, an Original, in the *Privy Chamber*; and another *Judith* over the Door. In the *Gallery*, over the Door, is the *Roman* Daughter giving Suck to her Father in Prison. In the *Bed-*

Chamber is another *Judith* over the Closet-Door, and the *Innocents* over that of the Chamber. In the Cieling of the *Closet* the Story of *Leda* and the *Swan* is wonderfully performed. In the *Dining Room* all Sorts of *Fish* and *Poultry*, and *Fruit* are very naturally presented; and in the *Gallery* there is a Picture much taken notice of for the Liveliness of the Light of a *Candle*, by which an old Woman is seen reading. In the Room of Audience, over the Chimney, is her Royal Highness the Princess of *Orange*, Mother to King *William*, and the Dutchess of *Richmond*, with this Inscription;—*Numero Deus impare gaudet*. In the Cieling is King *Charles* II, supported by *Peace* and *Victory*. In short, every Apartment that composes this Palace is spacious and noble: the Canopies of State, under which the late Queen gave Audience, are as rich as Embroidery can make them; and the Pictures in the Closet, and little Gallery, with that of *English* Beauties, are worth a Stranger's coming to *England* on purpose to see.

From that Guard-Room, where we said before was a Picture of the late King of *Sweden*, we pass into St *George's Hall*, the finest Room in the World. This Hall is very large and long, and designed from the first Institution for the Entertainment of the Knights of the Garter at their Installation; and the Sovereign us'd to give a Feast to his Twenty Five Knights Companions every St *George's* Day. But this latter Custom has not been observed since the Reign of King *Charles* II. who made the last Feast of that kind at the Installation of the present Duke of *Buckingham*, then Earl of Mulgrave.

On one Side of the Hall is painted King *Edward* III. sitting on a Throne, receiving his triumphant Son *Edward* the *Black Prince*, with the Kings of *France* and *Scotland* Prisoners, full as big as the Life …

On the Cieling are painted the Triumphs of King *Charles* II over Faction, Rebellion, and Sedition, where the Painter has put the Picture of the Earl of *Shaftesbury*, Lord Chancellor in that Reign, representing Sedition with Libels in his Hand, a Man, who served all Times and Parties, according to his Interest, and was named as one of the King's Judges, though he had the Wit not openly to appear. At the upper End of the Hall is the Picture of King *William* III. seated on a Throne, ten Steps high, five of which only are painted; and above this is St *George* killing the Dragon.

1. George Wharton, an astrologer who supported Charles I, and William Lilly, a strongly republican astrologer, were rivals at the time of the Civil War, but were eventually reconciled and helped each other at times when one or other of them was in danger of persecution for his political position. Lilly developed a particularly successful business as an astrologer and produced an almanac, *Merlini Anglici Ephemeris*, from the year 1647 till his death in 1682. It became very popular in the 1650s, not only in England but, in translation, on the Continent, but declined in the more rigorous intellectual times following the Restoration. Ashmole held him in high esteem, being present at his deathbed and paying for his tombstone.
2. *Sigils*, occult signs.
3. Backhouse (1593-1662) was a secretive adept whose life was uneventful, but who did much to encourage others in alchemy. Ashmole is the main source of information about him.
4. The Tradescants are the subject of a later chapter of this book.
5. Ashmole's first wife, Eleanor Mainwaring, died three years after the marriage. Some years later, in 1649, he married another Mainwaring, Mary, a relative of his late first wife, and a thrice-widowed woman twenty years his senior. The family had opposed the match and it proved not to be a happy one, but it made Ashmole wealthy enough to pursue his interests freely. Mary died in 1668.
6. Published in 1719 by E. Curll. It is not dated but since the description includes mention of a painting of King William III, it may be concluded that it was written in the last year of Ashmole's life, unless it was completed by another antiquary after his death.

IV

Oxfordshire: Robert Plot (1640–1696)

One of the most accomplished scholars of the period in which scientific research began its significant development, Robert Plot was a pioneer in the study of the natural world. The works for which he is remembered are *The Natural History of Oxfordshire* (1677) and *The Natural History of Staffordshire* (1686). After the publication of the first of these, he was appointed Professor of Chemistry at Oxford University, was chosen by Elias Ashmole as the first Keeper of the Ashmolean Museum, and was elected to the Royal Society, of which he soon became secretary. The second book, which was dedicated to King James II, led to his appointment as Historiographer Royal. Plot was born in Borden, Kent, and was educated at Wye and at Magdalen Hall, Oxford. He completed his BA, MA, and doctorate of civil law between 1661 and 1671. He entered University College in 1676, where he resided until 1690, when he married and retired to his property in Kent. In both of his professional posts he was enthusiastic, diligent, and productive, although the reason he gave for his eventual resignation was that the stipend was insufficient. To continue his ambitious project to produce further studies of natural history, he collected data in Kent, Middlesex, and London, but his death came before any of this could be applied in writing.

Indeed, it had been Plot's intention to emulate John Leland and William Camden in surveying the whole nation, but with respect to its natural history rather than its topography, genealogies and tenancies, and civic history. The study of Oxfordshire, then, was to be the first of a series which would include all the counties. He explained his aims on the first page of the book:

> … I shall consider, first, *Natural Things*, such as either she hath retained the same from the beginning, or freely produces in her ordinary Course; as *Animals, Plants*, and the *universal Furniture of the World*. Secondly, her *extravagancies* and *defects*, occasioned either by the Exuberancy of Matter, or Obstinacy of Impediments, as in *Monsters*. And then lastly, as she is restrained, forced, fashioned, or determined, by Artificial Operations. All which, without Absurdity, may fall under the general

> Notation of a *Natural History*, things of *Art* (as the Lord *Bacon* well observeth) not differing from those of *Nature* in *form* and *essence*, but in the *efficient* only; Man having no Power over *Nature*, but in her Matter and Motion, *i.e.* to put together, separate, or fashion Natural Bodies, and sometimes to alter their ordinary Course.[1]

As we will see in the work of John Aubrey, the scope of Plot's survey was greater than such as would later be thought of as 'natural history'. As well as examining normal natural things Plot also took account of the abnormal. In the chapter *Of Men and Women* he made clear at the opening that he would not deal with ordinary cases, 'there being no new *Species* of *Men* to be produced', but instead deal with 'the unusual *Accidents*' experienced by people. Again, the interest in the abnormal is also evident in Aubrey's enquiries, and indicates a curiosity especially aroused by the mysterious and the unexpected. Plot went further in considering the 'arts' of Man and '*things artificial*, which have either been *invented* or *improved* in this *County*' to be appropriately encompassed by a study of natural history. The *Oxfordshire* covers meteorological, geological, botanical, and zoological topics; the chapter on humans, their 'accidents' including strange ailments, unnatural conditions, monstrous births, folk customs, superstitions, supernatural phenomena; a chapter on the arts, including agriculture, astronomy, physics, architecture; and a chapter on antiquities. This last inclusion was perhaps made out of deference for the antiquarian tradition, in which his work represented a new direction, but, as with the other objects of his investigations, Plot aimed to treat antiquities scientifically, and he collected and described coins, urns, lamps and other artefacts.

The Natural History of Oxfordshire was innovative both in its conceptions and its methodology. It was the first substantial regional study of natural history and thus it was a county survey which eschewed the approach and directions of antiquarian chorographies. Its influence was immediate and far-reaching, and it was greeted with enthusiasm by the contemporary scholarly scientific community. For the modern reader it is a fascinating example of early modern naturalistic thinking, preceding as it does the system of classification which was to be developed by Linnaeus,[2] and embracing not only naturally-occurring phenomena but also the works of humans as part of the valid field of natural history. In a pre-industrial world, the now-familiar anxieties about the effects of human development on nature had not emerged: since the Industrial Revolution, and the accelerating growth of industry, it is difficult to appreciate the position that the cultivated and built environments are natural, and that the world is not in any way endangered by Man's 'arts'.

The three following extracts illustrate different ways in which Robert Plot, as a naturalist, 'saw' Oxfordshire. The first is from his examination of farming methods, one of the topics included in the chapter on the 'Arts', and illustrates a working landscape which may well have been familiar to many of his readers. He notes that his purpose has been to describe 'the most uncommon *Arts* I have met with concerning *Plants* related to *Husbandry*', explaining that by 'uncommon' he means that they would seem so to 'strangers', that is, readers from outside Oxfordshire, in which county the practices he describes are typical. Other practices were to be described in subsequent surveys of other counties. His account of the harvesting and storing of the grain is detailed and offers a lively view of work on a seventeenth-century farm. In the short second extract, taken from his descriptions of Oxfordshire plants, we are with the scientific naturalist in the field, and we see examples of the close study of particulars in which most of his investigations consist. At this stage the main direction of botanical and zoological studies was classification, and it is interesting to compare the approach with that of Gilbert White, the observer of how plants and animals actually lived, a hundred years later. Whatever the limitations of his methodology, Plot was meticulous, adhering faithfully to the new Baconian principles of observation and experimentation, and a pioneer in his discipline.

Finally, a sample from his chapter on 'formed stones' reveals the scientist using the same approach in addressing one of the greatest mysteries that was to be encountered in the seventeenth-century landscape. These objects were mineral crystals and fossils, for which he produced exact descriptions and a number of beautiful illustrations. In an earlier chapter on stones, Plot had set himself the guideline that he should confine his investigations to that which was useful to Man. Although the formed stones could not easily be said to meet this criterion, they seemed 'rather to be made for his *admiration* than *use*', and so were worthy of study.[3] The work on fossils was Plot's most celebrated venture, and warrants some explanation. His great achievement was the recognition and extensive documentation of specimens, while his greatest challenge was in trying to address the perplexing question of their origin:

> Whether the Stones we find in the Forms of *Shell-fish*, be *Lapides sui generis*,[4] naturally produced by some extraordinary *plastic virtue*, latent in the Earth or Quarries where they are found? Or, whether they rather owe their Form and Figuration to the *Shells* of the *Fishes* they represent, brought to the *places* where they are now found by a *Deluge, Earth-quake*, or some other such means, and there being filled with *Mud, Clay*, and petrifying *Juices*, have in tract of time been turned into *Stones*, as we now find them, still retaining the same Shape in the whole, with the same *Lineations, Sutures, Eminences, Cavities, Orifices, Points*, that they had whilst they were Shells?[5]

In a climate of controversy, Plot stated at the outset that he was inclined to the former option, that the stones were indeed *sui generis*, for it seemed to him to present fewer, and less insurmountable, difficulties. Yet in considering the matter, he wrote, 'I intend not any peremptory *Decision*, but a *friendly Debate*', in which he opposed one side to the other over a discussion occupying ten pages.[6]

Plot began by explaining the view which he himself maintained. Firstly, he reasoned, had the stones once been shellfish that had been brought to where they are now by a flood, it would not have been Noah's flood, because that was not a universal event, but was confined to Asia. Even supposing this not to have been the case, and the flood to have been universal, then since the flood was produced by rain, the shells would have been driven downwards and could not have ended up on the tops of hills. Also, the shells would have been 'indifferently scattered' and not found in groups with similar striations and of similar types. What was more commonly found seemed to be groupings, say, beds of cockles, as if in a breeding-place. In the mere forty days of the flood, they would not have had time to 'get together and sequester themselves from all other Company'. Moreover, he continued, there was no other known flood which would have effected England to a sufficient degree. So it could only have been by the actions of earthquakes raising low places up, a phenomenon practically unknown in England, that the shells could have come to be on hilltops. Yet even if, in the past, there had been a strange earthquake or flood which might have placed shells in the hills, there are further difficulties to be explained and, with some relish, Plot keeps the questions coming. How was it that some of the stones resemble shellfish which always stick to rocks, and so would not have been moved? While many shells, which are the remains of animals which cannot move around, are to be found, why are there so few remains, in the same places, of many other sea-creatures which have locomotion, and could conceivably get to the higher places, crustaceans being especially rare? How can many of the stones, resembling bivalves, not be species which continue to exist? Surely it seems unlikely that a species would have been lost in Noah's flood, because 'Providence' would not have let something made by Nature be wasted. Why are those stones, which look like shells, in fact striated on the outside only, not within? And moreover how could the numerous inconsistencies between living animals and the stones be explained?

Opposed to this torrent of objections, Plot outlines, on behalf of its supporters, the main points of the case that the stones were produced by the fossilization of the remains of plants and animals.[7] They noted, he writes, that the formed stones were remarkably similar to living shellfish, and amongst the stones there were sometimes found shell-shaped specimens with the same colours and surface substances as the actual shells; there was even a case of an oyster-like stone still having a pearl stuck to it. To explain why large numbers of similar stones might be found together, it was observed that in some places in England, away from the sea, large quantities of oyster-shells had been found together; one such being near Reading. Such deposits may well have been locations in which large numbers of people had in the past been eating seafood. That near Reading may have been left by an ancient garrisoned army. Finally, it seems contrary to Nature that it should produce something which has no purpose 'than only to exhibit a form'. These arguments, it must be said, are not very compelling, so the debate turns out not to be so impartially presented as promised.

Taking all into account, it must be granted that considerable imagination would have been needed to accept that the fossils were petrified plants and animals, since there appears not to have been an awareness of the possibility of species becoming extinct, and there was no formulation of the possibility of evolution of species. Nor was there any conception of the time over which fossilization might occur. The world in 1676 was thought to be 5,680 years old, as Plot himself specified elsewhere in his book.[8] There was no awareness of geological change to the profile and shape of the land, nor even of the glacial impact of the Ice Age. It is not difficult to see why he adopted the position he did and it was a case of the evidence being misleading. Yet the detail with which he described specimens was a scientific achievement of real value.

Corn

From *The Natural History of Oxford-Shire*, pp.255–260

98.[9] There are also several *Arts*, used about the *Corn* in this *County*, whil'st in the *Blade*, and *Straw*, that belong to this place, such as eating it off with *Sheep*, if too *rank*, to make it grow strong and prevent lodging: whil'st the *Corn* is young they also weed it, cutting the *Thistles* with a hook; but *rattles* they handweed as soon as in *flower*, and so they do *cockles* when they intend the *Corn* for *seed*.[10] If the *Crows* towards *Harvest* are any thing mischievous, as they many times are, destroying the *Corn* in the outer limits of the *Fields*, they dig a *hole* narrow at the bottom, and broad at the top, in the *green swarth* near the *Corn*, wherein they put *dust*, and *cinders* from the Smith's forge, mixt with a little *Gun-powder*, and in and about the *holes* stick *feathers* (*Crow-feathers* if they can get them) which they find about *Burford* to have good success.
99. They cut their *Wheat* here rather a little before, than let it stand till it be over-ripe; for if it be cut but a little too soon, the *shock*[11] will ripen it, and the *Corn* will be beautiful, whereas if it stand too long, much will shatter out of the head in *reaping*, especially if the *wind* blow hard, and that the best *Corn* too; the worst only remaining, which will be pale in the hand, an unpardonable fault where the *Baker* is the *Chapman*.[12] In reaping *Wheat* and *Rye* they use not the *sicle*, but a smooth edged *hook*, laying their *Corn* in small

hand-fulls all over the *Field*; I suppose that it may the sooner dry, in case wet come before they *bind* it, which they do in very small *sheaves*, and very loose in comparison of some other *Counties*: They *shock* it rafter-wise, ten *sheaves* in a *shock*, which if set wide in the but-end, will be very copped and sharp at the top, and will bear out rain beyond hope, or almost credit.[13]

100. They count their *Barly* ripe (as they do their *Wheat*) when it hangs the head and the *straw* has lost its *verdure*, which they mow with a *sithe* without a *cradle*,[14] never binding but raking it together, and cocking[15] it with a *fork*, which is usually a *trident*, whose teeth stand not in a row, but meet *pyramidally* in a *center* at the staff: They let it lie in the *swathe*[16] a day or two, which both ripens the *Corn* and withers the *weeds*. *Oats*, and all *mixed Corns* called *Horse-meat*, are Harvested somtimes with two reaping *hooks*, whereof the manner is thus: The *Work-man* taking a *hook* in each hand, cuts them with *that* in his right hand, and rolls them up the while with *that* in his left, which they call bagging of *Peas*: Others they cut with a reaping *hook* set in a *staff* about a yard long, and then they cut and turn the *Peas* before them with both hands till they have a *wad*, which they lay by, and begin again; and this they call cutting with the *staff-hook*: But the *sithe* they say is much the speediest way, which if used with care, cuts them as well and clean, as either of the other.

101. After the *sithe* they *wad* both *Beans* and *Peas*, and so turn them till they are throughly withered and dry, and then *cock* and fit them for *carriage*, only with this difference, that *Beans* while they are *cocked* and *carryed*, have the loose *stalks* pickt up by *hand*, the rake being apt to beat the *Beans* out of the *pods*, as they are drawn up against the leg. All sorts of *Cocks* are best made of a middleing *cize*, and well top'd; the advantages are, that these are apprehended at least to take less wet with the same *rain* than greater, and will dry again without breaking; whereas the great *cocks*, after *rain*, must be pulled to pieces, which cannot be done without great loss, for in the opening and turning much *Corn* will be beaten out, and that certainly the best too.

102. If their *Corn* be brought home a little *moister*, or *greener* than ordinary, or the *weeds* be not let lie to be throughly shrunk or wither'd, that they suspect it may *heat* in the *Barn* more than ordinary (for it is kind[17] for *Corn* and *fodder* to *heat* a little) then they draw a *Cubb* or *Beer-lip*[18] (which others call a *Seed-cord*) up the middle of the *mow* or *stack*, and through the *hole* that this leaves, the *heat* will ascend and so prevent *mow-burning*; Or if it *heat* in the *Barn* beyond expectation, and be like to do amiss, they then pull a *hole* in the middle from the top to the bottom, which will also help it much. They draw an old *Axel-tree* of a *Cart* up a *Hay-rick* to the same purpose, if they think their *Hay* of the *greenest*, or over *moist* when *stacked*.

103. But the best contrivance I ever yet saw to prevent the *fireing* of *Ricks* of *Hay*, or *Sainct-foin*, I met with at *Tusmore*, at the Worshipful *Richard Fermors* Esq;

where they let in *square pipes* made of *boards* of a foot *diagonal*, to the middle of their *stacks*, to give them *Air* perpetually; the number of *pipes* bearing proportion to the bigness of the *Ricks*, which no question may also be as rationally applyed to *stacks* of *Corn*, whenever thought subject to the same danger.

104. To preserve their *Ricks* of *Corn* lyable to *rats* and *mice*, they commonly place them in this *County*, on *standers* and *caps* of *stone*; the *standers* being four *Obeliscs* about two foot high, and the *caps* as many *Hemispherical stones* placed upon them, with the flat sides downwards, on which having laid four strong pieces of *Timber*, and other *Joists* to bear up the *Corn*, they place their *Ricks*, which then are not annoyed by *mice* or *rats* (at least not so much) as *stacks* on the ground, by reason the *Hemispherical* stones being *planums* at the bottom, though they may possibly ascend the *standers* well enough, yet can scarce get up the *caps*, whose broad bottoms hang so over them *in plano Horizontis*, that they must needs fall in the attempt.

105. The *Cart* they most use to bring home their *Corn*, is the two-wheeled *long Cart*, having *shambles*[19] over the *shafts* or *thills*, a *Cart Ladder* at the breech, and *hoops* over the *wheels*, on which they will lay great and very broad *loads*, though it go not so secure and steady as a *Waggon*, which notwithstanding that advantage is but little use here, only amongst *Carriers, &c.* They use also a sort of *Cart* they call a *Whip-lade*, or *Whip-cart*, whose hinder part is made up with *boards* after the manner of a *Dung-cart*, having also a head of *boards*, and *shambles* over the *thills*; which *head* being made so as to be taken out or left in, the *Cart* may be indifferently used to carry *dung* or other *matters*; *dung*, when the *head* is in, and *Corn, &c.* when taken out.

106. About *Banbury* most of their *Carts* have *Axel-trees* of *Iron*, made *square* at one end and *round* at the other; at the *square* end they are made fast into one of the *wheels*, and move round together with it; and at the other end they move within the *box* of the *wheel*, and the *wheel* round them too: With this sort of *Axel* some are of opinion that the *Cart* moves much lighter for the *Cattle*, than with a wooden *one*, to whom I should much rather assent, did the *round* end of the *Axel* move in a *box* of *brass*, and were the places where the *Cart* rests on it, lined with *brass plates*, for then a small matter of *oil* (as 'tis in the *oiling* of *bells*) would cause the heaviest weight to be moved with great ease: however as they are, much less *grease* serves the turn; and one of them made of good tough *iron*, will last a mans *age*, and somtimes *two*, whereas the wooden *ones* are frequently at reparations: nor does there any inconveniency attend *them* that I could hear of, but that the *wheels* have not so much room to play to and fro on *these*, as on the *others* of *wood*, and therefore not so good where either the *ways* or *Cart-routs* are deep.

107. Their way in this *Country* to bring the *corn* from the *straw*, is for the most part by the *flail*, only in some *places* when their *wheat* is very *smutty*, they have

a way of *whipping* it first, and then *threshing* it afterwards: their manner of *whipping* is striking the *corn* by a handful at a time, against a *door* set on its edge; and when a *sheaf* is thus *whipt*, they bind it up again for the *flail*: which way indeed is troublesom and tedious, but by this means the *smut bags* or *balls*[20] are preserved unbroken, and by the strength of a good wind, and care in the *raying*, most part of them may be gotten forth, and the *wheat* is left clear. ...[21]
110. Which is all concerning *Corn*, whil'st in the *blade* or *straw*, what remains relates to the separating the *seed* from the *chaff*, and preserving it in the *stores*. As to the first, they either do it in a good *wind* abroad, or with the *fan* at home, I mean, the *leaved fan*; for the *knee fan*,[22] and casting the *corn* the length of the *Barn*, are not in use amongst them. They that have but small quantities, when no *wind* is stirring, will do it with a *sheet*; the manner thus: Two *persons* take a *sheet*, and double it at the *seam*, then rolling in each end a little, and holding one hand at the top, and the other a foot or 18 inches lower, they strike together and make a good *wind*, and some speed. But the *wheel fan* saves a *mans* labor, makes a better *wind*, and does it with much more expedition.
111. They preserve it in their *stores*, as well as *ricks*, from *mice* and *rats* by many *ordinary* means used in other places: but I met with one way somewhat *extraordinary*, performed by a peculiar sort of *Rats-bane*, that kills no creatures but those for which it is designed, except *poultry*; so that it is an excellent *remedy*, especially within doors, where *Fowls* seldom come, or any other place where they may be kept from it; all *Cats*, *Dogs*, *&c.* tasting it without hurt. To secure their *Corn* from musting, I have heard of some that have laid it in *Chambers* mixt with *Pebble-stones* of the larger cize *stratum super stratum, viz.* after every six inches thickness of *Corn*, a *stratum* of *Pebbles*, placed about a yard distance from each other, then *Corn* again to the same thickness, and so *S S S* to ten *lains* apiece:[23] by which method, as I was told, *Corn* had been preserved sweet and free from *must*, ten years together, only removing it once a year, and laying it again as before; and in the *Summer* time when the weather was dry, setting open the *windows* in the day time and shutting them at night.
112. To recover it from *mustiness*, to its pristin *sweetness*, some have laid it out all *night*, thin spred on *cloaths*, to receive the Evening and Morning *dews*, with so good success, that being dryed again next day in the Sun, the ill smell has been quite removed. And thus I have done with the most uncommon *Arts* I have met with concerning *Plants* related to *Husbandry*, and the whole *Herbaceous* kind: where by the way let it be noted, as in *Chap. 6.* §.23. that these *Arts* are called *uncommon*, not so much in respect of this, as of other *Counties*, where indeed they will seem so: and that I have written of them rather for the information of *strangers*, than the *Inhabitants* of *Oxford-shire*, as I must hereafter in other *Counties*, for information of this. Wherein if through my own *ignorance*, or *frowardness* of some *Husbandmen* (I dare not

say all) I have failed of that *accuracy*, that might otherwise have been expected, I beg the *Readers* pardon, and promise amendment in the following *Counties*, provided I have encouragement to go on in my design.[24]

Herbaceous plants indigenous to Oxfordshire and not previously described

From *The Natural History of Oxford-Shire*, pp.146–148

3. *Viola Martia hirsuta major inodora.* Which large *Violet* from a fibrous Root sendeth forth many Leaves, each upon his own Foot-stalk, neither creeping as the common *March*, nor branched as the common *Dog-Violet*; its Leaves and Stalks are all *hairy*, especially on the back-side; they are also broader, larger, and more *pointed* than the ordinary *March Violets*, which occasioned (as some think) the Ingenious Dr. *Merret* to note it by the name of *Viola Trachelii folio*, but that certainly must be some different kind, the Leaves of ours being all *invecked* ... whereas the *Trachelia* are all *indented*: Amongst the Leaves grow large *Flowers*, upon Foot-stalks (as other *Violets*) of a pale Blue Colour, with White *Lines* or *Rays* issuing from the middle of them, but wholly without *Scent*. They flower in *March* and *April*, and are commonly, but abusively sold to the *Shops* amongst other *Violets*, they not being good for any of those Uses the *Apothecary*'s put them to, as other *Violets* are. They grow plentifully in *Magdalene College* Coppice, on *Shotover* Hill, *Stow-Wood*, and many other *places*.

4. *Viola palustris rotundifolia.* From the Root of this Plant, which is *white*, and at equal Distances *knotted* (whence only it sends forth its *Fibers*, not downward, but *Horizontally*) arise 3 or 4 (sometimes more) feeble small *Stalks*, each bearing at its top only a round Leaf ... Among which, about *April* come up the *Stalks* of the *Flowers*, Slender, like those of the *Leaves*; the whole *Plant* being weak, and beholding to neighbouring *ones* for its Support. The *Flowers* are small and Blue, which being past, a long *Prismatical Seed-vessel* succeeds, opening its self when ripe into three parts, and shewing a rank of brown *Seeds*, appended to each Angle by white *Nerves*: This is easily distinguished from all other *Violets* by its native *place*, wherein 'tis supposed they will not grow; and by the Smallness of its *Flowers*, which are considerable *less* than any of the rest; whereunto add the remarkable *roundness* of its Leaves, which are so far from drawing to *Points*, that the longest way of them is side to side. *Clusius* indeed seems to describe a Plant like this, by the name of *Viola Alpina altera*, but makes its Flower as much *greater*, as ours is *less* than the common *one*; adding beside, that it flowers about the latter end of *June*, a Month before which time the Seed of *ours* is ripe; which are Differences so irreconcilable, that we cannot but pronounce *ours* as distinct from *his*, as from any other

Violets before described by *Authors*, whereof we have consulted *most*, if not *all* the best. It grows sparingly in the Boggs about *Stow-Wood*, and on the Banks of the *Cherwell* between *Oxford* and *Water-Eaton*; but most plentifully at *Chilswell* in *Berkshire*, amongst the moistest Boggs.

Of Formed Stones

From *The Natural History of Oxford-Shire*, pp.132–133

157. … I have [a stone] dug out of a Quarry in the Parish of *Cornwell*, and given me by the Ingenious Sir *Thomas Pennyston*,[25] that has exactly the Figure of the lowermost part of the *Thigh-Bone* of a *Man*, or at least of some other *Animal*, with the *capita Femoris inferiora*, between which are the *anterior* … and the larger *posterior Sinus*, the seat of the strong *Ligament* that rises out of the *Thigh*, and that gives safe passage to the *Vessels* descending into the *Leg*: And a little above the *Sinus*, where it seems to have been broken off, shewing the *Marrow* within of a shining *Spar-like* Substance, of its true Colour and Figure, in the *hollow* of the *Bone* … In compass near the *capita Femoris* just two Foot, and at the Top above the *Sinus* (where the *Thigh-Bone* is as small as any where) about 15 Inches; in weight, though representing so short a part of the *Thigh-Bone*, almost 20 Pounds.
158. Which are *dimensions*, and a *weight*, so much exceeding the ordinary course of *Nature*, that by *Agricola*, *Cæsalpinus*, and *Kircher*, such *Stones* have been rather thought to be Formed either in hollows of Rocks casually of this *Figure*, and filled with *materials* fit for *Petrification*; or by some other sportive *plastic Power* of the Earth, than ever to have been real *Bones*, now *Petrified*.[26]
159. And that indeed there are *Stones* this naturally fashioned, must by no means be doubted, since no question the stony Teeth of which there are Cart-loads to be had in a *Cave* near *Palermo*, beside others in the shape of *Leg* and *Thigh-Bones*, and of the *Vertebræ* of the *Back*, are no others than such. None of them, as the judicious *Charles* Marquess of *Ventimiglia* well observed, having any signs of *hollowness* for the place of the *Marrow*, much less of the *Marrow* it self.
160. Which has fully convinced me that this *Stone* of ours was not so produced, it having those *Signs* exquisitly expressed; but must have been a real *Bone*, now *Petrified*, and therefore, indeed, not properly belonging to this place. However, it being now a *Stone*, and not coming into my Hands whilst I was treating of *Petrifications*, I have rather thought fit to throw myself upon the *Reader*'s Candour, and *mis-place* it here, as I did the *Adarce*, than altogether to omit so considerable an Instance.[27]
161. But against this Opinion of its having been once a *real Bone*, there lies a considerable *Objection*, *viz.* that it will be hard to find an *Animal* proportionable to *it*, both *Horses* and *Oxen* falling much short of *it*.[28] To

which if it be Answered, that it may be much encreased in the *Petrification*; it may again be replied, that though indeed there be an *Augment* in some *Petrifications*, yet that it is not so in *all*: for though in all *Petrifications* there be an Ingress of *Steams* and *Particles* that were not there before, and therefore either a Cession of some other Body required, or a necessary *Augmentation*; yet that those *petrifying Steams* are sometimes so thin and fine, that they require only the *Cession* of some *Airy* or *Æthereal Atoms*, contained before in the porous parts of the *Body* to be changed, as indeed it appears to have been in this *Instance* of our *petrified Bone*: for with it was found a *Tooth* … weighing two Ounces and ¼, not at all *petrified*, but perfect *Bone* still, rather exceeding than any thing short of it in *proportion*; whence it must necessarily be concluded, that there could be but little if any *Augmentation* at all.

162. And if it be asked, how it should come to pass that the *Thigh-Bone* should be *petrified*, and not the *Tooth*, it may be answered, and that *experimentally* too, that *Teeth* admit not so easily of any Change or *Petrification*, because they are much more closely compacted *Substances* than any other *Bones*; whence 'tis, that we so often find them sound and good, when all other *Bones* are consumed. Thus at *Bathendown*, or *Bannerdown* (the *Mons Badonicus* of *Nennius*) not far from *Bath* in *Somerset-shire*, there have been Cap-fulls of *Teeth*, picked up by such as followed the Plough, but we are told of no other *Bones* found there. And we are informed by *Fazellus*, in his History of *Sicily*, that of two *Giant's Skeletons*, one found by *Johannes a brachiis fortibus*, in the Field *Gibilo*, a Mile South of the Town *Mazarenum*, now *Mazara*; and the other by *Paulus Leontinus*, not far from *Palermo*, that when they came to be touched, all fell into Dust but the *dentes molares*, or the greater Teeth called the *Grinders*, sufficient Arguments (I had almost said) of their unalterable State.

163. Since then it seems to be manifest, that the Size of the *Bone* has been scarce alter'd in its *Petrification*: It remains, that it must have belong'd to some greater *Animal* than either an *Ox* or *Horse*; and if so (say almost all other *Authors* in the like Case) in probability it must have been the *Bone* of some *Elephant*, brought hither during the Government of the *Romans* in *Britain* …

1. *The Natural History of Oxford-Shire*, Second Edition, Oxford, 1705, facsimile reproduction, Menston, Yorkshire: Scolar Press, 1972, pp.1–2.
2. Carl Linnaeus, later Carl von Linné (1707–1778), Swedish naturalist, was the founder of the modern system of botanical taxonomy. He visited England and the acceptance of his system amongst English naturalists and gardeners was an important factor in its universal adoption.
3. *The Natural History of Oxford-Shire*, p.81.
4. Of a unique kind.
5. *The Natural History of Oxford-Shire*, p.112.

6. *Ibid. et seq.*
7. From amongst his contemporaries, Plot especially mentioned Hooke and Ray. Robert Hooke (1635–1703), natural philosopher, was the Curator of Experiments for the Royal Society and professor of geometry at Gresham College. His scientific research and invention encompassed many fields including mechanics, optics, properties of gases, microscopic observations, philosophy and architecture. John Ray (1647–1705) was a theologian and naturalist. His first specialty was the collection, cataloguing and classification of plants, for which he travelled widely in the British Isles and in Europe. He later broadened his interests to include insects and other animals. He collected and classified thousands of species, and his work is notable for its accuracy and detail.
8. *The Natural History of Oxford-Shire*, p.229.
9. Plot numbered his paragraphs throughout each chapter.
10. *Rattles*, plants whose seeds form in a pod and rattle when ripe. *Cockles*, pink-flowering plants which grow amongst the corn.
11. *Shock*, stook.
12. *Chapman*, a merchant, hence, poor corn is a problem if the baker is the one who is buying it.
13. Beyond belief.
14. *Cradle*, an attachment on a scythe which allows the cut grain to be laid in bunches on the ground.
15. *Cock*, a conical pile.
16. That is, where it has been cut.
17. *Kind*, in the nature of.
18. *Cubb, beer-lip*, types of carrying-basket.
19. *Shambles*, the wooden frame hanging over the shafts, otherwise called thills, in which the cart-horse was harnessed.
20. *Smut*, a black deposit caused by fungal growth.
21. Plot describes here 'straw-works', the fabrication by a certain artist in Oxford of decorations using painted straw.
22. These were contrivances to create a draught for winnowing.
23. That is, continuing till there are ten layers.
24. This was to be the first of numerous counties about which the author would write.
25. In this passage Plot refers to several classical authors and contemporary collectors who had reported observations of 'formed stones'.
26. With regard to the specimen in question, Plot observes that it does indeed look like part of a thigh-bone, and in the next paragraph comments that earlier writers (both classical and more recent) have argued that such formations are likenesses of bones formed either by chance or by some unknown 'power' in the world.
27. Certainly it might be a stone, continues the author, as there are known examples of stones which look like teeth and like vertebrae, but these are readily discounted because there is no sign of them having contained marrow. But this one does present a different appearance within. Plot refers to p.127, where he included an illustration of the 'Ardace' although it did not correctly belong with the other items in the illustration. The illustration is of accretion on a water-plant, which has in subsequent time hardened into a stony formation.
28. The main problem is the great size of the bone. Others encountering such specimens had argued that perhaps the process of fossilization had made them become larger, but Plot notes that a large tooth was found also and it is unlikely that so compact a body as the tooth would be enlarged by the process. He can only conclude that the specimen must have been the bone of an elephant.

THE SOUTH-WEST

V

Wiltshire: John Aubrey (1626–1697)

Of all the English antiquaries of the seventeenth century, John Aubrey is the one whom we may come to know most vividly, and the personality which his writings reveal is at once both engaging and eccentric. Few approached the breadth of his range of interests, the acuteness of his observation, the ingeniousness of his analyses, and his mastery of prose. The dominant intent of his work was the conservation of things past, and his observations of ancient structures, notably Stonehenge and Avebury, justify claims that he might be thought of as England's first archaeologist. As well as descriptions of these monuments, his writings offer, albeit in a fragmentary way, yet with remarkable immediacy, records of county people, their occupations, beliefs and customs, so providing information about his times of which we would otherwise now know very little. While he was an early exponent of the value of scientific observation to the degree of accuracy that could be achieved in the seventeenth century, he is more familiar as a biographer than as an antiquary, and his collection of lively accounts of contemporaries, now known as *Brief Lives*, has long been popular. He was moreover a man of tolerance and generosity, counting amongst his friends some of the greatest scientific minds of the time. Yet he was constantly dogged by ill fortune, his work was disorganised, his financial affairs badly managed, and, of all that he wrote, only one slim volume was published in his lifetime.[1]

Aubrey's editors have much admired his writing. K.G. Ponting, in his 1969 edition of the *Natural History of Wiltshire*, stated that he was 'one of the great masters of English prose', praising his attention to the 'actual': his ability to 'give the ephemeral beauty, the pride of the eye, the lust of the flesh'.[2] Likewise, John Fowles in 1980 drew attention to the freshness of his texts and the vividness with which he captured the feeling of the seventeenth century.[3] His remarks describing the people of his county have a liveliness and economy which combine with his observations and speculations about the natural and supernatural to produce an inimitable vignette:

> In North Wiltshire, and like the vale of Gloucestershire (a dirty clayey country) the Indigenæ, or Aborigines, speake drawling; they are phlegmatique, skins pale and livid, slow and dull, heavy of spirit; hereabout is but little tillage or hard labour, they only milk the cowes and make cheese; they feed chiefly on milke meates, which cooles their braines too much, and hurts their inventions. These circumstances make them melancholy, contemplative, and malicious; by consequence whereof come more law suites out of North Wilts, at least double to the Southern parts. And by the same reason they are generally more apt to be fanatiques: their persons are generally plump and feggy: gallipot eies, and some black: but they are generally handsome enough.[4] It is a woodsere[5] country, abounding much with sowre and austere plants, as sorrel, &c. which makes their humours sowre, and fixes their spirits. In Malmesbury Hundred, &c. (the wett clayy parts) there have ever been reputed witches.
>
> On the downes, sc. the south part, where 'tis all upon tillage, and where the shepherds labour hard, their flesh is hard, their bodies strong: being weary after hard labour, they have not leisure to read and contemplate of religion, but goe to bed to their rest, to rise betime the next morning to their labour.[6]

John Aubrey was born in 1626, to parents who were of the minor gentry, at Easton Piercy, near Malmesbury, and had a childhood marked by loneliness and ill-health. He went to Oxford in 1642, but after a few months, with the start of the Civil War, his father called him home again. The following year he persuaded his father to allow him to return to 'beloved Oxford',[7] but he was soon home once more, to his great disappointment, for there he 'conversed with none but servants and rustiques, … and soldiers quartered', and he grieved 'not to have the benefitt of an ingeniouse conversation', and had 'scarce any good bookes'. In 1646 he began, but again did not complete, studies in law at Middle Temple. He inherited a share of his father's estate in 1652, but after fifteen years of poor management of his finances and many lawsuits (the most lengthy and bitter of which resulted from his failing to honour an offer to marry a woman named Joan Sumner) he was nearly penniless. This condition of penury was to continue throughout his life, and he survived by the kindness of friends who were in turn grateful for his company, his wit, his gossip, his ideas, his store of antiquarian knowledge.

Amongst these friends were such eminent figures as Thomas Hobbes, Isaac Newton, Edmund Halley, Robert Boyle, Christopher Wren, Thomas Browne, Robert Hooke, and John Locke. The most frequently-mentioned of Aubrey's friendships, however, is the one that proved to be the least happy: that with Anthony Wood, the historian of Oxford University. Aubrey gave Wood access to some of his biographical work to assist him in the preparation of his *Athenae Oxoniensis*, only to have the material used indiscreetly and returned in a mutilated and incomplete condition. Wood is remembered also for his damning characterisation of Aubrey as 'a shiftless person, roving and maggoty-headed, and sometimes little better than crazed. And being exceedingly credulous, would stuff his many letters to A.W. with fooleries, and misinformations, which sometimes would guide him into paths of error.' It is unfortunate that Wood's authority as a biographer of his times meant that his comment should have had an unduly significant part in determining Aubrey's reputation in the later seventeenth and the eighteenth centuries.

In spite of the fecundity of his ideas, Aubrey left few of his works in a fit state for publication, so that only the *Miscellanies* was actually brought into print in his lifetime. Its subject was folklore and it was a collection of mainly ghostly and magical phenomena. The works unpublished in his lifetime included topographical studies of Wiltshire, a guide to antiquities (mainly tombs) in Surrey, his biographical writings, books on education, ethics, and natural science, *Monumenta Britannica*, and another collection of notes on folklore, *Remains of Gentilisme and Judaisme*. Due both to the nature of the *Miscellanies* and to the damning comments recorded by Wood, Aubrey was regarded during much of the eighteenth century as a misguided and deluded author of irrelevant material on the periphery of antiquarian studies.

John Britton in his 'Memoir of John Aubrey, F. R. S.', written in 1845, noted that Thomas Hearne, a significant eighteenth-century commentator on antiquarian scholarship, acknowledged Aubrey's research skills and his ability to write well, yet felt that he had limited his capacity to do more because he 'too much indulged his fancy, and wholly addicted himself to the whimseys and conceits of astrologers, soothsayers, and such like ignorant and superstitious writers, which have no foundation in nature, philosophy, or reason.'[8] Indeed, the study of Aubrey was justified only by his association with more famous figures, 'men illustrious in science, philosophy, literature, and art'.[9] In mitigation, however, Britton went on to argue that Aubrey's superstitions and his belief in 'all the absurdities of the so-called *science* of astrology' were shared with many others of his time as 'a failing incidental to the age in which he lived', and that 'the same aberration of good sense prevailed in the poet Dryden, the statesman Clarendon, the monarch Charles I., and many other eminent and illustrious men.'[10]

In introducing his 1847 edition of the *Natural History of Wiltshire*, Britton tempered his criticisms with the admission that Aubrey's collections provided 'interesting memorials of his times' and that they therefore had considerable value. He summed up the critical attitudes to Aubrey thus: 'It has long been customary to regard John Aubrey as a credulous and gossiping narrator of anecdotes of doubtful authority, and as an ignorant believer of the most absurd stories.'[11] Yet Aubrey's survey of Wiltshire, when set alongside those written by Robert Plot for Oxfordshire and Staffordshire, both of which were well received, is seen to deserve 'superior merits'.[12] In the twentieth century Aubrey has at last been appreciated as an innovative thinker and perceptive observer to whom we owe thanks for giving us a vivid picture of life in the seventeenth century in England, and for recording so much—monuments, customs, remains of the distant past—of which we would otherwise know nothing.

The first of the following extracts is from the *Natural History of Wiltshire*, and is, superficially, in keeping with a typical formula for the opening of a seventeenth-century county survey: a general regional description under such subject-headings as 'the air' (the weather), 'the soil', 'rivers', and so on. The model for this approach was the method of William Lambarde in opening *A Perambulation of Kent*, published in 1576.[13] Aubrey's survey of the 'air' of Wiltshire begins conventionally enough, but the reader is soon diverted to comments on the mouldiness of leather book-covers stored in Aubrey's house, and as the text continues it takes other tangents into *ad hoc* ideas and experiences. The reader is acutely aware not only of a sense of the haphazard, as if what is being read is really just notes and memoranda, but also of the lively versatility of a mind which is constantly seeking to discover and understand. Recollections of unusual events invoke questions about nature, juxtaposed with fragments of folklore, and speculation on the origins of observed features of the countryside.

A quite different description, from the same book, is of Wilton House, the country seat of the Earl of Pembroke. It was a place well known to Aubrey and much admired by him, and his comments on the impression made by the building and its setting suggest majesty rather than intimacy. The collection of paintings within evokes a more detailed treatment, with Aubrey noting not aesthetic qualities but the significance of the subjects portrayed. The pictures were viewed not as works of art, but as historical data. When it comes to the gardens, the architect's description is offered, these presumably being words of which Aubrey had approved and which he regarded as being more authoritative than his own, an approach consistent with the endeavour to make a reliable record for the future.

The next examples demonstrate Aubrey's more singular interests. The third, from *Monumenta Britannica*, is from his account of one of his most celebrated discoveries: the stone circle at Avebury.[14] The remarks are concise and succinct, consisting mainly of observations and measurements, but imbued with excitement and satisfaction in being the first to recognise an undistinguished group of stones, which had hitherto been overlooked, as the remnants of a coherent yet mysterious ancient structure. Following this is a passage from one of Aubrey's collections of folklore, *Remaines of Gentilisme and Judaisme*, which describes the custom of making garlands in Newnton, near Malmesbury, on Trinity Sunday. Here is the antiquarian passion to preserve the past which, as Aubrey adds, has changed since 'the late warres', that is, the English Civil Wars between Royalists and Parlimentarians, an event which, for many antiquaries, was the a boundary behind which so much of what had once been was lost.

The Air

From *The Natural History of Wiltshire*, pp.14–18

This shire may be divided as it were into three stories or stages. Chippenham vale is the lowest. The first elevation, or next storie, is from the Derry Hill, or Bowdon Lodge, to the hill beyond the Devises, called Red-hone, which is the limbe or beginning of Salisbury plaines. From the top of this hill one may discerne Our Lady Church Steeple at Sarum, like a fine Spanish needle. I would have the height of these hills, as also Hackpen, and those toward Lambourn, which are the highest, to be taken with the quicksilver barometer, according to the method of Mr. Edmund Halley in Philosophical Transactions, No. 181.

Now, although Mindip-hills and Whitesheet, &c., are as a barr and skreen to keep off from Wiltshire the westerly winds and raines, as they doe in some measure repel those noxious vapours, yet wee have a flavour of them; and when autumnal agues raigne,[15] they are more common on the hills than in the vales of this country.

The downes of Wiltshire are covered with mists, when the vales are clear from them, and the sky serene; and they are much more often here than in the lowest story or stage.

The leather covers of bookes, &c. doe mold more and sooner in the hill countrey than in the vale. The covers of my bookes in my closet at Chalke would be all over covered with a hoare mouldinesse, that I could not know of what colour the leather was; when my bookes in my closet at Easton-Piers (in the vale) were not toucht at all with any mouldiness.

So the roomes at Winterslow, which is seated exceeding high, are very mouldie and dampish. Mr. Lancelot Moorehouse, Rector of Pertwood, who was a very learned man, say'd that mists were very frequent there: it stands very high, neer Hindon, which one would thinke to stand very healthy: there is no river nor marsh neer it, yet they doe not live long there.

The wheat hereabout, sc. towards the edge of the downes,[16] is much subject to be smutty,[17] which they endeavour to prevent by drawing a cart-rope over the corn after the meldews fall.

Besides that the hill countrey is elevated so high in the air, the soile doth consist of chalke and mawme,[18] which abounds with nitre, which craddles[19] the air, and turns it into mists and water.

On the east side of the south downe of the farme of Broad Chalke are pitts called the Mearn-Pitts,[20] which, though on a high hill, whereon is a sea marke towards the Isle of Wight, yet they have alwaies water in them. How they came to be made no man knowes; perhaps the mortar was digged there for the building of the church.

Having spoken of mists it brings to me remembrance that in December, 1653, being at night in the court at Sr. Charles Snell's at Kington St Michael in this country, there being a very thick mist, we sawe our shadowes on the fogg as on a wall by the light of the lanternes, sc. about 30 or 40 foot distance or more. There were several gentlemen which sawe this; particularly Mr. Stafford Tyndale. I have been enformed since by some that goe a bird-batting[21] in winter nights that the like hath been seen: but rarely.

The north part of this country is much influenc't by the river Severne, which flowes impetuously from the Atlantick Sea. It is a ventiduct, and brings rawe gales along with it; the tydes bringing a chilnesse with them.

On the top of Chalke-downe, 16 or 18 miles from the sea, the oakes are, as it were, shorne by the south and south-west winds; and do recline from the sea, as those that grow by the sea-side.

A Wiltshire proverb:—

'When the wind is north-west,
The weather is at the best:
If the raine comes out of east
'Twill raine twice twenty-four howres at the least.'

I remember Sr. Chr. Wren told me, 1677, that winds might alter, as the apogæum:[22] *e.g.* no raine in Egypt heretofore; now common: Spain barren; Palæston sun-dried, &c. Quære, Mr. Hook de hoc.[23]

A proverbial rithme observed as infallible by the inhabitants on the Severne-side:—

'If it raineth when it doth flow,
Then yoke your oxe, and goe to plough;

But if it raineth when it doth ebb,
Then unyoke your oxe, and goe to bed.'

It oftentimes snowes on the hill at Bowden-parke, when no snow falles at Lacock below it. This hill is higher than Lacock steeple three or four times, and it is a good place to try experiments. On this parke is a seate of my worthy friend George Johnson, Esqr., councillor at lawe, from whence is a large and most delightfull prospect over the vale of North Wiltshire.

Old Wiltshire country prognosticks of the weather:—

'When the hen doth moult before the cock,
The winter will be as hard as a rock;
But if the cock moults before the hen,
The winter will not wett your shoes seame.'

In South Wiltshire the constant observation is that if droppes doe hang upon the hedges on Candlemas-day that it will be a good pease yeare. It is generally agreed on to be matter of fact; the reason perhaps may be that there may rise certain unctuous vapours which may cause that fertility.

At Hullavington, about 1649, there happened a strange wind, which did not onely lay down flatt the corne and grasse as if a huge roller had been drawn over it, but it flatted also the quickset[24] hedges of two or three grounds of George Joe, Esq.—It was a hurricane.

Anno 1660, I being then at dinner with Mr. Stokes at Titherton, news was brought in to us that a whirlewind had carried some of the hay-cocks over high elmes by the house: which bringes to my mind a story that is credibly related of one Mr. J. Parsons, a kinsman of ours, who, being a little child, was sett on a hay-cock, and a whirlewind took him up with half the hay-cock and carried him over high elmes, and layd him down safe, without any hurt, in the next ground.

Anno 1581, there fell hail-stones at Dogdeane, near Salisbury, as big as a child's fist of three or four yeares old; which is mentioned in the Preface of an Almanack by John Securis, Maister of Arts and Physick, dedicated to . . . . . Lord High Chancellor. He lived at Salisbury. 'Tis pitty such accidents are not recorded in other Almanacks in order for a history of the weather.

Edward Saintlow, of Knighton, Esq. was buried in the church of Broad Chalke, May the 6th, 1578, as appears by the Register booke. The snow did then lie so thick on the ground that the bearers carried his body over the gate in Knighton field, and the company went over the hedges, and they digged a way to the church porch. I knew some ancient people of the parish that did remember it. On a May day, 1655 or 1656, being then in Glamorganshire, at

Mr. Jo. Aubrey's at Llanchrechid, I saw the mountaines of Devonshire all white with snow. There fell but little in Glamorganshire.

Wilton House

From *The Natural History of Wiltshire*, pp.83–87

The old building of the Earl of Pembroke's house at Wilton was designed by an architect (Hans Holbein)[25] in King Edward the Sixth's time. The new building which faced the garden was designed by Monsieur Solomon de Caus,[26] tempore Caroli Imi., but this was burnt by accident and rebuilt 1648, Mr. Webb[27] then being surveyor.

The situation of Wilton House is incomparably noble. It hath not only the most pleasant prospect of the gardens and Rowlindon Parke, but from thence over a lovely flatt to the city of Salisbury, where that lofty steeple cuts the horizon, and so to Ivychurch; and to add further to the glory of this prospect the right honourable Thomas, Earle of Pembroke, did, anno 1686, make a stately canal from Quidhampton to the outer base-court of his illustrious palace.

The house is great and august, built all of freestone, lined with brick, which was erected by Henry Earle of Pembroke. Mr. Inigo Jones told Philip, first Earle of Pembroke, that the porch in the square court was as good architecture as any was in England. 'Tis true it does not stand exactly in the middle of the side, for which reason there were some would have perswaded his Lordship to take it down; but Mr. Jones disswaded him, for the reasons aforesayd, and that we had not workmen then to be found that could make the like work.—(From Dr. Caldicot.)

King Charles the first did love Wilton above all places, and came thither every summer. It was he that did put Philip first Earle of Pembroke upon making this magnificent garden and grotto, and to new build that side of the house that fronts the garden, with two stately pavilions at each end, all *al Italiano*. His Majesty intended to have had it all designed by his own architect, Mr. Inigo Jones, who being at that time, about 1633, engaged in his Majesties buildings at Greenwich, could not attend to it; but he recommended it to an ingeniouse architect, Monsieur Solomon de Caus, a Gascoigne, who performed it very well; but not without the advice and approbation of Mr. Jones: for which his Lordship settled a pension on him of, I think, a hundred pounds per annum for his life, and lodgings in the house. He died about 1656; his picture is at Mr. Gauntlet's house at Netherhampton. I shall gladly surcease to[28] make any further attempt of the description of the house, garden, stables, and approaches, as falling too short of the greatness and excellency of it. Mr. Loggan's graver will render it much more to the life, and leave a more fixt impression in the reader.[29]

The south side of this stately house, that was built by Monsieur de Caus, was burnt ann. 1647 or 1648, by airing of the roomes. In anno 1648 Philip (the first) re-edifyed it, by the advice of Inigo Jones; but he, being then very old, could not be there in person, but left it to Mr. Webb, who married his niece.

THE PICTURES. In the hall (of old pieces) were the pictures of the Ministers of State in Queen Elizabeth's time, and some of King Henry the Eighth. There was Robert, Earle of Essex, that was beheaded, &c.

At the stairecase, the picture of Sir Robert Naunton, author of 'Fragmenta Regalia'; his name was writt on the frame. At the upper end was the picture of King Charles I. on horseback, with his French riding master by him on foot, under an arch; all as big as the life: which was a copie of Sir Anthony Vandyke, from that at Whitehall. By it was the picture of Peacock, a white racehorse, with the groom holding him, as big as the life; and to both which Sir Anthony gave many master touches. Over the skreen is a very long picture, by an Italian hand, of Aurora guiding her horses, neigheing, and above them the nymphes powring down out of phialls the morning showres. Here was the 'Table' of Cebes, a very large picture, done by a great master, which the genius describes to William, the first earl of this family, and lookes on him, pointing to Avarice, as to be avoyded by a noble person; and many other ancient pieces which I have now forgott.

The long gallery was furnished with the ministers of estate and heroes of Queen Elizabeth's time, and also some of the French. In one of the pictures of Sir Philip Sydney are these verses, viz.—

'Who gives himselfe may well his picture give,
Els were it vain, since both short time doe live.'

At the upper end is the picture of King James the First sitting in his throne, in his royall robes; a great piece, as big as the life; by him on the right hand wall is the picture of William Herbert, first earle, at length, as big as the life, and under it the picture of his little dog, of a kind of chestnut colour, that starved himselfe for his master's death. Here is the picture of Henry Earle of Pembroke and his Countesse; and of William Earle of Pembroke, Lord Chamberlain; severall Earles of Oxford; and also of Aubrey Earle of Oxford, now living; the pictures of Cardinal Wolsey; Archy (King James's jester); . . . . . . , governour to Sir Philip Sydney; Mr Secretary Walsingham, in his gown and wrought cap; Mary Countess of Pembrok, sister of Sir Philip Sydney; the last Lady Abbess of Wilton (Lady Anna Gawen),[30] a pretty, beautiful, modest Penelope; and many others forgotten by me and everyone else.

I was heretofore a good nomenclator of these pictures, which was delivered to me from a child eight yeares old, by old persons relating to this noble family. It is a great and a generall fault that in all galleries of pictures the names are not writt underneath, or at least their coates of armes. Here was also the picture of Thomas Lyte, of Lytes Cary; and a stately picture of King Henry the eighth.

The genius of Philip (first) Earle of Pembroke lay much to painting and building, and he had the best collection of paintings of the best masters of any peer of his time in England; and, besides those pictures before mentioned, collected by his ancestors, he adorned the roomes above staires with a great many pieces of Georgeon,[31] and some of Titian, his scholar. His lordship was a great patron of Sir Anthony Van Dyck, and had the most of his paintings of any one in the world; some whereof, of his family, are fixt now in the great pannells of the wainscot in the great dining roome, or roome of state; which is a magnificent, stately roome; and his Majesty King Charles the Second was wont to say, 'twas the best proportioned room that ever he saw.[32] In the cieling piece of this great roome is a great peece, the Marriage of Perseus, drawn by the hand of Mr. Emanuel De Cretz; and all about this roome, the pannells below the windows, is painted by him, the whole story of Sir Philip Sydney's Arcadia. Quære, Dr. Caldicot and Mr. Uniades, what was the story or picture in the cieling when the house was burnt. At the upper end of this noble roome is a great piece of Philip (first) Earle of Pembroke and both his Countesses, and all his children, and the Earle of Carnarvon, as big as the life, with landskip[33] beyond them; by the hand of that famous master in painting Sir Anthony Van Dyk, which is held one of his best pictures that ever he drew, and which was apprized at 1,000 *li.* by the creditors of Philip the third earle of Pembrok. Mr. Uniades told me that he heard Philip (first) Earle say, that he gave to Sir Anthony Van Dyk for it five hundred Jacobuses. 'Tis an heir-loome, and the creditors had nothing to doe with it, but Mr Davys the painter, that was brought from London to apprize the goods, did apprize it at a thousand pounds. Captain Wind tells me that there is a tagliedome[34] of this great picture: enquire for it.

The anti-roome to the great roome of state is the first roome as you come up staires from the garden, and the great pannells of wainscot are painted with the huntings of Tempesta, by that excellent master in landskip Mr. Edmund Piers. He did also paint all the grotesco-painting about the new buildings.

In the roome within this great roome is the picture of King Charles the First on his dun horse, by Van Dyk; it hangs over the chimney. Also the Dutchess of Richmond by Van Dyk. Now this rare collection of pictures is sold and dispersed, and many of those eminent persons' pictures are but images without names; all sold by auction and disparkled[35] by administratorship:

they are, as the civilians term them, *bona caduca*.[36] But, as here were a number of pictures sold, with other goods, by the creditors of Philip (the second), so this earle hath supplied it with an admirable collection of paintings by great masters in Italy, when his lordship was there, and since; as he also did for prints, and bookes of fortification, &c.

THE LIBRARIE.—Here was a noble librarie of bookes, choicely collected in the time of Mary Countesse of Pembroke. I remember there were a great many Italian bookes; all their poets; and bookes of politie and historie. Here was Dame Julian Barnes of Hunting, Hawking, and Heraldry, in English verses, printed temp. Edward the Fourth. (Philip, third earle, gave Dame Julian Barnes to Capt. Edw. Saintlo of Dorsetshire.) A translation of the whole book of Psalmes, in English verse, by Sir Philip Sydney, writt curiously, and bound in crimson velvet and gilt; it is now lost. Here was a Latin poëme, a manuscript, writt in Julius Cæsar's time. Henry Earle of Pembroke was a great lover of heraldrie, and collected curious manuscripts of it, that I have seen and perused, *e.g.* the coates of armes and short histories of the English nobility, and bookes of genealogies; all well painted and writt. 'Twas Henry that did sett up all the glasse scutchions about the house: quære if he did not build it? Now all these bookes are sold and dispersed as the pictures.

THE ARMORIE. The armory is a very long roome, which I guesse to have been a dorture[37] heretofore. Before the civill warres, I remember, it was very full. The collection was not onely great, but the manner of obtaining it was much greater; which was by a victory at the battle of St Quintin's, where William the first Earle of Pembroke was generall, Sir George Penruddock, of Compton Chamberlain, was Major Generall, and William Aubrey, LL.D. my great-grandfather, was Judge Advocat. There were armes, sc. the spoile, for sixteen thousand men, horse and foot. (From the Right Honourable Thomas Earle of Pembroke.)

Desire my brother William Aubrey to gett a copy of the inventory of it. Before the late civill warres here were musketts and pikes for … hundred men; lances for tilting; complete armour for horsemen; for pikemen, &c. The rich gilt and engraved armour of Henry VIII. The like rich armour of King Edward VI. In the late warres much of the armes was imbecill'd.[38]

WILTON GARDEN: by Solomon de Caus.

'This garden, within the inclosure of the new wall, is a thousand foot long, and about four hundred in breadth; divided in its length into three long squares or parallellograms, the first of which divisions, next the building, hath four platts embroydered; in the midst of which are four fountaines, with statues of marble in their middle; and on the sides of those platts are the platts of flowers; and beyond them is a little terrass raised, for the more advantage of beholding those platts. In the second division are two groves or woods, cutt with diverse walkes, and through those groves passeth the river Nader, having a breadth in this place 44 foote, upon which is built the bridge, of the breadth of the great walke: and in the middest of the aforesayd groves are two great statues of white marble of eight foot high, the one of Bacchus, and the other of Flora; and on the sides ranging with the platts of flowers are two covered arbours of three hundred foot long, and divers allies. At the beginning of the third and last division are, on either side of the great walke, two ponds with fountains, and two columnes in the middle, casting water all their height; which causeth the moving and turning of two crowns at the top of the same; and beyond is a compartment of green, with divers walkes planted with cherrie trees; and in the middle is a great ovall, with the Gladiator of brasse, the most famous statue of all that antiquity hath left. On the sides of this compartment, and answering the platts of flowers and long arbours, are three arbours of either side, with turning galleries, communicating themselves one into another. At the end of the great walke is a portico of stone, cutt and adorned with pyllasters and nyckes, within which are figures of white marble, of five foot high. On either side of the said portico is an ascent leading up to the terrasse, upon the steps whereof, instead of ballasters, are sea-monsters, casting water from one to the other, from the top to the bottome; and above the sayd portico is a great reserve of water for the grotto.'

The grotto is paved with black and white marble; the roofe is vaulted. The figures of the tritons, &c. are in bas-relieve, of white marble, excellently well wrought. Here is a fine jeddeau and nightingale-pipes[39]. Monsieur de Caus had here a contrivance, by the turning of a cock, to shew three rainbowes, the secret whereof he did keep to himself; he would not let the gardener, who shewes it to strangers, know how to doe it; and so, upon his death, it is lost. The grott and pipes did cost ten thousand pounds. The garden is twelve acres within the terrace of the grott.

The kitchin garden is a very good one, and here are good ponds and a decoy. By the kitchin garden is a streame which turns a wheele that moves the engine to raise the water to the top of a cisterne at the corner of the great garden, to serve the water-workes of the grotto and fountaines in the garden.

Avebury

From John Aubrey, *Monumenta Britannica*, pp.33–41

I take this old, illshapen Monument of Aubury to be the greatest, most considerable, and the least ruinated of any of this kind in our British Isle. It is very strange that so eminent[40] an Antiquitie should lye so long unregarded by our Chorographers. Mr … [41] only names it.[42]

It is environned with an extraordinary great Vallum (or Rampart) as great, and as high as that at Winchester (which is the greatest Bulwark that I have seen) within which is a Graffe[43] of a depth and breadth proportionable to it: Wherefore it could not be designed for a Fortification, for then the Graffe would have been on the outside of the Rampart.

From the entrance at A, to that at β is sixty paces.[44]

From the entrance at γ, to that at δ the same distance; and the breadth of the rampart is fower perches: and the breadth of the Graff the same distance.

Round about the Graffe (sc. on the edge or border of it) are pitched on end huge Stones, as big, or rather bigger than those at Stoneheng: but rude, and unhewen as they are drawn out of the earth: whereas those of Stoneheng are roughly-hewen. Most of the stones thus pitched on end are gonne:[45] only here and there doe still remain some curvilineous segments: but by these one may boldly ghesse,[46] that heretofore they stood quite round about like a Corona.[47]

Within this circumvallation are also (yet) remaining segments (of a roundish figure) of two (as I doe conjecture) Sacella—one, the fig. 1 the other fig. 2[48] and their ruines are not unlike Ariadne's Crowne:[49] and are no neerer to a perfect circle than is that Constellation. So within our Christian churches are severall Chapelles respective to such, or such a Saint: and the like might have been here in those dayes.[50]

This old monument does as much exceed in bignes[51] the so renowned Stoneheng, as a Cathedral doeth a parish Church: so that by the[52] grandure one might presume it to have been an Arch-Temple of the Druids.

It is situated in the countrey of the stones called the Grey-weathers: of which sort of stones, both this Antiquity, and that of Stoneheng[53] were built.

From the south entrance runnes a solemne Walke, sc. with[54] Stones pitched on end about seven foot high, which goes as far as Kynet[55] (which is (at least) a measured mile from Aubury) and from Kynet it turnes with a right angle eastward crossing the River, and ascends up the hill to another Monument of the same Kind (but less) as in plate II.[56] The distance of the stones in this Walk, and the breadth of it, is much about the distance of a noble walk of Trees of that length: and very probable this Walke was made for Processions.[57]

Perhaps at this angular turning, might be the Celle (or Convent) of the Priests belonging to these Temples: to be sure, they did not dwell far from them: and their Habitations might hapily be the occasion of the rise of this Village.[58]

Within the circumference, or Borough of this Monument, is now the Village of Aubury, 8which stands per crucem, as is to be seen by scheme the Ist.[59] The Houses are built of the Frustrum's[60] of those huge Stones, which they invade with great Sledges, for hereabout are no other stones to be found (except Flints).[61] I have verbum Sacerdotis[62] for it, that these mighty stones, as hard as marble, may be broken in what part of them you please; without any great trouble: sc. Make a fire on that line of the stone, where you would have it crack; and after the stone is well heated, draw over a line with cold water, & immediately give a knock with a Smyths sledge, and it will break, like the Collets at the Glass house.[63]

The Houses of this Village are built with the Frustrum's of the stones of this Monument:[64] for hereabout are are [*sic*] no other stones to be found (except Flints).[65] The Church is likewise built of them: and the Mannour-house which was built by the Dunches tempe Reg. Elizabeth: and also another faire House not far from it.[66]

By reason of the crosse-streetes, Houses, Gardens, orchards, and severall small Closes; and the Fractures made in this Antiquity for the building of those Houses; it was no easy Taske for me to trace out the Vestigia, and so to make this Survey. Wherefore I have un-pestered[67] the Scheme of[68] the Enclosures, and Houses etc: which are altogether foreigne to this Antiquity, and would but have clowded and darkned the reall Designe. The crosse-street within this Monument was made in process of time for the convenience of the Rodes.

One of the Monuments in the Street that runnes East and West like that above Holy-head, is converted into a Pigstye, or Cow-house: as is to be seen in the Roade.

I am enformed, that as you ride[69] from Marleborough to Compton-Basset (a village not far from hence Westward) are to be seen Houses, part whereof are Stones pitched on end, as big as those of Stoneheng.

Garlands

From *Remaines of Gentilisme and Judaisme*, pp. 136–138

The Custome at Newnton on Trinity-Sunday

King Athelstan having obtained a victory over the Danes by the assistance of the Inhabitants of this place, riding to recreate himselfe, found a woman bayting[70] of cowe upon the waye called the Fosseway (which is a famous way and runnes through this parish, and goes from Cornwall to Scotland). This woman sate on a stoole, with the cowe fastened by a rope to the legge of the stoole. The manner of it occasioned the king to ask why she did so? She answered the king, that they had no common belonging to the towne. The Queen being then in his company, by their consents it was granted, that the towne should have so much ground in common next adjoining to this way as the woman would ride round upon a bare-ridged horse; she undertakes it, and for ascertaining the ground, the king appointed Sir Walter, a knight that wayted on him, to follow the woman or goe with her; which being donne, and made known to the monks at Malmesbury (they to show their liberality upon the extent of the Kings charity) gave a piece of ground parcell of their Inheritance and adjoyning to the churchyard, to build a house upon, for the Hayward[71] to live in, to look after the Beasts that fed upon this common. And for to perpetuate the memory of it, appointed the following Prayers to be sayd upon every Trinity-Sunday, in that house, with the Ceremony ensueing; and because a Monke of that time, out of his devotion, gave a Bell to be rung here at this house before prayers began, his name was inserted in the Petitions for that guift.

The Ceremonies.—The Parishioners being come to the Dore of the Haywards house, the Dore was struck thrice, in honour of the holy Trinity, then they entred; the Bell was rung; after which, silence being, the Prayers aforesayd. Then was a Garland of Flowers made upon a hoop brought forth by a Mayd of the Towne upon her Neck; and a young man, a Batchelour, of another parish, first saluted her three times (the Kiss of Peace) in honour of the holy Trinity, in respect of God the Father. Then she putts the garland upon his neck and kisses him 3 times in honour of the Trinity, particularly God the Sonne. Then he putts the Garland on her neck again and kisses her 3 times, and particularly in honour of God the holy ghost. Then he takes the garland from her neck again, and by the custome must give her a penny at least, which (as fancy leades) is now exceeded, as 2*s.* 6*d.*, &c.

The method of giving this Garland is from house to house annually, till it comes round.

In this Evening every Commoner sends his supper up to this house, which is called the *Tele-house*, and having before layd-in there, equally a stock of mault, which was brewed in the house, they suppe together, and what was left was given to the Poor.

The Forme of Prayer.—'Peace goodmen peace; this is the house of charitie, and house of peace; Christ Jhesus be with us this day & evermore. Amen.

'You shall pray for the good prosperity of our soveraigne lord King Hen. 8 and his Royall Issue (of later dayes K. Ch. 2d, Queen Katherine, Duke of Yorke, & the rest of the Royall progenie), with all the nobility of this Land, that Almighty God would give then such grace wisdome & discretion, that they may doe all things to the glory of God, the kings honour & the good of the kingdome.

'You shall pray to God that moved the hearts of King Athelstan, and Dame Mawd his good queen, to give this ground to our forefathers & to us, and to all them that shall come after us, in Fee for ever.

'You shall pray for the sowle of Sir Walter, the good black knight, that moved his heart to our forefayers[72] and us this ground both to tread and tite,[73] and to them that shall after [*sic*] us, in Fee for ever.

'You shall pray to God for the sowle of Abbot *Loringe* that moved his heart to give us this ground to build this house upon, to our forefathers and to us and to them that shall come after us, in Fee for ever.

'You shall pray to God for the sowle of *Dan*[74] *Alured*, the black Monke, that moved his heart to give the Bell to this house.[75]

'For sowles of these Benefactors whom the Lord hath moved their hearts to bestow these benefitts upon us, let us now and ever pray, Pater noster &c.'

In the late warres this Howse was burned down by the Soldiers; and the Custome of Supping is yet discontinued, togeyer with brewing that quantity of drinke. The rest of the ceremonies are yet continued on the Toft, and on the old dore of the Howse, which yet remains, which they doe carry thither; and a small quantity of drinke, of 6 or 8 gallons, is yet drunke after the Garland is given.[76]

1. The volume was *Miscellanies*, a collection of accounts of superstitions and the supernatural, which detrimentally influenced perceptions of Aubrey in the eighteenth century. It appeared in 1696, the year before his death.
2. *Aubrey's Natural History of Wiltshire*, introduced by K. G. Ponting, Newton Abbot, Devon: David & Charles (Publishers) Limited, 1969, 'Introduction to the 1969 printing', unpaginated.
3. *John Aubrey's* Monumenta Britannica, edited by John Fowles, annotated by Rodney Legg, 2 volumes, Sherborne, Dorset: Dorset Publishing Company, 1980, p.606. Aubrey's book is presented as a facsimile of his manuscript with annotations, to which reference is made in several of the following endnotes.
4. *Feggy*, perhaps a variant of *foggy*, flabby; *gallipot*, a small glazed pot used by apothecaries for medicines, perhaps suggesting eyes that are blank and expressionless.
5. *Woodsere,* of the ground: loose and spongy.
6. *The Natural History of Wiltshire*, p.11.
7. *Monument Britannica*, p.635. Autobiographical notes found in the manuscript of Aubrey's *Lives of Eminent Men* were included by John Britton in his *Memoir of John Aubrey*, which is reproduced in *Monumenta Britannica*, pp.633–638.
8. *Ibid.*, p.627. Thomas Hearne (1678–1735), an antiquarian scholar who edited many Anglo-Saxon and medieval manuscripts, was also a prominent Oxford gossip of the time.
9. *Ibid.*, p.623.
10. *Ibid.*, p.629.
11. *The Natural History of Wiltshire*, p.v.
12. *Ibid.*, p.vi.
13. Part of the opening of *A Perambulation of Kent* is given in the chapter on Lambarde.
14. The text from which this passage has been transcribed is accompanied by diagrams to which Aubrey refers when he mentions a measurement or a specific feature of the monument. He spelt the name of the place in the same way as his own name.
15. *Ague*, a cold, characterised by shivering.

16. *sc.*, abbreviation for *scilicet*, that is to say.
17. *Smutty*, effected by a fungus which gives the crop a sooty appearance.
18. *Mawme* a soft, friable, chalky rock, also called 'firestone'.
19. *Craddles*, the meaning of this is unclear.
20. Britton notes that *marne* is an old French word for marle.
21. *Bird-batting*, the meaning is unclear.
22. *Apogæum*, apogee, the sun's meridional altitude on the longest day of the year. Christopher Wren (1632–1723) was the greatest English architect of his time, but he was also a leading astronomer and mathematician. He was a founding member of the Royal Society.
23. *Quære ... de hoc*, query about this: 'quære' is Aubrey's indication of a question to be investigated. Mr Hook was his friend Robert Hooke (1635–1703), natural philosopher, who was a pioneer of the use of the microscope to make observations, made numerous discoveries in astronomy, concerning the properties of light, the nature of gases, and the mechanical properties of springs, and invented a number of devices such as the balance wheel and spring regulation in watches.
24. *Quickset*, a plant planted to grow as a hedge, usually hawthorn.
25. John Britton notes that 'There is no authority for the assertion that Holbein designed more than the porch mentioned elsewhere.'
26. The building and gardens were designed in 1632 by Isaac de Caus, assistant to Inigo Jones. Salomon de Caus, who was his elder brother, was an engineer, who designed some gardens in England, but not this one (he died in 1626).
27. After the fire Inigo Jones (1573–1652) was again consulted for restoration works. He was assisted by his son-in-law, the architect John Webb (1611–1672).
28. *Surcease to*, desist from.
29. Britton notes that this refers to an illustration 'contemplated' by Aubrey.
30. Britton notes that the abbess at the time of the Dissolution was Cecily Bodenham, so Aubrey is here mistaken.
31. Giorgione.
32. The room is now known as the Double Cube Room, from its proportions.
33. *Landskip*, landscape.
34. *Tagliedome*, perhaps *taille-douce*, a type of engraving, is intended.
35. *Disparkled*, scattered, portioned out.
36. *Bona caduca*, a legacy which has lapsed because the beneficiary has not taken it up.
37. That is, a monastic dormitory. Before the Dissolution, there was a Benedictine monastery on the site.
38. *Imbecilled*, stolen (embezzled).
39. *Jeddeau, jet d'eau*, fountain; *nightingale pipes*, tremolo pipes once used in organs, hence, here, perhaps a contrivance to make a musical sound.
40. Aubrey has added 'such' above the last two words.
41. The name is here omitted, but reference to a later page of Aubrey's manuscript shows that he was referring to Camden. (See *Monumenta Britannica*, p.33)
42. Aubrey wrote an alternative opening sentence: 'Aubury is four miles west from Marleborough in Wiltshire, and is peradventure the most eminent and most entire Monument of this Kind in the Isle of Great Britaigne.' (See *Monumenta Britannica*, p.33)
43. *Graffe*, a trench or ditch for fortification.
44. In this and the following sentence, Aubrey is referring to an accompanying plan of the site, headed 'Survey of Aubury' (Figure 10). It shows the shape of the monument, consisting of the 'rampire' (rampart) and the 'graffe' within it. A path crosses laterally from an entrance α on the western side to another, β, on the eastern side. The latter entrance is annotated with the words 'way to Marlborough'. As this path crosses the monument, a branch leads off to an entrance γ in the south and another path leads to δ in the north. The southern entrance is marked 'way to Kinnet' (presumably Kennet). In

writing that the distance from α to β was sixty paces, Aubrey meant sixty perches, which is the distance specified on the plan.

45. Aubrey has added above the last word: 'taken away'.
46. Aubrey has added above the last word: 'conclude'.
47. Aubrey has added above the last word: 'Crowne'. At this point he has inserted a line from Ovid, which may be translated as '... but great antiquity destroys and a long old age comes to the stone'. See *Monumenta Britannica*, p.35.
48. Further reference to the plan.
49. In the margin at this point Aubrey again quotes Ovid, meaning, 'Now that gold sparkles in nine stars', *Monumenta Britannica*, p.36.
50. Aubrey has added above the last two words: 'the old time'.
51. Aubrey has added above the last word: 'greatness'.
52. Aubrey has added above the last word: 'its'.
53. Aubrey has noted in the margin, '15 miles from Grey weathers'. The 'grey wethers' of the Marlborough Downs are sarsen stones which are a feature of the district. They are also known as 'druid stones'.
54. Aubrey has added above the last word: 'of'.
55. Kennet.
56. This is a reference to another plan, which shows the relative positions of the Avebury circles, Silbury Hill, and the Sanctuary, which was another stone circle, which no longer remains.
57. Here Aubrey has a marginal note, partly obscured, which mentions that a great stone at the beginning of the walk fell in 1684 and broke into two or three pieces.
58. Aubrey has added above the last two words: 'Kynet'.
59. Reference to a diagram apparently not included .
60. *Frustrum*, a fragment left after a solid (in this case a rock) has been cut.
61. There are two marginal notes accompanying this sentence and the following one; they are partly obscured; the first is probably 'Stanton Drew' and the second has the name 'Brunsdon', followed by 'Munckton'. Legg lists a certain Brunsdon as being the minister at Winterbourne Monkton, in Wiltshire. (*Monumenta Britannica*, p.108).
62. Legg gives the meaning for *Sacerdotis*: word of the priest, hence, 'unimpeachable evidence'. (*Monumenta Britannica*, p.38.) From *sacerdote*, a priest.
63. *Collet*, ring, collar. Legg gives its meaning as 'circular mould'.
64. 'Antiquity' is given as an alternative word.
65. This sentence has been crossed out, presumably because the same thing has been said earlier.
66. Aubrey has added above the last word: 'that'.
67. Aubrey had added as an alternative, 'dis-empestred'. 'Pester' meant to muddle, confuse, hence it seems that Aubrey meant that he could clarify his plan by omitting irrelevant items.
68. Aubrey has added, above this word, 'from'.
69. Aubrey has added, above the last two words 'one rides'.
70. *Bayting of cowe*, allowing the cow to feed.
71. The hayward was responsible for the maintenance of the fences of an enclosure.
72. The editor seems in some places to have transcribed 'th' as 'y'.
73. *Tite*, grant; so the whole means that Sir Walter granted the land for their use in fee (that is, in return for service to him) for ever.
74. The editor indicated uncertainty in transcribing this word.
75. Aubrey here notes that the bell is, at the time he is writing, kept at the home of a gentleman of the parish.
76. *Toft*, hillock.

VI

Cornwall: Richard Carew (1555–1620)

One of the most genial and engaging of all county descriptions is *The Survey of Cornwall*, written in 1602 by Richard Carew. Cornwall was his native county, and he described it in lively detail and with great affection. More than any other of the seventeenth-century antiquaries, he writes of everyday events and activities, of all classes of inhabitants, and of the unique landscape and environment of his homeland. Further, his is the most personal of such accounts, he is constantly present in the pages of his text, his delights, interests, and concerns inform his narrative, and we become, to a degree, familiar with him as he guides us through his much loved county.

Richard Carew was born on 17 July 1555 at Antony, by the River Lynher in the south-east corner of Cornwall. He went to Oxford when he was eleven, and at Christ Church was a friend of Sir Philip Sidney, with whom, on an occasion when he was fourteen, he disputed *extempore* in the presence of his friend's uncles, the earls of Leicester and Warwick. He subsequently trained for a legal career, entering firstly Clement's Inn and, subsequently, Middle Temple at the Inns of Court. He was the son of a leading family of the county, and he inherited the estate at Antony early in his life. He undertook the duties expected of a country gentleman, taking a succession of public offices: Justice of the Peace in 1581, Sheriff in 1586, Member of Parliament (1584 and 1597), and (during hostilities with Spain) Deputy-Lieutenant of the county under Sir Walter Raleigh. In his leisure time he conducted his research into the history and antiquities of Cornwall and studied foreign languages (Greek, Italian, German, French, and Spanish, according to the epitaph he wrote for himself). During the years in which he was working on his description of Cornwall, Carew was an active member of the Society of Antiquaries, and he could count both William Camden and Henry Spelman amongst his close friends. Indeed his scholarship was praised by numerous contemporaries.

The characteristic which most distinguishes Carew's county description from others is that while his gentlemanly achievements were in scholarship and public office, his text is most memorable for its expression of simple pleasures and the observation of ordinary things. He is at his most enthusiastic in writing of his pond for breeding fish, and is moved to portray his feelings in verse:

> I wayt not at the Lawyers gates,
> Ne shoulder clymers downe the stayres;
> I vaunt not manhood by debates,
> I envy not the misers fears:
> But meane in state, and calme in sprite,
> My fishfull pond is my delight.

Whether such passages are beguiling personal glimpses into a seventeenth-century life or simply droll contrivances, they set this work apart from its contemporaries and successors.

Prior to the publication of the *Survey*, Carew produced several translations, essays and poetry. *Godfrey of Bulloinge*, a translation of Tasso's *Gerusalemme Liberata*, an epic of the First Crusade, was published in 1594. The verse was modelled on that of Edmund Spenser, using the same archaic vocabulary, but while Carew's poem does indeed have some beautiful passages, it is not a masterpiece such as *The Faerie Queen*.[1] In the same year he published *An Examination of Men's Wits*, a translation of an Italian translation of a Spanish treatise by the physician Juan de la Huarte. Based on the medical system of Galen, it seeks to relate physiology and psychology, concluding with a chapter on eugenics. Unlike *Godfrey of Bulloigne*, it achieved a degree of popularity, going through three editions in subsequent years. *A Herring's Tail*, a mock-heroic account of a snail's attack on a weathercock, was published in 1598. It is at once a fantasy influenced by Sidney's *Arcadia*, Spenser's *Faerie Queen*, Tasso, Pliny, Ovid, Virgil, and Arthurian romance, and a satirical skit on the seriousness of works such as Spenser's. While it is not a great English poem, it was the first of any length composed in rhyming hexameters, possibly influencing Drayton's choice of metrical form for his *Poly-Olbion*.

While a brief review of Carew's major works serves to show the variety of his interests, a reading of his description of Cornwall gives even more extensive evidence both of his scholarly pursuits and of his knowledge of many facets of life in the county.[2] Regarding the latter, he is primarily concerned with the people of the present and what they do, rather than with their ancestors and their antiquity. The genealogy which came eventually to dominate the seventeenth-century county descriptions is not absent, but certainly it is not to any degree prominent in the narrative. Those matters which do predominate include mining (appropriate for Cornwall, the great producer of tin for centuries past), fishing (again a significant Cornish industry, but also, clearly, one of Carew's favourite pastimes), and his profile of the people of the county: their language, their lives, work, and leisure. Of religion and piety Carew has little to say, church-ales and saints' days taking up more space in the narrative than worship and devotion. He does list the knights of the county by hundreds, and his accounts of particular hundreds (in the Second Book) include some brief historical details of some families and estates, but these seem very much to be of secondary importance.

There is so much of interest in *The Survey of Cornwall* that it is difficult to choose outstanding examples. The extracts given below present two vivid pictures of life in that landscape, one taken from a very lengthy section describing the fish of the county and fishing both as an industry and as a pastime; the other describing a somewhat more vigorous pastime, the game of hurling. They are, however, appropriate, for Richard Carew is consistently more interested in the people that inhabit the landscape than in the landscape itself. The first extract deals with fishing at sea, and is the latter part of a very long account of fishing in Cornwall both as an industry and as a pastime. The county has one of the longest coastlines of any in England, and fishing was clearly of great importance to the economy. More than the provision of factual information, Carew takes his reader out on the boats with the fishermen, and onto the harbour where the catch is processed. The narrative is vivid, fast-moving, and wonderfully evocative. It is with even more rustic humour that the game of hurling is explained in a passage requiring little annotation. This game, which is clearly an early antecedent of rugby, is still played in two Cornish towns, St Columb and St Ives, as part of annual festivals.

Fishing at sea

From *The Survey of Cornwall*, pp.31v–35r

… Now from within the harbour, wee will launch out into the deepe, and see what luck of fish God there shall send us, which (so you talke not of Hares or such uncouth things,[3] for that proves as ominous to the fisherman, as the beginning a voyage on the day when Childermas day fell,[4] doth to the Mariner) may succeed very profitable: for the coast is plentifully stored, both with those foreremembred, enlarged to a bigger size, & divers other, as namely of shelfish, Sea-hedge-hogs, Scallops & Sheathfish.[5] Of flat, Brets, Turbets, Dornes, Holybut. Round, Pilcherd, Herring, Pollock, Mackrell, Gurnard, Illeck, Tub, Breame, Oldwife, Hake, Dogfish, Lounp,[6] Cunner, Rockling, Cod, Wrothe, Becket, Haddock, Guilthead, Rough-hound, Squary Scad, Seale, Tunny, and many others, *quos nunc, &c.*[7]

The Sheath, or Rasor-fish, resembleth in length and bignesse a mans finger, and in taste, the Lobster, but reputed of greater restorative.

The Sea-hedge-hogge, of like or more goodnesse, is enclosed in a round shell, fashioned as a loafe of bread, handsomely wrought and pincked,[8] and garded by an utter skinne full of prickles, as the land Urchin. But the least fish in bignes, greatest for gaine, and most in number, is the Pilcherd: they come to take their kind of the fresh (as the rest) betweene harvest and Alhallontyde,[9] and were wont to pursue the Brit, upon which they feede, into the havens, but are now forestalled on the coast by the Drovers and Sayners. The Drovers hang certaine square nets athwart the tyde, thorow which the schoell of Pilchard passing, leave many behind intangled in the meashes. When the nets are so filled, the Drovers take them up, clense them, and let them fall againe.

The Sayners complayne with open mouth, that these drovers worke much prejudice to the Commonwealth of fishermen, and reape thereby small gaine to themselves: for (they say) the taking of some few, breaketh and scattereth the whole schoels, and frayeth them from approaching the shore: neither are those thus taken, marchantable, by reason of their brusing in the meash. Let the crafts-masters decide the controversie.

The Sayne, is in fashion, like that within harbour, but of a farre larger proportion. To each of these, there commonly belong three or foure boates, carrying about sixe men apeece: with which, when the season of the yeere and weather serveth, they lie hovering upon the coast, and are directed in their worke, by a Balker, or Huer, who standeth on the Cliffe side, and from thence, best discerneth the quantitie and course of the Pilcherd: according whereunto, hee cundeth[10] (as they call it) the Master of each boate (who hath his eye still fixed upon him) by crying with a lowd voice, whistling through his fingers, and wheazing certing diversified and significant signes, with a bush, which hee holdeth in his hand. At his appointment they cast out their Net, draw it to either hand, as the Schoell lyeth, or fareth, beate with their Oares to keepe in the Fish, and at last, either close and tucke it up in the Sea, or draw the same on land, with more certaine profit, if the ground bee not rough of rockes. After one companie have thus shot their Net, another beginneth behind them, and so a third, as oportunitie serveth. Being so taken, some, the Countrie people, who attend with their horses and paniers at the Cliffes side, in great numbers, doe buy and carrie home, the larger remainder, is by the Marchant greedily and speedily seized upon. They are saved three maner of wayes: by fuming, pressing, or pickelling. For every of which, they are first salted and piled up row by row in square heapes on the ground in some seller, which they terme, Bulking, where they so remaine for some ten daies, until the superfluous moysture of the bloud and salt be soked from them: which accomplished, they rip the bulk, and save the residue of the salt for another like service. Then those which are to bee ventred[11] for *Fraunce*, they pack in staunch hogsheads, so to keep them in their pickle. Those that serve for the hotter Countries of *Spaine* and *Italie*, they used at first to fume, by hanging them up on long sticks one by one, in a house built for the nonce,[12] & there drying them with the smoake of a soft and continuall fire, from whence they purchased the name of *Fumados*: but now, though the term still remaine, that trade is given over: and after they have bene ripped out of the bulk, reffed[13] upon sticks, & washed, they pack them orderly in hogsheads made purposely leake, which afterward they presse with great waights, to the end the traine[14] may soke from them into a vessell placed in the ground to receyve it.

In packing, they keepe a just tale of the number that every hogshead contayneth, which otherwise may turne to the Marchants prejudice: for I have heard, that when they are brought to the place of sale, the buyer openeth one hogs-head at adventures; and if hee finde the same not to answere the number on the outside, hee abateth[15] a like proportion in every other, as there wanted in that. The trayne is well solde, as imployed to divers uses, and welneere acquiteth the cost in saving, and the saving setteth almost an infinite number of women and children on worke, to their great advantage: for they are allowed a peny for every lasts carriage (a last is ten thousand) and as much for bulking, washing, and packing them, whereby a lusty huswife may earne three shillings in a night; for towards the evening they are mostly killed.

This commoditie at first carried a very lowe price, and served for the inhabitants cheapest provision: but of late times, the deare sale beyond the seas hath so encreased the number of takers, and the takers jarring and brawling one with another, and for closing the fishes taking their kind within harbour, so decreased the number of the taken, as the price daily extendeth to an higher rate, equalling the proportion of other fish: a matter which yet I reckon not prejudiciall to the Commonwealth, seeing there is store sufficient of other victuals, and that of these a twentieth part will serve the Countries need, and the other nineteen passe into forraine Realmes with a gainefull utterance.

The Sayners profit in this trade is uncertayne, as depending upon the seas fortune, which hee long attendeth, and often with a bootlesse travaile: but the Pilcherd Marchant may reape a speedy, large, and assured benefit, by dispatching the buying, saving and selling to the transporters, within little more then three moneths space. Howbeit, divers of them, snatching at wealth over-hastily, take mony beforehand, and binde themselves for the same, to deliver Pilcherd ready saved to the transporter, at an under-rate, and so cut their fingers. This venting[16] of Pilcherd enhaunced greatly the price of cask, whereon all other sortes of wood were converted to that use: and yet this scantly supplying a remedie, there was a statute made 35. *Eliz.* that from the last of June 1594. no stranger should transport beyond the seas any Pilcherd or other fish in cask, unlesse hee did bring into the Realme, for every sixe tunnes, two hundred of clapboard fit to make cask, and so rateably, upon payne of forfeyting the sayd Pilcherd or fish. This Acte to continue before the next Parliament, which hath revived the same, untill his (not yet knowne) succeeder.

The Pilcherd are pursued and devored by a bigger kinde of fish, called a Plusher, being somewhat like the Dog-fish, who leapeth now and then above water, and therethrough bewrayeth them to the Balker: so are they likewise persecuted by the Tonny, and he (though not verie often) taken with them *damage faisant*. And that they may no lesse in fortune, then in fashion, resemble the Flying fish, certaine birds called Gannets, soare over, and stoup to prey upon them. Lastly, they are persecuted by the Hakes, who (not long sithence) haunted the coast in great abundance; but now being deprived of their wonted baite, are much diminished, verifying the proverb, *What we lose in Hake, we shall have in Herring*. These Hakes and divers of the other forerecited, are taken with threds, & some of them with the boulter, which is a Spiller of a bigger size. Upon the North coast, where want of good harbours denieth safe roade to the fisherboats, they have a device of two sticks filled with corks, and crossed flatlong, out of whose midst there riseth a thred, and at the same hangeth a saile; to this engine, termed a Lestercock, they tie one end of their Boulter, so as the wind comming from the shore, filleth the sayle, and the saile carrieth out the Boulter into the sea, which after the respite of some houres, is drawne in againe by a cord fastened at the neerer end. They lay also certaine Weelyes in the Sea, for taking of Cunners, which therethrough are termed Cunner-pots.[17] Another net they have long and narrow meashed, thwarted with little cords of wide distance, in which the fish intangleth it selfe, and is so drawne up.

For Bait they use Barne, Pilcherd, and Lugges. The Lugge is a worme resembling the Tagworme or Angletouch, and lying in the Ose somewhat deepe, from whence the women digge them up, and sell them to the Fishermen: They are descried by their working overhead, as the Tagworme. And, for lacke of other provision, the Fishermen sometimes cut out a peece of the new taken Hake, neere his tayle, and therewith baite their hookes, to surprise more of his *Canniballian* fellowes.

The Seale, or Soyle, is in making and growth, not unlike a Pigge, ugly faced, and footed like a Moldwarp, he delighteth in musike, or any lowd noise, and thereby is trained to approach neere the shore, and to shew himselfe almost wholly above water. They also come on land, and lie sleeping in holes of the Cliffe, but are now and then waked with the deadly greeting of a bullet in their sides.

The Fishermens hookes doe not alwayes returne them good prise: for often there cleaveth to the baite, a certaine fish like a Starre, so farre from good meate, as it is held contagious.

There swimmeth also in the Sea, a round slymie substance, called a Blobber, reputed noysome to the fish.

But you are tired, the day is spent, and it is high time that I draw to harbour: which good counsell I will follow, when I have onely told you, in what manner the Fishermen save the most part of their fish. Some are polled (that is, beheaded) gutted, splitted, powdred and dried in the Sunne, as the lesser sort of Hakes. Some headed, gutted, jagged, and dried, as Rayes, and Thornbackes. Some gutted, splitted, powdred, and dried, as Buckhorne made of Whitings, (in the East parts named Scalpions) and the smaller sort of Conger, and Hake. Some, gutted, splitted, and kept in pickle, as Whiting, Mackrell, Millet, Basse, Peall, Trowt, Sammon, and Conger. Some, gutted, and kept in pickle, as the lesser Whitings, Pollocks, Eeles, and squarie Scads. Some cut in peeces, and powdred, as Seale and Porpose. And lastly, some boyled, and preserved fresh in Vineger, as Tonny and Turbet.

Hurling

From *The Survey of Cornwall*, (pp.73v–75v)

Hurling taketh his denomination from throwing of the ball, and is of two sorts, in the East parts of *Cornwall*, to goales, and in the West, to the countrey.

For hurling to goales, there are 15. 20. or 30. players more or lesse, chosen out on each side, who strip themselves into their slightest apparell, and then joyne hands in ranke one against another. Out of these ranks, they match themselves by payres, one embracing another, & so passe away: every of which couple, are specially to watch one another during the play.

After this, they pitch two bushes in the ground, some eight or ten foote asunder; and directly against them, ten or twelve score off, other twayne in like distance, which they terme their Goales. One of these is appoynted by lots, to the one side, and the other to his adverse party. There is assigned for their gard, a couple of their best stopping Hurlers: the residue draw into the midst betweene both goales, where some indifferent person throweth up a ball, the which whosoever can catch, and cary through his adversaries goale, hath wonne the game. But therein consisteth one of *Hercules* his labours: for hee that is once possessed of the ball, hath his contrary mate waiting at inches, and assaying to lay hold upon him. The other thrusteth him in the brest, with his closed fist, to keepe him off; which they call Butting, and place in weldoing the same, no small poynt of manhood.

If hee escape the first, another taketh him in hand, and so a third, neyther is hee left, untill having met (as the Frenchman says) *Chausseura son pied*, hee eyther touch the ground with some part of his bodie, in wrastling, or cry, Hold; which is the word of yeelding. Then must he cast the ball (named Dealing) to some one of his fellowes, who catching the same in his hand, maketh away withall as before; and if his hap or agility bee so good, as to shake off or outrunne his counterwayters, at the goale, hee findeth one or two fresh men, readie to receive and keepe him off. It is therefore a very disadvantageable match, or extraordinary accident, that leeseth[18] many goales: howbeit, that side carryeth away best reputation, which giveth most falles in the hurling, keepeth the ball longest, and presseth his countrary neerest to their owne goale. Sometimes one chosen person on eche party dealeth the ball.

The Hurlers are bound to the observation of many lawes, as, that they must hurle man to man, and not two set upon one man at once: that the Hurler against the ball, must not *but*, nor hand-fast under girdle: that hee who hath the ball, must *but* only in the others brest: that he must deale no Fore-ball, *viz.* he may not throw it to any of his mates, standing neerer the goale, then himselfe. Lastly, in dealing the ball, if any of the other part can catch it flying between, or e're the other have it fast, he thereby winneth the same to his side, which straightway of defendant becommeth assailant, as the other, of assailant falls to be defendant. The least breach of these lawes, the Hurlers take for a just cause of going together by the eares, but with their fists onely; neither doth any among them seek revenge for such wrongs or hurts, but at the like play againe. These hurling matches are mostly used at weddings, where commonly the ghests undertake to counter all commers.

The hurling to the Countrey, is more diffuse and confuse, as bound to few of these orders: Some two or more Gentlemen doe commonly make this match, appointing that on such a holyday, they will bring to such an indifferent place, two, three, or more parishes of the East or South quarter, to hurle against so many other, of the West or North. Their goales are either those Gentlemens houses, or some townes or villages, three or foure miles asunder, of which either side maketh choice after the neernesse to their dwellings. When they meet, there is neyther comparing of numbers, nor matching of men; but a silver ball is cast up, and that company, which can catch, and cary it by force, or sleight, to their place assigned, gaineth the ball and victory. Whosoever getteth the seizure of this ball, findeth himselfe generally pursued by the adverse party; neither will they leave, till (without all respects) he be layd flat on Gods deare earth: which fall once received, disableth him from any longer detayning the ball: hee therefore throweth the same (with like hazard of intercepting, as in the other hurling) to some one of his fellowes, fardest before him, who maketh away withall in like manner. Such as see where the ball is played, give notice thereof to their mates, crying, Ware East, Ware West, &c. as the same is carried.

The Hurlers take their next way over hilles, dales, hedges, ditches; yea, and thorow bushes, briers, mires, plashes and rivers whatsoever; so as you shall sometimes see 20. or 30. lie tugging together in the water, scrambling and scratching for the ball. A play (verily) both rude & rough, and yet such, as is not destitute of policies, in some sort resembling the feats of warre: for you shall have companies layd out before, on the one side, to encounter them that come with the ball, and of the other party to succor them, in maner of a fore-ward. Againe, other troups lye hovering on the sides, like wings, to helpe or stop their escape: and where the ball it selfe goeth, it resembleth the joyning of the two mayne battels: the slowest footed who come lagge, supply the showe of a rere-ward: yea, there are horsemen placed also on either party (as it were in ambush) and ready to ride away with the ball, if they can catch it at advantange. But they may not so steale the palme: for gallop any one of them never so fast, yet he shall be surely met at some hedge corner, crosse-lane, bridge, or deepe water, which (by casting the Countrie) they know he must needs touch at: and if his good fortune gard him not the better, hee is like to pay the price of his theft, with his owne and his horses overthrowe to the ground. Sometimes, the whole company runneth with the ball, seven or eight miles out of the direct way, which they should keepe. Sometimes a foote-man getting it by stealth, the better to escape unspied, will carry the same quite backwards, and so, at last, get to the goale by a windlace:[19] which once knowne to be wonne, all that side flocke thither with great jolity: and if the same bee a Gentlemans house, they give him the ball for a *Trophee*, and the drinking out of his Beere to boote.

The ball in this play may bee compared to an infernall spirit: for whosoever catcheth it, fareth straightwayes like a madde man, strugling and fighting with those that goe about to holde him: and no sooner is the ball gone from, but hee resigneth this fury to the next receyver, and himselfe becommeth peaceable as before. I cannot well resolve, whether I should more commend this game, for the manhood and exercise, or condemne it for the boysterousnes and harmes which it begetteth: for as on the one side it makes their bodies strong, hard, and nimble, and puts a courage into their hearts, to meete an enemie in the face: so on the other part, it is accompanied with many dangers, some of which doe ever fall to the players share. For proofe whereof, when the hurling is ended, you shall see them retyring home, as from a pitched battaile, with bloody pates, bones broken, and out of joynt, and such bruses as serve to shorten their daies; yet al is good play, & never Attourney nor Crowner troubled for the matter.

1. Edmund Spenser (1552–1599) was one of the great English poets of the Elizabethan period. He lived in Ireland, where he was in the service of the Lord Deputy, Arthur Grey. He held controversial ideas about the government of Ireland, proposing, in a pamphlet not published during his lifetime, subjugation of the Irish through the suppression of their culture, customs, and language. His epic poem 'The Faerie Queen' is a masterpiece in which he devised a verse form which has been influential in the works of many succeeding poets.
2. May McKisack in *Medieval History in the Tudor Age* (p.140) comments that Carew was not deeply read in history, for he cites only Howden, 'Matthew of Westminster' and Froissart, fewer authorities than the more scholarly antiquaries would have called upon.
3. There are many superstitions associated with fishing at sea. The one concerning hares or rabbits originated in Cornwall.
4. *Childermas*, Holy Innocents' Day (28 December).
5. '*those foreremembred*', Carew has earlier in this section listed freshwater fish, and here he offers another marvellous and enchanting list of names, some still familiar, some slightly disguised (such as *holybut* for halibut), some archaic, and some, such as *illeck*, unique to Cornwall.
6. *Lounp*, lump-sucker, or sea-owl: a fish with a suctorial disc on its belly.
7. *Quos nunc*, literally, means 'to whom now', and is presumably used here before *etc.* just to mean that the names of the 'many others' needn't be mentioned.
8. *Pincked*, in the best condition, i.e., most handsome.
9. 'Harvest' meant autumn, and Alhallontide (All Hallows) is 1 November.
10. *Cund*, to guide a ship.
11. *Ventred*, ventured, sent by sea at the sender's risk.
12. *For the nonce*, for the express purpose.
13. *Reffed*, past participle of 'revve', to break in pieces, to split.
14. *Traine*, stream of liquid.
15. *Abateth*, reduces.
16. *Venting*, selling, marketing.
17. *Weely*, a wicker trap for catching fish, especially eels; *cunner*, gilt-head.
18. *Leese*, lose.
19. *Windlace*, a circumventive route.

VII

Devon: Thomas Westcote (1567–1636)

Thomas Westcote was one of a group of three friends, each of whom worked towards writing a description of Devon.[1] While they did not make a collaborative effort, they exchanged ideas, shared information, and helped one another. Of the three, Westcote and Tristram Risdon each finished the task, although neither work was published until the nineteenth century; the third, Sir William Pole, who spent over thirty years collecting data, left an incomplete manuscript which was published in 1791. These men were county gentlemen, not scholars, although Risdon spent some time at Oxford, and Pole studied at the Inner Temple, practised law and at different times was a member of parliament and became High Sheriff of his county. Little is known biographically of Westcote: born in Devon, he was self-educated and was variously a soldier, a traveller, and a courtier. He did not himself attempt to have his work, *A View of Devonshire in MDCXXX*, published, evidently having compiled it more for his own pleasure and the entertainment of his friends than anything else. Like his two fellow antiquaries, he was a gentleman of leisure, and his writing was a labour of love.

Westcote's book, then, is an example of an amateur county description. It is certainly a substantial book, but unlike the serious and dogged surveys of scholarly antiquaries such as Dugdale, it is a lively and individual work in which the reader is escorted around the county by a genial and animated guide. Of earlier surveys, it is to the study of Cornwall by Carew that it is probably closest in spirit, and which may indeed have been an influence on Westcote's approach. The larger part of the Devonshire description is concerned with tenancy of land and family descents, material which is less evident in Carew's book, but the earlier sections deal with the geography of the county, its produce and commodities, its people, and its antiquities and curiosities. Westcote relates some county traditions and folklore as well as gossipy reports about certain individuals, and he conveys an impression of great pride in and love for his native shire.

The first of the two extracts which follow is a description not of a landscape but of a sector of Devon society. In a sequence of chapters Westcote gives accounts of the different 'degrees of inhabitants' of the county, these being the nobility and gentility, the yeomanry and husbandmen, the merchants, and lastly 'Day-Labourers in Tin-works and Hirelings in Husbandry'.[2] In Devon, one of the main industries was the mining of tin, and this provided the work undertaken by many of the county's men. Westcote was one of the few authors who bothered to write about labourers. The differentiation of classes was, to most authors, wholly unremarkable, and the lower classes, who owned no land and made no noble achievements, were ignored. Of course this is not to say that the majority of writers of county descriptions were unaware of the labouring classes and never encountered them, but Westcote is unusual in not only acknowledging them (as do Carew and Aubrey) but also seeking to understand how life might have been for them. And with surprising frankness he expressed a degree of envy for the simplicity of their lives.

The second extract is a place description of the forest of Exmoor.[3] Here Westcote is like an affable host, proudly conducting his guest around his estate, savouring the pleasure of showing the special attractions and teasing out the anticipation of what is yet to come. Like a precursory travel-guide writer, Westcote offers the vicarious experience of an arm-chair visit. Yet he is oblivious to the scenery, attending only to that which may be found in it, which is either useful or related to the past: the whimsical narrative evokes the effort of traversing the way but lacks any depiction of the forest, dwelling instead on certain historical mysteries pertinent to ancient stone monuments. The forest 'yieldeth no metal as yet found', is good only for 'pasture and summering' of sheep and cattle, and so, but for 'certain stones', we should 'search it no farther'. He gives some historical speculation, together with a translation, evidently his own, of a stanza of Welsh poetry, on the purpose of one of the monuments.

Of Day-Labourers in Tin-works, and Hirelings in Husbandry

From *A View of Devonshire in MDCXXX*, Chapter XI,[4] pp.52–54

The common day-labourer, or hireling, as meanest, is last remembered. I speak of them that work by week or day in husbandry labour, or thereunto belonging, or in tin-works. Of the last are two sorts; one named a spador or searcher for tin, than whom (as it seems to me) no labourer whatsoever undergoes greater hazard of peril or danger, nor in hard or coarse fare and diet doth equal him: bread, the brownest; cheese, the hardest; drink, the thinnest;

yea, commonly the dew of heaven; which he taketh either from his shovel, or spade, or in the hollow of his hand; as Diogenes, the cynic, was taught by a boy. He spends all day (or the major part thereof) like a mole or earth-worm underground, mining in deep vaults or pits, as though he intended (with noble Sir Francis Drake) to find a way to the antipodes; yea, a nearer, and so to surpass him: for it is sometime of that profundity, that notwithstanding the country (so they term the earth over their heads,) is propped, posted, crossed, traversed, and supported with divers great beams of timber to keep them in security, yet all is sometimes too little; they perish with the fall thereof notwithstanding.

Miserable men! may some men say in regard of their labour and poverty; yet having a kind of content therein, for that they aim at no better, they think not so; for having sufficient to supply nature's demand, they are satisfied; sleep soundly without careful thoughts, which most rich men want not, which are either greedy of more, or press nature with superfluities of provoking sauces, hot wines, waters, and spices: for, as Horace speaketh,—

———'Multa petentibus
Desunt multa; bene est cui Deus obtulit
Parca quod satis est manu.'

Who much do crave, of much have need;
But well is he whom God indeed,
Though with a sparing hand, doth feed.

But if you will not give credit to him, hearken what the kingly prophet, David, saith,

'Doubtless the poor man's just estate
Is better, a great deal more,
Than all the lewd and worldly man's
Rich pomp and heated store.'

The other is also a day-labourer, but at husbandry or at work belonging thereunto. He labours without danger and much more easily, dieteth more liberally and after a better sort. Both are generally of a strong constitution of body to undertake any painful action, by their rustic, un-nice, and laborious education.

Their holy-days' exercises were also toilsome and violent, as wrestling, hurling, foot-ball, leaping, running, dancing with music, especially in their festivals, to exhilarate their hearts and such like; which made them fit for the wars or any other employment whatsoever, wherein hardiness, or strength, or agility was required. But these exercises are, by zeal, discommended and discountenanced, and so utterly out of use;[5] yet no better, nor any so good, used in their stead; which may in time breed some inconveniencies: but no more of his lest it bring me some also.

These people though the most inferior, are yet, notwithstanding, liberi homines—free-men of state and condition: no slaves. Of these the man saith, 'they are not asked nor sought for in public council, nor yet high in the congregation, nor are they placed in the judge's seat, nor understand they the order of justice. They cannot declare matters according to the form of law; nor are they meet for hard parables: yet without these cannot a city be inhabited or occupied.'

Of the Forest of Exmoor

From *A View of Devonshire in MDCXXX*,
Chapter XXIII, pp.88–92

Without danger, at length, though not void of tedious and wearisome travel, are we freed out of the liberty of tin-warrants; and a simple and unskilful pilot though I be, (so you find, and so I frankly confess myself, and would never have so boldly undertaken to be your guide had not the more sufficient slid back or fainted,) you are disembogued of the large gulf of land, the forest of Dartmoor; and under my conduct safely and securely escaped the peril of deep tin-works, steep tors, high mountains, low valleys, bogs, plains, being neither in any hazard or fear of danger, without wetting your foot in the many meers, or fouling your shoes in the many mires. Now I suppose you hope and expect more delightsome objects, pleasant ways, and comfortable travel, (after these uneven, rocky, stumbling, tiring, melancholy paths,) but I cannot promise you presently: I see a spacious, coarse, barren, and wild object, yielding little comfort by his rough, cold, and rigorous complexion. I doubt you will say with the poet—

> 'Incidit in Scyllam cupiens vitare Charibdim.'

> In shunning of Charibdes' paws
> He falleth into Scylla's jaws.

Have a little patience, your stay will not be long; I will shorten the way by directing you by a straight line without any turning or needless ambages; you shall not have a bough of a tree to strike off your hat, or drop in your neck: it is the other forest I have formerly told you of, part of which lies in this county, and is called Exmoor Forest. The greatest part belongeth to Somersetshire, and yieldeth no metal as yet found, only good pastures and summering, for sheep and cattle, in quantity and quality. We should therefore search it no farther, were I not to seek and show you certain stones, supposed (as I am informed,) by no simple evidence, to be there erected, some in triangle wise, others in circle, as trophies of victories gotten of or by the Romans, Saxons, or Danes; on which also are engraven certain Danish or Saxon characters. Thought of some to be there erected and fixed in memory of the great victory at the overthrow and slaughter of Hubba, the Dane; who, with Hungar, his associate, having harried over all the country, from Eglisdon (now St Edmondsbury,) to this country, was here utterly vanquished, and with his whole army slain, anno 879, and the banner (wherein was curiously wrought, by the fingers of the daughters of King Loth-brook, (in English, Leather-breech,) a raven, which they called Rephan, whereon they reposed so small confidence for good success, having been so oftentimes fortunately and with so happy success displayed,) taken, and the place since that time called Hubbleston. But for that place we may perchance find it hereafter near the mouth of Torridge.

Other there be that affirm them rather to be set as guides and directions, the better to conduct strangers in their way over those wastes. But let us forbear to inquire farther of the cause, and find the stones, which I cannot as yet, neither can they which I have purposely employed in quest of them, learn of any such, either in the north moor between Hore-oak-ridge and Snabhill; nor southward from Exaborough to Exridge; or in the middle moor westward, between the long chain to Rexable and Settacombe; or in the south from Druslade to Vermy-ball; neither from Wester Emmot to Lydden-moor; and all the other noted hills and valleys (which we term coombes,) therein. To reckon up all I doubt would be over-wearisome unto you, as the journey unto myself; for I was vexed with a jealous care to a serious and particular inquisition of what occurs in reading taken up of the writers (as the subject of our corantoes,)[6] upon the credit of the reporters.

For I find only near Porlock Commons a stone, not pitched but lying, which they call the long stone; but that may breed another question, why it should be so named, being not five feet in length and much less in crassitude.[7] Also in the west from Woodborough to Rodley-head, which we call Collacumb Commons, is a plain stone erected, in height near six feet, in thickness, two; yet without any antique or other engravings. But somewhat nearer to our purpose do I find in the parish of East Down, in the farm of Northcot the seat sometime of a generous family of the same denomination, John Northcot, whom was sheriff of this county in the 29th year of Edward

III. 1355; and though it be now out of the name, we shall find one of his name and of his posterity, his equal, in the 2nd year of our now Sovereign Lord King Charles I. 1626. In a large spacious field enclosed, by the name of Mattocks, or Maddocks Down, near five miles from the forest, certain great stones are erected in this manner:—first, there stand two great stones in nature or fashion (yet not curiously cut,) of pyramids, distant the one from the other 147 feet; the greatest above the ground nine feet and a half, every square bearing four feet; the height of the other stone is five feet and a half, but in every square near equals the other, being somewhat above three feet. These two stones, pyramids and pillars, stand in direct line one opposite to the other, sixty-six feet; on the side of each of these is laid a ridge, a row, or bank of three-and-twenty large (yet not equalling by half the other) stones, stretching out in length even with the other two, in straight and equal line, making a reciprocal figure, as having the sides equally proportioned, but double as long in length than square and more, (which, as I am told, is called a parallelogram.) But on none of these stones are there any characters to be seen, neither are they to be engraven they are so hard and rough.

That these stones should naturally grow here it cannot be thought by any spectator; neither can I as yet satisfy myself with any reason or occasion (by reading or tradition,) why they should be thus erected, but for some victory here gotten, and the monument of the interment of some famous person or eminent place or worth.

But to conjecture by the name of Maddock or Mattock I know not how to allude to any authentical history or person: for first to think upon Madock who, anno 23rd Edward I., 1294, raised an uproar and rebellion in Wales, from whom, in time, the king won the Isle of Anglesea, and after anno 25 of the said king was taken, drawn, and hanged; his rebellion being in Wales and his death in London; it holds with no congruity. To fetch it as far as Madock, the fourth son of Owen Grisneth, Prince of Wales, who, seeing his three elder brethren strive and violently to contend for the government of the country, or equal partition of their shares therein, could not endure it, and therefore rigged a fleet of ships and adventured the seas to seek some waste or desert place where he might inhabit quietly; who is supposed, by great probability, to be the first discoverer of the West Indies, and inhabiter thereof; imposing British names to divers things, which continue to this age. (440 years since, for he lived anno 1170.)[8] Of him Meredith, the son of Rhesi, (als ap Rhese,) who lived 1477, hath this written,—

'Madoc wif mw y die wed,
Jawn genan Owen Gwyneth,
Ni funnum dir fy enridd oedd
Ni da mowr ondy moroedd.'

It is Englished thus,—

Madoc, I am the son of Owen Guynedd,
With stature large, and comely grace adorned:
No lands at home, or store of wealth me please,
My mind was whole to search the ocean seas.

Thus Englished in Mr. Herbert's travels,—

'Madoc ap Owen was I call'd,
Strong, tall, and comely; not enthrall'd
With home-bred pleasure, but for fame
Through land and sea I sought the same.'

This man, employing himself in search of strange and uninhabited countries, I cannot, with any likelihood, place him here, but will leave it to him that hath dived deeper in the British tongue than myself; and so will take our leave of Exmoor …

1. The biographical information offered here on Westcote and his friends is derived from the work of Stan A. E. Mendyk, in his *'Speculum Britanniae': Regional Study, Antiquarianism, and Science in Britain to 1700*, University of Toronto Press, 1989, pp.90-98.
2. Book I, chapters VIII–XI.
3. Book I, chapter XXIII.
4. This is preceded by a chapter on 'the degrees of the Inhabitants', and then chapters on the gentry, the yeomanry, and the merchants.
5. While Sunday outdoor activities were much encouraged by James I and Charles I as a means of diverting their subjects' energies from more disruptive pursuits, they were regarded with disapproval by Puritans.
6. *Coranto*, a dance, a *courante*; but in this case, a newsletter or gazette.
7. *Crassitude*, thickness, density.
8. The tradition that there was a twelfth-century Prince of Wales, Madoc, who discovered the West Indies and established a Welsh-speaking settlement, perhaps in Alabama, first appeared in *A True Reporte*, written by Sir George Peckham in 1583. It was possibly devised to give Elizabeth I an early claim to territory in the New World. It was believed that there was a Welsh-speaking tribe of North American Indians, but no such phenomenon has ever been demonstrated. Peckham was the author of a treatise entitled *The Advantages of Colonization* (1582).

LONDON

VIII
London: John Stow (1525–1605)

John Stow was born, bred, and lived till his death in London, where he conducted a business as a tailor, although his consuming interest for most of his life was the study of the past. He was self-educated and of modest means, but eventually he could count leading scholars, such as William Camden and William Lambarde, amongst his friends, and he became an honoured member of the Society of Antiquaries. This other, scholarly career he established in 1561 with an edition of works of Chaucer; it continued with several compilations of chronicle histories of England and culminated in 1598 with his most enduring achievement, the *Survay of London*. It was based on extensive studies of archives and chronicles, which he used judiciously, tempering deference to authority with critical consideration. He brought thorough research together with his lifelong familiarity with the wards and streets, the buildings, river, markets, and people to create a vivid and detailed celebration of London's tumultuous past, its great monuments, and its colourful everyday activity. After four hundred years his book is still the best record of the Elizabethan city.

Stow's intimate knowledge of his subject was framed in a structure and method which were new, for this was the first town survey of such scope, or indeed the first study to offer such topographical detail about a particular place.[1] It was not a static description: he took account of change and development, both in urban needs, such as the location of markets, supply of water, shifts in residential profiles; and as a result of the political and religious innovations of the Tudor era. His personal experience of London was more than topographic; it also comprehended events going back to the Dissolution, so that Stow was able to remember a very different regime from that under which he had lived in his maturity. He had had first-hand experience of the changes which followed the Reformation, having even himself been under suspicion for having a library of antiquarian books, and subsequently having had his home searched on two occasions. While he refrained in his published works from giving opinions on religion or politics, his narrative sometimes echoed the instability of the times in its expression of nostalgia for the past.

Stow was diligent in his use of archives to verify historical details and he made judgments about their reliability when he found that they conflicted. He allowed, in his histories of England, a degree of credit to the account of the Trojan origins and subsequent line of succession of the nation's kings given in the 'Brut', although he judged Caesar's Commentaries to be more useful than Geoffrey of Monmouth's history. As an antiquary, he was a seeker of facts, so that he put truth before rhetoric to the point of admitting his ignorance, or of referring his readers to a better authority (such as his younger friend Camden) when he was unsure of his information. Stow's work, like that of Camden, indicates the emergence of a new type of writing about the past.

As an early example of an antiquarian chorographical study, *The Survay of London* exemplifies certain features of this methodology, in which the subject place is described by the geographical ordering of historical information. Stow himself acknowledged that his approach was influenced by Lambarde's book on Kent, and it can be seen that, after the preliminary sections of the survey, London is arranged in the book as if this author also is perambulating, accompanying his readers about the streets. The book begins with descriptions of those features of the city which relate to the whole rather than particular wards: the city wall, the rivers and water supply, bridges, gates, fortifications, places of learning; and then certain observations about the citizenry. With each detail thus encountered and in the ensuing traversal of successive wards, pertinent items of history are evoked and recounted.

The most striking effect of a chorographical description, then, is the insistent recalling of the past, to the degree that, at times, the reader might forget that the text is actually about the present. This illusion, generated by the frequent referencing of archives, brings the past into the present so that the two tend to blur one into the other. The following extract is the entire description of one of the twenty-six wards into which London was divided. Bread Street Ward is first delineated in detail, with reference to the streets which formed its boundaries. These specifications have the very distinct sense of guiding a walker pacing out the ward's extent, but they also have the effect of being like a depiction on a map, but without actually being able to see the map. A number of maps of towns and cities had been produced in the two or three decades prior to the *Survay*, but Stow did not include one in his book.[2] His narration intrinsically provides a kind of map, but it is textual, rather than visual.

Even while giving the boundary definitions Stow begins to include historical details—that Bread Street is so named because bread was sold there and in

1302 a decree determined that the bread should be sold in the markets and not from bakers' shops and houses. Then the description proper begins: 'The Monuments to bee noted here, are …' And so, following street after street, Stow points out the notable buildings, markets, and great houses. Churches are given particular attention, especially as the burial places of prominent citizens of the ward, and these listings give us an idea of the commercial profile of the area. A few places are given special attention. The first is Allhallows Church, regarding which a tale about the shortening of the steeple is related; the next is Gerard's Hall, a great house with which was associated a legend of a giant, which Stow dismisses with some scorn, but in spite of his personal attitude his narrative evokes the evidently extant credulity with which such stories were received; and the third is a former prison, the mention of which calls forth some comments about the maltreatment of those detained.

In common with most seventeenth-century antiquarian surveys, the application of the term 'description' to Stow's narrative requires some qualification. Passages which describe in any real sense a particular feature of the urban landscape are both terse and infrequent. In Bread Street Ward, the most expansive description is that of Goldsmiths' Row, 'the most bewdifull frame and front of faire houses, and shops, that be within all the walles of London, or elsewhere in England'. He gives no more than a few details of the size of the building and the appearance of the roof decoration. This and a couple of phrases about a row of fishmongers' houses in Knightriders Street, developed over time in the place where originally fish was sold in the street, are the only descriptive passages offered. Other remarks about places do no more than indicate their existence, with perhaps some brief pertinent anecdote.

The urban landscape is presented in terms of names, events, and dates: places are described by past associations and tenancies. So the appearance of places and buildings, which is experienced by the walker in the streets, is subsidiary to that information which has been found in the archives: the transactions conducted by of a set of people who have interconnections such as tenancy, succession, inheritance, patronage. But was this 'archival' view a special, legalistic, antiquarian view, or was it the normal view, that would be envisaged by a Londoner as he or she traversed the streets and observed the buildings? Certainly, if Stow's *Survay* is a distillation of archives, it cannot be expected that it will contain the observed, everyday background: the prospect of a streetscape, the clamour of a market, the cries of the stallholders, the warmth of an inn, the smell of a cesspit. But it may be asked what of these phenomena would indeed have been *noticed* by those in the streets. In describing an urban landscape now we would not point out as highlights the sound of the passing traffic, the brightness of the street lights, the existence of car-parks, the presence of advertising hoardings. These things have an unremarkable presence and are taken for granted, so it may well be expected that they will not be given prominence in a description. Nevertheless, there is in the narrative one fleeting glimpse of community life in Bread Street Ward, and that is evoked by the mention of a maypole being set up in the summer, although this custom belonged not to the present but the not-too-distant past.[3]

Since the urban landscape presented by Stow is so much delineated in terms of people, his enumerations of the tombs in the parish churches help to flesh out the picture. There are goldsmiths, salters, tailors, fishmongers, and one each of a blader,[4] a vintner, a cleric, a draper, a skinner, an ironmonger, as well as a pewterer and a surgeon each having royal custom. It was a mercantile part of London, and the supposition that many inhabitants enjoyed a comfortable lifestyle is borne out by Stow's references to wealthy citizens and 'fayre and large houses'. The number of city officials mentioned is another indication of the standing of the ward: either commemorated in the parish churches or mentioned as having been in the ward are ten mayors, eight sheriffs, and three other aldermen of the city of London.

Bredstreete Warde

From *The Survay of London*, pp.279–285

Bredstreete Ward beginneth in the high streete of West Cheape, to wit, on the South side, from the Standard, to the great Crosse.[5] Then is also a part of Watheling street of this ward, to wit, from over against the Red Lyon on the North side up almost to Powles gate, for it lacketh but one house of S. *Augustins* Church. And on the South side, from the Red Lyon gate to the Old Exchaunge, and down the same Exchaunge on the East side, by the West end of Mayden Lane, or Distar Lane, to Knightrydars streete, or as they call that part thereof, Old Fishstreete.[6] And all the North side of the said Old Fishstreete, to the South ende of Bredstreete, and by that still in Knightridars streete, till over against the Trinitie Church, and Trinitie Lane. Then is Bredstreet it selfe so called of bread in old time there sold: for it appeareth by records, that in the yeare 1302. which was the 30. of *Ed.* the 1. The Bakers of *London* were bounden to sell no bread in their shops or houses, but in the Market, and that they should have 4. Hall motes in the yeare, at foure severall termes, to determine of enormities belonging to the said Company.[7]

This streete giving the name to the whole Warde, beginneth in West Cheape, almost by the Standard, and runneth downe South, through or thwart Watheling streete, to Knightridars street aforesaid, where it endeth. This Bredstreete is wholly on both sides of this Warde. Out of which streete on the East side, is Basing Lane, a peece whereof, to wit, too and and [*sic*] over against the backe gate of the Red Lyon in Watheling streete, is of this Bredstreete Warde.

Then is there one other streete, which is called Friday streete, and beginneth also in West Cheape, and runneth downe South through Watheling streete, to Knightridar streete (or Old Fishstreet). This Friday streete is of Bredstreete Warde, on the East side from over against the Northeast corner of saint *Mathewes* Church, and on the West side from the South corner of the said Church, downe as aforesaid.

In this Fryday streete on the West side thereof, is a Lane, commonly called Mayden lane, or Distaffe Lane, corruptly for Distar lane, which runneth West into the olde Exchange: and in this lane is also one other Lane, on the South side thereof, likewise called Distar lane, which runneth downe to Knightridars Streete, or old Fishstreete: and so be the boundes of this whole Warde. The Monuments to bee noted here, are first, the most bewtifull frame and front of faire houses, and shops, that be within all the walles of *London*, or elsewhere in *England*, commonly called Godsmithes rowe, betwixt Breadstreet end, and the Crosse in Cheape, but is within this Breadstreete Warde: the same was builded by *Thomas Wood* Goldsmith, one of the Sheriffes, in the yeare 1491. It continueth in number, tenne faire dwelling houses, and foureteene shops, all in one frame uniformely builded, foure stories high, bewtified towards the streete, with the Goldsmithes Armes, and the likenesse of woodmen (in memorie of his name) riding on monstrous beasts, all which is cast in Leade, richly painted over, and guilt: these hee gave to the Goldsmithes, with stockes of money to be lent to young men, having those shops &c.

This said front was againe new painted and guilt over, in the yeare 1594. Sir *Richard Martin* being then Maior, and keeping his Maioraltie in one of them, and serving out the time of *Cutbert Buckle* in that office, from the second of Julie, til the 28. of October. Then for Watheling Streete, which *Leyland* calleth Atheling or Noble street: but since he sheweth no reason why it was so called, I rather take it so named of the great high way of the same calling.

True it is, that at this present as of olde time also, the inhabitants thereof were and are, wealthy Drapers, retailors of woollen cloathes both broad and narrowe, of all sortes, more then in any one streete of this Citie. Of the olde Exchange, heere I have noted in Faringdon Warde: wherfore I passe downe to Knightriders street, wherof I have also spoken in Cordwainer streete Ward, but in this part of the said Knightriders streete, is a fishmarket kept, and therefore called old Fishstreete, for a difference from new Fishstreete.

In this olde Fishstreete, is one rowe of small houses, placed along in the middest of Knightriders streete, which rowe is also of Bredstreete Warde, these houses now possessed of Fishmongers, were at the first but moovable boordes (or stables) sette out on market dayes, to shewe their fish there to be sold: but procuring license to set up sheads,[8] they grewe to shops, and by litle and litle, to tall houses, of three or 4. stories in heigth, and now are called Fishstreete. Bredestreet, so called of bread solde there (as I sayd) is now wholely inhabited by rich Marchants, and divers faire Innes be there for good receipt of carriers, and other travellers to the citie. On the East side of this street, at the corner of Watheling Streete, is the proper church of Alhallowes in Bred street, wherin are the monuments of *James Thame* Goldsmith, *John Walpole* Goldsmith 1349. *Thomas Beamount* Alderman, one of the Sheriffes, 1442. Sir *Richard Chaury* Salter Maior, 1509. Sir *Thomas Pargitar* Salter Maior, 1530. *Henry Sucley* Marchantailor, one of the Sheriffes 1541. *Richard Reade* Alderman, that served & was taken prisoner in *Scotland*, 1545 *Robert House* one of the Sheriffes, 1586. *William Albany*: *Richard May*, and *Roger Abde* Marchantaylors. The steeple of this church had sometime a faire speere of stone, but taken downe upon this occasion. In the yeare 1559. the fifth of September, about noone or midday, fell a great tempest at *London*, in the ende whereof, happened a great lightening, with a terrible clap of thunder, which strooke the said speere about nine or tenne foote beneath the top thereof: out of the which place fell a stone, that slew a dogge, and overthrew a man that was playing with the dogge: the same speere being but litle damnified hereby, was shortly taken downe, for sparing the charges of reparation. On the same side is Salters Hall, with sixe almes houses in number, builded for poore decayed brethren of that company: This Hall was burned in the yeare 1539. and againe reedified.

Lower downe on the same side, is the parish church of Saint *Mildred* the Virgine. The monuments in this Church bee of the Lord *Trenchaunt*, of Saint *Albons* knight, who was supposed to be eyther the new builder of this Church, or best benefactor to the works therof, about the year 1300. & odde. *Cornish* gentleman 1312. *William Palmer* Blader a great benefactor also 1356. *John Shadworth* Mayor, 1401. who gave the parsonate house, a revestry, and Churchyard, in the yeare 1428. and his monument is pulled down. *Stephen Bugge* Gentleman, his Armes be 3. water bugges, 1419 *Roger Forde* Vintoner, 1440. *Thomas Barnwell* Fishmonger, one of the Sheriffes, 1434. Sir *John Hawlen* Clarke, Parson of that Church, who built the Parsonage house newly, after the same had bene burned to the ground, togither with the Parson and his man also, burned in that fire, 1485. *John Pranell* 1510. *William Hurstwaight* Pewterer to the King, 1526. *Christopher Turner* Chirurgian to King *Henry* the 8. 1530. *Raphe Simonds* Fishmonger, one of the Sheriffes, in the yeare 1527. *Thomas Laugham* gave to the poore of that Parish foure Tenements, 1575. *Thomas Hall* Salter, 1582. *Thomas Collins* Salter, Alderman. Sir *Ambrose Nicholas* Salter, Maior, 1575. was buried in Sir *John Chadworths* Vault.

Out of this Bredstreet, on the same East side, is a Basing lane, a part whereof (as is afore shewed) is of this Warde, but howe it tooke the name

I have not read: other then that in the 20. yeare of *Richard* the second, the same was called the Bakehouse: whether ment for the Kings Bakehouse, or of Bakers dwelling there, and baking bread to serve the Market in Bredstreete, where the bread was iolde, [*sic*] I knowe not: but sure I am, I have not reade yet of any Basing, or of *Gerrarde* the Gyant, to have any thing there to doo.

On the South side of this Lane, is one great house, of old time builded upon Arched Vaultes of stone, and with Arched Gates, now a common Ostrey for receit of Travellers,[9] commonly and corruptly called Gerardes Hall, of a Gyaunt saide to have dwelled there. In the high Rooffed Hall of this house, sometime stood a large Firre Pole, which reached to the roofe therof, and was said to be one of the staves that *Gerarde* the Gyant used in the warres, to runne withall.[10] There stoode also a Ladder of the same length, which (as they say) served to ascende to the toppe of the Staffe. Of later yeares this Hall is altered in building, and divers roomes are made in it. Notwithstanding the Pole is removed to one corner of the Hall, and the Ladder hanged broken up on a Wall in the yarde. The Hostelar of that house saide to me, the Pole lacked halfe a foote of fortie in length: I measured the compasse, and founde it to bee fifteene inches. Reason of the Pole, coulde the maister of the Hostrey give me none, but badde me reade the great Chronicles, for there he had heard of it. Which aunswere seemed to me insufficient, for hee meant the description of *Brittaine*,[11] before *Reinwoolfes* Chronicle, wherein the Authoure writing a Chapter of Gyaunts, and having beene deceived by some Authours, too much crediting their smoothe speeche, hath set downe more matter then troth, as partly (and also against my will) I am enforced to touch. *R. G.* in this briefe collection of Histories hath these wordes.[12] I the writer hereof, did see the tenth day of March, in the yeare of our Lord 1564. and had the same in my hande, the Toothe of a man, which waighed tenne Ounces of *Troy* waight. And the skull of the same man is extant and to be seene, which will holde five Peckes of wheate. And the shinne bone of the same man is sixe foote in length, and of a marvellous greatnesse. Thus farre of *R. G.* Whereunto is added in the saide discription, that by conjecturall simetrie of those partes, the bodie to be twentie eight foote long or more. From this hee goeth to an other matter, and so to *Gerard* the Gyant and his staffe. But to leave these fictions and to return where I left, I will note what my selfe have observed concerning that house.

I reade, that *John Gisors* Mayor of *London*, in the yeare 1245. was owner thereof, and that Sir *John Gisors* Knight Mayor of *London*, and Constable of the Tower, one thousand three hundreth and eleven. And divers others of that name and family since that time owed it. For I reade that *William Gisors* was one of the Sheriffes, one thousand three hundreth twentie nine. More, that *John Gisors* had issue, *Henry* and *John*. Which *John* had issue, *Thomas*. Which *Thomas* deceasing in the yeare one thousand three hundreth and fiftie, left unto his sonne *Thomas*, his Messuage called *Gysors* Hall, in the Parish of Saint *Mildred* in Bredstreete: *John Gisors* made a Feofment[13] thereof, one thousand three hundreth eightie sixe, &c. So that it appeareth that this *Gisors* Hall of late time by corruption hath bin called *Gerards* Hall, for *Gisors* Hall, as Bosomes Inne for Blossoms In. Bevis Markes, for Buries Marke. Marke Lane, for Marte Lane: Belliter Lane, for Belsetters Lane: Gutter Lane, for Guthuruns Lane: Cry church, for Christes church: S. Mihell in the Querne, for Saint Mihell at Corne, and sundrie such others. Out of this Gisors Hall, at the first building thereof, were made divers Arched doores, yet to be seene, which seeme not sufficient for any great monsture, or other then men of common stature to passe through, the Pole in the Hall might be used in olde time (as then the custome was in every parish) to be set up in the streete, in the Summer as a Maypole, before the principall Hall, or house in the parish, or streete, and to stand in the Hall before the scrine,[14] decked with Holme & Ivie, all the feast of Christmas.[15] The lader [16] served for decking of the Maypole, & Roofe of the Hall. Thus much for Gisors Hal & for the side of Bredstreet, may suffice. Now on the West side of Bredstreet, amongst divers fayre and large houses for merchants, and faire Innes for passengers, had yee one prison house pertaining to the Sheriffes of *London*, called the compter in Bredstreete:[17] but in the yeare 1555 the prisones were remooved from thence, to one other new Compter in Woodstreete, provided by the cities purchase, and builded for that purpose: the cause of which remoove was this. *Richard Husband* Pastelar,[18] keeper of this Coumpter in Bredstreet, being a wilful and headstrong man, dealt for his own advantage, hardly with the prisoners under his charge, having also sernants [*sic*] such as himselfe liked best for their bad usage, and woulde not for any complaint bee reformed: whereupon in the yeare 1550. Sir *Rowland Hill* beeing Mayor, by the assent of a court of Aldermen, he was sent to the gayle of Newgate, for the cruell handling of his prisoners: and it was commaunded to the keeper to set those irons on his legges, which are called the widows almes: These he ware from Thursday, till Sunday in the afternoone, and being by a court of Aldermen released, on the Tuesday, was bound in an hundred markes, to observe from thenceforth an act made by the common councell, for the ordering of prisoners in the Compters: all which notwithstanding, hee continued as afore: whereof my selfe am partly a witnesse: for being of a Jurie to enquire against a Sessions of Gayle deliverie, in the yeare one thousand five hundred fiftie two, wee found the prisoners hardly dealt withall, for theyr achates[19] and otherwise, and that theeves and strumpets were there lodged for foure pence the night, whereby they might be safe from searches that were made abroad: for the which enormities, and other not needfull to bee recited, he was indighted at that Session, but did rubbe it out, and could not be reformed, til this remove of the prisoners for the house in Bredstreete was his owne by Lease, or otherwise, so that he could not bee put from it. Such Gaylors buying their offices, will deal hardly with pittifull prisoners. Now in Fryday streete, so called of Fishmongers dwelling there, and serving frydayes market, on the East side, is a small parish church, commonly called S. *John Evangelist*, the monuments therein, be of *John Dogger* Marchantaylor, one of the Sheriffes, in the yeare 1509. Sir *Christopher Askew* Draper, Mayor, 1533. Then lower downe, is one other parish church of S. *Margaret Moyses*, so called (as seemeth) of one *Moyses*, that was founder, or new builder thereof. The monuments there, bee of sir *Richard Dobbet* Skinner, Mayor, 1551. *William Dane* Ironmonger, one of the Sheriffes, 1569. Sir *John Allet* Fishmonger, Mayor 1591.

On the West side of this Fryday streete, is Mayden Lane, so named of such a signe, or Distaffe Lane, for Distar Lane, as I reade in record of a Brew-house, called the Lambe in Distar Lane, the sixteenth of *Henry* the sixt. In this Distar Lane, on the North side thereof, is the Cord-wayners, or Shoemakers Hall, which company were made a brotherhood or fraternitie, in the eleventh of *Henry* the fourth. On the South side of this Distar Lane, is also one other Lane, called Distar Lane: which runneth downe to Knightriders streete, or olde Fishstreete, and this is the ende of Bredstreete Warde: which hath an Alderman, his Deputie, Common Councell tenne, Constables ten, Skavengers eight, Wardmote Inquest thirteene, and a Beadle.[20] It standeth taxed to the fifteene in *London*, at thirtie seven pound, and in the Exchequer at thirtie sixe pound tenne shillings.

1. An example of an earlier town history was John Hooker's (unpublished) *Description of the Citie of Excester*, but it consisted for the most part of transcriptions of source documents.
2. For example those by Ralph Agas (see Fig. 4).
3. Maypole dancing is first mentioned in England around 1350. It was banned by the Long Parliament in 1644, but the custom was resumed at the Restoration in 1660. Stow's remarks, however, suggest that maypoles were no longer usual in 1598.
4. *Blader*, cutler.
5. 'West Cheap' was an early name given to Cheapside, distinguishing it from the market which was once held at the Eastern end of the street. Before the fire in 1666 it was very wide, and the market was held in the middle of the street. It contained three significant monuments: the Standard, which was a fountain, which was there in the reign of Edward I and was rebuilt in the reign of Henry VI; the Cross, which was one of the nine Eleanor Crosses erected by Edward I in 1290 on the death of his queen; and a conduit, providing flowing water.
6. The 'Old Change' existed in the reign of Edward I. It was the place at which gold was bought and sold.
7. *Hall mote*, the court of a trade guild or company, in this case the bakers' company; *enormity*, a breach of the law.
8. *Shead*, (shed) a lean-to structure, probably, in this case, without front and sides.

9. *Ostrey*, hostelry.
10. Marginal note here: A Pole of 40. foote long, and 15. inches about, fabuled to be the justing staffe of Gerarde a Giant.
11. In the 1603 edition it is made clear that this is a reference to Leland.
12. Marginal note here: R.G. A stone said to be a toothe, and so by conjecture, a man to be 28. foote of height.
13. *Feofment*, the action of investing a person with a fief or fee, i.e., an estate held on condition of homage and service.
14. *Scrine*, shrine, a box for the keeping of valuables.
15. Marginal note here: Every mans house of olde time was decked with holly and Ivie in the winter, especially at Christmas.
16. *Lader*, ladder.
17. *Compter*, a debtors' prison. There were two in London, one of which was the one to which Stow refers here, and which, as he goes on to say, was moved to a different location in 1555.
18. *Pastelar*, pastry-cook.
19. *Achates*, purchases made for provisions from outside the prison.
20. *Scavenger*, a person employed to clean streets; *wardmote*, a group of liverymen (freemen of the city entitled to wear the livery of their company), presided over by the alderman; *beadle*, town-crier.

IX
Hertfordshire: Henry Chauncy (1633–1719)

Sir Henry Chauncy was a person who would seem to exemplify the typical antiquary of his time. He was a gentleman of comfortable circumstances, who had pursued a successful career in law; he inherited the family estates at Ardeley; he had official responsibilities in the administration of his county; he was honoured with a knighthood. He was educated at schools in Hertfordshire, for a short time at Cambridge, and at Middle Temple in London. Called to the bar in 1656, he eventually became a Justice of the Peace, reader of Middle Temple, Recorder of Hertford, and, in 1688, Sergeant-at-Law. He married three times and was widowed twice, and had altogether nine children. His survey of Hertfordshire was a labour of love, although because he was a busy person he paid assistants to do much of the research. While it was finally a very substantial work, it was unadventurous in its conception, adhering closely to the antiquarian methods which had developed over the past hundred years in the hands of William Lambarde, Sampson Erdeswicke, William Burton, William Dugdale, Robert Thoroton, James Wright, and others.[1]

The Historical Antiquities of Hertfordshire is not a description which affords even glimpses of the county landscape. Its contents, ordered by parishes within the hundreds of the county, are family genealogies, estate tenancies, histories of successful Hertfordshire aristocrats and gentry, foundations of monasteries, schools and hospitals, and inscriptions on tombs. It also offers numerous accounts on a variety of subjects such as Roman history (especially with regard to Verulamium, the Roman remains near St Albans); the origins and histories of church institutions, such as parishes, vicarages, parish registers, church buildings, consecration rites, first-fruits, the use of saints' names for churches, and funerary monuments; the histories of bells, clocks, and the use of music in public celebrations; the origins and histories of legal offices, such as sergeants, mayors, burgesses, and judges; of manors and their lords; and of university degrees. Such were the interests of the author and of the levels of society in which he moved.

That the style and subject-matter of this county survey should be so remarkably similar to those of Leicestershire by William Burton and of Warwickshire by William Dugdale written, respectively, about eighty years and fifty years earlier, suggests a strong gentry need for continuity and stability. Many of those Hertfordshire gentry who would have been appreciative subscribers to Chauncy's book would have remembered times of civil war and, more recently, experienced the disturbances of the plots and revolutions which characterised the final decade of the Stuart monarchs. Like those earlier essays in county genealogy, the *Hertfordshire* looks back and recreates a past of piety, nobility, and honour. But unlike them, it is not rooted in the past, for it also celebrates its contemporaries and so, somewhat incongruously, allows prominent county figures to become part of the 'antiquities' of Hertfordshire.

The qualities which emerge belong to a new age of stability and promise, and are more proper to successful men of affairs, government, and commerce, than to the valiant knights and pious monks who populate the pages of Dugdale's *Warwickshire*. The following comments, about Francis Flyer, a High Sheriff of Hertfordshire in the reign of Charles I, were drawn from personal knowledge and were doubtless intended as a special tribute, as he was the father of Chauncy's first wife.

> [He] was very grave in his Deportment, reserved in his Discourse, excellent at Accounts in Merchandise, punctual to his Word, and just in his Dealings, which gave him a good Reputation: He loved Hospitality, was noble in Entertainments, bountiful to Strangers, and liberal to the Poor: He was very strict in all his Acts of Religion, always valuing a Clergyman by the Severity of his Duty, and the Rules of his Life: He observed an excellent Method for the Government of his Family, and kept great Order in this Parish.[2]

Gentlemanly virtues are worldliness, reasonableness, wisdom, and discretion. Complementary qualities were admirable in a lady, such as exemplified by a certain Lady Susan Cecill, 'a proper comely Lady, endowed with a most rare and pregnant Wit, a florid and ready Tongue, very sharp, but witty in her Repartees; her common Discourse did much exceed the ordinary Capacity of her Sex'.[3] Such a description throws into relief, even more than those given for gentlemen, the liveliness of the present in Chauncy's 'historical antiquities'. A more complete sketch of a modern woman is that offered for Margaret, the widow of Sir Thomas Hewyt,

> whose Life was a Pattern to her Sex: She was endowed with a comely Presence, a grave Aspect, a graceful Deportment, a smart and witty Tongue, and a wise

> Understanding; she govern'd her Family with great Prudence and Discretion; was neat and curious in her House, choice and delicate in her Kitching, free and generous at her Table, hospitable to the Gentry, courteous to her Neighbours, fed the Poor at her Door, and educated their Children at School; was strict to her own; exact in the Performances of her Servants; very regular in her Life, most devout in her Duty to God. [4]

The womanly virtues of Lady Godeva and other such saintly ladies praised by Dugdale—piety, chastity, silence—are displaced by godliness, wit, hospitality, and a good sense of domestic management. Country houses are not described (there are illustrations of some of them) but a few words sometimes make mention of the orderly plenitude, security, and comfort which they might exude. James Forester (who became one of Chauncy's sons-in-law) improved his house with

> a fair Gallery and Lodging-chambers on the West Side thereof, pav'd the Hall with Stone, erected a fair Screen, beautify'd the House, made a fair Garden, enclos'd it with a Brick Wall, planted with excellent Fruit, and adorn'd his Seat with a pleasant Walk double set on either Side with Lime-Trees.[5]

While Chauncy described little of the Hertfordshire landscape, he did record a striking event associated with the county, in a passage which brings the splendour of the past into the world of the late seventeenth century. It must be admitted that he did not actually see what he recounted, for it occurred in the same year that he was born, and moreover it actually took place in London. It was a Lord Mayor's parade, and found its way into the text ostensibly because the Lord Mayor concerned, Sir Ralph Freeman, had his seat in Hertfordshire and, as well, because this was clearly the sort of thing that Chauncy really enjoyed. The heirs of Freeman were subscribers to the *Hertfordshire*, so an engraving of the family seat, Aspeden House, is included along with the wonderful account of the parade whose source, presumably, was in the archives at Aspeden.

The parade was provided by the Lord Mayor as an entertainment for King Charles I and his queen, and was followed by a banquet at the Merchant Taylors' Hall. It is an example of the stunning aristocratic entertainments favoured in the courts of James I and Charles I, with masquers in fabulous costumes pantomiming and dancing, liveried officers, horsemen, sumptuously painted and gilded scenes, burning flambeaux, trumpeters, chariots, and magnificent music and song. The sheer detail and insistence of Chauncy's account brilliantly and nostalgically recreates this past experience.

The Lord Mayor's Parade

From *The Historical Antiquities of Hertfordshire*, Vol. I, pp.244–248

... in [1623] *Ralph Freeman* ... was elected the first Sheriff in **London**. And *An.* 1633, 9 *Car.* I. Lord Mayor of that City. About the 10th Day of *January* in the same Year, he invited the King and Queen, and all the Maskers[6] of the Inns of Court, to a Banquet, who, clothed in rich and glorious Apparel, attended in a most solemn and splendid Parade, from the Court to **Merchant Taylor's Hall** in the City of **London**.

The first that marched were twenty Footmen in scarlet Liveries, with Silver Lace, each one having his Sword by his Side, a Battone in one Hand, and a Torch lighted in his other; these were the Marshal's Men, who cleared the Streets, made Way and waited on the Marshal;[7] after, and sometimes in the midst of them, came Mr. *Darrel* the Marshal: He was an extraordinary proper Gentleman of **Lincoln's Inn**, mounted upon one of the King's best Horse, and richest Saddles; his own Habit was exceeding rich and glorious; his Horsemanship very gallant, and besides his Footmen, he had two Lacquies[8] who carried Torches by him, and a Page his Cloak: The King knighted him for his brave Deportment.[9]

After followed one hundred Gentlemen of the Inns of Court, five and twenty chosen out of each House, of the most proper and handsome young Gentlemen of the Societies, every one gallantly mounted on the best Horses, and with the best Furniture[10] that the Stables of the King, and all the Noblemen in Town would afford.

Every of these Gentlemen were attired in very rich Cloaths, cover'd with Gold and Silver Lace, had a Page and two Lacquies, waiting on him in his Livery by his Horse Side; the Lacquies carried Torches, and the Pages their Masters' Cloaks. The Richness of their Apparel and Furniture glittering by the Light of a Multitude of Torches attending on them, with the Motion and stirring of their mettled Horses;[11] and the many and various gay Liveries of their Servants; but especially the personal Beauty and Gallantry of the handsome young Gentlemen, made the most glorious and splendid Shew that ever was beheld in **England**.

These Horsemen had for their Musick, about a dozen of the best Trumpeters in their Liveries sounding before them; After whom came the Antimaskers,[12] representing Cripples and Beggars on the poorest leanest Jades the Dirt-Carts could afford,[13] who had their Music of Keys and Tongs,[14] and the like snaping,[15] and yet playing in a Consort before them; the Variety and Change from such noble Musick and gallant Horses as went before, unto the proper[16] Musick and pitiful Horses of these Cripples made the greater Divertisement. [*sic*]

Next came Men on Horseback, playing on Pipes, Whistles, and Instruments sounding Notes like those of Birds of all sorts, in excellent Consort. Then the Antimasque of Birds followed: This was an Owl in an Ivy Bush, with many several sorts of other Birds in a great Flock gazing upon the Owl. These were little Boys put into Covers of the Shapes of those Birds rarely fitted, and sitting on small Horses, with Footmen going by them, carrying Torches in their Hands, and others to look unto the Children, which was very pleasant to the Spectators.

Other Musicians on Horseback followed this Antimasque, playing upon Bagpipes, Hornpipes, and such kind of Northern Musick,[17] speaking the succeeding Antimasque of Projectors,[18] to be of the Scotch and Northern Quarters; these had many Footmen with Torches waiting on them.

First in this Antimasque rode a Fellow upon a little Horse with a great Bit in his Mouth, and another upon his Head, also Headstall and Reins fastened: This signify'd a Projector, who begg'd a Patent that none in the Kingdom might ride their Horses with such Bits, but such as they should buy of him.

After him came another Fellow with a bunch of Carrots upon his Head, and a Capon upon his Fist; describing a Projector who begg'd a Patent of Monopoly, as the first Inventor of the Art to fat Capons with Carrots, and that none but himself might make Use of that Invention, and have the Priviledge of fourteen Years, according to the Statute.[19]

Several other Projectors were personated in a like Manner in this Antimasque, which were the more acceptable to the Spectators, for that they represented to the King the Unfitness and Ridiculousness of these Projects against the Law.

After this and the other Antimasques (which are here omitted) were past, there came six of the chief Musicians on Horseback, upon Footclothes,[20] and in the Habits of Heathen Priests, and Footmen carrying Torches by them.

Then an open large Chariot followed these Musicians, drawn by six brave Horses, with large Plumes of Feathers on their Heads and Buttocks; the Coachman and Postilion in rich Antick Liveries. There were above a dozen Persons in several Habits of the Gods and Goddesses sitting in the Chariot, and many Footmen by them on all sides bearing Torches.

Six more of the Musicians followed this Chariot on Horseback, habited with Footclothes, and attended with Torches as the former were.

Then came another large open Chariot like the former, drawn with six gallant Horses, set forth with Feathers, Liveries, and Torches, as the others had, in which were about a dozen Musicians in like Habit as those in the first Chariot, but all with some Variety or Distinction.

These going immediately next before the Grand Masquer's Chariots, play'd upon excellent and loud Musick all the Way as they went.

Then six more Musicians on Footclothes followed this Chariot with Horses habited and attended as the other.

After them came the first Chariot of the grand Masquers, which was not so large as those that went before, but most curiously framed, carved, and painted with exquisite Art for this very Purpose: The Form was after that of the Roman Triumphant Chariots, as near as could be made by some old Prints and Pictures of them; The Seats in it were made of an oval Form in the back End of the Chariot, so that there was no Precedence in them, and the Faces of all that sate in it might be seen together.

The Colours of the first Chariot were Silver and Crimson, given by the Lot to **Gray's Inn**, the Chariot and the very Wheels were richly painted all over with the same Colours, and the carved Work of it was as curious for that Art; it made a stately Shew, drawn by four Horses all on breast, covered to their Heels all over with Cloth of Tissue,[21] of the Colours of Crimson and Silver, with Plumes of white Feathers on their Heads and Buttocks; the Coachman's Cap and Feather, his long Coat, and very Whip and Cushion, were of the same Stuff and Colour; In this Chariot sate the four grand Maskers of **Gray's Inn**, their Habits, Doublets, Trunk-hose, and Caps of most rich Cloth of Tissue, and wrought as thick with silver Spangles as they could be placed, large white silk Stockings to their Trunk-hose, and rich Sprigs in their Caps, themselves proper and beautiful young Gentlemen.

On each Side of the Chariot were four Footmen in Liveries of the Colour of the Chariot, carrying huge Flambuoys[22] in their Hands, which with the Torches gave such a Lustre to the Paintings, Spangles, and Habits, that hardly any thing could be invented to appear more glorious.

Six more Musicians on Footclothes, in the like Habits, followed this Chariot; after whom came the second Chariot, which by Lot fell to the **Middle Temple**, and differ'd from the former only in Colours, which were Silver and Blue; the Chariot and Horses were cover'd and deck'd with Cloth of Tissue, of Blue and Silver: In this Chariot were the four grand Masquers of the **Middle Temple**, in the same Habits as the former Masquers were, and with the like Attendance, Torches, and Flambuoys with the former.

The third and fourth Chariots followed after these, and six Musicians between each Chariot, habited on Footclothes and Horses as before; both the Chariots of the same Form and like Carving and Painting, differing only in the Colours; in the third rode the Grand Masquers of the **Inner Temple**; and in the other those of **Lincoln's Inn**, according to their several Lots.

The Habits of all the Grand Masquers were the same, their Persons most handsome and lovely; their Equipage so full of State and Height of Gallantry, that it was never outdone by any Representation mentioned in former Stories.

The Torches and huge flaming Flambuoys, born by the Sides of each Chariot, made it seem lightsome as at Noonday, but more glittering, and gave a full and clear Light to all the Streets and Windows as they passed by. The March was slow, in Regard of the great Number, but more interrupted by the Multitude of Spectators in the Streets, besides the Windows, unwilling to part from so glorious a Spectacle.

The King and Queen stood at a Window, looking into the Street to see the Masque pass by, and when all were gone, they, with all their noble Train, came to the Hall, where the Masque began, and was incomparably performed in the Dancing, Speeches, Musick, and Scenes; the Dances, Figures, Properties[23] the Voices, Instruments, Songs, Aires, Composures;[24] the Words and Actions were all of them exact, and none of them failed in their Parts; and the Scenes were most curious and costly.

The Queen did the Honour to some of the Masquers to dance with them, and did judge them as good Dancers as ever she saw, and the great Ladies were very free and civil in Dancing with all the Masquers, as they were taken out by them.

Thus they continued in their Sports till it was almost Morning; then the Lord Mayor entertained the King and Queen, the Lords and Ladies, and the Masquers, and Inns of Court Gentlemen with a noble and stately Banquet; and after that was dispersed, every one departed to their Homes.

1. The authors of surveys of Kent, Staffordshire, Leicestershire, Warwickshire, Nottinghamshire, and Rutland respectively. *The Historical Antiquities of Hertfordshire* was produced in a print run of only 500 copies and consequently has become a very rare book. A reprint was made in 1826. On Henry Chauncy, see the introduction by Carola Oman in the 1975 reprint, listed in the bibliography.
2. Chauncy, *Hertfordshire*, v.1, p.281.
3. *Ibid.*, p.287.
4. *Ibid.*, p.346.
5. *Ibid.*, p.147.
6. A *masque* was a costumed dance performance, usually by noble and titled people of the court, accompanied by a narration by a professional actor. It probably had its origins in traditions of mumming and disguising, and also in masked festivities held at court as early as the time of Edward III. Masques were, by Tudor and Stuart times, usually performed at balls. It was Ben Jonson (1572–1637) who infused the genre with a dramatic spirit which, combined with the use of remarkable costuming, gave it a sophistication quite unlike its more humble origins. By the time of the event described here, masquing was being integrated into processional celebrations, although obviously the dramatic aspect must have been somewhat compromised.
7. *Marshal*, the legal officer responsible for keeping order.
8. *Lacquies*, footmen, liveried attendants.
9. *Deportment*, manner of conduct.
10. *Furniture*, the harness and trappings of a horse.

11. *Mettled*, mettlesome, hence, lively and spirited.
12. An *antimasque* was a comical masque, parodying rather than glorifying its subject.
13. *Jade*, a draught-horse, a hack, a horse in poor condition.
14. *Music of Keys and Tongs*, probably meaning the striking of metal implements against one another.
15. *Snaping*, perhaps snapping.
16. *Proper Musick*, i.e., their own music.
17. *Northern Musick*, Scottish music.
18. *Projector*, one who plans and undertakes some enterprise or project, especially one which is unscrupulous, hence, a schemer.
19. The Statute of Monopolies of 1623 provided that an inventor of an item had exclusive rights to exploit the invention for fourteen years.
20. *Footcloth*, a large caparison; a rich cloth draped over a horse, hanging to the ground on both sides.
21. *Tissue*, a rich cloth woven with gold or silver.
22. *Flambouy*, a lighted torch made of several thick wicks dipped in wax.
23. *Properties*, stage props.
24. *Composures*, literary, artistic, or musical compositions.

X

Seeing the World: The Tradescants

Amongst a series of readings of English people seeing England, this reading is an interlude in which we are concerned with a different experience, that is, English people looking *out* of England. Naturally this might have been achieved by going overseas, but for those who were not able to travel, the display of collections of exotic items was a vicarious means of seeing and touching upon other places. The Tradescant collection was not the first of these but it was the best-known, and it formed the basis of the first English museum, that is, a presentation of a collection for public viewing. The story of how this museum, the Ashmolean, in Oxford, came into being has been considered in the foregoing account of the career of the antiquary Elias Ashmole, who came to be closely associated with the two John Tradescants, each of whom was both gardener and collector of 'rarities', especially of a botanical nature.

The birth date of John Tradescant the Elder is unknown, but the record of his marriage is dated in 1607, and he was shortly afterwards working for Robert Cecil, the son of Lord Burghley, the first Earl of Salisbury, and chief minister to Elizabeth I and then James I, at Hatfield House in Hertfordshire.[1] In this employment he travelled to France and the Netherlands to obtain plants new to England to be planted in the Hatfield park and gardens. He brought back fruit trees, berries, vines, rose bushes, and bulbs. Some were gifts from similarly great houses of nobility and royalty, and Tradescant developed friendships with his counterparts in some of these establishments. The new specimens were planted in great quantities: Hatfield accounts indicate that there were over 30,000 vines, and in 1611 Tradescant sent 1,000 new fruit trees from France in December alone. On the accession of the earl's son as the second earl in 1611, Tradescant began a period of work on his new master's other residences: Salisbury House in London, and at Cranborne in Dorset.

In subsequent years and with different employers, Tradescant continued to be given opportunities to travel and collect. He was engaged by Lord Wotton[2] to establish the gardens at St Augustine's Palace in Canterbury, which had been purchased from the Earl of Salisbury. He also worked at Chilham for Sir Dudley Digges, whom he accompanied to Russia in 1618. In 1620 he was travelling in the Mediterranean, visiting Algiers and possibly reaching Constantinople, all the while collecting plants for Lord Wotton. By 1623 he had been taken on by George Villiers, the Duke of Buckingham, to lay out the gardens at Newhall in Essex. He was sent by Buckingham to Flanders to acquire plants in 1623 and accompanied him to Paris in 1625 when he went there to escort the king's bride, Henrietta Maria, back to England. Even when he went to give military support as his master laid siege to La Rochelle he was able to return with plants. After Buckingham's assassination in 1628, Tradescant was given charge of the gardens of the king's palace at Oatlands, Surrey, and in 1637 he was appointed Custodian of the Botanical Gardens at Oxford, but he died before the latter appointment could be taken up.

Tradescant and his son, also John Tradescant, lived on a property of several acres in Lambeth, where they had developed a garden and orchard which became widely, indeed internationally known, and from which they may have sold plants and fruit. Contemporary records indicate that the garden, which came to be known as The Ark, was famous not only for its exotic specimens but also for lesser-known English plants.[3] It was here that they built up the collection which was later to form the basis of the Ashmolean Museum. The younger Tradescant was also a traveller, and in 1637, 1642, and 1654 he visited Virginia. In England, he had been appointed to the position at Oatlands left vacant by his father's death, while accumulating more items for the cabinet of curiosities, or *Wunderkammer*, at Lambeth.

While the profession of the Tradescants was botanical, they were also collectors of other items: zoological specimens, artefacts, and unusual natural phenomena such as geological specimens. The collection at Lambeth included all these types of exhibits, a presentation for which there were, in the seventeenth century, several precedents both in England and in European countries. The first significant museum-like collections were formed in Italy, notably by the Medici, who also patronised the Bolognese botanist Ulisse Aldrovandi (1522–1605), the founder of an early botanic garden. Michele Mercati (1541–1593), curator of the Vatican botanic garden, made a collection of natural rarities and antiquities including mummies; and Athanasius Kircher (1601–1680), also of Rome, made a collection in which Egyptian objects, such as obelisks, had a prominent place alongside the classical remains and natural specimens. The intention to represent as many aspects of the world as possible had grown from the theory expounded in 1565 by Samuel von Quicchelberg of Antwerp, that the museum should be like a model of the world, divided into five sections: the nature of the museum itself; artefacts; natural specimens; instruments and machines; and conceptual figures and symbols. Other great collections were associated with academic institutions of the sixteenth century, and yet others were developed by European princely families such as the Hapsburgs. Most celebrated of all was the collection in Denmark of Ole Worm (1588–1654), which later was incorporated into the collection of King Frederick III in Copenhagen.

It is likely that the Tradescants had visited such exhibitions both in England and in other countries, but The Ark became one of the most celebrated to be seen anywhere. In a move considered unusual at the time, the collection could be visited, for a fee, by anyone who was willing to pay. A hundred years earlier, the places where 'rarities' might be viewed by the public were cathedrals and churches: apart from the stained glass and precious ornaments and vestments, sacred relics were an obvious attraction but other secular marvels might sometimes be displayed, such as giant bones and strange stones. With the reform of the Church, relics formerly sacred became mere curiosities, and about the same time the discovery of the New World produced an influx of objects never seen before. This new availability of the unusual engendered a widening desire to see the curiosities and experience the wonder of the exotic. Thus it led both to the opening of collections and the unscrupulous sale of items of questionable provenance to the gullible.

At some time before 1650 John Tradescant the Younger became acquainted with the antiquary Elias Ashmole, whose interests covered various esoteric fields including astrology, alchemy, the masonic orders, and the collection of rare things. A friendship developed and between 1650 and 1652 Ashmole and another friend, the anatomist Thomas Wharton, assisted Tradescant in the creation of a catalogue of the contents of The Ark, which was eventually published in 1656 as *Musæum Tradescantianum: Or, A Collection of Rarities Preserved at South-Lambeth neer London by John Tradescant*.[4] In an earlier chapter on Elias Ashmole we have seen that Tradescant's items came later to form a substantial part of the Ashmolean Museum; our concern here is the first view of the rarities as listed in this 1656 catalogue. It is divided into fourteen different categories, the largest sections being botanical. There are sections listing artefacts, such as '*Mechanick artificiall Works in Carvings, Turnings, Sewings and Paintings*', '*Warlike Instruments*', and '*Garments, Vestures, Habits, Ornaments*'. The section given below is that headed '*Variety of Rarities*', which title suggests that it includes everything which did not find a place elsewhere, and is therefore the most miscellaneous group in the catalogue.

The museum phenomenon was the result of people being able to go to look at the unfamiliar, at new and different things not seen in everyday life. Further, it was an opportunity to learn and, indeed, it was especially thought beneficial for the young to visit collections such as The Ark.[5] One visitor in 1634 was Peter Mundy of the East India Company, himself a traveller, who recorded spending a whole day examining the collection, concluding that 'I am almost perswaded a Man might in one daye behold and collecte into one place more Curiosities than hee should see if hee spent all his life in Travell.'[6] The enthusiasm for such displays as that of the Tradescants can easily be understood, for people are always fascinated by that which is strange and has never before been seen. Items from other countries have the added intrigue that they might never be seen again. Certain items had the enticing quality of having been used personally by the famous, such as '*Edward the Confessors* knit gloves', '*Anne* of *Bullens* Night-vayle embroidered with silver', and '*Henry* 8. hawking-glove, hawks-hood, dogs-coller'.[7] Such exhibits are to be found in museums still, as they were in medieval collections of saintly relics.

Few of the items included by the Tradescants in The Ark are still in existence. Arthur MacGregor's *Tradescant's Rarities* contains a catalogue of the surviving items from the seventeenth-century catalogues, produced in 1656 (from which the following extract is taken) and 1683. The survivors of those which are listed in the following extract are: a partially lacquered white marble image of the Buddha,[8] listed as 'Indian Pa God'; an amber carving,[9] listed as 'A Gamaha of a Deaths head'; a gamahe, an inscribed grey mudstone pebble,[10] listed as 'A Gamaha with *Jesus, Joseph & Mary*, in Italian capitall letters'; and a jet pendant amulet,[11] listed as 'A Hand of Jet usually given to Children, in *Turky*, to preserve them from Witchcraft'. All of the surviving items from the seventeenth-century catalogues (there are 446 in all) are now displayed in the Tradescant Room of the Ashmolean Museum, set up in 1976. This room has been designed to give the impression of a seventeenth-century museum, yet using modern display techniques.

Variety of Rarities

From John Tradescant the Younger, *Musæum Tradescantianum*, 1656, pp.42–44

Indian morris-bells of shells and fruits.[12]
Indian musicall Instruments.
Indian Idol made of Feathers, in shape of a Dog.
Indian fiddle.
Spanish Timbrell.
Instrument which the Indians sound at Sun-rising.
Portugall musicall Instrument like a hoop, with divers brasse plates.
A choice piece of perspective in a black Ivory case.
A Canow[13] & Picture of an Indian with his Bow and Dart, taken 10 leagues at Sea, *An*°.—76.
A bundle of Tobacco, *Amazonian*.
Birds-nests from *China*.
Indian Conjurers rattle, wherewith he calls up Spirits.

Indian *Pa* God.[14]
The Idol *Osiris*. *Anubis*, the Sheep, the Beetle, the Dog, which the Ægyptians worshipped. Mr. *Sandys*.
A Gamaha with *Jesus*, *Joseph* & *Mary*, in Italian capitall letters.[15]
A Gamaha with a Fish in it.
A Gamaha of a Deaths-head.[16]
A Circumcision Knife of stone, and the instrument to take up the *præputium*, of silver.
Jewes Philacteries with the Commandments, writ in Hebrew.
A piece of Stone of Saint *John Baptists* Tombe.
A piece of the Stone of *Sarrige*-Castle where *Hellen* of *Greece* was born.
A piece of the Stone of the Oracle of *Apollo*.
A piece of the Stone of *Diana*'s Tomb.
An Orange gathered from a Tree that grew over *Zebulon*'s Tombe.[17]
Severall sorts of Magnifying glasses: Triangular, Prismes, Cylinders.
Antient Iron-Money in crosse-plates, like Anchors, preserved in *Pontrefract*-Castle, *Yorke-shire*.
Severall Assayes of Money.
A Brazen-ball to warme the Nunnes hands.
A piece of one of the Logges of *Bagmere* in *Cheshire*, neer *Breereton*.[18]
A Trunion of Capt: *Drake*'s Ship.[19]
Divers sorts of Indian Jakes.[20]
Severall sorts of Cymballs.
Cassava Bread 2 sorts.[21]
The Padre Guardians staffe of *Jerusalem* made of a branch of one of the 70 Palme-Trees of Elam, which he gave to Sir *Tho: Roe*.
A glasse-horne for annointing Kings.
2 Roman Urnes.
A Roman sacrificing-earthen-Cup, with the word *CAMPANION* printed in the bottome.
Tarriers of Wood made like our Tyring-Irons.[22]
Tarriers of Wood like Rolles to set Table-dishes on.
Indian Tresles to hang a payr of Skales on, of black varnisht wood.
The plyable Mazer wood, being warmed in water will work to any form.[23]
Blood that rained in the *Isle of Wight*, attested by Sir *Jo: Oglander*.[24]
A Hand of Jet usually given to Children, in *Turky*, to preserve them from Witchcraft.[25]

1. For a detailed study of the Tradescants, see Arthur MacGregor, 'The Tradescants: Gardeners and Botanists', in *Tradescant's Rarities: Essays on the Foundation of the Ashmolean Museum*, 1683, with a catalogue of the Surviving Early Collections, ed. by Arthur MacGregor, Oxford: Clarendon Press, 1983, pp.3–16.
2. Edward Wotton (1548-1626) was in the service of Sir Francis Walsingham. In 1602 he was made comptroller of the royal household, and in 1603 was created Baron Wotton of Marley.
3. *Tradescant's Rarities*, p.10. The Tradescants are interred at the nearby church of St Mary, which was made redundant in 1972. It has now become the Museum of Garden History, thanks to the work of the Friends of the Tradescant Trust.
4. Thomas Wharton (1614–1673) gave the first explanation of glands and the secretory system, and was the first anatomist to identify and understand the salivary duct. He should not be confused with George Wharton (1617–1681), another of Ashmole's friends, who was responsible for engendering his interest in astrology and alchemy.
5. T*radescant's Rarities*, p.22.
6. Cited in *ibid.*, p.21. from *The Travels of Peter Mundy, in Europe and Asia*, 1608–1667, ed. by R. C. Temple, Hakluyt Society ser. 2, vols. 45–46, 1919, pp.1-3.
7. *Musæum Tradescantianum,* p.49.
8. *Tradescant's Rarities*, item 79, p.183.
9. *Ibid.*, item 178, p.244.
10. *Ibid.*, item 189, p.248.
11. *Ibid.*, item 190, p.249.
12. Presumably made like the bells sewn onto the costumes of morris-dancers.
13. *Canow*, canoe.
14. A marble image of the Buddha, probably from Burma. This item is still at the Ashmolean Museum.
15. A *gamaha*, usually spelt 'gamahe', is a stone bearing natural markings resembling some recognisable pictorial or ornamental figure, and therefore valued as a talisman. The first of the three gamahas here listed is one of the items which is still in the museum.
16. Another item still in the museum.
17. *Zebulon,* in the Old Testament, was the tenth son of Jacob.
18. *Bagmere* is a Cheshire mere containing peat, in which organic material may be preserved.
19. *Trunnion*, the two small cylindrical projections on a cannon, forming the axis on which it pivots.
20. *Jakes*, perhaps 'jackets' was intended, referring to some articles of clothing. The word as printed referred at the time to a privy or dunghill.
21. *Cassava*, starch made from the root of the plant cassava, or manioc.
22. *Tarrier*, a pair of tiring-irons. Tiring-irons are metal rings and a wire which form a puzzle: the wire is bent back on itself in a long loop and a number of rings, usually seven or ten, is passed over this loop. Another piece of metal, the same length as the loop, holds the rings in place, but they may be removed by a complex series of manoeuvres. This game is very ancient, and is sometimes called 'Chinese Rings', but not necessarily with any substantiated justification. It was described by the mathematician Girolamo Cardano (known in English as Jerome Cardan) in the sixteenth century. It is a difficult puzzle, hence the name 'tiring-irons', and for the same reason it might also be given the name 'tarrier', as something which causes time to be passed without anything being achieved. It may only be speculated what the wooden tarriers referred to here and in the next item were actually like.
23. *Mazer*, maple or other fine-grained hardwood which may be used as a material for making drinking vessels.
24. Sir John Oglander (1585–1655) was a diarist and historian of the Isle of Wight. His work is published as *A Royalist's Notebook: The Commonplace Book of Sir John Oglander, Kt. of Nunwell, born 1585, died 1655*, transcribed and edited by Francis Bamford, with an introduction by C. F. Aspinall-Oglander, London: Constable, 1936.
25. Still in the Ashmolean Museum.

WEST MIDLANDS

XI
Warwickshire: William Dugdale (1605–1686)

William Dugdale was one of the most accomplished and influential antiquaries of the seventeenth century. He was the writer of voluminous, detailed collections of historical data pertaining to significant elements in gentry life in his times: the church, his county, the law, offices and honours. His first major undertaking was *Monasticon Anglicanum*, a three-volume collection of documents concerning monastic foundations in England and their histories, which he began in collaboration with Roger Dodsworth, who died while the project was in progress. In its usefulness as a source it is perhaps his most enduring achievement. The first volume of this work was followed in 1656 by *The Antiquities of Warwickshire Illustrated*, the survey of his native county, which will be discussed in more detail below; after which his more notable publications were: the other two volumes of the *Monasticon Anglicanum*, in 1661 and 1673 respectively; *The History of St Paul's Cathedral in London*, which also contains numerous engravings by Wenceslaus Hollar,[1] in 1658; *The History of Imbanking and Drayning of divers Fenns and Marshes*, written to promote a Commonwealth project but published after the Restoration, in 1662; *Origines Juridiciales*, in 1666; and *The Baronage of England* in two volumes, in 1675 and 1676 respectively.

These titles give some idea of the matters which concerned both author and readers. Dugdale also left an autobiography, which is mainly a rather cursory third-person account of his career, offering little insight into the development of his personal life. He claimed that he understood his vocation even in childhood, recording that 'his naturall inclination tend[ed] chiefly to the Study of Antiquities', and through family connections he was soon introduced to some influential mentors: William Burton, who had published a description of Leicestershire, and Simon Archer, who was collecting material on Warwickshire. From there he went on to meet some of the leading antiquaries of the land, including Henry Spelman, Roger Dodsworth, and Christopher Hatton.[2] The career of the author followed the two closely related paths of antiquary and herald: in the latter pursuit he was a servant of the Crown, responsible for matters of rank, honours, precedence and ceremony. This office took him to Oxford when the King was based there in the Civil War, yet even in these dangerous years he found time to pursue his research in the Bodleian Library and amongst other archives in the vicinity. Late in his life, after the restoration of the monarchy, he was knighted and became Garter King at Arms, the highest of heraldic offices.

Dugdale's account of Warwickshire is, as its title suggests, concerned chiefly with the county's antiquities, these being the remains of its past: estates, castles, monasteries, churches, tombs. These might be thought of, most immediately, as historical data, but, to the gentry antiquary, they had another even more significant function, in that they provided evidence of origins and pedigree, and so affirmed the most valued of qualities: ancientness and continuousness. Antiquarian scholarship had been strongly motivated in the sixteenth century by the desire to establish a credible and national history which could replace the widely discredited 'Brut' which had come down from Geoffrey of Monmouth. At the levels of county, town, manor, and parish, county survey writers were contributing to this process, both in the discovery of historical information and in the development of methods for the historical process. *The Antiquities of Warwickshire* was not the first study of its type, but it was the most comprehensive and sophisticated example in the seventeenth century and was regarded as a model by subsequent authors. Its inclusion in this collection, then, is as a representative of the county descriptions which took the genealogical approach and presented the county as consisting of landed families and their estates. Its main predecessors were Sampson Erdeswicke's *Survey of Staffordshire* (1593–1603) (which was eventually edited by Dugdale but not published till 1717), William Burton's *Description of Leicester Shire* (1622) and Thomas Habington's *Survey of Worcestershire* (which was not published till the nineteenth century); its main successors were Robert Thoroton's *Antiquities of Nottinghamshire* (1677), James Wright's *History and Antiquities of the County of Rutland* (1684), and Henry Chauncy's *Historical Antiquities of Hertfordshire* (1700).

The reader will search in vain in *The Antiquities of Warwickshire* for descriptions of county landscapes, and it must be concluded that, beautiful as such scenes might have been, they did not form part of the view which Dugdale took of his county. The countryside is ignored even as a mere background to the histories of events, births, deaths, marriages, agreements, and transactions of gentry life. This genealogical view, moreover, looks into the past more closely than into the present. Yet its perspective of the past is not purely chronological, for the more immediate historical dimension in Dugdale's work is place, which provides the framework and index of the survey as the reader is taken from manor to manor and, at each, led through the changes in tenure which trace the history of the estate and its holders. These events are all marked by regnal dates, so they move each story of each estate on through time, usually beginning with the period of the earliest reliable archive Dugdale could use, Domesday Book, and continuing up into the sixteenth or early seventeenth century.

The extract given below demonstrates some significant facets of Dugdale's approach to seeing his county. Firstly, it is about land-holding people and the lands that they held. In this view, land which is not so held doesn't, in effect, exist: there is no wilderness in Dugdale's Warwickshire. Secondly, the survey's narrative is insistently about the past, and thirdly—and this is a crucial element in the antiquarian methodology which Dugdale brought to maturity in his county survey—every occurrence which is recorded corresponds to an archive. Indeed, the entire county, on this basis, might be seen through the proxy of a vast collection of archives in libraries, courts, family chests, and on the tombs in parish churches. As well as being records, archives have another important function, which Dugdale exploited and perfected: they are an extension of historical memory, allowing us to reach ever further back into the past. When the memories to be found in that past are of the same estates and families that continue to exist at the time of Dugdale's book, what is achieved is not only the affirmation of pedigree but also a link from the present to the past, bringing present readers in touch with the world that existed then. And why would they want to have such a link? Because, Dugdale believed, the world of the past was a better one, which he called 'those flourishing Ages past', a more noble and more secure world than that in which he and his peers suffered in the times of the rebellion, iconoclasm, and sacrilege of the mid-seventeenth century.

The Antiquities of Warwickshire contains accounts of nearly five hundred locations and of more than five hundred families. The longest entry deals with Warwick, seat of the Earls of Warwick, and gives details of the several successive families whose heads took that title. Some entries, for which Dugdale had not been able to find much information, amount to no more than a short paragraph. The text below is taken from the moderately lengthy entry for Sutton, now known as Sutton Coldfield, on the outskirts of Birmingham. The particular feature of the place was the great chase that had been maintained in the manor park, and for this reason it does indeed contain a flicker of awareness of the countryside. The extract demonstrates several characteristics of the antiquarian genre. The formal style of writing reflects the legal significance attached to being able to use evidence of lineage of titles and properties in a time when litigation was frequent and lengthy. Words in, say, a stained-glass window in a parish church were admissible in a court of law but, in the uncertain times of the mid-seventeenth century, such windows had a precarious existence. The collections of evidence put together in printed form by antiquaries were therefore of real value to those who might need to verify their entitlements.

In spite of this, Dugdale is always present in his narrative, a somewhat ingenuous guide through the maze of archives, being careful to point out his uncertainties where appropriate. Commenting, for example, on the exchange of the manor of Sutton by King Henry I with the Earl of Warwick for certain other manors, which agreement he quotes, he notes the absence of any provision of rent to the Crown, continuing, 'therefore 'tis probable that by some other Agreement with that King, or King *H*. 2. it might be'. The admission of such reservations about the completeness of his information served to reassure his readers of the reliability of that information which he did provide, and gave his work a degree of credibility. A related feature of the antiquarian method was the meticulous inclusion of many thousands of citations from archive sources. These impart to the writing an undeniably pedantic quality, but they make it trustworthy, a matter of considerable importance to gentry readers. Dugdale's notes (which appeared, in Latin, as marginalia in the first edition, but as footnotes in the 1730 edition) are included in the extract below. He used a wide range of sources; those relevant below include Domesday Book, Exchequer Rolls, Patent Rolls, Fine Rolls, accounts and cartularies of the Earldom of Warwick, manuscript documents in the possession of other gentlemen, and John Leland's *Itinerary*.

Dugdale's survey, as well as being a mine of information, is a celebration of the Warwickshire gentry. There were those that were pious, those that were powerful, those that were valiant fighters, those that were loyal, those that were disloyal, those that were wise scholars and those that were magnanimous lords. Most are from the past; apart from some of Dugdale's antiquarian associates, few of his contemporaries have a place in a collection of 'antiquities'. In looking back to that golden age of whose passing he seems to be so nostalgically aware, Dugdale affirms the gentry lineage which confers still the esteem and honour that are evident throughout his narratives. Especially of the monasteries does he write with the greatest respect and an acute sense of loss. As he states in the very opening of his introduction to the collection, the benefit of history is that it expands our experience of the world and enables us to learn from the lives of those who have gone before. This didactic note is most clear when he gives accounts of pious benefactors and of kings who faced rebellion, especially Henry III, who takes a role as a kind of prefiguration of the tragic Charles I, in whose service Dugdale was employed while he was collecting the material for this book.

As with Michael Drayton, Dugdale's writings became outmoded in his own lifetime. In one of his late works he lamented errors in heraldic usage, a preoccupation which has some poignancy when it is considered that it comes only four years before William III and Mary II ceased to issue warrants for heraldic visitations for the examination of arms. He strove to recapture the past in his writings and to continue its glories in a new and modern world, which he perceived to be less honourable and less secure. His writing is tinged with a sense of nostalgia and melancholy which was to persist and find new expression in English aesthetic movements of the succeeding centuries.

The Chase at Sutton

From *The Antiquities of Warwickshire*, pp.663–667

Having now done with **Bermingham**, and tracing **Rhea** through the Parish of **Aston**, I come to its confluence with **Tame**; following which River about two miles lower, I find the accession of a pretty torrent from the North west, at the head whereof stands **Sutton**,[3] being a large Parish, but a barren soil, and containeth divers Hamlets and places of note; *viz.* **Wigginshill**, **Maney**, **Hill**, **Little Sutton**, **Warmley**, **Langley**, **Newhall**, and **Pedimore**; of all which in their order.

That this **Sutton** was originally so called from its situation, there is no doubt; and therefore as it stands South to **Lichfield**, I am inclin'd to believe that the name at first arose. In *Edw.* the Confessor's days, *Edwine*, Earl of **Mercia**, was owner[4] of it; but after the Norman invasion the Conqueror held it in his own hands, as appeareth by the generall Survey[5] shortly after made, wherein it is rated at *viii* hides,[6] the Woods extending to two miles in length and one in breadth, and all valued at 4*l.* But it continued not long in the Crown; for I find[7] that K. *H.* 1. past it away in exchange unto *Roger* Earl of **Warwick**, for the Mannours of **Hocham** and **Langham** in **Rutland**; …[8]

The next thing, in order, to be spoke of, is the *Chase*, whereof the bounds extended (as by the before recited authoritie[9] is evident) to the banks of **Thame** and **Bourne** (which Rivers are described by the Map[10]) and so consequently out of the bounds of this Countie, aswell as into other Lordships within it, that are no members of **Sutton**: to give some reason therefore for this, I have look't further into the antiquitie thereof; and do find, that whilst this Lordship continued in the King's hand, that which afterwards bore the name of the *Chase*, was then a Forest; and this appears by a speciall Inquisition[11] taken in 3. *E.* 2.[12] where the Jury say upon their Oaths, that they had heard their Ancestors affirm the same: for, that the antient Kings of **England**, before they limited themselves by *Carta de Foresta* in 9. *H.* 3. might and did make Forests where they pleased, *Manwood*, in his treatise of *Forest Laws* (whereunto I refer my Reader) doth sufficiently declare. …[13]

That the Earl of **Warwick** so held it, with all the privileges thereto antiently belonging, may appear by sundry testimonies, some of which I shall here point at. About the beginning of K. *John*'s time, the Lord *Basset* of **Draiton** (a great Baron in these parts) erected a Park at **Draiton** *Basset*, which being within the precincts of this *Chase*, and questioned by *Waleran* then Earl of **Warwick**, necessitated the said Lord *Basset*, rather than he would pull down his pales again, to come to an Agreement with the Earl; ...[14]

... And that the succeeding Earls of **Warwick** still held it as their free *Chase*, the severall Licenses[15] that they granted to sundry persons in their own peculiar lands and Woods, lying within the precincts thereof, do sufficiently manifest; *viz.* to *Raph de Limesi*, by *Will. de Beauchamp* Earl of **Warwick**, to make a Park at **Weford** of his Wood called **Ashehay**, in 17. *E.* 1. In 18. *E.* 1 to *Raph* Lord *Basset*, to hunt in his Woods at **Draiton**. In 21. *E.* 1. to *Will. de Odingsells*, to hunt in the Woods and fields of **Weford**, **Thickbrome**, and **Hynts**: so also to *Will. Meignill* and *Rob. de la Ward*, in their lands and Woods at **Hynts**, &c. And that this *Chase* was of high esteem with those great Earls (who had here a very goodly Mannour House, with fair Pools near unto it) is evident, as I shall now further manifest.

In 17. *E.* 1. the last recited Earl obtained a speciall Patent[16] of the King, that during his life he might have free libertie to follow and pursue such of his Deer, as, being hunted within this *Chase*, fled into the Forest of **Kanc**, and there to kill and bring them away, without any disturbance of the said King's Verderers[17] or other Officers of the Forest: nay, the Earl was so tender[18] in preserving his game, that though he had given libertie to the Lord *Basset* for hunting in his own Woods at **Draiton**; yet to the end it might appear that he excluded not himself, he questioned the same Lord *Basset* for his Keepers over boldness in those Woods; so that *Basset* coming to an agreement[19] with him, it was concluded, that from thenceforth his Forester for **Draiton** woods, for the time being, should make Oath to the said Earl and his heirs, for his faithfull custodie of the Venison, and to make Attachments, and Presentments in the said Earl's Court at **Sutton**,[20] touching the same: and that the Ranger to the said Earl and his heirs, for the time being, should oversee the Keepership of the Deer in those Woods, at his own pleasure, and make attachments for the same: as also that the Earl should have one half of all Amerciaments,[21] and recompence for Trespasses done to the Deer in those Woods, to be received by his Bayliff of **Sutton**. Which Accord was made at **Sutton** on the Eve of *Holy Rood* day, in the presence of Sir *John Clinton* the younger Kt. *Thomas Prior* of **Canwell**, *Ankerill de L'isle*, *Rob. de Scheldon*, *Henr. de Mabely*, *Will. de Lee*, *John Russell*, and others.

In 21. *E.* 1. there being a complaint[22] made to the King, by the before specified Earl, that some misdemeanours had been committed by certain lewd persons in killing of Deer within this *Chase*, a speciall Commission was directed to *Roger* Lord *Strange*, to find them out, and to punish them according to their demerits. And in 25. *E.* 1. *John* Lord of **Little Barre** came to an Accord[23] with the before specified Earl, for license to inclose his Woods at **Little Barre**; as also to improve them by assarting,[24] and for cutting of underwood there, they being within the bounds of this *Chase*: for which libertie so granted, he covenanted for himself and his heirs, to pay yearly to the said Earl and his heirs, six barbed Arrows on the Feast day of St *Michaell*, at his Mannour of **Sutton**.

… in 17.*E.* 2. there was a notable Robberie[25] committed upon a certain Road, thwarting that part of the *Chase* called **Colfeild**, then, and yet known by the name of **Rugewey**, the partie rob'd being one *Elias le Collier*, and the summe of money taken from him *CCC l.* about nine of the Clock in the morning: whereupon he commenced his suit against the Inhabitants of this Hundred of **Hemlingford**, and those of the Hundred of **Offlow** in **Staffordshire**, according to the Statute of **Winchester**,[26] for not prosecuting the Felons; in regard that the same Way, as the record saith, divideth the Counties of **Warwick** and **Stafford**, *viz.* leaving **Sutton** and **Aston** *juxta* **Bermingham**, on the one side of it (of this Countie) and **Barre**, **Alrewich**, with part of **Shenston** in *Com. Staff.* on the other side; and had Judgment to recover the money accordingly: whereupon Writts being directed to the Shiriffs of both Shires, to levie the said summe, return was made, that the people were so much indebted to the King, and impoverisht by Murrein of their Cattel, dearth of Corn, and other accidents, that they were not able to pay it. Nevertheless, it seems that the Shiriff pressing hard upon them, by virtue of severall Writts to him directed, at the procurement of the partie rob'd, levied *xl.* marks of it. Much ado there was about this Money, the Bishop of **Cov.** and **Lich.** pleading, for himself and his Tenants, immunitie from such charges; and the Countie still shifting the payment; so that at length, they procured a *Suspersedeas* from the King[27] to stop any farther proceeding therein …

… Perhaps the Tuesday **Mercate**,[28] formerly granted (as is before exprest) grew to be discontinued; for in 27. *E.* 3. *Thomas de Beauchamp*, then Earl of **Warwick** (and Lord of this Mannour) obtained another Charter[29] for it upon the same day: by which he had likewise a grant of two **Faires** to be yearly kept here; *sc.*[30] the one on the Eve of the *Holy Trinitie* and two days after, the other on the Eve and day of St *Martin*. With the other lands belonging to these great Earls, this Mannour, at length, came to *Ric. Nevill*, in right of *Anne* his wife (as in **Warwick** is shewed[31]) but towards the later end of *H.* 6. reign, when this haughty spirited Earl sided with the House of **York**, it was seized by the King, and demised[32] to Sir *Edm. Mountfort* Knight, one of his Carvers, for the terme of x. years; and the Rangership of the *Chase* disposed[33] of by the same King, to

John Holt Esq; one of his Household servants, to hold for terme of life, with the Fees and profits thereof antiently due and payable. How it was afterwards (*sc.* in 14. *E.* 4.) taken from the said *Anne*, with the rest of the lands of her inheritance, and setled by Act of Parliament upon *Isabell* and *Anne* her Daughters, I have in **Warwick** fully shewed; as also how by a speciall grant, and Act of Parl. likewise, to strengthen the same, it came to the Crown: it now therefore remains to shew the course of it since: in which disquisition I find, that K. *H.* 7. in 5. of his reign, assigned[34] it to the before specified *Anne*, to hold during her life.

After which, e're long, the **Mercate** being utterly forsaken,[35] the Town fell much to ruin; and the Mannour place was totally pulled[36] down by one *Wingston*, who being imployed as an Officer there for the King, made use of most of the timber for himself, selling the intire fabrick of the Hall unto the Marq. *Dorset*, which was set[37] up at **Bradgate** in **Leicestershire**. And in this decayed condition did **Sutton** continue, till[38] that *John Harman, alias Veisy*, Bishop of **Exeter**, bearing a great affection thereto, in respect it was the place of his birth, having obtained[39] of the King in 19. *H.* 8. certain parcells of Inclosure here, called **More crofts**, and **Hethe yards**, and more than xl. acres of wast, with License to inclose it, the next year ensuing procured Letters Pat.[40] dated 16. *Dec.* for the making it a Corporation, by the name of a *Warden and Societie*, to consist of xxiiii. persons besides the Warden: as also another yearly **Faire** on *Simon* and *Jude*'s day, with a weekly **Mercate** upon the Munday (the Tuesday **Mercate** being discontinued) together with a Common Hall or *Moote Hall*, for their assemblies, a Clerk of the **Mercate**, and a Steward, and one or two Sergeants at Mace; the Warden for the time being to be Coroner within the same Corporation; and that no Shiriff nor Bailiff shall medle within their Liberties: granting besides unto them the whole Town and Mannour of **Sutton Colfeild**; as also the *Chase* and Park, to hold to them and their successors for ever in Fee ferm, at the Rent of Lviii *l. per an.* in which sort it continueth to this day.

1. Wenceslaus Hollar was born in Prague in 1607, and was brought to England in 1636 by Thomas Howard, Earl of Arundel, under whose patronage he worked until 1642. During the Civil War he went to Antwerp, returning in 1651. He won various commissions, including several from Dugdale. He died in Westminster in 1677. For details of his life and a selection of his work in England see Graham Parry, *Hollar's England, a mid-Seventeenth-Century View*, Salisbury, Wiltshire: Michael Russell (Publishing) Ltd, 1980.
2. William Burton (1575–1645) was the central figure amongst a group of Midlands antiquaries; Simon Archer (1581–1662), magistrate and antiquary of Tamworth, Warwickshire, began a study of the history of his own family which developed into the much wider project which he eventually handed over to Dugdale; Henry Spelman (1563–1641) was a leading historical scholar of his time; Roger Dodsworth (1585–1654) began a history of the monasteries, *Monasticon Anglicanum*), and invited the

participation of Dugdale, who completed the task after Dodsworth's death; Christopher Hatton (1605–1670), Dugdale's patron, son of the Elizabethan lord chancellor of the same name, was a royalist member of the Long Parliament who became King Charles I's Comptroller of the Royal Household.

3. Now called Sutton Coldfield. Note the font convention used by Dugdale: names of people are given in italics, and names of places are given in blackletter. This is reproduced in this extract, except that the blackletter is here presented simply as bold.
4. Dugdale's note: Domesday lib.
5. Dugdale's note: Domesday lib.
6. *Hide*, an area of land deemed adequate for the support of a household: it varied between 60 and 120 acres, according to local usage.
7. Dugdale's note: Ex pervetusto Cod. MS. penes Rob. Arden ar. Vide Esc. 26. E. 1. n. 41.
8. Dugdale here quotes the source of this information.
9. That is, the document which he has just quoted.
10. Dugdale's book is divided into four parts, each dealing with one of the four hundreds of the county, and each commencing with a map of the hundred.
11. Dugdale's note: Ex vet. exempl. penes præf. R. Arden.
12. Dugdale uses regnal dates; this example, 3. *E.* 2, is year 3 of Edward II.
13. Dugdale here quotes the specifications of the boundaries of the chase, as determined by the Inquisition.
14. Dugdale here quotes the words of the agreement 'because 'tis very memorable', and lists the signatories.
15. Dugdale's note: Ex præf. vet. cod. MS. penes R. Arden ar.
16. Dugdale's note: Pat. 17. E. 1. m. 9.
17. *Verderer*, a judicial officer responsible for dealing with trespassers into a forest.
18. *Tender*, careful.
19. Dugdale's note: Cartul. Warw. Com. f. 101. a.
20. *Attachments*, means by which a defendant might be made to answer a charge, such as *distraint*, the seizure of some of his possessions; and *presentments*, the required reporting, to the court, by a member of a 'tithing', or group of peers and neighbours, crimes committed by another member.
21. *Amerciaments*, fines.
22. Dugdale's note: Pat. 21. E. 1. m. 2.
23. Dugdale's note: Ex præf. cod. MS. penes R. Arden
24. *Assarting*, grubbing up trees and bushes in order to make the land arable.
25. Dugdale's note: Plac. coram. R. 17. E. 2. rot. 107.
26. The Statute of Winchester, of 1285, required sheriffs to keep arms and horses ready to deal with attacks on villages by roaming mercenaries, a significant problem at the time.
27. *Supersedeas*, a writ to stay legal proceedings.
28. *Mercate*, market.
29. Dugdale's note: Cart. de an. 25, 26, & 27. E. 3. n. 11.
30. Abbreviation for *scilicet*, meaning 'that is to say'.
31. That is, in the text on Warwick, elsewhere in the book.
32. *Demised*, transferred. Dugdale's note: Pat. 38. H. 6. p. 2. m. 14.
33. Dugdale's note: *Ibid.* m. 13.
34. Dugdale's note: Pat. 5. H. 7. m. 24.
35. Dugdale's note: Lel. Itin. vol. 4. f. 187.
36. Dugdale's note: *Ibid.*
37. Dugdale's note: *Ibid.*
38. Dugdale's note: *Ibid.*
39. Dugdale's note: Pat. 19. H. 8. p.1.
40. Dugdale's note: Pat. 20. H. 8. p.2.

XII
Memorial Warwickshire: William Thomas

In 1730 Dr William Thomas, a Worcester clergyman and antiquary who had become Rector of Exhall in Warwickshire, brought out a new edition of William Dugdale's county survey, originally published in 1656. It might be presumed that, after seventy-four years, tastes in county descriptions would have moved on to a degree that such a project would not have been warranted, but at the time this was a moot point. An earlier attempt to re-edit *The Antiquities of Warwickshire*, in 1718, had failed for lack of support, but Thomas was motivated by the scarcity of copies of the book, and his understanding that it 'was always thought by judicious Persons a valuable Book'.[1] The achievement of a second edition demanded both significant dedication and sufficient funding. Thomas was not daunted by the first of these challenges, for he was an indefatigable worker, and he addressed the other problem by financing the printing through the sale of subscriptions, a common procedure at the time. Unfortunately, despite the support of 218 subscribers, the venture proved not to be profitable, and the takings 'barely covered the cost of publication'.[2] Yet there was clearly a degree of interest, and we may conclude that there were indeed some, in the gentry community, who derived benefit from the availability of a comprehensive genealogical reference for the county.

Although Thomas embarked on the project with an associate, this other person failed to participate, so he was obliged to survey the entire county himself. In spite of the provision of some material by Peter le Neve (a herald and the then president of the Society of Antiquaries, to whom Thomas referred as 'the Ornament of his profession'[3]), it was a substantial task. His aim, he wrote in his preface, was to 'visit the Churches, transcribe the Epitaphs, note the Arms, and continue the Families down to our own Time'.[4] The objective was not to change, but to update and correct Dugdale's work. The result was an expansion of the book from about 800 to about 1300 pages, accounts of family and estate descents being continued into the eighteenth century, records of parish incumbencies being extended, and, most strikingly, a further 826 monumental inscriptions being added to Dugdale's original collection of 255.

These were taken from 177 churches across Warwickshire. Such thorough attention to family memorials in parish churches may have been in response to a perceived requirement of the expected readership, or it may have been a matter of expediency—that it was undoubtedly easier to get such information from church visits than to interview families and seek access to their records, a task which Dugdale had found difficult eighty years earlier.

Regardless of Thomas's other editorial initiatives, the new epitaphs broadened the scope of the survey to include not only saintly benefactors, manorial lords, famous knights, and powerful officials but also county clergymen, teachers, merchants, and other more ordinary gentlemen and their wives and children. Their epitaphs are more than terse, formulaic appeals for prayers for departed souls, but individual memorials of human lives. They speak with a new didacticism of attitudes and ideals which differ from those celebrated by Dugdale as he looked back to the medieval centuries; family honour is now manifested more in gentle and godly virtues than in military prowess and the bearing of arms.

The most obvious characteristic of Dugdale's survey was the preoccupation with the past. This is especially powerful because his accounts of people and places tend not to be carried forth even into the fifty years before he was writing. While this is not the case in Thomas's version, the narrative is concerned just as insistently with people who have died; his view was quite purposefully historical. It was not like Robert Atkyns's book *The Ancient and Present State of Glostershire*, published in 1712, which showed that a county survey could, as the title suggests, be relevant to the present as well as to the past. While there is plenty of historical data, Atkyns dealt conspicuously with the parishes of Gloucestershire as they were at the time he was writing.

The following extract is a sample of Thomas's records of epitaphs, which form a very significant part of his description of the county. It is taken from his account of the church of St Michael, at Coventry,[5] which is one of the most lengthy catalogues of epitaphs in the book. The inscriptions are not arranged in any order other than that in which they would be encountered by a visitor walking through the building, so that a random sample includes both earlier and more recent examples. To whom were they addressed? The intended readership was perhaps becoming more specific. While pre-Reformation epitaphs were often appeals to passers-by to pray for the soul languishing in Purgatory, the genre in later times was characterised more by statements of virtuous achievements, asserting family standing in the community. As with every other aspect of bringing Dugdale's book up to date, Thomas was scrupulously careful to be accurate. In his preface, he tells his readers, of the epitaphs, that 'they are generally printed with the same Lines and the same Letters as on the Monuments (except where the Dashes and Lines overhead would not admit of it) and with the same Spelling, though in some Places not true, being willing to represent Things as really they are, and not as they should be.' It was a very singular view of the county.

Funeral monuments in the Chancel, Drapers' Chapel, and Mercers' Chapel at St Michael's Church, Coventry.

From *The Antiquities of Warwickshire Illustrated*, 2nd edn, pp.167-171

On a brass plate fixed to the north wall of the Chancell, the portraiture of a woman kneeling:

HER ZEALOUS CARE TO SERVE HER GOD,
HER CONSTANT LOVE TO HVSBAND DEARE,
HER HARMLESS HARTE TO EVERY ONE,
DOTH LIVE ALTHOUGH HER CORPS LYE HERE.
GOD GRAVNTE VS ALL WHILE GLASS DOTH RVN,
TO LIVE in CHRIST AS SHE HATH DONE.

ANN SEWELL, THE WIFE OF WILLIAM SEWELL OF THIS CITTY, VINTNER, DEPARTED THIS LIFE 20TH DECEM. 1609 OF THE AGE OF 46 YEARS, AN HVMBLE FOLLOWER OF OVR SAVIOVR CHRIST, AND A WORTHY STIRROR VP OF OTHERS TO ALL HOLY VERTVES.[6]

On another, the portraiture of a Woman kneeling:
MARIÆ HINTON, FÆMINÆ LECTISSIMÆ, VXORI DILECTÆ, PROBÆ, ET PIÆ, MARITVS AMORIS HOC SVI MONVMENTVM POSVIT.

QVÆ PIETATIS ERAS, QVÆ RELLIGIONIS AMORE
ET MATRONALI CVNCTIS GRAVITATE PROBATA,
VIVENS ET MORIENS CONSTANS EXEMPLAR AMICIS
VIVENDI IN VITA, MORIENDI IN MORTE RELINQVIS.
SIC TIBI, SIC VIVIT VITÆ BONA FAMA PERACTÆ
SIC TIBI, SIC VITÆ CONSTAT SPES VIVA PERENNIS.
OBIIT ANNUM AGENS TRICESSIMUM.
APRILIS 27. 1594

On flat stones in the Chancell:

Here Lyeth the body of Ralph Flexney Gent. who departed this life Jan. 16. 1608. the 74 year of his Age.

On a cheveron three cross croslets fitche, between three annulets empaling barry a boar's head and vine branch in bend:[7]
James Smith of MAGHVIL Hall in Lancashire Esq; who departed this Life in hopes of a better the 24 of October, in the year of our Lord 1670. Aged 53.

Sable a cheveron arg. charged with three roses, gules, between three firelocks, or, emp. quarterly 1 *and* 4. *gules on a bend three pheons of the first,* 2 *and* 3. *gules a fess and border ingrailed between three wheatsheafs argent.*

Richard Hopkins Esq; who departed this life 1 Febr. 1707.

Quarterly, 1 *and* 4. *on a cheveron two crescents and a star between three heads errased.* 2 *and* 3. *barry of six, three roundells in cheif empaling a bend wavy, between two Staggs heads errased:*

Here Lyeth interred Thomas Bearcroft of the Citie of Coventry Gent. Descended from that Ancient family of Meargreen, in the Parish of Hanbury near Droitewich, in the County of Worcester; who married two wives, the first Alicia, the fourth daughter of Samuel Harwar, of Stoke near Coventry Gent. his second was Mary Grey, Daughter to the Honorable Job Grey, second son to the Right Honorable Anthony Earl of Kent. He departed this life on the 20. of August 1689, in the 90 year of his Age.

Here also Lyeth the body of Mrs. Mary Bearcroft, Relict of the said Mr. Thomas Bearcroft, who departed this Life 29 July 1717. Aged 60.[8]

HERE LYETH THE BODY OF MRS. KATHERINE LOWE, THE WIFE OF HUMPHREY LOWE ESQ; IN THE COVNTY OF WORCESTER, SHE DEPARTED THIS LIFE OCTOBER 8. 1695. AGED 74 YEARS.

In Drapers Chappell, at the east end of a raised Tomb, *on a bend cotiz'd three staggs heads, emp. quarterly,* 1 *and* 4. *a fess wavy between three harts tripping,* 2 *and* 3 *ermin three storks.*

On a black marble table on the foreside:
Vnto the Memorie of William Stanley, late Citizen and Maister of the worshipful Company of Merchant Taylers London, and one of the Maisters of St Bartholomew Hospitall in Smithfield in the said Citie. Born in this Citie of Coventry, and late Maister of the worshipfull Companie of Drapers here. He gave sundrie Legacies to the good of the aforesaid Hospitall, and of this Citie, and departed this Life the XVIII of December 1640. Ætatis suæ LXXXI. ii. Monthes.[9]

Joan his mournfull widowe hath erected this Monument.

On a flat stone a plate of brass, *a cheveron between three roundells, and three roundells in cheif*:

HERE LYETH MR. THOMAS BOND DRAPER, SOMETIME MAJOR OF THIS CITTIE, AND FOVNDER OF THE HOSPITALL OF BABLAKE, WHO GAVE DIVERS LANDS & TENEMENTS FOR THE MAINTENANCE OF TEN POOR MEN SO LONG AS THE WORLD SHALL ENDVRE, & A WOMAN TO LOOK TO THEM, WITH MANY OTHER GOOD GIFTS, AND DYED THE XVIII DAY OF MARCH IN THE YEARE OF OUR LORD GOD MDVI.[10]

On other flat stones in the same Chappell:

Here Lyeth the body of John Lapworth gent. who departed this life Aug. 26. 1720. in the 59 year of his age.

Edward Lapworth Alderman, Nov. 9. 1703. Aged 78. also Thomas Lapworth Chirurgeon, who departed this life 18 March 1716. Aged 52.

Mrs. Anne Roach, widow of Captain Philip Roach, Commander of the Smyrna Merchant, who died Dec. 29. A. D. 1707. Aged 50.

John Wright Gent. sworn Clarke of the High Court of Chancery, who departed this Life July the 3. An. Dom. 1703. Aged 55. Elizabeth his wife, June 5. 1714.

A lion rampant emp. on a fess three fleurs de lis, between three cross Saltires:

Here Lie the bodies of Mr. Thomas Love, late Alderman of this Citie, aged 75. and Mrs. *Joan* his wife; and Mr. Edward Love, his son, aged 47. and Mrs. Prudence his wife. Also Mr. Thomas Love, the son of the said Mr. Edward Love, who departed this life June the 10. 1699. Aged 46. in hopes of a joyfull Resurrection.

In Mercers Chappell, a small monument fixed to the east wall, *argent a cheveron sable.*[11]

FORBID NOT LITTLE ONES TO COME UNTO CHRIST, FOR OF SUCH IS THE KINGDOM OF HEAVEN.
OUT OF THESE STONES SHALL GOD RAISE A CHILD OF WILLIAM STAUNTON OF STAVNTON, IN COM. NOTT, ESQ; AND ANNE HIS

WIFE, WHO HEAR OFFER UP AS HOLY TO THE LORD, THE FIRST FRVITS OF THE WOMBE, THEIR ELDEST DAVGHTER FRAVNCIS, WHO PERFORMED HER VOW TO FORSAKE THE WORLD A°. ÆTATIS 7. A. SALVTIS 1638. THIS, NO MONVMENT OF THEIR GRIEF, BUT A MEMORIAL OF THAT BLESSING, THE GUIFT WHEREOF THEY SO LOVED, THAT THEY HELD EVEN THE LOSSE DEARE.
DEAR LOSSE, WHO THIS REMAYNES ALONE,
THAT WE, BAD PARENTS, GIVE A STONE,
SINCE DESTINY, AS IT APPEARES,
BY METHOD KILLS NOT, NOR BY YEARS.
AND THOU WHO TOOKST OUR SHAPE AND BREATH,
ARE MADE OUR AUNCIENT NOW IN DEATH,
BE THOU OVR PLEDGE TO HEAVEN WHILST WE
HAST TO THE GRAVE TO FOLLOW THEE.

Somewhat lower:

TO LIVE, NOR KNOW LIFE DID ADVAUNCE,
THY LIFE TO EXTASY AND TRAUNCE,
THAT WHAT WAS DREAME BEFORE PAST ON,
CONSUMATED IN VISION.
THE TREE OF KNOWLEDGE SCAPD UNTASTED IS,
THY PLEA TO INNOCENCE AND PARADICE.

On a raised tomb below it, there are on the side seven sheilds of coats of arms defaced, among the rest, *a cheveron frete, a cheveron between three* ... motto RYEN SAVNCE TRAVAYLE, with nine images in *basso relievo*; at the head *azure on a bend, two strip'd carnations empaling* 1 *and* 4. *a cheveron frette,* 2 *and* 3. *on a cheveron, two mullets and a crescent between three roundlets.* This is called *Wade*'s Tomb.

On a raised tomb of marble, *or a cheveron azure on a canton sable, a boar's head emp. Harewell:*

Sacrum memoriæ suavissimæ & charissimæ conjugis Elizabethæ, ornatissimæ Matris Judaethæ, & trium Infantulorum, posuit mœstissimus Maritus, Filius, Pater, Josephus Moore Med. D^{r}. Oxon. Anno Dom^{ni}. 1640. Qui jam orbus donec cognati conjungantur pulveres, meliorari non ambit, non obnixe rogat, quam similiter Vivere, Mori, Esse.

Sleepe, Saints, and when your Easter's come about,

A trump will call, the world will light you out.

Elizabetha Filia Henrici Harewell,
de Civitat. Covent. in Comitant.
Civit. Coventr Armig. Obiit
puerpera 15. Maii eodem quo & nata
est.de Comitat.
Anno Domini 1640

Judaetha Filia Thomæ Edmonds,
de Comitat. Devon Armig.
Vxor Johannis Moore, Dorcest.
Generosi. Obiit xi. die
Septembr.
Anno Domini 1636.
Ætatis suæ 72.

Memento Mori.

On a monument on the south wall, *Argent three bulls heads errased sable, empaling gules three bears paws argent.*

AN ELEGIACALL EPITAPH MADE UPON THE DEATH OF THAT MIRROR OF WOMEN, ANN NEWDIGATE LADY SKEFFINGTON, WIFE TO THAT TRUE MOANEING TURTLE SR. RICHARD SKEFFINGTON KT. & CONSECRATED TO HER ETERNAL MEMORIE BY THE VNFEIGNED LOVER OF HER VERTVES, WILL. BULSTRODE KNIGHT.

VERTVE HVMBLE, BEAVTY CHASTE, PIOVS WIT,
HVSBANDS HONOVR, WOMENS GLORY SWEETLYE KNIT,
AND ALL COMPRISED FAIRELYE IN THS ONE,
SAD FATE HATH HERE INSHRINED WITH THIS STONE,
VIRTVE TRIVMPH, FOR THOU HAST WON THE PRIZE,
BEAVTIE TEACH WOMEN TO BE CHASTE & WIZE;
MAKE HER YOUR PATTERNE OF A VERTVOVS LIFE,
WHO LIVED & DYED A FAIR VNSPOTTED WIFE.
SHE WAS THE MIRROR OF HER AGE AND DAYS,
AND NOW THE SVBJECT OF TRANSCENDENT PRAISE.
O WHAT A HARMONIE MANS LIFE WOVLD BE,
WERE WOMEN ALL BVT NEARE SO GOOD AS SHE!
HER LIFE WAS SVCH AS FEARED NO STING OF DEATH,
BVT DAR'D HIM BY SO STRONG VNDOVBTING FAITH,
AS THAT HE DID BVT MILDLY STEAL VNTO HER,
AND GENTLYE WHISPER'D AS HE MEANT TO WOE HER.
AND SHE AS GENTLYE YEILDED STRAIT TO GOE,
BEFORE 'TWAS KNOWNE IF SHE WERE DEAD OR NO.
NOR IS SHE DEAD, HER SOVLE TO HEAVEN STEPT,
THE REST STAYES HERE TILL IT A WHILE HATH SLEPT.
AND HER FAME HERE STILL LIVES & STILL SHALL WAKE,
TILL ALL GOOD MEMORIE SHALL EARTH FORSAKE.
THRICE BLESSED SOVL, WEE'LE NOT OVR GREIF BELYE,

WEE WAYLE NOT THEE, BVT OVR OWN DESTINYE.
YET IN OVR LOSS OF THEE THIS IS OVR GLORYE,
THAT 'TIS THY HAPPINESS THAT MAKES VS SORYE.
W.B.[12]

Obiit. Maii. 21. Ætatis suæ 29.
Anno Dni. 1637.

On a flat stone in the same Chappell, *a cheveron between three snails:*

Here lieth the body of William Snell, Alderman of this City, he departed this life the 24. of October 1711. Aged 84. also Abigail his wife, who departed this life the 10th of September 1709, Aged 66.

1. 'The Editor's Preface', William Dugdale, *The Antiquities of Warwickshire Illustrated*, edited by William Thomas, London, 1730, p.ix.
2. The price was three guineas, 350 copies were printed, and there had been 218 subscribers (whose names appear in the prefatory material to the book).
3. Thomas's preface, p.x.
4. *Ibid.*, p.ix.
5. Later Coventry Cathedral.
6. Even a small sample of the tombs which Thomas recorded shows a variety of styles of epitaph. Ann Sewell is presented as the godly wife in words appropriate to the reformed church, while the adjacent tomb of Mary Hinton is written in Latin, retaining the more mystical and remote gravity of the Catholic liturgy.
7. A coat of arms was evidence of ancestry of title and therefore it was important data for the antiquary to record. This could be done by including a likeness (with the colours indicated by abbreviations) or, as here, by specifying the blazon, or heraldic description. In this example, the terms are as follows: *cheveron*, the representation of the two rafters of a house meeting at a middle, higher point; *cross croslet*, a cross with its ends crossed; *fitché*, cut to a point; *annulet*, little circle; *empale* (or *impale*), combine with in a coat of arms; *barry*, separated by a *bar*, a wide horizontal band; *bend*, a diagonal band extending from the *dexter chief* (upper right) to the *sinister base* (lower left).
8. Mary, Thomas Bearcroft's second wife, was only 32 when her 90-year-old husband died.
9. This and the next are examples of more personal, didactic memorial statements.
10. This last date is probably transcribed erroneously.
11. This poignant memorial to a child who died at the age of seven reveals something of contemporary attitudes to death. Presumably the child died because of illness and probably had realised her fate (hence her 'vow to forsake the world'). Destiny is unknowable and the child's death is just a matter of chance, but now she has become 'ancient' relative to her parents, and they must follow where she leads rather than she, as their child, following them.
12. The memorial to Ann Newdigate, the Lady Skeffington, who died aged twenty-nine 'a fair unspotted wife' was erected by another man, William Bulstrode, the 'unfeigned lover of her virtues'. While the story of the relationships between these people may not be known to us, we may reflect on the shifting sense of 'antiquity' that admitted the inclusion of personal epitaphs such as this.

XIII
Myddle, Shropshire: Richard Gough (1634–1723)

Richard Gough differs from the other antiquaries represented in this collection in that his interest was principally not in a place but in the people who dwelt in a place. It was moreover not so much landholdings, honours, and rank that he detailed, but ordinary matters pertaining to ordinary individuals. The place was his own village of Myddle and he was not in any professional sense a writer, so he may readily be characterised as an amateur local historian. Gough referred to himself as a yeoman, which was the social level just below that of the gentry. He inherited a farm on the death of his father in 1661, and he also undertook employment in various posts; he had been trained in law while serving as a clerk to a local Justice of the Peace. As well, his social standing required that he serve in local administrative positions, all of which would have given him good acquaintance with the community in which he lived. By the time he wrote he was probably one of the most elderly folk in Myddle, and he wrote nothing more afterwards. Through his education and his work he developed a sound knowledge of Latin and the classics, from which he quoted constantly in his text. He was certainly familiar with Camden's *Britannia*, for he referred to it frequently, but he did not make use of other well-known antiquarian county surveys.

The study of Myddle was composed as two separate essays (which together are usually called *The History of Myddle*), the first being the much shorter *Antiquityes and Memoyres of the Parish of Myddle,* which adopts the usual scheme of an antiquarian place description. It gives information about the manor, the church, the boundaries, and matters of local administration. The second, written two years later, in 1702, *Observations concerning the Seates in Myddle and the familyes to which they belong*, was much more unusual, and assured its author a unique place in the evolution of local history-writing in early modern England.[1] Taking each pew in the parish church in turn (and even including a diagram of their layout), Gough wrote about the occupants, thus dealing with each of the local households and effectively ranking them according to their standing.[2] But the antiquarian details of genealogy and tenancy are subordinated by lively, gossipy stories, sketching the personalities and foibles of the subjects with vivid and pithy succinctness. A few examples will show how very different they are from the terse and distant narratives normally presented by more scholarly authors:

> Thomas Jukes was a bauling, bould, confident person; hee often kept company with his betters, but shewed them noe more respecte than if they had beene his equalls or inferiors. Hee was a great bowler, and often bowled with Sir Humphrey Lea att a Bowling Greene on Haremeare Heath, neare the end of Lea Lane; where hee would make noe more account of Sir Humphrey, than if hee had beene a plow-boy. Hee would ordinarily tell him hee lyed, and sometymes throw the bowle att his head, and then they parted in wrath. But within a few dayes, Sir Humphrey would ride to Newton, and take Jukes with him to the bowles; and if they did not fall out, would take him home and make him drunk.[3]

Of a later generation of the same family,

> Richard, the eldest son, and heire of Thomas, was a sort of morose, lofty, imperious person, and was beloved of few. Hee married Elinor, the daughter of Roger Bird ... this Elinor was a comely proper woman, of a friendly and curtuouse disposition ...[4]

Thomas Ash served as a corporal on the side of the king in the Civil Wars and when he returned

> ... hee brought nothing home but a crazy body and many scarrs, the symptomes of the dangerouse service which hee had performed, and besides, hee found litle of his debts payd, for the payment of taxes and charges of repaires had taken up the most part of the rent; but hee being minded that none shouald lose by him, sold his lease to William Formeston. Hee had some money to spare when hee had satisfied his debts, and with that hee took a lease of Mr Crosse of Yorton, of severall peices of ground neare Yorton Heath, and there hee built a litle warme house, made a neate litle garden, planted a pretty horcyard, built severall outhouses, and made everything very handsome and convenient, and there hee and his loveing wife spent theire old age, though not in a plentifull, yet in a peaceable and contented condition. There was but litle space betweene the time of their deceases.[5]

These remarks are frank and direct in their economy, and the pictures they present are sometimes unexpected: particularly arresting is the cross-class familiarity between the companions who go bowling and drinking together, tempering historical preconceptions about class interrelationships. Thomas Jukes had inherited a cottage from his father, who had bought it from a Shrewsbury draper. He married the daughter of 'an ancient and substantiall family', and had two sons and two daughters. The elder son was 'a good ingeniouse person, well skilled in any country afaries', and became a churchwarden in Myddle. The daughters married holders of small tenements: one was a weaver; the other, whose trade is not mentioned, was 'pritty rich'. The second son went to London as an apprentice, 'but for some misdemeanor, came to an untimely end'. Yet it is clear from his narrative that Gough, like the professional antiquaries, had done his genealogical research properly and that he did not invent it, noting points at which he had been unable to find details. We see this in frequent admissions: for example, in tracing the tenancy of the property which the Jukes family eventually came to own, he remarks: 'How these lands came to Banaster, of Church Eyton, in the county of Stafford, I cannot say, having noe deed to that purpose; but I have beene credibly informed by antient persons that ...' So his account is a blend of verified facts and remembered data.

Of course, as with all gossip, the stories of the bad people are the most entertaining. There are plenty of these amongst the inhabitants of Myddle, and the overall impression is decidedly negative. This is, however, to some degree misleading as a profile of seventeenth-century village life, for the people in Gough's account were by no means all contemporaneous. Of the three examples just quoted, only two describe characters whom Gough would ever have met: the Thomas Jukes in the first case was much earlier, being the son of a man who first bought a cottage at Myddle in 1572. As for Gough himself, his family had been at Myddle for a number of generations, so he wrote quite extensively about his many relatives, although he refrained from making any judgements on his own personality. Indeed, little is known of him from any source.

The first of the following extracts is taken from the first book, which is a more general description of the parish as a place. Myddle Castle was a ruin at the time of writing, so Gough drew upon his childhood memories to describe the former shell of the building and, more significantly, the uses to which it was being put by the village community, giving an evocative glimpse of country life in the mid-seventeenth century. The link from the present back to the past, so keenly sought by the antiquaries, is here ingenuously achieved in the observations of present-day businesses being conducted in an ancient ruin. Without any sense of heritage as it is now conceived, there is an unquestioned and almost unconscious continuity with the past. The description is fresh, informal, and personal, reminiscent of the writing of Richard Carew in Cornwall a hundred years earlier, yet there is neither emotive nor aesthetic judgement: however fondly Gough may have recalled his childhood visits to the castle, he ascribes to the scene no such quality as beauty, for example. And it was to be many more years till any author of a description of the landscape would do so.

The vignette dealing with Reece Wenlock is one of many in which Gough gives the impression that village life was often insecure and even hostile. He was severely critical of many villagers, variously characterising them as lazy, wasteful, selfish, or dishonest, but the main evil he constantly exposed was drunkenness. In this case we have a mocking portrait of a man who was envious, selfish, foolish, and superstitious: a bad neighbour and a petty thief. This is one amongst a very considerable catalogue of unsavoury characters accumulated by Gough over sixty-six years. He would moreover have had an abundance of further sources from which to draw. The parish had at the time a population of about 450, and it may be assumed that everyone knew everyone else. At the alehouse or wherever else people met, gossip would have been a prevalent activity, and the account of the village is constructed from information and pseudo-information derived from hearsay, popular opinions, Chinese whispers, and recollections of events and tales. Yet the portrait of Myddle as a whole is a faithful picture of village life, the environment in which it was lived, and the various available means of earning a livelihood.

Myddle Castle

From *The History of Myddle*, pp.27–29

The Manor of Myddle, was formerley beautifyed with a faire but small Castle, which now lyes in ruins. Mr Camden[6] saies, that the Lord Strange built the castle at Knockin, and wee may rationally conclude, that hee alsoe built this castle, haveing here the convenience of free stone, which is plentifull in this Manor. The stone wherewith the Castle was built, was gott on that end of Haremeare heath, which is next to Myddle. The walls of this castle about sixty years agoe were standing, soe that it might easyly bee perceived what manner of structure it was, of which I will give you an accompt, as well as my memory will serve.

This Castle was built four square, within a square moate, and had a square Court within it. There was a piece of ground, of almost an acre of land on the east side of the castle, which peice was moated about with a lesser moate than the castle.[7] The entrance into this peice was throw a Gate-house which stood neare the north-east corner of the Castle moate: the passage throw the Gate-house was about eight foot wide. There were foure Chambers in it beelow, to wit two on eyther side of the passage. Those two that were next the castle were, (when I first saw it,) made use of for a bake-house. There was alsoe, in the same peice of ground, another peice of building, which was supposed to have been a slaughter-house for the use of the Castle. The floore of this peice of building was of clay, and made high along the myddle of the Building, like a Bridge; it may bee for the ease of the slaughterman in falling his beeves,[8] and for laying them to bleed more freely. Almost over against this Building, I beeleive the Bridge was over the castle moate, for when I was a schoole-boy att Myddle, Mr. Gittins his servants, in a dry summer, when they were carrying of mudde out of the Castle moate, to manure theire meadows tooke up there two large sills[9] that wrought over crosse the castle moate; the sills were blacke, but not rotten, they were about two feet square, and the mortaces in them, that were to receive the posts that supported the bridge, were two feete long, and six inches wide. The passage from the end of the Bridge, went throw into the court which was in the myddle of the Castle; on the south side the passage was a large roome, supposed to have beene a Kitchen, by reason of a very large chimney in it, which seemed to have beene much used; on the south side of the Castle was a pleasante roome supposed to have beene a parlor; on the west side and just over against the passage, there were two roomes open togeather, onely parted with somewhat of a wall, that had severall large doore-places throw it; this was supposed to have been the hall. I doe not remember any chimney in it, butt I know the Court Leet[10] for this Manor was kept in that roome. I suppose this Castle was onely two storyes high, and flatt on the top or roofe; there was (and in part still is) a tower, and stairecase at the north-west corner of the inner Court, and a doore-place out of it, neare the top, to goe out on the Roofe of the castle. Part of the top of this Tower fell downe in an Earthquake, about the yeare 1688, at which time, alsoe part of the stone wall of Mr. Lloyd's garden in Myddle fell downe. There was another stairecase of stone at the south-west corner of the said Court. This Castle stood at, or in, the north-east corner of a pretty large Parke, which had a lane about it on the outside. On the east side, was a lane, called the Moor Lane. On the south side there is some lands, called the Lane, which ly between Myddle parke, and the lands belonging to Webscot Farme, which lane is held att a certaine rent by the tenants, or owners of Webscott. On the west side is the Linches lane, soe called from a certaine Hall, called the Linches' Hall, which stood upon a banke in Fennimeare ground, neare the side of this lane. On the north, is the roadway that goes through Myddle. In this parke, not far southward from the castle, stoode a dwelling house, perhapps a lodge or habytation for a keeper, but I never saw it inhabyted, but onely used for tying of cattle and bestoweing of fodder; it is now (1700) utterly gon to ruine. It was called the Harhouse, and the banke neare where it stood is still called the Harhouse Banke.

The Ninth Peiw on the North Side of the North Isle

From *The History of Myddle*, pp.61–62

This was a supernumerary peiw; for beefore the uniformeing of the church with wainscott seates, there was but eight seats on this side of the north isle, soe that this was a voyd seate;[11] and then those that lived in the Meare House, and Clarke of Haremeare Heath, and those that lived in a cottage in Myddle (which beelongs to the Castle Farme) wherein the widow Russell now dwelleth,—these persons, I say (although none of them payes any church leawan[12] but Clark, which is but 2d.), gott into this seate, and have ever since used it; and now, (happly) they plead prescription.[13]

The Meare House, at Haremeare, did stand over crosse the brooke that issueth out of Haremeare; butt when the Meare was lett dry, the house was removed, and sett by the side of the brooke, and one Spurstow dwelt in it, and was imployed by Sir Andrew Corbett to looke to the Heyment of Haremeare,[14] and to tend the catell that were in it, for when it was let dry, there were catell putt in it as a lay;[15] and after, as it beecame dry and sound, it was divided into severall peices. After Spurstow, one Reece Wenlocke dwelt in it. He was descended of good parentage, who were tenants of a good farme, called Whottall, in Eleesmeare Lordshipp. Butt the father of this Reece was a bad husband, and a pilfering, thievish person, and this son, Reece, and another son, named John, who lived at Bald Meadow, in this parish, were as bad as theire father. They never stole any considerable goods, but were night walkers, and robbed oarchyards and gardens, and stole hay out of meadows, and corne when it was cutt in the feilds, and any small things that persons by carelessnesse had left out of doors. Reece had a cow, which was stolen away, and it is reported that hee went to a woman, whom they called the wise woman of Montgomery, to know what was beecome of his cow; and as hee went, hee putt a stone in his pockett, and tould a neighbour of his that was with him that he would know whether she were a wise woman or not, and whether she knew that hee had a stone in his pockett. And it is sayd, that when hee came to her, shee sayd, thou hast a stone in thy pockett, but itt is not soe bigge as that stone wherewith thou didst knocke out such a neighbour's harrow tines.[16] Butt the greatest diskindenesse that hee did to his neighbours was, by tearing their hedges. And it is reported, that hee had made a new oven; and, according to the manner of such things, it was att first to bee well burnt, to make it fitt for use, and this hee intended to doe in the night. Att that time William Higginsons dwelt att Webscott, and hee had a servant, named Richard Mercer, a very waggish fellow. This Mercer did imagine that Reece would teare his master's hedges to burne the oven; and as hee walked by a hedge, which was near Reece's house, hee saw there a great dry sticke of wood, and tooke it home with him, and bored a hoale in the end of it with an augur, and putt a good quantyty of powder in it, and a pegge after it, and putt it againe into the hedge. And it happened, that Reece Wenlock, among other hedge-wood, tooke this stick to burne in his oven; and when hee cast it into the fire in the oven, it blowed up the topp of it, and sett fire on the end of the house. Reece went out and made a hideouse crying, fyre! fyre! William Higginson, being the next neighbour, heard him, and called Mercer, butt hee sayd I know what is the matter; however, they went both downe to the Meare House, but Reece had putt out the fyre that was in the end of the house, and the oven was broaken to peices.

1. The books were not published till 1834, when they appeared together under the title *Human Nature displayed in the History of Myddle*, edited by the antiquarian and book-collector Sir Thomas Phillips. Naturally it must be speculated, as it has for example by Hoskins, that the delay in publishing was the fear of offending members and descendants of families described in the text. See Richard Gough, *Human Nature Displayed in the History of Myddle*, with an Introduction by W. G. Hoskins, Fontwell, Sussex: Centaur Press Ltd., 1968, p.2. This edition, referred to as *The History of Myddle*, is used for all the following citations. There is a more comprehensive discussion of the book in a paperback edition: Richard Gough, *The History of Myddle*, edited with an Introduction and Notes by David Hey, Penguin Books, 1981.
2. Robert Mayer in his excellent essay on Myddle has discussed the role of Gough's text in empowering village families; see his *History and the Early English Novel*, Cambridge University Press, 1997, pp.54–74.
3. *The History of Myddle*, p.54.
4. *Ibid.*, p.56.
5. *Ibid.*, p.147.
6. William Camden.
7. Gough's spelling has consistent peculiarities, but in this sentence he has written 'piece' two different ways.
8. *Beeves*, beasts.
9. *Sills*, horizontal timbers.
10. *Court Leet*, manorial court.
11. An extra pew was added when the church was 'uniformed' after the removal of the communion rail. This refurbishment evidently included the installation of the wainscoting (oak panelling).
12. *Leawan*, a payment to the parish. Gough refers earlier to a 'book of Leawans' in which these were recorded. (*The History of Myddle*, p.15).
13. That is, to claim the right to the pew by virtue of having long used it.
14. *Heyment*, land used for pasture.
15. Perhaps the same as ley, an area of arable land temporarily sown with grass.
16. *Harrow*, a device which has a row of prongs (*tines*) and is pulled over ploughed land to level it.

XIV

Albion—Warwickshire: Michael Drayton (1563–1631)

Drayton's *Poly-Olbion* is a very long poem of some 15,000 lines, which describes the regions of England and the legendary and heroic past associated with them. Most of the descriptions, as might be expected, are imaginative and stylised, and much of the material is based not on the poet's experience but on his reading, notably of Camden's *Britannia*. While the inclusion of such a work in a collection of accounts of views of England might seem incongruous, there are nevertheless passages which evoke country scenes in a way which suggests a basis in first-hand experience, and which clearly testify to a deeply-felt love of the landscape of Great Britain in the heart of the poet.

Michael Drayton was born about 1563 at Hartshill, Warwickshire, probably to a yeoman family, but his upbringing was at nearby Atherstone. There is considerable uncertainty about his early life. It seems that he attended local grammar schools; there is no evidence of him having studied at either Oxford or Cambridge. He was taken into service as a page in the household of Sir Henry Goodere, a local gentleman, to whom Drayton later acknowledged a great debt for having guided his education. He read extensively: English, French and Italian poets, the classics, and chronicles. His poetic output was considerable, amounting to some two thousand pages, and he attempted almost all the kinds of poetry known at his time. He wrote sonnets and other short lyrical poems, heroic epistles (imagined verse letters from the pens of great English historical figures), odes, and long historical poems. For the most part, his poetry was written in praise of English heroes and England's past, and in *Poly-Olbion*, the greatest of such ventures, it is England itself that is the object of praise. This long work, on which he spent so much time and effort, was to be a celebration of England's legendary history, a monument to a noble past and, as well, a topographical survey of the wonders of the land. The collaboration of the much-admired antiquary John Selden, who provided accompanying notes to elucidate the references to ancient places and events, gave added substance to the matter of the past.

Poetry such as that which Drayton composed was also taken to have a particularly compelling didactic function. For Renaissance readers, poetry had an exalted status in literature, as being the finest means of expressing human ideas and as an approach, in a humanist context, to divine understanding and immortality. In such a cultural climate, *Poly-Olbion* would teach about England and its history, a function to which its chorographical framework was ideally suited. Likewise, in the tradition of his friends William Camden and John Stow, Drayton used the celebratory conjunction of the past and place to establish the origins and fame of England. Just as the civilizations of Athens and Rome could point to their classical beginnings, and just as Renaissance poetry and history could imitate the classical models, so also should England be able to claim a comparable antiquity.

Geoffrey of Monmouth's history of Britain, of course, provided appropriate origins. As well as accepting these, Drayton was able to point to another ancient tradition of knowledge, which had been passed down in the songs of the Bards and in the rites of the Druids. It has been observed that Drayton's use of the word 'song' for each section of his poem suggests that he saw himself as a successor to the Bards.[1] At the beginning of the first song of *Poly-Olbion*, Drayton calls upon the '*Genius*', a kind of eternal spirit of the land, as might have been invoked by the Bards and Druids, to guide him, the Poet. Drayton wrote of the ode which was perhaps his own favourite, 'The Ballad of Agincourt', that he saw the 'ballad' as being in the tradition of Petrarch and Chaucer, and that in writing such a poem he could take on 'the old English garb', suggesting a likening of his work with medieval ballads. It was dedicated 'To the Cambro-Britains and Their Harp', as he intended the odes to be accompanied with music, again recalling the performances of Bards.[2]

Poly-Olbion was a project which occupied a major proportion of Drayton's working life, from 1598 to 1618. He brought it out in two parts, but the public response was disappointing. The first part appeared in 1612, but it did not sell, and in 1622 he had trouble getting a publisher for the second part. He had envisaged a third part, which was to deal with Scotland, but he never wrote it. Commentators have discerned a slackening of the pace in the second part, perhaps indicative of a loss of confidence as Drayton pressed on. The first part is dominated by a lively contention between the fame of the Celts and that of the Anglo-Saxons, but there is less of this in the second part which is more topographical and in which the historical passages take on a similarity to chronicles. If there was a decline in the poet's enthusiasm, it was probably because he was becoming aware that popular appreciation was leaving him behind. A further source of disquiet for Drayton was the disapproving reception by King James I of his panegyric to welcome the new reign, probably because it not only failed to do honour to the late queen, but also was published before she was buried. Drayton never regained the ground he might have won in royal patronage, and he went on to view the reign in diminishing esteem. From his satirical poem *The Owl* of 1604 to the emergence, in successive works through to the 1620s, of a recurring nefarious figure, 'great Olcon', who has been taken to represent the king, Drayton's disillusionment with the nation's new directions becomes increasingly evident.

Citing the *Oxford English Dictionary*, Richard F. Hardin observed that 'the words *patriot* and *national* first entered our language in 1596 and 1597.'[3] Late in the reign of Elizabeth, England had come to be recognised as a leading sea power, a formidable champion of Protestantism in Europe, and an explorer and coloniser of other lands. These were all reasons for patriotism and nationalism, and it was amongst Drayton's social class of country gentry that these sentiments were held with special keenness. In the sixteenth century, this had been the governing class, but by the accession of James I, the Court was beginning to be more City-oriented, and a new breed of gentry was influencing fashions and ideas. In the long run, the rift between Country on the one hand and City and Court on the other was to engender a climate which would produce real political conflict, which was to come to a head in 1642. So at the same time that Drayton was composing *Poly-Olbion*, country values were being superseded by those of the sophisticated urban gentry: wit, fashion, flattery, idleness. It was a prospect which dismayed him, for the new attitudes detracted from the appreciation both of patriotism and of history.

In his preface to the First Part, Drayton wrote a disparaging appraisal of the new outlook, and in lamenting the loss that would be suffered, he invoked an ancient and mysterious spiritual kinship with the landscape and with the peoples who have inhabited it in the past.

> Then, whosoever thou be, possest with such stupidity and dulnesse, that, rather then thou wilt take paines to search into ancient and noble things, choosest to remaine in the thicke fogges and mists of ignorance, as neere the common Laystall of a Citie; refusing to walke forth into the *Tempe* and Feelds of the Muses, where through most delightfull Groves the Angellique harmony of Birds shall steale thee to the top of an easie hill, where in artificiall caves, cut out of the most naturall Rock, thou shalt see the ancient people of this Ile delivered thee in their lively images: from whose height thou mai'st behold both the old and later times, as in thy prospect, lying farre under thee; then convaying thee downe by a soule-pleasing Descent through delicate embrodered Meadowes, often veined with gentle gliding Brooks; in which thou maist fully view the dainty Nymphes in their simple naked bewties, bathing them in Crystalline streames; which shall lead thee, to most pleasant Downes, where harmless Shepheards are, some exercising their pipes, some singing roundelaies, to their grazing flocks: If as, I

> say, thou hadst rather, (because it asks thy labour) remaine, where thou wert, then straine thy selfe to walke forth with the Muses; the fault proceeds from thy idlenesse, not from any want in my industrie.[4]

But behind the rhetoric of these lines there is a striking contrast between Drayton's eager acceptance of the countryside as a source of knowledge and wisdom, and the critical apparatus of the introduction included by Selden, citing a plethora of documents and treatises, where truth in a new age is to be sought only in scholarship. There is, then, some irony in Drayton's inclusion of Selden's notes in his work, for it may well have been argued that changing values were the result not of 'idleness' but of a more sceptical intellect.

Drayton never married, and his association with the Gooderes continued through his life. He spent his last summer, in 1631, at the home of his boyhood master's daughter, Anne, and supposedly on the last night of his life wrote a poem of love addressed to her. He was given the honour of burial in Westminster Abbey, perhaps through veneration accorded to the one remaining poet from the days of Sidney, Spenser, and Marlowe, and perhaps because he had indeed become a spokesman for the Country, as opposed to the bureaucracy surrounding the throne. He has been seen as a bridge from medieval to modern England, linking the century of the Tudors and the century of the Stuarts, countering the great changes that were developing with his assertion of the continuity of past and present.

The first of the following extracts praises a part of England for which Drayton had a personal affection, the Forest of Arden, near the place where he was raised. These were lines derived not from *Britannia* but from the poet's experience. Of course it is unlikely that he would have encountered so multifarious a gathering of birds as he presents here, but he conjures up an exhilarating fantasy of the beauty and vivacity of the forest. The second extract is from the second part of *Poly-Olbion* and describes another part of England which may have been one of Drayton's favourites, the Peake District of Derbyshire. He had written of this place much earlier in 'An Ode Written in the Peak', a much shorter encapsulation of the 'wonders' there to be enjoyed. In *Poly-Olbion* the Peake is the mother of seven wonders, and hers is the voice lovingly presenting them in turn.

Birds in the Forest of Arden

From *Poly-Olbion*, the Thirteenth Song, lines 41-92

When *Phœbus* lifts his head out of the Winters wave,[5]
No sooner doth the Earth her flowerie bosome brave,
At such time as the Yeere brings on the pleasant Spring,

But Hunts-up to the Morne the feath'red *Sylvans* sing:[6]
And in the lower Grove, as on the rising Knole,
Upon the highest spray of every mounting pole,
Those Quirristers are pearcht with many a speckled breast.
Then from her burnisht gate the goodly glittring East
Guilds every lofty top, which late the humorous Night[7]
Bespangled had with pearle, to please the Mornings sight:
On which the mirthfull Quires, with their cleere open throats,
Unto the joyfull Morne so straine their warbling notes,
That Hills and Valleys ring, and even the ecchoing Ayre
Seemes all compos'd of sounds, about them every where.
The Throstell, with shrill Sharps; as purposely he song[8]
T'awake the lustlesse Sunne; or chyding, that so long
He was in comming forth, that should the thickets thrill:
The Woosell neere at hand, that hath a golden bill;[9]
As Nature him had markt of purpose, t'let us see
That from all other Birds his tunes should different bee:
For, with their vocall sounds, they sing to pleasant May;
Upon his dulcet[10] pype the Merle doth onely play.
When in the lower Brake, the Nightingale hard-by,[11]
In such lamenting straines the joyfull howres doth ply,
As though the other Birds shee to her tunes would draw.
And, but that Nature (by her all-constraining law)
Each Bird to her owne kind this season doth invite,
They else, alone to hear that Charmer of the Night
(The more to use their eares) their voyces sure would spare,
That moduleth her tunes so admirably rare,
As man to set in Parts, at first had learn'd of her.
　To *Philomell* the next, the Linet we prefer;[12]
And by that warbling bird, the Wood-Larke place we then,
The Red-sparrow, the Nope, the Red-breast, and the Wren,[13]
The Yellow-pate:[14] which though shee hurt the blooming tree,
Yet scarce hath any bird a finer pype then shee.
And of those chaunting Fowles, the Goldfinch not behind,
That hath so many sorts descending from her kind.
The Tydie for her notes as delicate as they,[15]
The laughing Hecco, then the counterfetting Jay,[16]
The Softer, with the (Shrill some hid among the leaves,[17]
Some in the taller trees, some in the lower greaves)
Thus sing away the Morne, untill the mounting Sunne,
Through thick exhaled fogs, his golden head hath runne,

And through the twisted tops of our close Covert creeps
To kisse the gentle Shade, this while that sweetly sleeps.
   And neere to these our Thicks, the wild and frightfull Heards,
Not hearing other noyse but this of chattering Birds,
Feed fairely on the Launds; both sorts of seasoned Deere:
Here walke, the stately Red, the freckled Fallowe there:
The Bucks and lusty Stags amongst the Rascalls strew'd,[18]
As sometime gallant spirits amongst the multitude.

1. Graham Parry, *The Trophies of Time: English Antiquarians of the Seventeenth Century*, Oxford University Press, 1995, pp.108-112; Graham Parry, "Sacred Bards' and 'Wise Druids': Drayton and his Archetype of the Poet', *English Literary History*, 51 (1984), 1-16.
2. Richard F. Hardin, *Michael Drayton and the Passing of Elizabethan England*, The University of Kansas Press, 1973, p.7.
3. *Ibid.*, p.25.
4. *The Works of Michael Drayton*, edited by J. William Hebel, Kathleen Tillotson, B. H. Newdigate, and B. E. Juel-Jensen, Oxford: Basil Blackwell, 1931-1941, Vol. IV, *To the Generall Reader,* p.*v.*
5. *Phoebus* was another name for Apollo, associated with the sun, hence the reference here refers to the coming of sunny weather.
6. *Hunts-up*, a call on a hunting-horn to signal the commencement of the hunt; *sylvan*, a woodland dweller.
7. *Humorous,* capricious, given to whims.
8. *Throstell*, song thrush.
9. *Woosell*, ouzel, that is, blackbird. *Merle* is another name for the same bird.
10. Drayton's marginal note: Of all Birds, only the Blackbird whistleth.
11. *Brake*, thicket.
12. *Philomell*, Philomena, in Greek mythology, was changed into a nightingale.
13. *Nope*, bullfinch.
14. *Yellow-pate*, yellow-hammer, a yellow finch.
15. *Tydie*, meaning obscure.
16. *Hecco*, woodpecker.
17. The opening parenthesis is misplaced.
18. *Rascalls*, young deer.

1. St Pauls': Wenceslaus Hollar's etchings of the exterior and interior of old St Paul's, produced for Dugdale's *History of St. Paul's Cathedral in London*, which was published in 1658, are a unique record of the building which was destroyed in the Great Fire of London eight years later. *Reproduced by courtesy of the Guildhall Art Gallery, City of London*

2. Albury, Surrey: a rural scene by Hollar, depicting part of the country seat of his patron Thomas Howard, Earl of Arundel. *Reproduced by courtesy of the Guildhall Art Gallery, City of London*

3. London view: In contrast, a city scene: one of Hollar's numerous depictions of London, this shows part of the city from Southwark, across London Bridge. Unlike the more personal picture at Albury, this is made into a public statement by the angelic embellishment above. *Reproduced by courtesy of the Guildhall Art Gallery, City of London*

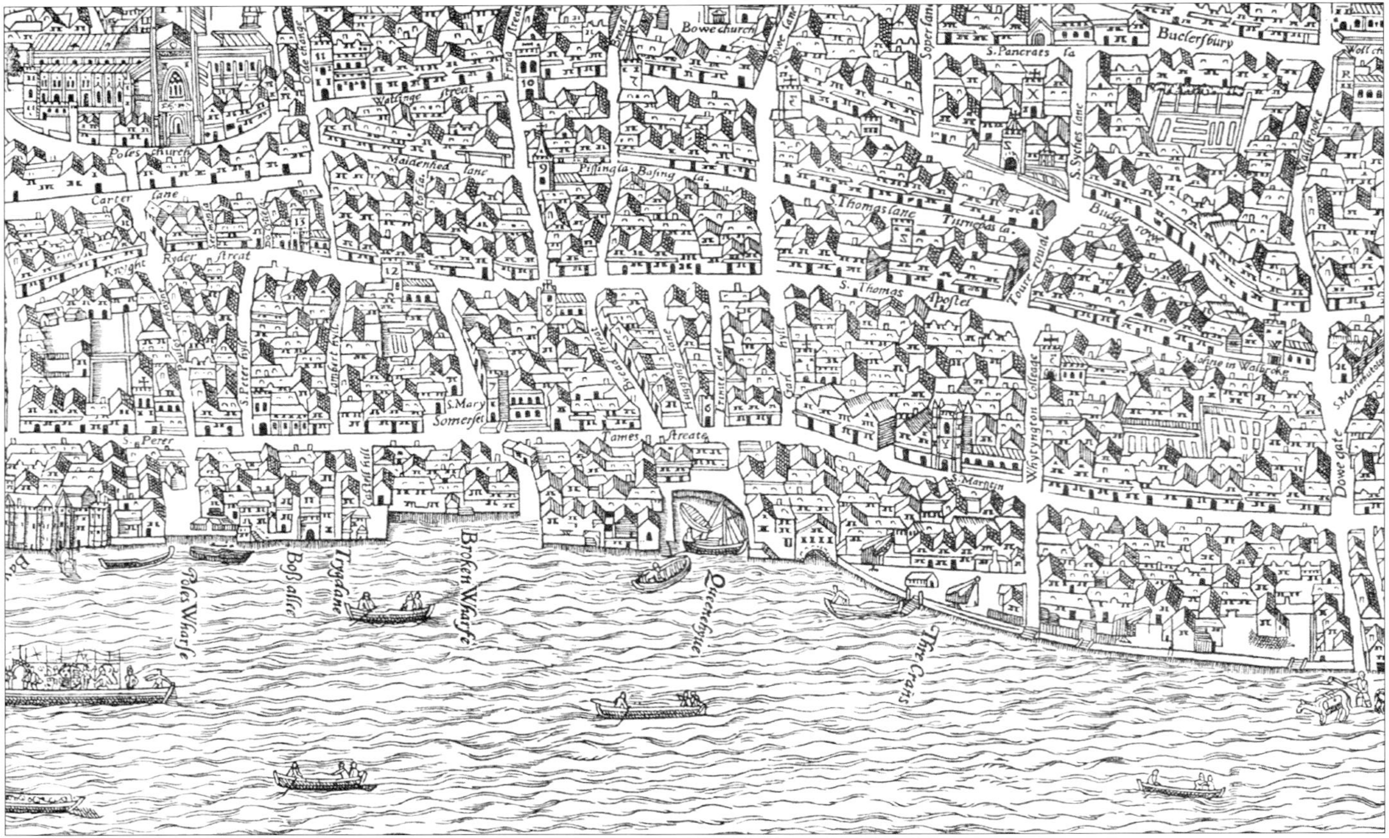

4. A detail from Ralph Agas's map of London, made about 1561, showing part of Bread Street approximately in the centre, running from bottom to top. *Reproduced by courtesy of the Guildhall Art Gallery, City of London*

CHEAPSIDE CROSS
Copied from the Original Print of the Procession of Mary de Medices, on a visit to her Daughter Henrietta Maria.
This Cross was erected 1290 by Edward the 1st in 1441 being very much damaged John Hatherley then
Mayor procured a licence of King Henry ye 6th to re-edify the same in a more beautiful manner for the
honor of the City, this Cross was then curiously wrought, John Fisher, Mercer, gave 600 Marks towards it, the same
was erecting from 1484 to 1486, it was gilt all over in 1522, was new burnished in 1553, gilt again in 1554.
Was again repaired 1595. In 1599 the top of the Cross was taken down it being in a very rotten state, a new
one was put up 1600 covered with lead & gilt. the body of the Cross cleansed of dust: during the grand Rebellion, all the Crosses and Images about the Town were demolished
See Strypes Stow, p 553 & 654 & Pennants London
Pubd May 10.1792 by N Smith Great Mays Buildings St Martins Lane.

5. An eighteenth-century copy of what was perhaps a contemporary picture of the procession of Marie de Medici, who visited her daughter Queen Henrietta Maria in 1638, passing through Cheapside. The Cross and the Little Conduit are in the midst of the thoroughfare. *Reproduced by courtesy of the Guildhall Art Gallery, City of London*

6. Another example of Hollar's work: Windsor Castle. *Reproduced by courtesy of the Guildhall Art Gallery, City of London*

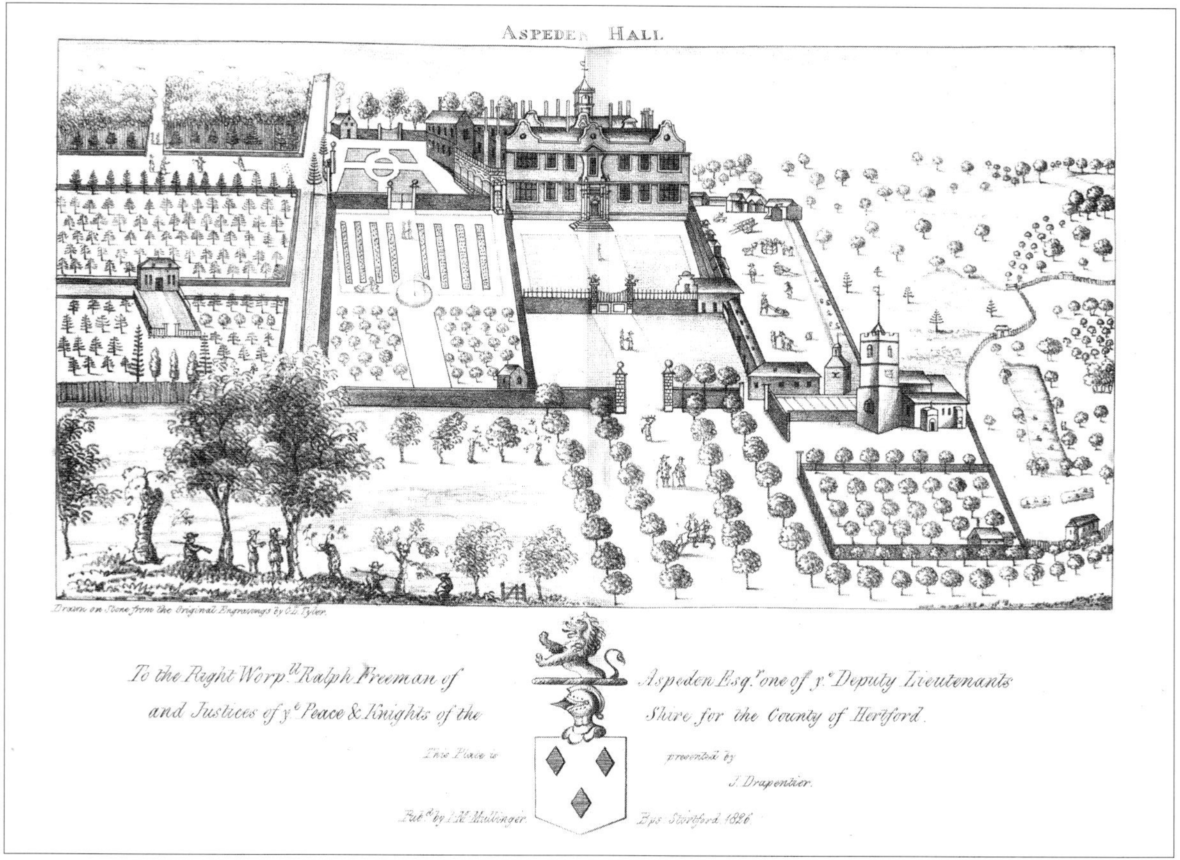

7. Aspeden, Hertfordshire, the seat of Ralph Freeman, from Chauncy's *Historical Antiquities of Hertfordshire.* County surveys normally contained numerous engravings of country houses, paid for by the families who occupied them. *Reproduced with the permission of the Hertfordshire County Council*

Pl. XIII. pa. 174.
To the Rev.d Charles Lyttelton L.L.D. Dean of Exeter This Tolmen in Constantine Parish in Cornwall
is most gratefully inscrib'd by Wm: Borlase.
WB
J. Green Sculp Oxon

8. A dolmen in Cornwall, from Borlase's *Antiquities of Cornwall.* Plates were contributed by subscribers, this one dedicated to the Dean of Exeter Cathedral.
Reproduced with the kind permission of the Cornwall County Council

9. The title page of the 1594 edition of Camden's *Britannia*. The figure of Britannia (which was used on Roman coins) is at the top; the map of Britain is flanked by Neptune, the Roman god of the sea and Ceres, the Roman goddess of agriculture, while below are historical British scenes. The regions named on the map of are those of the various tribes named by the Romans. *Reproduced by courtesy of the Dean and Chapter of Hereford Cathedral*

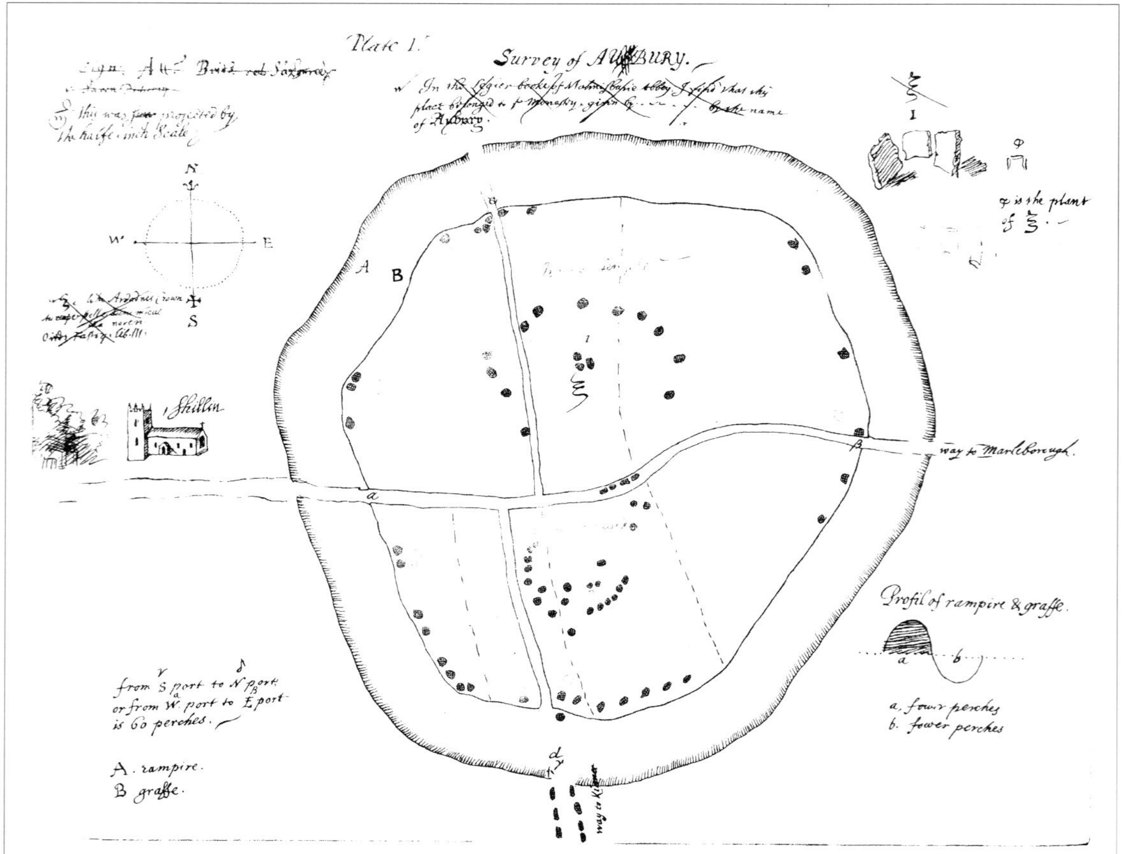

FAC-SIMILE of JOHN AUBREY'S PLAN of the GREAT EARTHWORK, FOSS within it (tinted), and STONES at AVEBURY in WILTSHIRE.

Taken about A.D. 1663. From "Aubrey's Monumenta Britannica," M.S. in the Bodleian Library.

10. Aubrey's plan of Avebury, showing the surrounding ditch both in plan and in profile, and the remaining standing stones. *Reproduced by courtesy of Wiltshire County Council Libraries & Heritage*

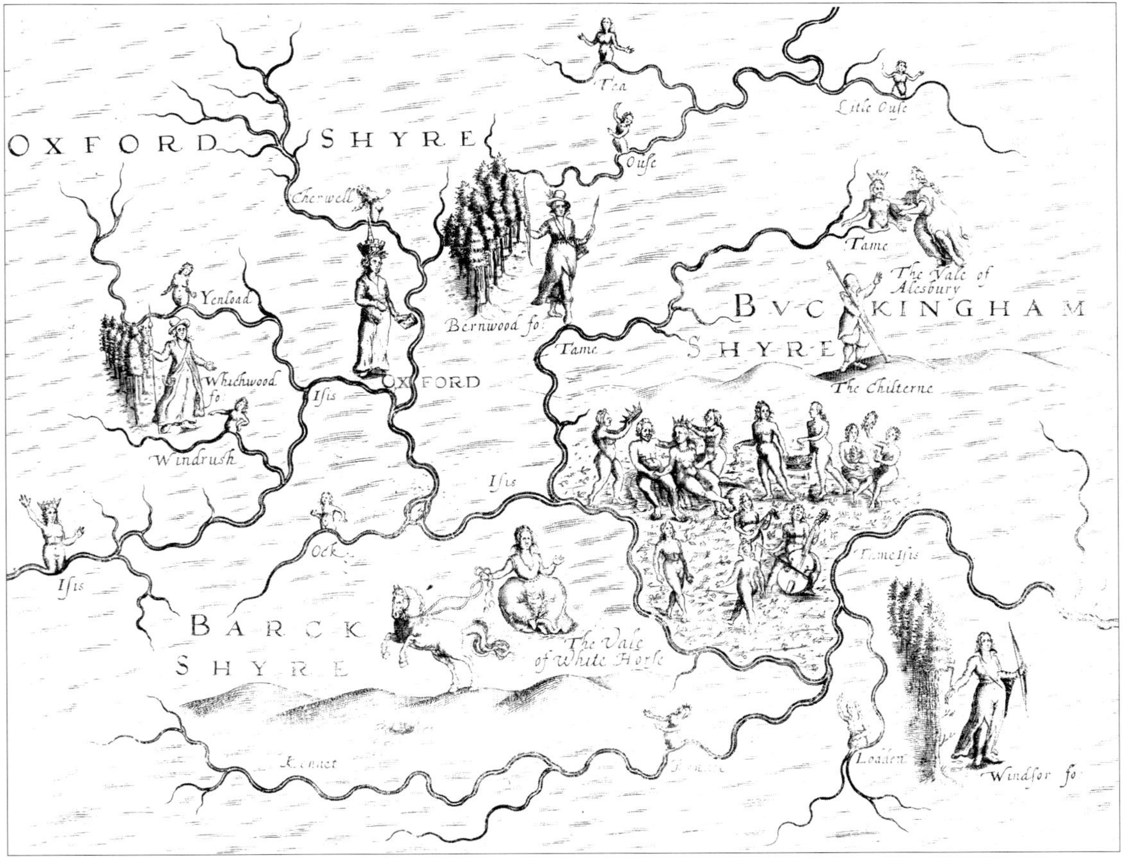

11. A map from *Poly-Olbion*: Oxfordshire. The rivers, participants in singing the 'songs' in Drayton's poem, as well as certain other features, are represented by anthropomorphic pastoral figures. In this case the main event is the 'marriage', that is, the confluence of the Thames and the Isis. *Reproduced by courtesy of the Oxfordshire County Council Photographic Archive*

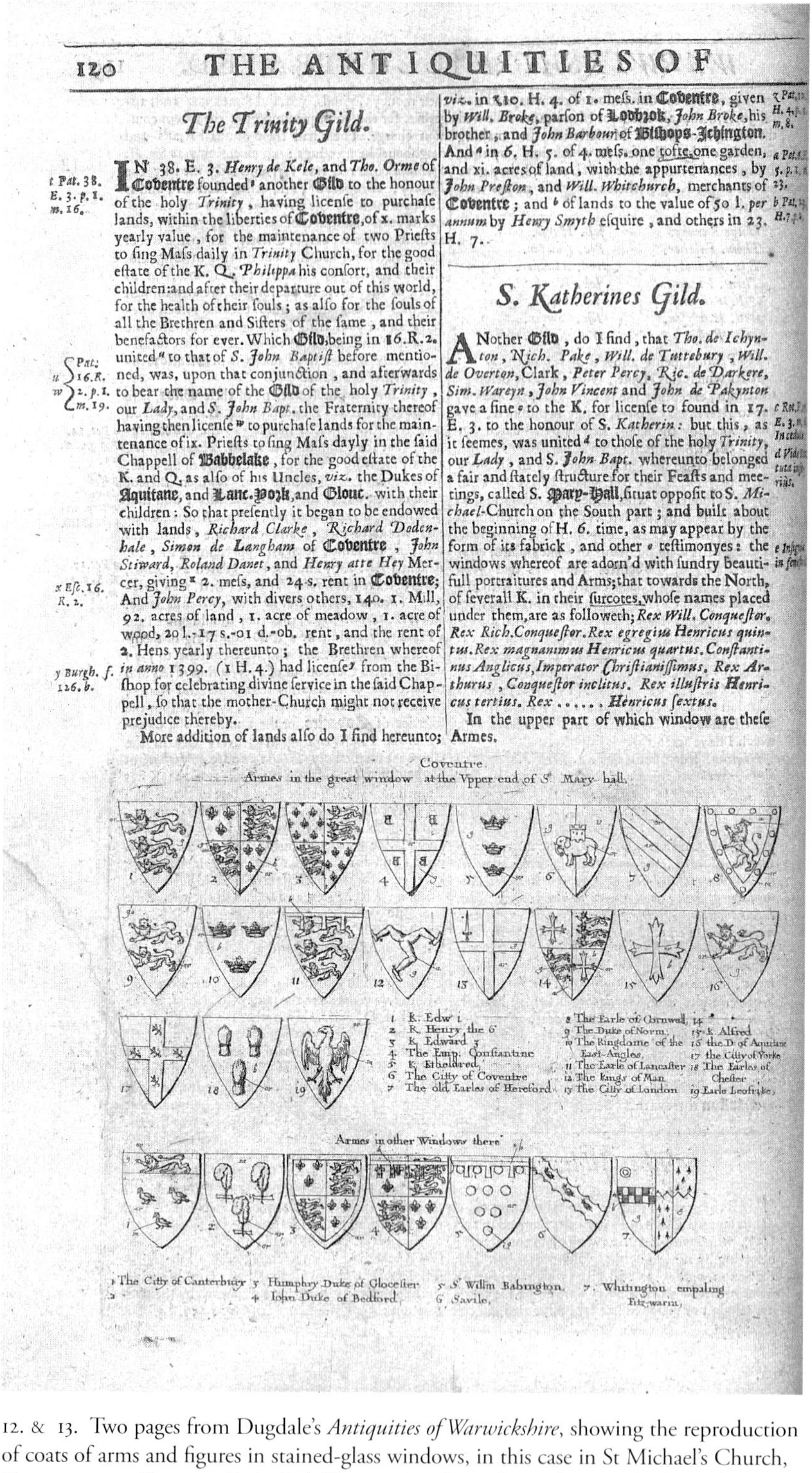

The Trinity Gild.

t Pat. 38. E. 3. p. 1. m. 16. IN 38. E. 3. *Henry de Kele*, and *Tho. Orme* of **Coventre** founded[t] another **Gild** to the honour of the holy *Trinity*, having licenſe to purchaſe lands, within the liberties of **Coventre**, of x. marks yearly value, for the maintenance of two Prieſts to ſing Maſs daily in *Trinity* Church, for the good eſtate of the K. Q. *Philippa* his conſort, and their children: and after their departure out of this world, for the health of their ſouls; as alſo for the ſouls of all the Brethren and Siſters of the ſame, and their benefactors for ever. Which **Gild**, being in 16. R. 2. united[u] to that of *S. John Baptiſt* before mentioned, was, upon that conjunction, and afterwards to bear the name of the **Gild** of the holy *Trinity*, our *Lady*, and *S. John Bapt.* the Fraternity thereof having then licenſe[w] to purchaſe lands for the maintenance of ix. Prieſts to ſing Maſs dayly in the ſaid Chappell of **Babbelake**, for the good eſtate of the K. and Q. as alſo of his Uncles, *viz.* the Dukes of **Aquitane**, and **Lanc. York**, and **Glouc.** with their children: So that preſently it began to be endowed with lands, *Richard Clarke*, *Richard Dodenhale*, *Simon de Langham* of **Coventre**, *John Stiward*, *Roland Danet*, and *Henry atte Hey* Mercer, giving[x] 2. meſs, and 24 s. rent in **Coventre**; And *John Percy*, with divers others, 140. 1. Mill, 92. acres of land, 1. acre of meadow, 1. acre of wood, 20 l.-17 s.-01 d.-ob. rent, and the rent of 2. Hens yearly thereunto; the Brethren whereof *in anno* 1399. (1 H. 4.) had licenſe[y] from the Biſhop for celebrating divine ſervice in the ſaid Chappell, ſo that the mother-Church might not receive prejudice thereby.

u w { Pat. 16. R. 2. p. 1. m. 19.

x Eſc. 16. R. 2.

y Burgh. f. 126. b.

More addition of lands alſo do I find hereunto; *viz.* in [z]10. H. 4. of 1. meſs. in **Coventre**, given by *Will. Broke*, parſon of **Lodbrok**, *John Broke*, his brother, and *John Barbour* of **Biſhops-Ichington**. And[a] in 6. H. 5. of 4. meſs. one tofte, one garden, and xi. acres of land, with the appurtenances, by *John Preſton*, and *Will. Whitchurch*, merchants of **Coventre**; and[b] of lands to the value of 50 l. *per annum* by *Henry Smyth* eſquire, and others in 23. H. 7.

z Pat. 10. H. 4. p. 1. m. 8.

a Pat. 6. H. 5. p. 1. m. 23.

b Pat. 23. H. 7. p. 3.

S. Katherines Gild.

ANother **Gild**, do I find, that *Tho. de Ichynton*, *Nich. Pake*, *Will. de Tuttebury*, *Will. de Overton*, Clark, *Peter Percy*, *Ric. de Darkere*, *Sim. Wareyn*, *John Vincent* and *John de Pakynton* gave a fine[c] to the K. for licenſe to found in 17. E. 3. to the honour of S. *Katherin*: but this, as it ſeemes, was united[d] to thoſe of the holy *Trinity*, our *Lady*, and S. *John Bapt.* whereunto belonged a fair and ſtately ſtructure for their Feaſts and meetings, called S. **Mary-Hall**, ſituat oppoſit to S. *Michael*-Church on the South part; and built about the beginning of H. 6. time, as may appear by the form of its fabrick, and other[e] teſtimonyes: the windows whereof are adorn'd with ſundry beautifull portraitures and Arms; that towards the North, of ſeverall K. in their ſurcotes, whoſe names placed under them, are as followeth; *Rex Will. Conqueſtor. Rex Rich. Conqueſtor. Rex egregius Henricus quintus. Rex magnanimus Henricus quartus. Conſtantinus Anglicus, Imperator Chriſtianiſſimus. Rex Arthurus, Conqueſtor inclitus. Rex illuſtris Henricus tertius. Rex* ..... *Henricus ſextus.*

c Rot. Fin. E. 3. m. ... In cedula.

d Vide ... tuta ... riis.

e In ... in fen...

In the upper part of which window are theſe Armes.

Coventre.
Armes in the great window at the Vpper end of St Mary hall.

1 K. Edw 1
2 R. Henry the 6
3 K. Edward 3
4 The Emp: Conſtantine
5 K. Etheldred,
6 The Citty of Coventre
7 The old Earles of Hereford
8 The Earle of Cornwall,
9 The Duke of Norm:
10 The Kingdome of the East-Angles,
11 The Earle of Lancaſter
12 The kings of Man
13 The Citty of London
14
15 K. Alfred
16 the D. of Aquitane
17 the Citty of Yorke
18 The Earles of Cheſter
19 Earle Leofrike,

Armes in other Windows there

1 The Citty of Canterbury
2
3 Humphry Duke of Gloceſter
4 Iohn Duke of Bedford
5 Sr Willm Babington,
6 Savile,
7 Whitington empaling Fitzwarin,

12. & 13. Two pages from Dugdale's *Antiquities of Warwickshire*, showing the reproduction of coats of arms and figures in stained-glass windows, in this case in St Michael's Church, Coventry, now Coventry Cathedral. The sample of text shows the use of italic and blackletter fonts for personal and place names respectively. *Kindly reproduced from the Warwickshire Collection with the permission of Warwickshire Library and Information Service*

And in those towards the East and West, of divers eminent persons that were admitted of this Fraternity: amongst whom I have made choise of these here placed, to shew the magnificence and state, antiently, of our English nobility; which, through the favour of that learned, and truly noble gentleman *Charles Nevill* Esquire, now Vice-Provost of *Kings-Coll.* in Cambridge (whose lineall Ancestors * most of them be) are out of his speciall honour to their memory, and singular affection to Antiquities, thus, in the formalitie of their habits, lively represented.

* *As a branch of* Bergaveny *descended from the one; and through the heires of* Gresham, Thwaits, Savile, Paston, *and* Beaufort *D. of* Somerset, *from the other.*

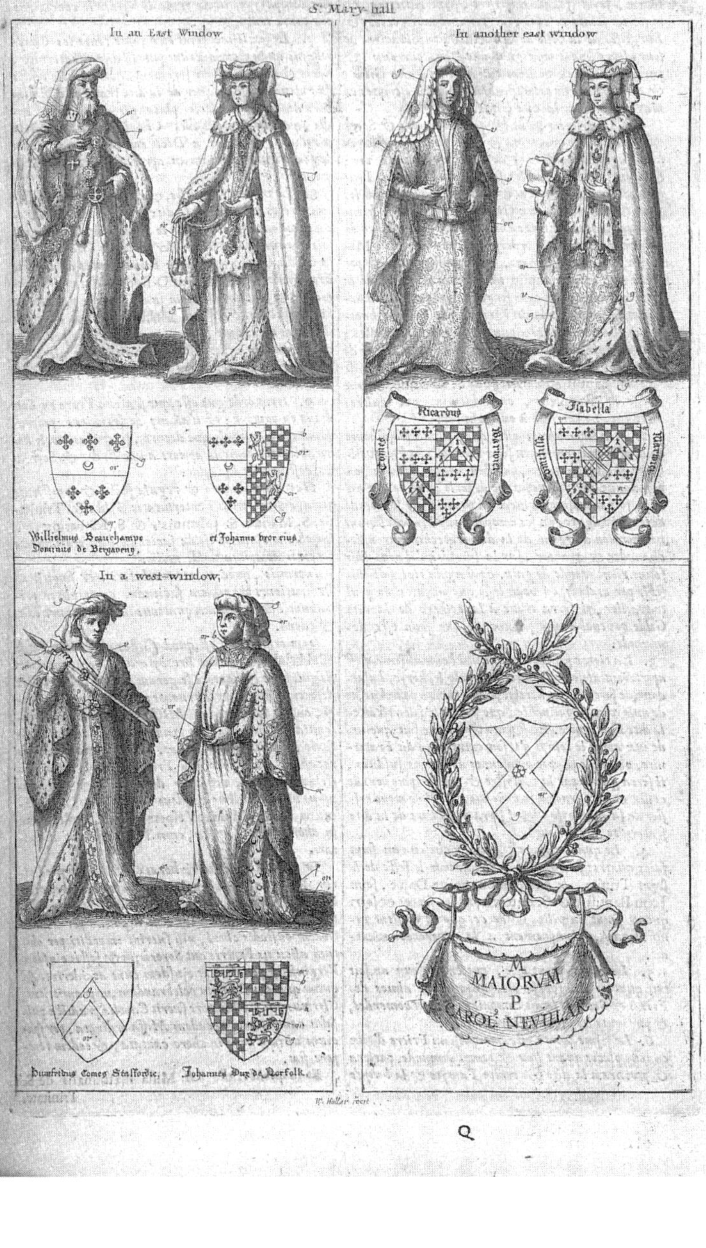

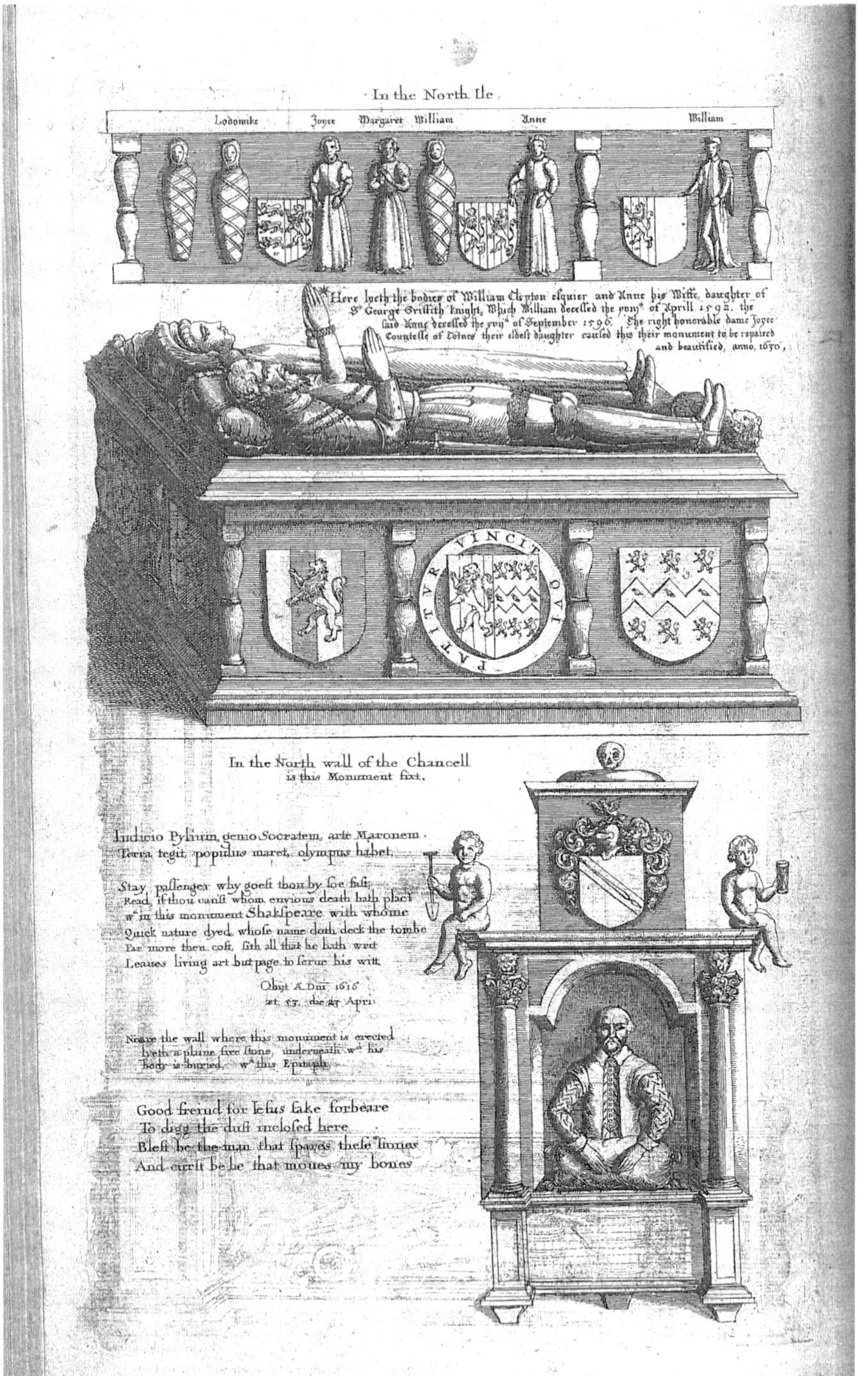

14. Another page from Dugdale's survey of Warwickshire, showing the memorial to William Shakespeare, less famous then than now, in Holy Trinity Church, Stratford-upon-Avon. The bust is not the same as that seen today, which was erected in 1748 and which shows the playwright holding a pen and paper. *Kindly reproduced from the Warwickshire Collection with the permission of Warwickshire Library and Information Service*

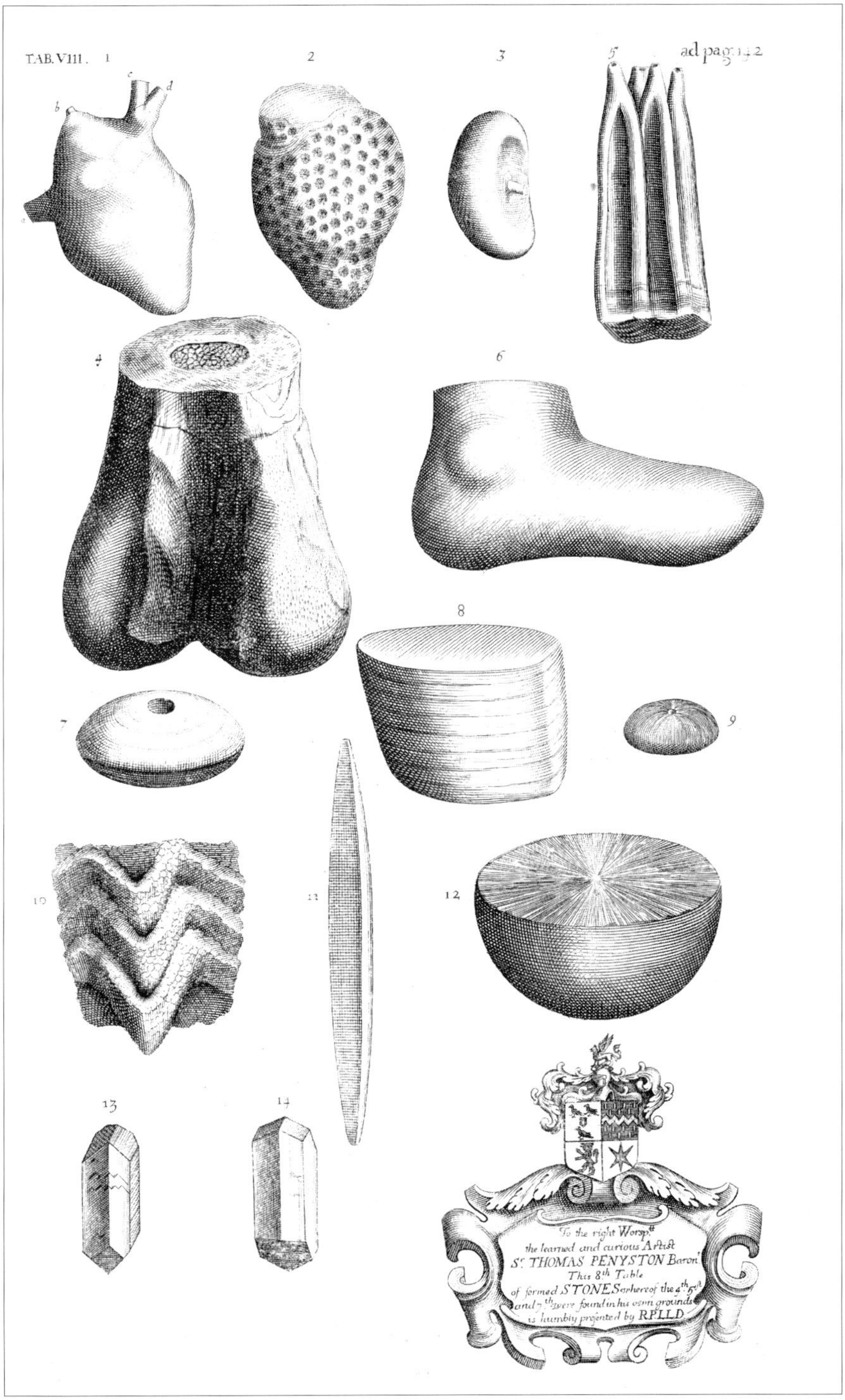

15. Illustrations of 'formed stones' from Robert Plot's *Natural History of Oxfordshire*. The stone discussed in the included extract is that numbered 4. *Reproduced by courtesy of the Oxfordshire County Council Photographic Archive*

16. A picturesque scene from the pages of William Gilpin's book on the lakes and mountains of Cumberland and Westmorland. This illustration is amongst the pages in which Derwentwater and Windermere are described. *Reproduced with permission of the Cumbria County Council*

17. The Wakes, Gilbert White's house and garden at Selborne, photographed by the author in 2004.

EAST MIDLANDS

XV
Albion—Derbyshire: Michael Drayton

The wonders of the Peake

From *Poly-Olbion*, the Twenty-sixth Song, lines 397-494

My dreadfull daughters borne, your mothers deare delight,
Great Natures chiefest worke, wherein shee shew'd her might;
Yee darke and hollow Caves, the pourtratures of Hell,
Where Fogs, and misty Damps continually doe dwell;
O yee my onely Joyes, my Darlings, in whose eyes,
Horror assumes her seat, from whose abiding flyes
Thicke Vapours, that like Rugs still hang the troubled ayre,
Yee of your mother *Peake*, the hope and onely care:[1]
O thou my first and best, of thy blacke Entrance nam'd
The *Divels-Arse*, in me, O be thou not asham'd,[2]
Nor thinke thy selfe disgrac'd, or hurt thereby at all,
Since from thy horror first men us'd thee so to call:
For as amongst the *Moores*, the Jettiest blacke are deem'd
The beautifulst of them; so are your kind esteem'd,
The more ye gloomy are, more fearfull and obscure,
(That hardly any eye your sternnesse may endure)
The more yee famous are, and what name men can hit,
That best may ye expresse, that best doth yee befit:
For he that will attempt thy blacke and darksome jawes,
In midst of Summer meets with Winters stormy flawes,
Cold Dewes, that over head from thy foule roofe distill,
And meeteth under foot, with a dead sullen Rill,
That *Acheron* it selfe, a man would thinke he were
Imediately to passe, and stay'd for *Charon* there;[3]
Thy Flore drad Cave, yet flat, though very rough it be,
With often winding turnes: then come thou next to me,

My prettie daughter *Poole*, my second loved child,[4]
Which by that noble name was happily enstild,
Of that more generous stock, long honor'd in this Shire,
Of which amongst the rest, one being out-law'd here,
For his strong refuge tooke this darke and uncouth place,
An heyre-loome ever since, to that succeeding race:
Whose entrance though deprest below a mountaine steepe,
Besides so very strait, that who will see't, must creepe
Into the mouth thereof, yet being once got in,
A rude and ample Roofe doth instantly begin
To raise it selfe aloft, and who doth so intend
The length thereof to see, still going must ascend
On mightie slippery stones, as by a winding stayre,
Which of a kind of base darke Alabaster are,
Of strange and sundry formes, both in the Roofe and Floore,
As Nature show'd in thee, what ne'er was seene before.
For *Elden* thou my third, a Wonder I preferre[5]
Before the other two, which perpendicular
Dive'st downe into the ground, as if an entrance were
Through earth to lead to hell, ye well might judge it here,
Whose depth is so immense, and wondrously profound,
As that long line which serves the deepest Sea to sound,
Her bottome never wrought, as though the vast descent,
Through this Terrestriall Globe directly poynting went
Our *Antipods* to see, and with her gloomy eyes,
To glote upon those Starres, to us that never rise;
That downe into this hole if that a stone yee throw,
An acres length from thence, (some say that) yee may goe,
And comming backe thereto, with a still listning eare,
May heare a sound as though that stone then falling were.
   Yet for her Caves, and Holes, *Peake* onely not excells,
But that I can againe produce those wondrous Wells
Of *Buckston*, as I have, that most delicious Fount,[6]
Which men the second Bath of *England* doe account,
Which in the primer raignes, when first this well began
To have her vertues knowne unto the blest *Saint Anne*,
Was consecrated then, which the same temper hath,
As that most daintie Spring, which at the famous *Bath*,
Is by the Crosse enstild, whose fame I much preferre,
In that I doe compare my daintiest Spring to her,
Nice sicknesses to cure, as also to prevent,

And supple their cleare skinnes, which Ladies oft frequent;
Most full, most faire, most sweet, and most delicious sourse.
To this a second Fount, that in her naturall course,
As mighty *Neptune* doth, so doth shee ebbe and flow.
If some *Welsh* Shires report, that they the like can show,
I answere those, that her shall so no wonder call,
So farre from any Sea, not any of them all.
My Caves, and Fountaines thus delivered you, for change,
A little Hill I have, a wonder yet more strange,
Which though it be of light, and almost dusty sand,
Unaltred by the wind, yet firmly doth it stand;
And running from the top, although it never cease,
Yet doth the foot thereof, no whit at all increase.[7]
Nor is it at the top, the lower, or the lesse,
As Nature had ordain'd, that so its owne excesse,
Should by some secret way within it selfe ascend,
To feed the falling backe; with this yet doe not end
The wonders of the *Peake*, for nothing that I have,
But it a wonders name doth very justly crave:
A Forrest such have I, (of which when any speake,
Of me they it enstile, The Forrest of the *Peake*)
Whose Hills doe serve for Brakes, the Rocks for shrubs and trees,
To which the *Stag* pursu'd, as to the thicket flees;
Like it in all this Isle, for sternnesse there is none,
When Nature may be said to show you groves of stone,
As she in little there, had curiously compyld
The model of the vast *Arabian* stony Wyld.
The as it is suppos'd, in *England* that there be
Seven wonders: to my selfe so have I here in me,
My seaven before rehearc'd, allotted me by Fate,
Her greatnesse, as therein ordain'd to imitate.

1. The description of natural features in Derbyshire as the 'Wonders of the Peak' was well established in the seventeenth century. The philosopher Thomas Hobbes, in 1636, wrote a poem so entitled, after a visit to the area, and a satirical poem of the same title was published in 1681 by Charles Cotton, a poet and horticulturalist. The designation of features such as the moors as 'wonders' was treated with scepticism by many visitors from other parts of the country.
2. The Devil's Arse is a popular name for Peak Cavern, a natural cave at Castleton, Derbyshire.
3. *Acheron*, in Greek mythology, the branch of the river Styx over which Charon, the ferryman, took newly-dead souls to Hades.

4. Poole's Cavern, named after an outlaw who was said to have lived there in the fifteenth century.
5. Elden Hole is a cavern which was traditionally thought to be bottomless.
6. Buxton, a spa town, was established by the Romans with facilities similar to those at Bath. It was developed again in the eighteenth century, especially by the Dukes of Devonshire, whose seat at Chatsworth is nearby. St Anne's Well, in Buxton, is the geothermal spring, from which water rises at a constant temperature of 28°C.
7. Drayton is presumably referring to Mam-Tor, the 'Shivering Mountain' which consists of unstable layers of shale and gritstone which are constantly slipping.

XVI

Stamford, Lincolnshire: Richard Butcher (1586/7–1664)

Stamford in Lincolnshire has been the subject of antiquarian studies by several of its citizens, the first being Richard Butcher, whose book, *The Survey and Antiquities of the town of Stamford*, was printed in 1646, with a slightly enlarged edition appearing in 1660. It was republished in 1717 in a volume which also included Wilhelm Bedwell's description of Tottenham High Cross, London, which had first come out in 1631. The next appearance of Butcher's book (taken from its 1660 edition) was as an appendix to a very much more substantial work, *Academia Tertia Anglicana, or, The Antiquarian Annals of Stanford*, compiled by Francis Peck and published in 1727.[1]

Little can be said of Butcher because little is known of him. He was an innkeeper, victualler and, from 1626, Town Clerk. From town records he seems to have had numerous conflicts with other officers of Stamford, one of which was the reason for his dismissal from his post in 1634. In 1646 he became a Capital Burgess of the town (that was, a member of the second of the two chambers of the town's council), but was forced to resign in 1648. From then till 1660 he was prominent in a series of local disputes, but by 1663 had managed to recover his position in the town chambers, and even became Town Clerk again in 1664, not long before his death in the same year. His book is short, some of his history is imaginative, and he includes criticisms of some of his fellow councillors, but his work is valuable in that it gives an idea of the structure and processes of local government at the time.

The rather unusual extract which follows is one of the 1660 additions to Butcher's book, but it is not a description of a particular place, rather it is one which gives some fleeting images of village life in the 1640s. It is the story of a miraculous cure wrought by a mysterious visitor, and its inclusion in the town survey suggests that it had made a strong impression on members of the community, or at least those members with whom Butcher was sympathetic. Both the reading-matter which the subject of the cure mentions and the mantra-like refrain to fear God indicate a puritan sense of godliness and piety, but the method of the cure involves rituals which belong more to the realm of folklore and superstition. Butcher himself was insistent that it was evidence of the intervention of God, commenting:

> It is a farther memorable thing here to sett downe the uncharitable censures of those that call themselves ministers of the gospel, as touching this occasion. Some say, that this old man was a witch; others, that he was a divell changed into an angell of light. (As if the divell would advise any man to serve God, & to trust in him!) disclaiming all miracles as being ceased, & (as if God limited) never considering the infinite mercy of the Omnipotent, in shewing himself miraculously in this atheisticall age, in which men think there is neither God nor divell, heaven nor hell, angel nor spirit, day of resurrection or day of judgment or of account, which, if they did suppose, they would never dare to doe what is done dayly amongst us. …[2]

In the telling of the story some tantalising background details may be glimpsed. The door of the poor man's house opens directly onto the street, and, once the visitor has entered, the two men sit with the door open. We learn something of what food and drink the poor man had in his home, and of the clothing a man might be wearing. The sick man has received a medical opinion but cannot have treatment because he is so poor. We learn what might have been regarded as physical exercise, and how hospitality might have been offered. None of these is something which the story was intended to convey, but it is in texts such as this that we can glean some impression of how village life might have been lived. And while great houses of England still stand and may even still be furnished as they were in the past, the village houses of ordinary people are gone and cannot be brought back.

Samuel Wallis's miracle

From *The Survey and Antiquitie of the Towne of Stanford* (from Francis Peck, *Academia Tertia Anglicana,* separate pagination, pp.14–16)

Upon Whitsunday, which was in the year of our Lord God 1658. about six of the clock in the afternoone, after evening sermon, I being newly up, &, as I sat by the fire, reading in that little book called Abrahams suit for Sodom,[3] about halfe an hour; so it was that the woman who kept me was gone forth, & had shut the doores upon me. [*There being no body in the house then with him, & his wife gone into the country to seek relief of some friends; finding himself a little lightsome, he crept to the fireside. And as he was reading …*][4] In the mean time, whilst I was reading in the book, I heard one rapp at the doore. I thought it to be a stranger, because it was sabbath day. So I was constrained to go to the door my self; & I took my stick in my hand, & by the wall with my other hand, as well as the Lord God did enable me, I went to the door. There I beheld a proper, tall, grave, old man. Thus he said, friend, I pray thee give an old pilgrime a cup of small beere.[5] And I said, Sir, I pray you come in, & welcome. And he said, I am no Sir, therefore call me not Sir; but come in I must, for I cannot pass by thy door before I come in. And I said, come in I pray you, and welcome: For I thought he could not passe by my door untill he had dranke, he was so drye; So we both came in together, & left the door open. So as well as the Lord God did enable me, with my stick in one hand & the wall in my other hand, I went & drew him a cup of small beer [*in a little jug-pot*], & gave it him in his hand, & satt me downe. And he walked twice or thrice to & fro; & then he drank, & walked againe as before, & drank againe. And so he did likewise three times, before he had drank it all [*who took it by the bottom, & drank a little, & then walked*]. Then he set the cup in the window by me. All this while he said nothing to me, nor I to him. Then I thought he would have been goeing; but he was not. He walked twice or thrice as he did before. And, when he came almost at me, he said, friend, thou art not well? I said, no, truly, Sir, I have not beene well this many years. He said, what is thy disease? I said, a deep consumption, Sir; our doctors say past cure.[6] He said, there they said well: But what have they given thee for it? I said, Sir, truly nothing. For indeed I am a very poor man, & not able to follow doctors councell. Therefore I do commit my selfe to the almighty God; what his will is, I am content with it. He said, in that thou sayest very well. Then I will tell thee what thou shalt doe, & by the helpe and power of almighty God above, thou shalt be well (do but remember my words, & observe to doe them; but however thou dost, above all things fear God, & serve him) To morrow, when thou risest up, go into thy garden, & get there two leaves of red sage & one of bloodworte; & put these three leaves into a cup of thy small beer, & let them lie in it three dayes. Drink as often as need requires; &, when the cup is empty, fill it again. But this remember, that thou lett the leaves lye in still untill the fourth day in the morning; then cast them away, & put in thereto the fourth day in the morning three more fresh leaves. I pray thee remember my words, & observe, & do them, but however thou dost, above all things fear God, & serve him. The fourth day in the morning is the first day of the three againe. And so continue thus doeing every fourth day in the morning, for the space of twelve dayes together; neither more, nor less. I pray thee remember my wordes, & observe, & doe them; but howsoever thou dost, above all things, fear God, & serve him. And for the space of these twelve days, thou must drink noe strong beer or ale. But afterwards thou mayest; a little to suffice [*strengthen*] nature. And thou shalt see, through Gods great goodness & mercy unto thee, before these twelve days be past, thy disease to be cured, & [*the frame of*] thy body altered. I doubted the truth of these things, that they could do me small good. I said, Sir, be these good for all consumptions? He said, I tell thee remember my words, & observe to do them. But howsoever thou dost, above all things, fear God, & serve him. Then he said, friend, this is not all; thou must change the aire too for thy health. And I said, what mean you by saying that I must change the aire? He said, you must go three, four, five miles or more [*or if it be twenty miles off*]; the further, the better. And there you must continue in the fresh aire by the space of one month. And thou must goe as speedily as thou possibly canst doe [*after the twelve days are over*]; or else a very grievous fit of sickness will follow very suddenly; yet, through Gods great goodness & mercy unto thee [*by doing this*], thou mayest avoid this likewise. And thou shalt see, through Gods great goodness & mercy unto thee, & that before the month be up & within these twelve days [*ended*], that the cloaths which thou now wearest, thou shalt not be able to wear with ease [*thy body will be grown so much*]. I said, Sir, but if it may please the almighty God so far to enable me as to goe into our owne fields two or three times a day, will that not serve? He said, I tell thee it will not. For this aire, where the infection was taken, is not so properly good to cure the same disease. Therefore I pray thee remember my words, & observe, & doe them; but however thou dost, above all things, fear God, & serve him. I said, Sir, I had thoughts to be let blood, as weak a creature as I am? He said, no, friend; by no means possibly. For thou'lt see the great goodness of God unto thee, & that before the month be up, & within these twelve days, thy blood shall be as good as ever thou hadst it in thy life. But this observe, thy joynts will be weak as long as thou livest. I pray thee remember my words, & observe to doe them; but however thou doest, above all things, fear God, & serve him: So, friend, I must be going. So when I saw that he was a going indeed, I thought he might as well be an [*sic*] hungry as dry. So I said, Sir, if it please you to eat any bread & butter, or bread & cheese, you shall be very wellcome. For truly I am a very poor man, & have no other food in the house. For, if I had, you should have it, & wellcome. But he said, no, friend; I will not eat any thing: the Lord Christ is sufficient for me. Very seldome doe I drink any beer neither, but that which comes from the rocke.[7] So, friend, the Lord God of heaven be with thee. I said likewise, God in heaven be with you. [*When Wallace saw him go out of doors, he went to shut them after him. But the old man returned half way into the entry again, & said, friend, I pray thee remember what I have said unto thee, & do it; but above all things, whatsoever thou dost, fear God, & serve him. And so they parted. Wallace adds, that he saw him pass along the street, some half a score yards from his door; & so he went in. But he was not seen of any body else, though some neighbours were standing at their door, opposite to the said Wallaces house.*][8] My condition was such at that time that the skin clave to my bones for want of flesh. It was parcht & dry; with a yellow skin & white scurf, upon it. Upon the fourth day [*four days after Wallace had made use of the leaves aforementioned, there arose a scurfe upon his body, &, when that came off, under it a new skin, like that of a sucking child*] afterwards (when I was rising out of my bed) the aforesaid white scurfe came off of my bosome, & I wondred what it was? I rubb'd my hand upon my body, & the more I rubb'd my hand there, the more it came off. So that day, & that night, it all came off. The next morning, when I arose, I lookt upon my body: The yellow skin was dryed, which nobody ever saw but I: & the same was broke into little scales, but a little bigger than the white scurfe was. So the yellow skin & white scurfe came both off together in three days time; & under them was a young tender skin all over my body, like as a young child born of his mother. And so, blessed be God, I grew every day in flesh more & more, until that my cloaths (as the old man said unto me) were so little that I could not weare them with ease. And, blessed be God, I do continue both in health & strength from day to day. [*By the end of the twelve days he was as healthful & strong as ever he was; only this he says, that when he came to sit down, his knees would smite together; so that he still found a weakness in his joynts, as was foretold him. He said also, that one day within the time prescribed, by the solicitation of some friends, he drank a little strong drink, & immediately his speech was taken from him for a space of twenty four hours.*] The habit of the old man was as followeth. [*As for the description of this old mans person & habit, thus he related it. He was tall & antient. His hair as white as wool, &c. He wore a fashionable hat, & a little narrow band. His coat & hose [that is, his breeches] were both of a purple colour; his stockings pure white, &c.*] His hatt was fashionable. His hair of his head was white, curl'd up to his hatt. His beard was white & broad. But a little hair upon both sides his cheeks; & of a fine ruddy complexion. His band but a little turn'd from his coller. His coat was of a purple couler, button'd down to his waste. His britches of the same couler & cloth; all new to see to. His britches had no trimming at the knees. His stockens was very white; whether linnen, or jersey, I know not. His shooes was black, tyed with the same colour'd strings that his suit was. His hand was pure white. No gloves that I know of; nor cuffs that I saw. He had a white stick in his hand. The day was rainy, from morning untill night [*as many remember'd*]; but he had not one spott of dirt upon his shooes or stockings, that I could perceive; or raine upon his cloaths.

1. This last edition is the most accessible, because it was republished as a facsimile in 1979 by EP Publishing Limited. This edition also contains an introduction by A. Rogers and J. S. Hartley, which is the source of biographical information used here.
2. Francis Peck, *Academia Tertia Anglicana*, second pagination, p.16.
3. *Abrahams suite for Sodome A sermon preached at Pauls Crosse the 25. of August. 1611,* by the Lincolnshire preacher Robert Milles, was printed in London in 1612. Sodom is likened to the society of contemporary times, warning how few are amongst the elect and lamenting how many are sinners and how profligate their sins: it is a veritable treatise of 'fire and brimstone'.
4. Italicised text in square brackets is that which is included as footnotes, as Peck explains thus:

   The famous presbyterian divine Mr. Samuel Clerk, Minister of St Benet Fink, in his examples, Lond. 1671. fol. vol. 2. p. 18. has inserted, 'a true & faithful relation of one Samuel Wallace, &c. whereof he gave this account, with much affection & sensibleness of the lords mercy & goodness to him, upon April 7. 1659.' Which account in Mr. Clerk is much the same with this in Mr. Butcher. I shall not therefore tire the reader with a repetition of it in Mr. Clerks words, but only where any material difference, or enlargement, occurs, set down the same at the foot of the page.
5. *Small beer* was a low-alcohol beer, often drunk for breakfast and given to children. It was preferred by many to water as a drink because it was more likely to be clean.
6. *Consumption*, a disease causing wasting of the body, including, but not confined to, pulmonary tuberculosis.
7. Peck's footnote here:

   I heard my own father once speak of this story to some Stanford neighbours, with this remarkable circumstance, that the old man should tell Wallis, that he almost never drank any thing but water, & that the water he drank was sometimes the water of St Thomas's well. That well, said my father, was the well you know in such a place. I heard him describe the place, but being then very young, can only remember it was somewhere without Stanford on the east, not far from the Uffington road. I have since enquired of several persons, but they can none of them tell me of any such well.
8. Peck's footnote here:

   Now whereas Wallis here says no body saw the old man but himself, I understand him speaking to the best of his knowledge. For I was told by the Reverend Mr. Samuel Rogers now [1726] vicar of All Saints, in Stanford; that he once heard his father the late Mr. John Rogers affirm, that he heard the late lady Cust (who lived to a very great age) say, that she [being then a maiden, &] living at the black friers in Stanford when these things happened, walking forth to take the air [on Whitsunday evening, & returning homewards] met a venerable, comely old man, in his person & dress exactly the same as described by Wallis. Which is not impossible; only the day being rainy from morning to night, it is much any young lady should be abroad in the wet.

EAST ANGLIA

XVII
Norfolk: Thomas Browne (1605–1682)

Now remembered chiefly as the author of some of the most admired prose composed in the English language, Thomas Browne was a scholar of classical learning, science, and religion. While he was a respected practising physician in Norwich and the father of twelve children, he was the author of *Religio Medici*, one of the most celebrated personal confessions of religion of the seventeenth century; he was a distinguished natural philosopher, scientist, and antiquary who addressed an encyclopedic range of issues in his *Pseudodoxia Epidemica*, a calendar of popular false beliefs; and he created in *Urne-Buriall* and *The Garden of Cyrus*, meditations on death and life respectively, two of the masterpieces of contemplative thought in English literature. As well as his major works, he produced numerous miscellaneous tracts, essays, letters, and notes covering a vast array of topics.

Browne was born in London, and studied from the age of ten at Winchester College, where his education during six years consisted firstly in Latin and, later, also in Greek. He would have studied Lily's Latin *Grammar* and the then popular texts of Ovid, Virgil, Cato, and Mantuan, and Latin translations of the New Testament; these he would have analysed, memorised, translated into English and then back into Latin, while composing Latin sentences to develop skills in syntax, figures of speech, and prosody. Such were the rigours of the grammar school curriculum following the Renaissance, but Browne was obviously one for whom these studies were enormously beneficial and enjoyable. He matriculated to Pembroke College, Oxford University, whence he received his BA in 1626 and his MA in 1629. These courses were still based on the medieval *trivium* (grammar, logic, and rhetoric) and *quadrivium* (arithmetic, geometry, astronomy, and music), as well as the philosophies: moral, natural, and metaphysical. He then studied medicine for four years, attending successively the universities at Montpellier, Padua and Leiden. All these elements of his education contributed to the astonishingly comprehensive breadth of his mature thinking and writing.

Although he lived through a period of significant religious and social upheaval in English history, he seems neither to have participated in it nor been effected by it. That said, it may be simply that he chose not to write about the events, so we cannot know what he did and thought. His major works, however, were all completed during the two decades of civil war and interregnum (*Religio Medici* in 1643, *Pseudodoxia Epidemica* in 1646, and *Hydriotaphia*, or *Urne-Buriall* as it is usually known, and *The Garden of Cyrus* in 1658). *A Letter to a Friend upon Occasion of the Death of his Intimate Friend* and *Christian Morals*, composed in 1656 and the 1670s respectively, were published posthumously, as well as numerous shorter works which were still in manuscript at his death. His work was well received, especially *Religio Medici*, which had eight editions during his lifetime. His writings were much praised by subsequent literary critics, including Samuel Johnson, Coleridge, and Hazlitt. Browne was knighted in Norwich by King Charles II in 1671.

Religio Medici is thought to have been composed in 1634, some years before it first appeared in an anonymous and unauthorised edition in 1642. (Browne had circulated copies of the manuscript amongst friends.) It is a statement of personal belief, albeit one which is based on an adherence to the faith of the orthodox Church of England. It is a religion of latitude and moderation in which differences within the realm of Christianity are to be accepted and resolved by reason: '… where the Scripture is silent, the Church is my Text; where that speakes, 'tis but my Comment; where there is a joynt silence of both, I borrow not the rules of my Religion from *Rome* or *Geneva*, but the dictates of my owne reason …'[1] But religion does not reveal all, for God '…is wise in all, wonderfull in what we conceive, but far more in what we comprehend not, for we behold him but asquint upon reflex or shadow … to pry into the maze of his Counsels, is not onely folly in Man, but presumption even in Angels …'[2] Moreover God is revealed in other ways:

> … Thus there are two bookes from whence I collect my Divinity; besides that written one of God, another of his servant Nature, that universall and publik Manuscript, that lies expans'd unto the eyes of all; those that never saw him in the one, have discovered him in the other: This was the Scripture and Theology of the Heathens; the naturall motion of the Sun made them more admire him, than its supernaturall station did the Children of Israel; the ordinary effects of nature wrought more admiration in them, than in all his other miracles; surely the Heathens knew better how to joyne and reade these mysticall letters, than wee Christians …[3]

Browne's book was an immediate success: it was a time of considerable religious debate, and devotional literature was popular. But it was a time also of extremes, of Puritan beliefs ranging from the moderate to the apocalyptic, of iconoclasts defacing cathedrals, of Laudian reform ending with the execution of the Primate of the Church, and of the continuing fear of resurgent Catholicism. To many, Browne's text was a religious profession which was sensible, balanced, tolerant, compassionate. Several writers annotated and commented on *Religio Medici*, and it was praised for its wit and 'sweetness'.[4]

That 'Nature' should be a source of 'Divinity' was a tenet which complemented Browne's scientific research. He accepted, moreover, the Baconian program for natural philosophy: skepticism of accepted beliefs and of authorities from the past, and the adoption of a system of empirical enquiry based on experiment and inductive reasoning. The legacy of scholasticism was scientific knowledge to which nothing had been added since Aristotle, and which was the secret province of a few; Bacon prepared the way for open and shared research by a community of scholars who worked scientifically, and, indeed, after the restoration of the monarchy, Bacon became a kind of patron saint of the Royal Society. The particular scientific project which Browne took upon himself was a response to a call by Bacon for the exposure of popular errors of belief, and this he achieved in 1646 with his *Pseudodoxia Epidemica*, which came to be given the name 'Vulgar Errors'.[5] The book is divided into chapters dealing with major categories of knowledge: a general section on causes and origins of erroneous beliefs; then beliefs concerning minerals; then plants; insects; animals; Man; then misconceptions portrayed in pictures; customs; and finally geographical and historical knowledge. Thus the section on animals addresses questions such as: 'That an Elephant hath no joints'; 'That an Horse hath no gall'; 'That a Pigeon hath no Gall'; 'That a Bever to escape the Hunter bites off his testicles or stones'; 'That a Badger hath the Legs of one side shorter than of the other'. The analysis of this last is an example of one of the shorter discussions presented by Browne, but nevertheless shows how he applied his learning from the ancients, his observations, and his reasoning to the refutation of a 'vulgar error':

> That a Brock or Badger hath the legs on one side shorter then of the other, though an opinion perhaps not very ancient, is yet very general; received not only by Theorists and unexperienced believers, but assented unto by most who have the opportunity to behold and hunt them daily. Which notwithstanding upon enquiry I find repugnant unto the three Determinators of Truth, Authority, Sense, and Reason. For first, *Albertus Magnus* speaks dubiously, confessing he could not confirm the verity hereof; but *Aldrovandus* plainly affirmeth, there can be no such inequality observed. And for my own part, upon indifferent enquiry, I cannot discover this difference, although the regardable side be defined, and the brevity by most imputed unto the left.

> Again, It seems no easie affront unto Reason, and generally repugnant unto the course of Nature; for if we survey the total set of Animals, we may in their legs, or Organs of progression, observe an equality of length, and parity of Numeration; that is, not any to have an odd legg, or the supporters and movers of one side not exactly answered by the other. Although the hinder may be unequal unto the fore and middle legs, as in Frogs, Locusts, and Grasshoppers; or both unto the middle, as in some Beetles and Spiders, as is determined by *Aristotle*, *De incessu Animalium.* Perfect and viviparous quadrupeds, so standing in their position of proneness, that the opposite joints of Neighbour-legs consist in the same plane; and a line descending from their Navel intersects at right angles the axis of the Earth. It happeneth often I confess that a Lobster hath the Chely or great claw of one side longer than the other; but this is not properly their leg, but a part of apprehension, and whereby they hold or seize upon their prey; for the legs and proper parts of progression are inverted backward, and stand in a position opposite unto these.
>
> Lastly, The Monstrosity is ill contrived, and with some disadvantage; the shortness being affixed unto the legs of one side, which might have been more tolerably placed upon the thwart or Diagoniall Movers. For the progression of quadrupeds being performed *per Diametrum*, that is the cross legs moving or resting together, so that two are always in motion, and two in station at the same time; the brevity had been more tolerable in the cross legs. For then the Motion and station had been performed by equal legs; whereas herein they are both performed by unequal Organs, and the imperfection becomes discoverable at every hand.[6]

Religio Medici probes mysteries of religion; *Pseudodoxia Epidemica* enquires into mysteries of the world; *Urne-Buriall* and *The Garden of Cyrus* are concerned with mysteries of the human condition. The two complementary works were published together in 1658. While each takes as its point of departure certain observations in the physical world, such as could be made by an antiquary in the first case, and a naturalist in the second, they are meditations on the human experience of life, each framed by a structure which had special significance in the seventeenth century: the monument which assures the memory of a life after it is over, and the garden, which is the metaphor of an earthly paradise. The pieces are also similar in their symmetry, each comprising five chapters, the third being the longest; and in their dedication, each having been written for a friend.

Urne-Buriall opens with a consideration of the means whereby peoples of the past and of other nations have disposed of their dead, providing a context for the brief statement in the second chapter of a number of urns, containing the ashes of created bodies, having being found buried in a field in Norfolk.

Browne develops an argument that the urns are probably Roman remains, although this is not conclusively decided. (They were in fact Saxon.) In the third chapter Browne contemplates the inevitability of the corruption of our remains after death, in spite of whatever great monuments are erected to house them. And moreover he asks whether those who are to be interred in such circumstances be can be sure of being left undisturbed, as have the remains in these simple urns buried in a field? 'He who lay in a golden Urne eminently above the Earth, was not likely to find the quiet of these bones.'[7] It is a sombre meditation on mortality. In the following chapter Browne surveys the various efforts of peoples of past civilizations to provide for a continued existence after death, and considers all people's innate desire that death should not be 'the end … of nature'. The final chapter has been deemed by many to be one of the masterpieces of English prose. From the opening words, 'Now since these dead bones have already out-lasted the living ones of *Methuselah* …'[8] sounding out, as Jonathan Post puts it, 'in the portentous drumbeat of simple Anglo-Saxon diction'[9], Browne calls up the contrast between the present and eternity, the brevity of life on earth, the irrelevance of memorial celebration, and a recasting of Christian faith to embrace all who are godly, through all time, and in spite of anonymity in death. 'To be namelesse in worthy deeds exceeds an infamous history … Who knows whether the best of men be known? or whether there be not more remarkable persons forgot, than any that stand remembred in the known account of Time?' The triumph of Christianity is in quietness and humility.

The full title of the companion-piece is *The Garden of Cyrus, or, the Quincunciall, Lozenge, or Net-Work Plantations of the Ancients, Artificially, Naturally, Mystically Considered*. On the face of it, this is an essay about the quincunx, or the arrangement of the number five as the four points of a square together with the point at which the diagonals cross, as on a dice. As such, it gives considerable prominence to 'decussation', the formation of a cross, as in the letter X. Such arrangements are sought out in ancient architecture, in ancient gardens, in nature, in numerology. But the underlying argument is that there is an ordering of reality to be discovered: artistic imagination, scientific observation, and the sense of the divine in the universe may be brought together in an agreement which gives understanding of God's creation. In the construction of so visionary a concept from so trite a beginning, and with such elaborate diction, and with a concluding passage in which the author contentedly drops off to sleep, Browne contrived also to maintain an element of the comic, which provoked Samuel Johnson to count the essay amongst the mock epics of Homer and Virgil.[10]

The first of the following extracts is a note which Browne made of an unusual storm in Norwich. It is one of the few pieces of his writing which is an eyewitness account of his 'seeing' something in England. It is a concise report in which all the relevant observations are set down as if ready to be used in some possible future scientific investigation. The second extract concerns a much more 'antiquarian' matter: the continued role of an ancient language in English. It is perhaps more properly a case of 'hearing' England, but it is nevertheless a description of a feature of England, in particular East Anglia, concerning which Browne highlighted an emerging field of knowledge. (The first English dictionary of the Saxon language, compiled by William Somner, was published in 1659.) The extract is in fact taken from the middle of an essay on language, treating especially the contribution of Saxon to English. Browne gave a series of six examples to show how closely the two languages read and sounded; in this case only three of these have been included. The final extract is taken from the third chapter of *The Garden of Cyrus*. While it certainly describes the flora with which Browne was familiar in Norfolk, it is no more a botanical study than *Urne-Buriall* is an archaeologist's report of a dig. Yet it is another case of seeing England, and, in this case, seeing in order to seek out the secrets of the order of things in Nature. It consists only of a few paragraphs, but is enough to demonstrate the meditative method of the investigation as well as the sumptuousness and generosity of Browne's prose.

Account of a thunderstorm

From *The Works of Sir Thomas Browne*, vol. III, pp.239-240

June 28, 1665.

After 7 aclock in the evening there was almost a continued thunder untill 8, wherin the *Tonitru & Fulgur*,[11] the noyse & lightening were so terrible that they putt the whole citty into an Amazement, & most unto their prayers. The clowdes went lowe & the cracks seemed neere over our heads during the most part of the thunder.

About 8 aclock an *Ignis Fulmineus, pila ignea fulminans, Telum igneum fulmineum* or fire ball[12] hit agaynst the litle woodden pinnacle of the high Leucome windowe[13] of my howse toward the market place, brake the flewboards & caryed peeces thereof a stones cast of; whereupon many of the tiles fell into the street & the windowes in adjoyning howses were broaken. At the same time ether a part of that close bound fire or another of the same nature fell into the court yard & whereof no notice was taken till wee began to examin the howse, & then wee found a freestone on the outside of the wall of the entry leading to the kitchin, half a foote from the ground, fallen from the wall, an hole as big as a footeball bored through the wall which is above a foot thick, & a chest wch stood agaynst it on the inside split & caryed above a foot from the wall. The wall also behind the leaden cistern at 5 yards distance from it broaken on the inside & outside, the middle seeming intire. The lead on the edges of the cisterne turned a litle up, & a great washing boll that stood by it to receave the raync turned upside downe & split quite thorough. Some chimneys & tyles were struck downe in other parts of the citty. A fire ball also flewe downe the walk in the market place. And all this god bee thancked without mischief to any person. The greatest Terror from the noyse, answerable unto 2 or 3 canons. The smell it left was strong like that after the discharge of a canon. The balls that flewe were not like fire in the flame, butt the coale, & the people sayd twas like the sunne. It was *discutiens*, *terebrans*, butt not *urens*.[14] It burnt nothing, nor anything it touched smelt of fire, nor melted any lead of windowe or cisterne, as I found it to doe in the great storme about 2 yeares ago at Melton hall 4 miles of, at that time when the hayle broake 3 thousand pounds worth of glasse in Norwich in half a quarter of an hower. About four dayes after, the like fulmineous fire kild a man in Erpingham church by Aylisham, upon whom it brake & beat downe divers wch were within the wind of it. One also went of in Sr John Hobarts gallerie at Blickling: hee was so neere that his arme & thigh were nummed above an hower after. 2 or 3 dayes after a woeman & horse were killed neere Bungay; her hatt so shivered that no peece remained bigger than a groat, whereof I had some peeces sent unto mee. Granadas, crakers & squibbs do much resemble the discharge, & *Aurum Fulminans* the fury thereof.[15] Of other Thunderbolts or *Lapides Fulminei* I have litle opinion: some I have by mee under that name, butt they are *e genere fossilium*.[16]

Of Languages, and particularly of the Saxon tongue

(From *The Works of Thomas Browne*, vol.III, pp.75-80)

The Saxons settling over all England, maintained an uniform Language, onely diversified in Dialect, Idioms, and minor differences, according to their different Nations which came in to the common Conquest, which may yet be a cause of the variation in the speech and words of several parts of England, where different Nations most abode or settled, and having expelled the Britanes, their Wars were chiefly among themselves, with little action with foreign Nations untill the union of the Heptarchy under Egbert; after which time although the Danes infested this Land and scarce left any part free, yet their incursions made more havock in Buildings, Churches and Cities, than in the Language of the Country, because their Language was in effect the same, and such as whereby they might easily understand one another.

And if the Normans, which came into Neustria or Normandy with Rollo the Dane, had preserved their Language in their new acquists, the succeeding Conquest of England, by Duke William of his race, had not begot among us such notable alterations; but having lost their Language in their abode in Normandy before they adventured upon England, they confounded the English with their French, and made the grand mutation, which was successively encreased by our possessions in Normandy, Guien and Aquitain, by our long Wars in France, by frequent resort of the French, who to the number of some thousands came over with Isabel Queen to Edward the Second, and the several Matches of England with the Daughters of France before and since that time.

But this commixture, though sufficient to confuse, proved not of ability to abolish the Saxon words; for from the French we have borrowed many Substantives, Adjectives and some Verbs, but the great Body of Numerals, auxiliary Verbs, Articles, Pronouns, Adverbs, Conjunctions and Prepositions, which are the distinguishing and lasting part of a Language, remain with us from the Saxon, which, having suffered no great alteration for many hundred years, may probably still remain, though the English swell with the inmates of Italian, French and Latin. An Example whereof may be observ'd in this following,

ENGLISH I

The first and foremost step to all good Works is the dread and fear of the Lord of Heaven and Earth, which thorough the Holy Ghost enlightneth the blindness of our sinfull hearts to tread the ways of wisedom, and then leads our feet into the Land of Blessing.

SAXON I

The erst and fyrmost stæp to eal gode Weorka is the dræd and feurt of the Lauord of Heofan and Eorth, whilc thurh the Heilig Gast onlihtneth the blindnesse of ure sinfull heorte to træd the wæg of wisdome, and thone læd ure fet into the Land of Blessung…

…ENGLISH V

And though they were a deal less, and rather short than beyond our sins, yet do we not a whit withstand or forbear them, we are wedded to, not weary of our misdeeds, we seldom look upward, and are not ashamed under sin, we cleanse not ourselves from blacknes and deep hue of our guilt; we want tears and sorrow, we weep not, fast not, we crave not forgiveness from the mildness, sweetness and goodness of God, and with all livelihood and stedfastness to our uttermost will hunt after the evil of guile, pride, cursing, swearing, drunkenness, overeating, uncleanness, all idle lust of the flesh, yes many uncouth and nameless sins, hid in our inmost Breast and Bosomes, which stand betwixt our forgiveness, and keep God and Man asunder.

SAXON V

And theow they wære a dæl lesse, and reither scort thone begond oure sinnan, get do we naht a whit withstand or forbeare them, we eare bewudded to, noht werig of ure agen misdeed, we seldon loc upweard, and ear not offchæmod under sinne, we cleans noht ure selvan from the blacnesse and dæp hue of ure guilt; we wan teare and sara, we weope noht, fæst noht, we craf noht foregyfnesse fram the mildnesse, sweetnesse and goodnesse of God, and mit eal lifelyhood and stedfastnesse to ure uttermost witt hunt æfter the ufel of guile, pride, cursung, swearung, druncennesse, overeat, uncleannesse and eal idle lust of the flæsc, yis mænig uncuth and nameleas sinnan, hid in ure inmæst Brist and Bosome, while stand betwixt ure foregyfnesse, and cæp God and Man asynder.

ENGLISH VI

Thus are we far beneath and also worse than the rest of God's Works; for the Sun and Moon, the King and Queen of Stars, Snow, Ice, Rain, Frost, Dew, Mist, Wind, fourfooted and creeping things, Fishes and feathered Birds, and Fowls of either Sea or Land do all hold the Laws of his will.

SAXON VI

Thus eare we far beneoth and ealso wyrse thone the rest of Gods Weorka; for the Sun and Mone, the Cyng and Cquen of Stearran, Snaw, Ise, Ren, Frost, Deaw, Miste, Wind, feower fet and crypend dinga, Fix and yefetherod Brid, and Fælen auther in Sæ or Land do eal heold the Lag of his willan.

Thus have you seen in few words how near the Saxon and English meet.

Now of this account the French will be able to make nothing; the modern Danes and Germans, though from several words they may conjecture at the meaning, yet will they be much to seek in the orderly sense and continued construction thereof; whether the Danes can continue such a series of sense out of their present Language and the old Runick, as to be intelligible unto present and ancient times, some doubt may well be made; and if the present French would attempt a Discourse in words common unto their present Tongue and the old *Romana Rustica* spoken in Elder times, or in the old Language of the Francks, which came to be in use some successions after Pharamond,[17] it might prove a Work of some trouble to effect.

It were not possible to make an Original reduction of many words of no general reception in England but of common use in Norfolk, or peculiar to the East Angle Countries; as, Bawnd, Bunny, Thurck, Enemmis, Sammodithee, Mawther, Kedge, Seele, Straft, Clever, Matchly, Dere, Nicked, Stingy, Noneare, Feft, Thepes, Gosgood, Kamp, Sibrit, Fangast, Sap, Cothish, Thokish, Bide owe, Paxwax: of these and some others of no easie originals, when time will permit, the resolution might be attempted; which to effect, the Danish language new and more ancient may prove of good advantage: which Nation remained here fifty years upon agreement, and have left many Families in it, and the Language of these parts had surely been more commixed and perplex, if the Fleet of Hugo de Bones had not been cast away, wherein threescore thousand Souldiers out of Britany and Flanders were to be wafted over, and were by King John's appointment to have a settled habitation in the Counties of Norfolk and Suffolk.

The Quincunx in plants

From *The Garden of Cyrus*, in *The Works of Sir Thomas Browne*, vol I, pp.192-195

Now although this elegant ordination of vegetables hath found coincidence or imitation in sundry works of Art, yet it is not also destitute of naturall examples, and though overlooked by all, was elegantly observable in severall works of nature.

Could we satisfie our selves in the position of the lights above, or discover the wisedom of that order so invariably maintained in the fixed Stars of heaven; Could we have any light, why the stellary part of the first masse, separated into this order, that the Girdle of *Orion* should ever maintain its line, and the two stars in *Charles's* Wain[18] never leave pointing at the Pole-Starre, we might abate the *Pythagoricall* Musick of the Spheres, the sevenfold Pipe of *Pan*; and the strange Cryptography of *Gaffarell* in his Starrie Booke of Heaven.[19]

But not to look so high as Heaven or the single Quincunx of the *Hyades* upon the head of *Taurus*, the Triangle and remarkable *Crusero* about the foot of the *Centaur*;[20] observable rudiments there are hereof in subterraneous concretions, and bodies in the Earth; in the *Gypsum* or *Talcum Rhomboides*, in the Favaginites or honey-comb-stone, in the *Asteria* and *Astroites*,[21] and in the crucigerous[22] stone of S. *Iago* of *Gallicia*.

The same is observably effected in the *Julus*, *Catkins*,[23] or pendulous excrescencies of severall Trees, of Wallnuts, Alders, and Hazels, which hanging all the Winter, and maintaining their Net-worke close, by the expansion thereof are the early foretellers of the Spring, discoverable also in long Pepper, and elegantly in the *Julus* of *Calamus Aromaticus*, so plentifully growing with us in the first palmes of Willowes, and in the Flowers of Sycamore, Petasites, Asphodelus, and *Blattaria*, before explication.[24] After such order stand the flowery Branches of our best spread *Verbascum*, and the seeds about the spicous head or torch of *Tapsus Barbatus*, in as fair a regularity as the circular and wreathed order will admit, which advanceth one side of the square, and makes the same Rhomboidall …

… The white umbrella or medicall bush of Elder, is an Epitome of this order: arising from five main stemms Quincuncially disposed, and tollerably maintained, in their subdivisions. To omit the lower observations in the seminal spike of Mercurie, weld, and Plantane.

Thus hath nature ranged the flowers of Santfoyne, and French honey suckle; and somewhat after this manner hath ordered the bush in *Jupiters* beard, or houseleek; which old superstition set on tops of houses, as a defensative against lightening, and thunder. The like in Fenny Sengreen or the water Souldier;[25] which, though a militarie name from Greece, makes out the Roman order.

A like ordination there is in the faviginous[26] Sockets, and Lozenge seeds of the noble flower of the Sunne. Wherein in Lozenge figured boxes nature shuts up the seeds, and balsame which is about them.

But the Firre and Pinetree from their fruits doe naturally dictate this position. The Rhomboidall protuberances in Pineapples maintaining this Quincuncial order unto each other, and each Rhombus in it selfe. Thus are also disposed the triangular foliations, in the conicall fruit of the firre tree, orderly shadowing and protecting the winged seeds below them.

The like so often occurreth to the curiosity of observers, especially in spicated seeds and flowers, that we shall not need to take in the single Quincunx of Fuchsius in the grouth of the masle fern, the seedie disposure of Gramen Ischemon, and the trunk or neat Reticulate work in the coddle of the Sachell palme.[27]

For even in very many round stalk plants, the leaves are set after a Quintuple ordination, the first leaf answering the fifth, in lateral disposition. Wherein the leaves successively rounding the stalke, in foure at the furthest the compass is absolved, and the fifth leafe or sprout returns to the position of the other fifth before it; as in accounting upward is often observable in furze, pellitorye, Ragweed, the sproutes of Oaks, and thorns upon pollards,[28] and very remarkably in the regular disposure of the rugged excrescencies in the yearly shoots of the Pine.

But in square stalked plants, the leaves stand respectively unto each other, either in crosse of decussation to those above or below them, arising at crosse positions; whereby they shadow not each other, and better resist the force of winds, which in a parallel situation, and upon square stalks would more forcibly bear upon them.

And to omit, how leaves and sprouts which compasse not the stalk, are often set in a Rhomboides, and making long and short Diagonals, doe stand like the leggs of Quadrupeds when they goe: Nor to urge the thwart enclosure and furdling[29] of flowers and blossomes before explication, as in the multiplyed leaves of Pionie; And the Chiasmus in five leaved flowers, while one lies wrapt about the staminous beards, the other foure obliquely shutting and closing upon each other; and how even flowers which consist of foure leaves stand not ordinarily in three and one, but two and two crossewise unto the Stylus; even the Autumnal budds, which awaite the returne of the sun, doe after the winter solstice multiply their calicular[30] leaves, making little Rhombuses, and network figures, as in the Sycamore and Lilac.

1. *The Works of Sir Thomas Browne*, ed. by Geoffrey Keynes, London: Faber & Faber Limited, 1928, vol. I, p.14.
2. *Ibid.*, pp.21-22.
3. *Ibid.*, pp.25.
4. Jonathan F. S. Post, *Sir Thomas Browne*, Boston: Twayne, 1987, p.20.
5. The full title was *Pseudodoxia Epidemica: or, Enquiries into very many received Tenents and commonly presumed Truths.*
6. *Works*, vol II, pp.170–171.
7. *Works*, vol I, p.152.
8. *Ibid.*, p.164.
9. Post, p.128.
10. *Ibid.*, p.136.
11. *Tonitru & Fulgur,* thunder and lightning.
12. *Ignis fulmineus*, fire-ball. In this case, the other Latin phrases have the same meaning: *pila*, mortar; *telum*, missile.
13. *Leucome window*, skylight.
14. From *discutio*, to shatter; *terebro*, to bore; *uro*, to burn.
15. *Aurum Fulminans*, fulminating gold, an explosive substance obtained by dissolving gold in *aqua regia* and then mixing it with ammonium hydroxide; it was discovered by alchemists in the late sixteenth century.
16. *E genere fossilium,* dug out of the ground.
17. Pharamond (*c.*370–*c.*420) is regarded as having been the first king of the Salian Franks.
18. *Charles's wain*, the Big Dipper. (From Charlemagne's wain).
19. Jacques Gaffarel (1601–1681), French astrologer, proposed that letters of the Hebrew alphabet corresponded to constellations and the stars in the sky could be 'read' like a book.

20. The Southern Cross.
21. *Asteria,* astroites, literally, 'star-stones', gems in which the light forms the shape of a star.
22. *Crucigerous*, marked with a cross.
23. *Julus, catkin*, a tuft of small unisexual flowers, as in the willow, hazel, etc.
24. *Petasites*, butterbur; *verbascum blattaria*, moth mullein; *explication*, unfolding (of leaves, flowers). *Tapsus Barbatus* is another herb of the genus *verbascum*.
25. Browne's note: Stratiotes. Stratiotes, or Water Soldier, is an underwater plant growing in Europe and north-west Asia. Although it is an underwater plant, it rises to the surface when it flowers.
26. *Favaginous*, cellular, as honey-comb.
27. *Masle* fern, male fern, a common fern; *Gramen Ischemon*, a rare plant identified by James Petiver as a type of manna grass or edible cocksfoot, in a paper given to the Royal Society in 1713; *Sachell palme*, a date palm.
28. Browne's note: Upon pollard Oaks and Thorns.
29. *Furdling*, rolling up.
30. *Calicular*, cup-like.

YORKSHIRE AND THE HUMBER

XVIII
York: Francis Drake (1696–1771)

Eboracum, a description of the city of York, is a good example of a town survey as that genre developed in the eighteenth century. It is a six hundred-page volume offering, in the first place, copious information about the Roman origins of the city (whence the name 'Eboracum') and the remains from that period to be found in the vicinity. It also gives detailed data on the governance of the municipality and lists of past office-holders, and comprehensive accounts of the history and state of the Archbishopric of York and of York Minster, and the histories of the earls and dukes of York, and the Abbey of St Mary. In describing the streets and buildings of York, the narrative is historical and genealogical. There is little in the way of description, as may be exemplified by the paragraph devoted to one of the city's major buildings, the Castle:

> At the end of this street [Castlegate] stands the famous castle of *York*; situated at the confluence of the rivers *Ouse* and *Foss*; the later of which has been drawn in a deep mote quite round it; and made it inaccessible but by two draw-bridges. The larger of these lead to the ancient great gate from the county, the piles and foundations of which I saw lately dug up; the other to a postern-gate from the city. This has been a year ago rebuilt in a handsomer manner, and is at present the only entrance to the castle; except I mention a small postern near the *milns*.[1]

Francis Drake pursued a career in medicine and in 1717, at the age of twenty-one, he succeeded to the practice of the York surgeon to whom he had been apprenticed. But his main interest was in antiquities, the study of which he undertook not as an academic, but as a gentleman of amateur scholarly inclinations. He said of himself,

> … being bred a surgeon, and, possibly, allowed some share of knowledge in my profession, yet *History* and *Antiquity* were always, from a child, my chiefest tast;

nor could I stifle a *genius*, which as I take it was born with me, without being a kind of *Felo de se*, which I should not care to be guilty of.[2]

Like William Dugdale some ninety years earlier, Drake claimed a childhood passion for the past, perhaps nurtured in a family in which his father, uncle, and grandfather were all clergymen, as had been the grandfather's brother and father as well. The modern reader may dismiss this as an antiquarian conceit, for just the notion of a child being fascinated by tombs, arms, and family histories now seems impossibly remote. But it was evidently a credible claim, and so serves to remind us of the gap between the past and the present. For Drake, the past became so compelling an interest that he took some trouble to rationalise his preference for antiquarianism over medicine:

I take it, there are now, almost, as many books published on the cure of the body as there are of the soul; and the practice of the former, both externally and internally, is made so evident and clear, by them, to the meanest capacity, that in reading a common *Dispensatory* only, we may imagine that no body has occasion to dye; and we are now every day assured, in publick *Advertisements*, that the blind shall see, the deaf hear, the dumb talk, and the lame throw away their crutches by the slightest and most insignificant applications and remedies. In an age like this, when art is brought to such a perfection as even to work miracles upon nature, I should be highly presumptuous to pretend to exceed. Besides, I am rather a sceptick in the matter, and have so much of the *Antiquarian* in me that I cannot help thinking that the art of physick was as well known, except in one or two specificks, two thousand years ago as it is now; and that the divine *Hippocrates* saw as far into a diseased human system, and knew as well how to restore it, as the clearest sighted physician of this age … Under a diffidence like this, and, as I said, being naturally inclined to it, I have turned my skill in a quite different way …

He was surely exaggerating. But whatever he really thought of his chosen profession, he clearly believed that there was much to be discovered about the past, and in *Eboracum* he turned his hand to it. Moreover, in his view, surgery was work, while antiquarianism was pleasure.

While the examination of the past was the main business of antiquaries, the English in general became seemingly more and more fascinated by things ancient as the seventeenth and eighteenth centuries progressed. Perhaps it was motivated by the destruction of ancient buildings and institutions in the Reformation, and reinforced by the iconoclasm of the civil war years, but its culmination was in the romantic aesthetic of the later eighteenth century, realised in endeavours to recreate the Gothic and the Medieval and to experience the mystery and desolation of ancient ruins. It has been suggested that this sentiment is essential to the English imagination, a manifestation of a melancholy and nostalgic aspect of the English temperament.[3] Certainly the preferences of Francis Drake bear out this proposition.

Drake was appointed City Surgeon in 1727, suggesting that he was well regarded as a medical practitioner. The following year his wife of eight years died, having borne him five sons, and he remained a widower for the rest of his life. By this time he had read the manuscript of a history of York written by Sir Thomas Widdrington, and it inspired him to embark on 'a design to publish the antiquities of this city'. The project was supported by the city corporation—he was given access to all of their records—and attracted 540 subscribers. After the publication of *Eboracum* Drake was elected to fellowships of both the Society of Antiquaries and the Royal Society, and he continued to divide his time between his medical profession and his antiquarian interests. He was an anonymous, and possibly a major contributor to a 22-volume *Parliamentary or Constitutional History of England*, which appeared between 1751 and 1760. He died at the age of 76, having moved to Beverley, where his son Francis was the vicar of St Mary's Church, and it is there that he is buried and commemorated.

With true antiquarian purpose, Drake's aim was 'to revive the memory of a decayed city, at present the second in *Britain*, but of old the first, and in antiquity, the glory of the whole *Island*.'[4] In paying homage in his preface to earlier historians who had written about York, and acknowledging sources from which he had used material, he remarked upon a difficulty in publishing local history: put simply, such books, unlike the works of 'the more general historians', were not selling well.

> ... such a history as mine is must lag behind, be raised by the heavy method of *subscription*, thrust into the press and dragged through it by all the force and strength that the author, or his friends, can apply to the engine. This discouragement from the publick does not in the least abate in me a value for local histories.[5]

So the unusual love for antiquities, which he had sensed in his childhood, was no immature fancy, it was to become a guiding principle in his major endeavours: the preservation of the past was his enduring goal. But at the same time his remarks provide evidence that the appeal of such books had diminished, as William Thomas had discovered in 1730 when he re-edited Dugdale's *Antiquities of Warwickshire*.

The extract which follows is one of the descriptions in the book which addresses not the past, but the times which Drake observed himself. It is immediately preceded, in *Eboracum*, by a recounting of the numerous fairs held in the city, some associated with unusual customs. The Lammastide Fair was known as the 'bishop's fair' because it was marked by jurisdiction of the city being temporarily handed over to the Archbishop of York. On St Luke's Day was held a 'dish fair' at Micklegate, where wooden dishes and ladles were sold. The day was also known as 'whip-dog-day' because schoolboys traditionally whipped all the dogs that they saw in the streets. York was clearly an important commercial centre, and Drake's enumeration of the markets is a lively illustration of the variety and activity from day to day in the city streets. The local authorities were obviously kept busy monitoring the vendors' weights and measures and endeavouring to eliminate cheating. One of the market locations, the Shambles, is now one of the famous attractions of York. It is promoted as 'Europe's best-preserved medieval street'.

Markets in the City of York

From *Eboracum*, pp.219–220

There are several places within the city where markets are kept, but the principal are called *Thursday market* and the *Pavement*. The description of the places will come under another head, and I shall here only mention the days they fall on, *&c.*[6]

In the *Pavement* is kept a market three times a week, *Tuesdays*, *Thursdays*, and *Saturdays*; which is abundantly furnished with all sorts of grain, and vast variety of edibles, of which *wild fowl* is not the least. This last article is so plentiful that I believe, for a constancy, no market in *England* can produce the like, either for quantity, variety, or cheapness.

The stand for wheat always ranges on the north side of the *Pavement* market, the rye opposite. The place for pease, beans and oats is in *Coppergate*; and the barley market in upper *Ousegate*, all contiguous. The poulterers vend their wares at the *cross*.

The toll of this market is of corn only; and from every sack-load of corn, be it either two or three bushels, is taken two dishfuls for toll. Sixteen of these dishes are to contain a peck, as appears by an ordinance mentioned before.

No corn to be carried out of this market till the toll be gathered, and that the toll-bell be rung. This bell is hung in the turret of the new cross, and is usually rung at eleven o'clock. After which the market is free.

Flesh market[7] is weekly kept every *Saturday* in *Thursday market-place*, to which the country butchers have free resort. There is also in the common *shambles* and other butcher's shops of free citizens an open market kept every day; whereby this city is as well supplied with all sorts of shambles-meat as most markets in *England*.

Sea fish market is kept every *Wednesday* and *Friday* upon *Foss-bridge*, betwixt grate and grate, for panniermen[8] free of the city; where convenient stalls have been lately erected for them. For panniermen not free of the city, the market is kept in *Walmgate* at the east end of *Foss-bridge*.

Several good ordinances have been made for the regulation of this market, which may be seen in the fishmonger's ordinary;[9] one of which is this, no pannierman whatsoever is allowed to carry any fish out of this market before the citizens of this city be first served, til the market bell be rung. After which every person is free to carry his fish to any other market where he pleases.

The nearness of *York* to the *German* ocean and eastern sea-ports, causes this market to be exceedingly well stocked with sea-fish of most kinds. From whence it is bought up again and exported into the more inland parts by foreign panniermen; there being much more of this valuable blessing brought to the city than can be consumed in it. However it were to be wished that the abovementioned ordinance was more strictly kept, then I am afraid it now is, for the benefit of the citizens in general.

Fresh fish market is appointed to be held at a place known by the name of *Salter-greeses* upon the eastern end of *Ouse-bridge*, where all kinds of fresh fish took in the rivers *Ouse* and *Humber* are exposed to sale. Salmon caught in these rivers are accounted exceeding good; but when the season will not permit this kind of fish to be carried to *London*, the several fisheries on the *Derwent* and the *Tease* pour it in upon us very plentifully. Here are smelts too, which, at their season, are oft took in such numbers as to be cried about the streets in wheel-barrows, at three half pence a score. Oysters from the *Lincolnshire* and *Norfolk* coasts are here sold.

An order for this fish shambles is in the book of occupations, letter A, fol. 177.

In the fishmongers ordinary is an order that all strangers fisher-boats are to fasten their boats beneath the *Stayth*, with their fish in the water of *Ouse*, **annenst Thrush-lane-end**, and to sell their fish upon *Ouse-bridge* end in the place accustomed, and to sell the same betwixt seven and eleven a clock forenoon.

[*Butter* market] [i]s in *Micklegate*, and there kept on *Tuesdays, Thursdays* and *Saturdays*, but not prohibited any day of the week, for the benefit of the merchants of this city.

This market is only for firkin butter, a merchandize of the staple to be exported, sold in gross to free merchants of the city, and not to be bought or sold by any until it be brought to the standard of the said market, and there tried and examined, and after marked by the officer thereunto appointed by the lord-mayor for the time being. Who hath for the marking and weighing of every firkin a halfpenny.[10] There is a searcher[11] also appointed by the cheesemongers in *London*, who has an allowance from them of so much *per* firkin. The export of this commodity from the city itself, amounting to near sixty thousand firkins a year, is a great argument for the fertility of the soil about us.

[The *Linnen* market] was formerly kept in *Thursday market-place* every *Friday* weekly, for all sorts of linnen cloth, and of linnen yarn. The yarn is duly searched by the wardens of the company of linnen-weavers that it be true tale[12] from the reel, and well spun thread. The linnen cloth likewise ought to be searched and sealed by the said searchers of linen-weavers, before the same be sold, for the prevention of battling,[13] liming, chalking, or any other deceitful thickning of the same by bleachers or others, contrary to the statute in that case provided. Which, says my authority, if well observed, would be a great improvement to that manufacture in this city.

Upon a complaint to the lord-mayor by the country-websters,[14] an order was made *Feb.* 23. 1592, *Robert Askwith* mayor, as follows,

It is agreed that the said market shall be kept in the said market-place, called *Thursday market-place*, and not in any house or houses. And that the same shall not begin before one of the clock in the afternoon upon the *Friday* weekly. And that none resorting to the said market shall buy or sell there before the said hour, nor in any other place upon pain of the thing bought or sold. And that a standard of a true yard wand shall be set upon the market cross there, and that the inhabitants thereabouts shall be commanded not to suffer any to buy or sell in the houses any of the said cloth brought to the said market, upon pain of such fines as shall be thought meet. And proclamation shall be made in the said market-place to the effect aforesaid, two or three several market days. And that no yard wand shall there be used but such as shall be marked and burned with a burn in that behalf to be made, and agreeable to the said standard, *&c.*

Proclamation was made of the several articles accordingly, and an officer appointed by the mayor and aldermen for the execution of the premisses, and one moiety of the forfeitures allowed for seizure and presentments, *&c.*

[The *Leather* market] for all sorts of tanned leather, both of hides and calf-skins, is kept on *Thursday* every week in the *Thursday market-place* in this city; and the said leather to be searched and sealed there by the searchers of the several companies of cordwainers and curriers in this city, before the same be sold, as well upon the penalties of the ordinancies and by-laws of the city and companies, as of the statutes in that case provided.

[The *Wool* market] is kept on *Peasholm-green*; and was first established *anno* 1707, *Robert Benson* esquire, afterwards lord *Bingley*, lord-mayor. They have a convenient shed built for them where the wool is weighed.

[The *Herb* market] [u]sed to be kept close under the church in *Ousegate*; but, *anno* 1729, the city built and fitted up a neat little square, adjoining to the church-yard, where there is a pump in the midst, and stalls for the herb-women quite round. Pulse, roots and all sorts of garden-stuff are there daily sold as they come in season. And it is remarkable that, of late years, this city is so much improved in this way, that our little square is an epitome of *Covent-garden.*

1. *Eboracum*, p.286. The remnant of the castle is known as Clifford's Tower. *Miln*, corn-mill.
2. From the Preface to *Eboracum*. (*Felo de se*, a person who commits suicide.)
3. Peter Ackroyd, *Albion: the Origins of the English Imagination*, London: Chatto and Windus, 2002, chapter 30.
4. From Drake's Preface.
5. *Ibid.*
6. For the Thursday market, see *Eboracum,* pp.323–324:
   '... a handsome square, were it but all well built, called *Thursday-market*; anciently the chief market of the city; the old cross of which stood near the midst of it. How long the country butchers have had the privilege to bring and expose their meat for sale on *Saturdays* at this place, I shall not say, but formerly this market was on *Thursdays* ... *Anno* 1705, was finished a beautiful and useful structure, for the shelter of market-people in bad weather, which now stands on the west side of this square ...'
   For the Pavement, see p. 292:
   '... whether this was so called from being the first or last paved street in the city, I cannot determine. It has bore that name some hundred of years; yet I cannot find this place made use of for a market, by any regulation in the old registers of the city. It is but of late years since the cross was erected in it ...Being a square with a dome, ascended into by a pair of winding stairs, and supported by twelve pillars of the *Ionick* order, but ill executed ...'
7. Drake's footnote inserted here:
   Every *Christmas* even, *Easter* even and *Whitsun* even, the lord-mayor, aldermen and sheriffs have used to walk into the markets, and take notice of the measures of salt, oatmeal, and such like things. And if any shambles meat be rotten, or otherwise unwholesome, it is openly burnt in *Thursday-market*; and the butcher, or who offered such corrupted meat to sale severely fined. An admirable law to prevent sickness and diseases.
8. *Pannier*, a basket for carrying food, hence, *pannierman*, one who sells food, especially, a hawker of fish.
9. *Ordinary*, an ordinance, a rule.
10. *Firkin*, wooden container for butter.
11. *Searcher*, examiner.
12. *Tale*, numerical reckoning.
13. *Battling*, beating the cloth while it is being washed.
14. *Webster*, weaver.

XIX
Yorkshire: William Bray (1736–1832)

In making a distinction between antiquaries and other writers, the position of William Bray is ambiguous. While he was a solicitor who enjoyed a successful career, he was also a fellow of the Society of Antiquaries, and completed *The History and Antiquities of Surrey*, a substantial traditional county survey which he took over from Owen Manning, an antiquary who had lost his sight. As a younger man, Bray had been the author of a travel guide, *A Sketch of a Tour in Derbyshire and Yorkshire* (1777), in which a somewhat more personal view was taken of the countryside, yet certain critics at the time deemed that, *qua* travel guide, it contained too much historical material.[1] Having been appointed in 1761, through the patronage of John Evelyn,[2] to the Board of the Green Cloth, which oversaw domestic affairs of the royal household, he lived in London, and as a result had easy access to many archival sources: the Exchequer Office, the Rolls Chapel, the Tower, the Office of Augmentations, Lambeth Palace Library, and the British Museum. So when in 1800 Bray took up the Surrey survey, he was well placed to do the necessary research.

Bray also left a diary, which records a private life which belies the stereotype of the antiquary as a humourless pedant engaged in the examination of ancient musty tomes and decaying monuments. Especially before he was married he spent plenty of time in the pursuit of amusement: playing cards, drinking and dining out, and going to the theatre. He kept a diary, but its entries are terse and restrained, as on 28 September 1758, when he married Mary Stephens:

> At 8 went to Mrs. Norwood's, Miss Adee and Betsy Stevens breakfasted there; they went down the backway to Mr. Brewer's; I went home and down town; was married; sent Mr. Brewer's man for a chaise and came away directly; went afterwards to Mr. Brewer's and drank chocolate; dined at Epsom; to Mrs. C.'s at 5; I walked to Hatton Garden and with Mr. Boughton to Lincoln's Inn Coffee House; then home; at quadrille[3] before supper.

It was doubtless a busier day than usual. After his marriage his social life, as logged in the diary, was more moderate, perhaps because at this time he devoted more time to his legal career, although the nineteenth-century editor claimed that 'he continued for many years to live more like a bachelor than a married man, spending most of his evenings in the society of his numerous friends, or at a coffee-house.' They had eight children, and when Mary died at the age of 62, Bray was to note: '[she was] the most affectionate of wives, tenderest of parents, and most sincere of Christians; to her great prudence and discretion I owe the prosperity with which God has blessed me.'

Bray travelled frequently and widely in England and Wales between 1769 and 1799, and the *Sketch of a Tour in Derbyshire and Yorkshire* is the outcome of one of his earlier journeys. In the 1876 edition of his diary are listed twenty-six journeys altogether, some of them, such as to Wales, to Shropshire, to the Lake District, and in the south of England, extending more than five hundred miles. The *Sketch* is an example of an early travel guide, produced at a time when the genre was emerging. Travel had become popular amongst the aristocracy and more affluent gentry in England in the later seventeenth century, when it developed into a program intended for the education of young men, which is generally referred to as the Grand Tour. This was an extended visit to France, especially Paris; the Alps in Switzerland; and Italy, especially Florence, Venice, and sites of significance in the classical Latin literature which had been studied during formal education. The tourer would probably be accompanied by an entourage of servants and tutors. The young man was expected to experience a degree of independence, develop his taste as a connoisseur of art and culture, make liaisons with his social counterparts on the Continent, and even have the opportunity to sow his wild oats before returning to the family social circle and taking up new responsibilities.[4]

By Bray's time participation in the Grand Tour had broadened to include people of lesser means and social status, who travelled more modestly and perhaps as families with wives and children. The advent of war on the Continent, firstly the Seven Years War of 1756–1763 and then of the wars with France, which took place more or less constantly between 1790 and 1815, caused a significant decrease in the numbers of visitors from Britain, and consequently the Grand Tour began to give way to domestic travel. Coincident with this political change was the growth of interest both in the Celtic and in the emerging picturesque ideal in art.[5] Especially attractive were the wilder parts of the British Isles, such as the Scottish highlands, northern Wales, and the Lake District. Bray's *Tour* includes the Peake District of Derbyshire and the wild expanses of Yorkshire, both suitably adventurous and romantic destinations.

Bray's *Sketch* was to some extent similar to seventeenth-century county descriptions except that it was intended that the reader should actually visit the places of which accounts were given. Hence additional, useful, information was included, relevant to matters such as finding accommodation and stabling horses. The narrative combines the usual antiquarian observations—ancient buildings and estates with historical and genealogical notes—with aesthetic comments on the landscape, judging some scenes to be romantic and picturesque, as was the predilection of those who visited the countryside. The following extract demonstrates this clearly, as the antiquarian observations of the castle soon give way to rapturous admiration of the nearby rapids and falls in the river.

Bolton Castle and Askrig

From *Sketch of a Tour in Derbyshire and Yorkshire*, pp.162–169

Bolton castle was built by *Richard* Lord *Scroope*, the honest and spirited Chancellor of *Richard* II. but whose ancestors had an estate here at least as early as 24 *Edward* I. *Leland* says it was eighteen years in building, and the cost, 1,000 marks a year, which makes 12,000*l*. He says that the timber used about it was mostly fetched from the forest of *Engleby* in *Cumberland*, by relays of ox-teams placed on the road. He mentions chimnies made in the side of the walls for conveyance of the smoke, as a thing he had not been accustomed to see. He also mentions an astronomical clock being here.

The castle is of a quadrilateral figure; the greatest length being from north to south, but no two of its sides equal; the south is 184 feet, the opposite 187, the west 131, and the east 125. It has four right-lined towers, one at each angle, but neither their faces nor flanks are equal, each of the former measuring, on the north and south sides, forty-seven feet and an half, and on the east and west only thirty-five feet and an half. The latter vary from seven feet and an half to six feet. In the center, between the towers, both on the north and south sides, is a large projecting right-angled buttress or turret: that on the north-side is fifteen feet in front, its west-side fourteen, its east sixteen; on the south-side the front is twelve feet, its east nine, its west twelve.

The grand entrance was in the east curtain, near the southermost tower; there were three other doors, one on the north, two on the west-side. The walls are seven feet thick, ninety-seven high. It was lighted by several stages of windows. The chief lodging-rooms were in the towers. The east and the north sides are mostly in ruins, the west part is in good repair. One of the towers, which was the principal object of attack in the civil wars, fell down in the night in *November* 1761.[6]

Mary Queen of *Scots* was confined here, under the care of Lord *Scroope*, in 1568, but was soon removed to *Tutbury* Castle in *Staffordshire*. Her chamber is shewn.

In the civil wars this castle was gallantly defended for the King by Colonel *Scroope*, but at length surrendered on honourable terms.

In this parish lived that singular instance of longevity *Henry Jenkins*, who died 8 *December*, 1670, aged 169 years. After he was more than 100 years old he used to swim in the rivers, and was called upon as an evidence to a fact of 140 years past. He was once a butler to Lord *Conyers*, after that a fisherman, and at last a beggar.

In the road from hence to *Askrig* and *Richmond*, are the falls of the river *Eure*, called *Atte-scarre* (from the rocks between which the river runs) corruptly *Aysgarth-force*, or *The Force*, which are less known than they deserve to be, and which, indeed, exceed any expectation that can well be formed of them, and any description which I can give.

Cross the river at *Bolton-hall*, and the right-hand road leads to a small public-house near *Aysgarth* church; here the horses may be left. Go down a sharp descent to the bridge, turn on the right, and soon quitting the high road, go on the right again, through a little wood, and over three of four fields, to the bank from whence the principal fall is seen.

The romantic situation of the handsome church of *Aysgarth*, on an eminence, solitarily overlooking these cataracts (says the ingenious Mr. *Maude*, chief agent to the Duke of *Bolton* here), the decency of the structure within and without, its perfect retirement, the rural church yard, the dying sounds of water, amidst woods and rocks wildly intermixed, with the variety and magnitude of the surrounding hills, concur to render this scene at once aweful and picturesque, in a very high degree.

The falls that are above the bridge, are seen on descending to it, but are seen to greater advantage on the return. You there view them through a spacious light arch, which presents the river, at every step, in variety of forms. On the left is the steeple, emerging from a copse.

From the bridge the water falls near half a mile, upon a surface of stone, in some places quite smooth, in others worn into great cavities, and inclosed by bold and shrubbed cliffs; in others it is interrupted by huge masses of rock, standing upright in the middle of the current. It is every where changing its face, and exhibits some grand specimens before it comes to the chief descent, called *The Force*.

The whole river, which is of considerable breadth, here pours down a ledge of irregular broken rocks, and falling to a great depth, boils up in sheets of white foam, and is some time before it can recover itself sufficiently to pursue its course, which it does at last with great rapidity. No *words* can do justice to the grandeur of this scene, which was said by Dr. *Pococke* to exceed that of the cataracts of the *Nile*, nor is it much less difficult for the pencil to describe it; I do not think that the very accurate and judicious Mr. *Pennant* (excellent as his plates in general are) shews half its magnificence.

The bridge has on it the date of 1539, which is probably a stone of the old bridge, the present one seeming of much later date.

Returning back to the bridge, you have a full view of the falls above it, as mentioned before, and here your horses may meet you; for if you go to the public-house you must return and cross the river again to go on to *Askrig*.

This place is in a bottom, and for a mile or two before coming to the descent of the hill, the road runs along the edge of a steep declivity, guarded by a stone-wall. On the side of this bank is an old house, of Mr. *Weddell*, called *Nappe-hall*, which he has quitted for *Newby* near *Rippon*. This was formerly the seat of the *Medcalfs*, so numerous a family that *Camden* says Sir *Christopher Medcalf*, the chief of them, went with 300 horse, all of his family and name, and in the same habit, to receive the justices of assize, and conduct them to *York*.

Askrig is a small town, with decent accommodation at the *George*. The inhabitants are employed in knitting stockings, of which they make great quantities.

1. Rosemary Sweet, in *Antiquaries: the Discovery of the Past in Eighteenth-Century Britain*, London: Hambledon & London, 2004, notes this, referring to William Mavor, *The British Tourist, or Traveller's Pocket Companion, through England, Wales, Scotland and Ireland*, 6 vols (London, 1798), ii, p.303.
2. John Evelyn (1620–1703) is chiefly remembered, like his friend Samuel Pepys, as a diarist who kept records of the tumultuous times of the English Civil War, the Restoration, and the Great Plague of 1665 and the Great Fire of London. He wrote on many subjects, especially gardening and architecture, and accumulated a considerable library. He was one of the founders of the Royal Society. Bray's last major literary work, with William Upcott, was *Memoirs Illustrative of the Life and Writings of John Evelyn*, which included a transcription of Evelyn's diary, marred by some inaccuracies and bowdlerized.
3. *Quadrille*, a card game with four players.
4. *On the Grand Tour*, see James Buzard, 'The Grand Tour and after (1660–1840)', in Peter Hulme and Tim Youngs (editors), *The Cambridge Companion to Travel Writing*, Cambridge University Press, 2002, pp.37–52.
5. The aesthetic of the picturesque is discussed in the chapter on William Gilpin, below.
6. Bray's footnote here: These measurements are taken from Mr. Grose's very elegant work, to which I am indebted for much information.

THE NORTH-WEST

XX

Cheshire: William Smith (*c*.1550–1618) and William Webb

These two antiquaries of Cheshire, here presented together, in all probability had little or nothing to do with each other, for they lived at different times and pursued different careers. They came, however, to have two things in common: each wrote a descriptive account of the same native county and, in 1656, many years after they had been written, their two works were published together as the first two sections of Daniel King's compendium of Cheshire antiquities, *The Vale Royal of England*. Their surveys are neither lengthy nor scholarly, but they provide examples of gentlemanly writing about places clearly held in deep affection. These ingenuous early essays on Cheshire stand in refreshing contrast to the more meticulous and systematic chorographical surveys of Camden, Stow, and Dugdale.

William Smith was born in Cheshire about 1550, travelled widely, wrote books on history and topography, and wrote historical plays, but his greatest interest was heraldry and in 1597 he became a member of the College of Arms as Rouge Dragon Pursuivant. Although Anthony Wood in his *Athenae Oxoniensis* supposed that Smith had been at either Oxford or Cambridge, it seems that he was a London haberdasher. He began writing surveys of places while he was young, both in England and in Germany. Around 1580 he travelled to Nuremburg, where he married and had a family, returning to England several years later. His description of Cheshire dates from about 1586.[1] Only one of his plays, *The Hector of Germanie,* survives. Much less is known of William Webb: he attained an MA at Oxford, became clerk to the Mayor of Chester, and later Under-Sheriff. He referred to Henry Peacham (author of *The Compleat Gentleman*) as his cousin. His description of Cheshire seems, from his list of mayors and sheriffs, to date from 1617.[2] The editor of these two county surveys, Daniel King (*c*.1616–*c*.1661), also of Chester, was an artist who did etchings for the first volume of William Dugdale's great collection of monastic histories and documents, the *Monasticon Anglicanum*. He used his plates to produce a rival publication, *The Cathedrall and Conventuall Churches of England and Wales*, which did not however have any substantial text. *The Vale Royal of England* is another collection of borrowings: although the four texts in which it consists were written by authors who are named, the book also contains unacknowledged plates (against which King's efforts are readily seen to be inferior) by Wenceslaus Hollar.[3]

William Smith's description of Cheshire is particularly interesting because it was so early an attempt at the genre; indeed it was preceded only by Lambarde's *Perambulation of Kent*. Although Smith had obviously had to do some research, it would have been very straightforward: the whole work, which is only ninety-nine pages in length, consists of not more than twenty-three pages of descriptive text and twelve pages of historical data on the kings of Mercia, the earls of March, the earls of Chester and the bishopric of Chester. The remainder is made up of lists (mayors and sheriffs of Chester; places, knights and gentlemen in each of the hundreds), charters and petitions, and some material taken from Leland. All of this is ordered in a somewhat haphazard way, and is followed by a number of pages of county coats-of-arms. What was Smith offering his readers? For the most part, it seems not to be a book through which one would read, so it may have been intended to be used for reference. It was also an earnest but modest assertion of the standing and heritage of Cheshire in England.

Like Lambarde, Smith traced the courses of the county rivers, and his accounts read like verbal cartography. It was a time when maps were not commonly encountered, and his text was doubtless more readable than it is now. Here is a sentence from the description of the River Dee:

> From *Banger* it passeth to *Worthenbury*, where it receiveth a small River, that cometh from the East, having two principal Heads or Mears: The one at *Blackmer* in *Shropshire*, which runneth through *Whitchurch*: the other at *Coisley* in *Cheshire*, from thence it goeth to *Shocklich* in *Cheshire*, (where it hath *Cheshire* on the East, and *Denbighshire* on the West) not far from thence, it receiveth in a River that cometh from *Wrixham*, and also a little Brook, that cometh from *Old-castle*, not far from the town of *Malpas*.[4]

It is a method which demands unusual degrees of concentration and visualization of the reader, and is similar to Stow's specification of the layout of London's streets.[5] Elsewhere, Smith gives information about the more significant towns and villages, usually with great economy of words, as for Macclesfield:

> MACCLESFIELD is one of the fairest towns in *Cheshire*, and standeth upon the edge of *Macclesfield* Forest, upon a high Bank; at the foot whereof runneth a

> small River, named *Bollin*, distant 8. miles South from *Stopford*. It hath Market every Munday, and two yearly Fairs; that is to say, on *Barnabas* day, and *All-souls* day.
>
> There is a fair Church, with a very high Spire steeple, founded by *Thomas Savage*, Bishop of *London*, and after Arch-bishop of *York*; but the steeple thereof is not fully finished: therein are divers goodly Monuments of the *Savages*; and not far from the Church, is a huge place all of stone, in manner of a Castle, which belonged to the D. of *Buckingham*, but now gone much to decay.
>
> I find the name of this Town written *Macclesfield*, and Gentlemen of the same surname, which now are dead.[6]

This brief description, more expansive than many, illustrates the key strategies of Smith's method: he offers some practical information, he makes a remark about the church, and he endeavours to establish the place's connections with persons of title. Indeed, the final curious sentence links the town with prominent persons of whom no more is revealed but that they are no longer alive.

William Webb's survey was written some thirty years later and is more than twice as long. He presented many tables of similar data, such as a lengthy list of mayors and sheriffs, but he wrote much more expansively in his descriptions of places. In his introduction, Webb referred to antiquaries in whose steps he sought to follow: John Norden, John Stow, and John Speed, thanks to whose work there was an established structure upon which he could base his survey. So pleased has he been, he wrote, with earlier county histories, that '… I have been transported with I know not what longing desire, that some particular Descriptions of other parts and Countyes of the same Kingdome, not yet by any man published might be taken in hand …'[7] Moreover he embarked on his project with the express purpose of praising Cheshire: '… My Pen would here run into too spacious a field, if I should fall into the praises, either of the place, or of the people; the Soyl, or the Commodities; the Climate, or the wholesomness of the Ayr, and Scituation …'[8]

Webb's survey was arranged according to the seven hundreds of the county, and beginning with Broxton Hundred, he came almost at once to the city of Chester itself. Following the true antiquarian agenda, he began with a lengthy consideration of the origins and early history of the city. While Webb was clearly sceptical about ancient legends ('fables') he argued that the very obscurity of Chester's origins was sufficient evidence for its antiquity.[9] There were several traditions, variously attributing the foundation to the grandson of Noah; to Leon Gaure, a giant who had conquered the Picts; and to the Romans. Webb was generally impatient with antiquarian details, and at several points he noted that he had omitted data as being 'not so pertinent' in order to maintain his 'intended brevity'. Of the city's churches the cathedral warranted some comment, although Webb was mainly concerned to preserve 'worthy remembrances of many famous Persons ... by reciting their several Monuments'.[10] For the other churches, he opted to 'wade no further ... into the times of [their] foundations ... wherein I might spend a great deal of unprofitable discourse both in the doubtfull Collection of other men, and ungrounded conjectures of my own framing; which the Reader would happily think time ill bestowed upon ...'[11] Moreover he makes clear that his text is to be 'a plain Topographical Description', and 'no Historical Narration'.[12]

For all Webb's protestations, there is plenty in his survey that is genealogical, and therefore more 'historical' than 'topographical'. In describing places, he gave most attention to the gentry families there seated, and wherever he could, he gave their funerary epitaphs. He gave lengthy histories of the earls of Chester and of the bishopric of Chester. His list of mayors and sheriffs includes, in many cases, a few remarks on notable incidents of the year of tenure, vividly capturing moments of seventeenth-century life which seemed memorable when they occurred. In 1612, for example, the mayor, Robert Whitby, gentleman,

> did very strictly take care, that all Statutes and Orders within the City should be kept accordingly, and caused all that sold Ale or Beer for two pence the quart, to pay the full forfeiture of their recognisances; he appointed every man to bring their Quarts, and break in pieces all that were not full measure; he viewed the weights and measures of all the Tradesmen within the City, reforming those that were amisse, and caused many new bushels to be cut lesse; he sized the Wines, Muscadine at 7*d.* the quart, Sack at 10*d.* and other Wines at six pence.[13]

The previous year, the mayor was Joseph Ratcliffe, beer brewer, who

> ... being perswaded, that the Sabbath day should be truly performed and kept, [...] caused the Reapers to be removed that came every Sunday to the high Crosse in the Harvest time to be hired for the Week following.[14]

In 1606, the year of Philip Philips, hatmaker:

> In the moneth of *January* the Sword being carried before the Maior through the *Minster* Church, it was put down by one of the Prebends, which was the cause of some controversie, but the same was presently appeased by the Bishop.
>
> A Stranger did Dance and Vault upon a Rope, which was fastened a great height above the ground, overthwart the street at the high Crosse, which did seem strange to the beholders.[15]

The first extract which follows is a part of William Smith's description of the county as a whole. It is as rhetorical as factual, and reads more like a check-list of all the items to be mentioned in a topographical sketch than an eye-witness report. This is a basic county-survey method, and will be found to be remarkably similar to that written ten years earlier by William Lambarde for Kent, and which probably influenced Smith. Nevertheless we can sense the writer's love for his native county, which is given a certain degree of individuality, such as in the unusual nature of the peat-bogs and the abundance of salt. It is a place of plenitude and peace, better in most respects than every other county in England: Cheshire is the oldest, the most independent, the most beautiful, the most productive; it has the longest-established church, the noblest leaders, and makes the best cheese. The second extract is from William Webb's description of the city of Chester. Here are his descriptions of the walls and the streets of the city, both of which are still major attractions for visitors to Chester. The arcading of the footpaths, with the upper floors of the shops and houses overhanging, was apparently a novel arrangement. In explaining the benefits of this design, Webb gives a vivid idea of the traffic to be encountered in a seventeenth-century High Street. Far from being a detached observer, Webb emerges as a lively participant in the scenes he describes, sensitive to the conveniences and annoyances of the urban environment.

Cheshire (William Smith)

From the *Particular Description of Cheshire*, from *The Vale-Royal of England,* first pagination, pp.15–19

This County Palatine of *Chester*, which in our common speech is called *Chestershire*; and by corruption, more short, *Cheshire*, lyeth then on the North-West corner of that Countrey, which was sometimes under the Government of the Kings of *Marcia*; as is before declared:[16] Whose people were called by the Romans *Devani*; that is, bordering on the River *Dee*. The proportion thereof, is almost three-corner'd, or rather like to the Wing of an Eagle, being stretched forth at length …

By Natural Scituation, it lyeth low, nevertheless very pleasant, and abounding in plenteousness of all things needfull and necessary for mans use: insomuch, that it merited, and had the Name of *The Vale-Royal of* England: Which Name, King *Ed.* I. gave unto the Abbey of Vale-Royal, which he founded upon the River of *Weever*, in the midst of the same Shire. The ayr is very wholesome; insomuch that the people of the countrey are seldome infected with Diseases or Sicknesse, neither do they use the help of the

Physicians, nothing so much, as in other countries: For when any of them are sick, they make him a posset, and tye a kerchieff on his head;[17] and if that will not amend him, then God be merciful to him. The people there live till they be very old; some are Grand-fathers, their Fathers yet living; and some are Grand-fathers before they be married.

The Summer-time is temperate, and aboundeth not so much in heat, as in other places: Howbeit, the Winter is somewhat colder, and is oftentimes subject to great Tempests of winds, especially when it bloweth at the West or North-west; and namely, the countrey of *Wewal*,[18] by reason of the Sea at hand.

The Countrey, albeit it be in most places plat and even; yet hath it certain Hills of Name (besides the Mountains, which divide it from *Stafford-shire* and *Darby-shire*,) as *Frodshum* Hills, *Peckfarton* Hills, *Buckley* Hills, *Helsby* Tor, *Winecader* Hill, *Shutlingslow* Hill, *Penket* Cloud, *Congleton* Hedge, (or Edge) *Mowcop* Hill, which is a mile, from the foot, to the top, but standeth for most part in *Stafford-shire*.

It aboundeth chiefly in Arable Pasture, Meadow, and Woodland, Waters, Heaths, or Mosses: And first, of Woods, there is many, and of divers names and bigness; and namely, two famous Forests: that is, the Forest of *Delamer*, not far from *Chester*; and *Maxfield* Forest, hard by *Maxfield*: also great store of Parks; for every Gentleman, almost, hath his own Park.

Of Waters, there is also great store, in manner of Lakes, which they call Meres; as *Combermere*, *Bagmere*, *Comberbach*, *Pickmer*, *Ranstorn Mere*, *Okehanger-Mere*; and certain also which they call Pools; as *Ridley-Pool*, *Darnal-Pool*, *New-Pool*, *Petti-Pool*; and divers others, wherein aboundeth all kind of Fresh-Fish; as *Carpes*, *Tenches*, *Bremes*, *Roches*, *Daces*, *Trouts*, and *Eeles*, in great store.

The Heaths are common; so that they serve for *Cattel* to feed on, especially Sheep and Horses, a good help for the poorer sort.[19]

Out of the Mosses, they dig Turves[20] every Summer, every man as shall serve his turn, to burn all the Year: Which Turves in some places when they are dry, are redish and soft, much like a Sponge, which burneth fast away, and giveth not so good a light or heat, as the other sort which are black and very hard when they be dryed, and are much better than the other.

Moreover, in these Mosses (especially in the black) are Fir-trees, found under the ground, (a thing marvellous!) in some places 6. foot deep, or more, and in some places not one foot; which Trees are of a marvellous length, and straight, having certain small Branches, like Boughs, and Roots at one end, like as if they had been blown down with Weather; and yet no man can tell that ever such Trees did grow there; nor yet, how they should come thither. Some hold Opinion, that they have lain there ever since *Noahs* Floud.

These Trees being found (which the Owners do search out with a long Spit of Iron, or such like) they are then digged up: and first being sawed into short pieces (every piece of the length of a yard) then they cleave the said pieces very small; yea, even as the back of a knife, the which they use, instead of a candle to burn, and giveth a very good light: It hath a long snuff, and yet in falling, doth no harm, although it should light into Tow, Flax, or such like.[21]

Besides the Heaths, Mosses, Woods, and Commons, the rest is Inclosed Ground, both for Pasture and Tillage, but the third part thereof, in a manner, is reserved onely for Tillage, which bringeth forth corn in great quantity; (howbeit more in some places, than in other some) especially Wheat and Rye (which they sowe in *September*, and so lyeth in the ground all Winter): also, Oats and Barley, Beans, Pease, Fitches,[22] French Wheat[23], and such like.

The Pasture Ground is reserved, especially, for their Kine; (for their Sheep and Horses commonly go upon the *Commons*) The cause of their keeping of so many Kine, is, as well for breeding of *Cattel*, as for their milk; wherewith (besides that which they spend in their houses) they make great store both of Butter and Cheese. In praise whereof, I need not to say much, seeing that it is well known, that no other Countrey in the Realm may compare therewith, nor yet beyond the Seas; no, not *Holland* in goodness, although in quantity it far exceed.

Their young Cattel, which they breed and bring up, (their own turn being served) they bring the rest to the Market to sell, and many times are brought up as far as *London*, and further, by Grasiers, who buy them there; and, feeding them a certain time, do then sell them again.

Their Oxen are very large, and big of bone, and altogether with fair and long horns; so that a man shall find divers, whose horns at the tops, are more then three foot wide, or asunder, one from another; with the which oxen, they do all-labour; as Tilling of their Ground, Carring[24] of their Corn, Hey, Turves, and Wood, and some come to *London*, with their Wayns laden with Salt. They keep their Oxen all the Winter time in house, but not their Kine, as they do in some other Countries.

They keep nothing so many sheep, as in other Countries, because their ground serveth better to other purposes; for commonly, they keep but so many, as to serve in their own houses for provision, and to sell to the Butcher, and that the wool thereof may suffice to make apparel for their Houshold. Of which sheep, some have horns, and some not. Some are all black, and the wool thereof being spun and woven into cloth or kersey, as it is undyed, is not black, but more liker brown, such as we call, *A Sheeps Russet.*

Horses and Mares, they keep but so many as to serve their turn, to ride on, or to carry corn to the Mill; (Howbeit, in most places, the Millers have Carriers, which fetch the corn, and when it is ground, do bring it home again.) As for Horses and Mares to draw, they use not any, but onely one or two, at the most, to go before their Oxen: except in some certain places, and that is commonly amongst them that dwell on Sandy ground.

Swine, Geese, Ducks, Cocks, Capons, and Hens, there is like store, as in other Countries; but all things much better cheap there, then in the South part of *England*.

Besides the great store of Deer, both Red and Fallow, in the two Forests before named; there is also great plenty of Hares: In Hunting whereof, the Gentlemen do pass much of their time, especially in Winter: also, great store of Conies, both black and gray; namely, in those places, where it is Sandy ground: neither doth it lack Foxes, Fulmards, Otters, Basons,[25] and such like.

Wild-Foul aboundeth there in such store, as in no other Countrey have I seen the like; namely, Wild-Geese, and Wild-Ducks. Of which first sort, a man shall see sometimes flying, neer 200. in one flock; and likewise of the Ducks, 40. or 50. in a flock. And in other kinds also it hath like store; as Phesant, More-hen, Partridg, Woodcocks, Plovers, Teels, Widgins[26]; and of all kind of small Birds. So hath it on the contrary sort, Ravens, Crows, Choughs, Kites, Gleads,[27] and such like.

Of Fruits; as Apples, Pears, Wardens[28], Plums, Cheries, and such like, they have plenty in their Orchards, not onely to serve their own turn, but also to sell and give away. But Quinces have I not seen in any place of the *Countrey*, that I can remember.

Likewise, doth every man keep certain Hives of Bees; but no greater store, commonly, then to serve their own turn: yet some do bring to the Market both Wax and Honey.

The Soyl of the *Countrey* is, in most places, clay, both black and red: in the which, is found in some places, certain veins of Sand; in other places it is black Sand, which is neer unto Mosses. There is also found a certain kind of fat clay, called *Marle*, both white and red, which they dig up, and spread on their *Arable Ground*, which maketh it more ranker, and bringeth *Corn* in as great abundance, as that which is dunged.

There is in some places *Choak*,[29] *White-lime*, *Oker*, red and yellow, and a certain kind of fine red Earth, like unto red Lead, and in some places, *Cole*.

Likewise *Rocks*, and *Quarries of Stone*, out of which they dig very fair stones for Building, and all kinds of *Masonry*: also very broad Slates, wherewith they cover their houses, and blew Slate: But they that dwell far off, do use Shingle of Wood, instead of Slate.

Also, there are very fair Mill-stones digged up at *Mowcop* Hill.

And, to make an end, I must not forget the chiefest thing of all; and that is, the Salt-wells, which they call Brine-pits; out of the which, they make yearly a great quantity of fine white Salt: a singular commodity, no doubt, not onely to the *Countrey*, but also to the whole Realm; wherein this Shire excelleth (not onely all other Shires in *England*; but also) all other *Countries* beyond the Seas. For in no Countrey where I have been, have they any more then one Well in a Countrey: Neither at *Durtwich* in *Worcester-shire*, is there any more then one; whereas in this Countrey are four, and all within ten miles altogether; that is, one at *Nantwich*, another at *Northwich*, and two at *Middlewich*.

The City of Chester (William Webb)

From *A Description of the City and County Palatine of Chester*, from *The Vale-Royal of England*, second pagination, pp.15–19

The City of *Chester*, is built in form of a quadrant, and is almost a just square, inclosed with a fair stone-wall, high and strong built, with fair Battlements of all the four sides; and with the 4. Gates, opening to the four Winds: Besides some Posterns,[30] and many seemly Towers, in, and upon the said Walls. The four Gates, are, the East-gate, the North-gate, the Water-gate, and the Bridge-gate: Without the first two of these gates; namely, the East and North Gates: The City extends her self in her Suburbs, with very fair streets, and the same adorned with goodly Buildings, both of Gentlemens houses, and fair Innes for entertainment of all Resorts.

And the Bridge-gate opening into an antient part of the City, beyond the water, over the Bridge; or rather that part which some suppose was once the City it self, now called *Iland-bridge*; and the Water-gate onely leading forth to the side of the River *Dee*: Which River, even there, falls into the mouth of the Sea, having first as it were purposely turn'd it self aside, to leave a fine spacious piece of ground of great pleasure and delight, called *The Rood-Eye*; for the Citizens both profit and re-past a very delightful Meadow place, used for a Cow-pasture in the Summer-time; and all the year for a wholesome and pleasant Walk by the side of the *Dee*; and for Recreations of Shooting, Bowling, and such other Exercises, as are performed at certain times by men; and by running Horses, in presence and view of the Major of the City,[31] and his Bretheren; with such other Lords, Knights, Ladies, Gentlemen, as please at those times, to accompany them for that view.

That which we may call the chiefest passage into that City, giving entrance to all comers from the most part of that County of *Chester*, and the great Roads from other Shires, is the East-Gate, a goodly great Gate, of an antient fair Building, with a Tower upon it, containing many fair Rooms within it: At which, we begin the circuit of the Wall, which from that gate, Northward, extendeth to a Tower upon the said wall.

These Towers, whereof there are divers upon the said walls, were, as I suppose, made to be Watch-Towers in the day, and lodging places in the night, and in the time of storms, for the watchmen that kept watch upon the walls, in those times of danger, when they were so often besieged by Armies of Enemies, and in such perilous surprises; though now some of them be converted to other uses.

The North gate of the City is of a reasonable strong fair building, and used for the prison of the City ...[32]

From the North-gate, still Westward, the wall extendeth to another Tower; and from thence to the turning of the wall Southwards; at which corner, standeth another fine Turret, called, *The New Tower*, and was pitcht within the channel of *Dee* water; which *New Tower*, was built, as it is reported, in, or neer to the place in the River, which was the Key[33] whereunto Vessels of great burden, as well of merchandize, as others, came close up; which may the rather seem probable, as well by a deeper Foundation of Stonework, yet appearing from the foot of that Tower, reaching a good distance into the Channel; as also, by great Rings of Iron, here and there fastned in the sides of the said Tower, which if they served not for the fastening of such Vessels, as then used to approach to the same Key, I cannot learn what other use they should be for.

From this corner of the *New Tower*, the wall goeth South to the Water-gate; which Gate is less then any of the other three, serving onely for the passage to the *Rood-Eye*, formerly mentioned, and to the Bank of the River, where are brought into the City all such commodities of Cole, Fish, Corn, and other things; which Barks, and other small Vessels bring up so far, upon the water of *Dee*.

And still South from the same Water-gate, reacheth the wall in a straight line, before it hath gotten beyond the Castle, and then turns it self towards the East.

From that turning, is the Bridge-gate, scituate at the North-end, of a very fair and strong Stone-bridge; with another fair gate at the South-end of it.

The River of *Dee* doth here incline to enlarge it self, having gotten so near the Sea, but that it is soundly girt in on either side, with huge Rocks of hard stone, which restrain the pride of its force.

This Bridge-gate being a fair Strong Building of it self, hath of late been more beautified by a seemly Water-work of stone, built Steeple-wise, by the ingenuous industry and charge of a late worthy member of the City, *John Terer* Gent. and hath served ever since, to great use, for the conveying of River-water from the Cestern, in the top of that Work, to the Citizens houses, in almost all parts of the City, in Pipes of Lead and Wood, to their no small contentment and commodity.

The Wall thence continueth along the River side Eastward, to another remainder of a Turret, and then turneth it self Northward; and certain Paces from thence, is a Postern, of old, called *Woolfield gate*; but of latter-times, named *New-gate*, which in *Anno* 1609. was augmented and adorned with a fair Building, and made for a passage, both for Horse and Carts, serving to great use; and for a more compendious way to all Passengers, Horse, Foot, Carts, or Coaches, which either desire not to behold the beauty of the middle streets of the City, or delight not to be seen of many Eyes, but make more speed in their travel, then some do: and from this gate, our wall having another Turret now unto it, called *Wall-Tower*, stretcheth still along, till it meeteth with the East-gate, at which it began.

This wall is so fairly built, with Battlements on the outward part, as was said before, and with a foot-pace, or floor, a yard or four foot under the Notch of the Battlement,[34] that with the help of some stairs, to pass the breadth of one of the great Gates, you may go round about the walls, being a very delectable Walk, feeding the Eye, on the one side, with the sweet Gardens, and fine Buildings of the City; and on the other side, with a Prospect of many miles into the County of *Chester*, into *Wales*, and into the Sea ...[35]

Upon the South-side of the City, neer unto the said water of *Dee*, and upon a high Bank, or Rock of Stone, is mounted a strong and stately Castle, round in form; the *Base-Court* likewise inclosed with a circular wall, which, to this day, retaineth one testimony of the *Romans* magnificence, having therein a fair and antient square Tower; which by testimony of all the Writers, I have hitherto met withall, beareth the name of *Julius Cæsars* Tower: besides which there remain yet many goodly pieces of Building; whereof one of them containeth all fit and commodious Rooms, for the lodging and use of the Honourable Justices of Assize, twice a year. Another part is a goodly Hall, where the Court of the *Common-Pleas*, and Gaol-delivery; and also the Sheriffs of the Counties Court; with other businesses for the County of *Chester*, are constantly kept and holden: And is a place, for that purpose, of such state and comeliness, that I think it is hardly equalled with any Shire-Hall, in any of the Shires of *England*.

And then next unto the South-end of the said Hall, is a less, but fair, neat, and convenient Hall, where is continually holden the Princess Highness most honourable *Court of Exchequer*; with other Rooms, fitly appendant thereunto, for keeping of the Records of that *Court*. Within the Precincts of which *Castle*, is also the Kings Prison for the county of *Chester*, with the Office of *Protonothory*,[36] Convenient Rooms for the dwelling of the *Constables*, or Keeper of the said Castle and Gaol, with divers other Rooms of Stabling, and other uses, with a fair Draw-well of water, in the middest of the *Court*; divers sweet and dainty Orchards and Gardens; beside much of the antient Building, for want of use, fallen to ruine and decay ...

To step therefore from thence, into the city itself; The streets, for the most part, are very fair and beautiful, the Buildings on either side, especially towards the Streets, of seemly proportion, and very neatly composed; whether of Timber, whereof the most are builded; or of Stone, or Brick; and for a singular property or praise to this city, whereof I know not the like of any other, though there be towards the street fair Rooms, both for shops and dwelling houses; to which there is rather a descent, then an equal height with the floor or pavement of the street: Yet the principal dwelling houses and shops of the chiefest Trades, are mounted a Story higher; and before the Doors and Entries, a continued Rowe on either side of the street, for people to pass to and fro all along the said houses, out of all annoyance of Rain, or other foul weather, with stairs fairly built, and neatly maintained, to step down out of those Rowes into the open streets, almost at every second house; and the said Rowes built over the head, with such of the Chambers and Rooms, for the most part, as are the best Rooms in every of the said houses: Which manner of building, howsoever it may seem to have had beginning from some other cause: yet, indeed, approves it self to be of most excellent use, both for dry and easie passage of all sorts of people, upon their necessary occasions; as also, for the sending away of all, or the most Passengers on foot, from the passage of the street, amongst laden and empty Carts, loaden and travelling Horses, lumbring Coaches, and Beer-carts, Beasts, Sheep, Swine, & all annoyances, which what a confused trouble it makes in other Cities, especially where great stirring is, there's none that can be ignorant …

1. He included a list of the mayors and sheriffs of Chester, which goes as far as 1586.
2. Webb's list contains increasingly more information up to 1617, after which there are few details besides names and dates. The later records were probably added by Daniel King.
3. As well as Smith and Webb, the authors are Samuel Lee, whose text *Chronicon Cestrense* (1653) is a history of Chester in which events are dated by the method of synchronism, that is, making comparisons with the histories of other people, places, and events; and James Chaloner, whose text is a brief description of the Isle of Man. On Wenceslaus Hollar, see the Introduction and the chapter on William Dugdale.
4. *The Vale-Royal*, first pagination, p.20.
5. See Stow's description of Bread Street, *supra*.
6. *The Vale-Royal*, first pagination, p.45.
7. *The Vale-Royal*, second pagination, p.1.
8. *Ibid.*, p.4.
9. 'That there hath been so much wrastling and striving to find out antient Names, and the first Original of the City of *Chester*, is to me one Argument of the antientness thereof; for, where there is no certainty known, how can it be but beyond the reach of all intelligence, that the laborious Writers of all Ages have endeavoured after: Whereupon I hold it a conclusion, that many Monuments in this Kingdome, whereof there can be found no Memory for their Foundation, are more antient, than those who have had their Foundations either certainly known, or probably conjectured.' (*Ibid.*, p.7)

10. *Ibid.*, pp.24–25. Webb's narrative on the cathedral is interrupted by a five-page editorial insertion headed '*A Discourse of the Foundation and Endowment of the Abbie of St* Werburgs *in* Chester: *Written by N.N.*' (The former abbey church of St Werburg became the cathedral of Chester in the reign of Henry VIII.) It is a more scholarly piece, having a number of marginal references to sources, which include Dugdale's *Monasticon Anglicanum*, the first volume of which was published in 1655. Clearly this was added by Daniel King, but was done so clumsily that it comes in the midst of a quite unrelated discussion on the origins of Christianity in Britain.
11. *Ibid.*, p.33.
12. *Ibid.*, p.10.
13. *Ibid.*, p.213.
14. *Ibid.*
15. *Ibid.*, p.211.
16. Smith has earlier given an outline history of the kings of Mercia.
17. *Posset,* a drink made of hot milk curdled with ale or wine. The word is Old English, having meant 'a drink good for a cold in the head'. A *kerchief* (a Middle English contraction of 'coverchef') is a cloth worn to cover the head.
18. Probably 'Wirral' was intended.
19. Smith means that the heaths are common land which can be used by everyone.
20. *Turves*, blocks of peat.
21. The burnt wick remains long and does not fall until it is cold and so will be unlikely to cause a fire.
22. *Fitches*, perhaps vetches, leguminous plants grown for forage.
23. *French Wheat*, buckwheat.
24. *Carring*, carrying.
25. The meanings of 'fulmard' and 'bason' are obscure.
26. *Widgins*, widgeons (a type of freshwater duck).
27. *Gleads*, kites.
28. *Wardens*, cooking pears.
29. Perhaps 'chalk' was intended.
30. *Posterns*, minor gates.
31. *Major*, mayor.
32. In this paragraph, Webb explains the use of the building as the city prison.
33. *Key*, quay.
34. That is, under the crenels between the merlons, under the spaces formed by the crenellation of the wall.
35. Such a walk is still possible.
36. *Protonothory,* prothonotary.

THE NORTH-EAST

XXI
Britannia—Northumberland: William Camden (1551–1623)

William Camden was the outstanding historian and antiquary of the later Tudor and early Stuart periods: both with respect to his method and the scope of his undertakings, his profound influence on subsequent English historical scholarship was widely acknowledged. He was cited with deference throughout the seventeenth century; his *Britannia* was regarded as the model chorography, and his *Annales Rerum Anglicarum et Hibernicarum Regnante Elizabethae*, translated from Latin as *The History of the Renowned Princess Elizabeth*,[1] was a seminal work of early modern English historical scholarship, making a departure from the method of the medieval chronicle. He wrote in Latin as the language of scholarship, and his works were read in European countries as well as in Britain. Indeed, Camden corresponded with many Continental scholars, and it was on the urging of Abraham Ortelius, visiting England in 1577, that he undertook the writing of *Britannia*. The historian F. Smith Fussner described Camden as 'an intellectual aristocrat' whose distinguished career was characterised by dignity, courtesy, and restraint.

Born in London, Camden attended St Paul's School, and went on to Oxford when he was fifteen years of age. He was associated with several of the university colleges in succession, till, as a defender of the established religion, he became involved in controversy with certain influential Catholics and, because of this, failed to gain a fellowship at All Souls. He did not take a degree and, on leaving the university, spent a few years travelling and collecting material on antiquities, an interest which he had developed in his youth. Through his friendship with Dr Gabriel Goodman, Dean of Westminster, he obtained a position in 1575 as second master at Westminster School. He found this situation offered considerable amenity to his antiquarian pursuits, for the vacations allowed him to continue his travels, research, and writing. By 1593 he had become the headmaster of the school.

The first edition of *Britannia* was published in 1586, an octavo volume of modest size, but which was to grow considerably as Camden included more and more material, both from further travels and from further study of classical writers, as successive editions followed. The extract given below, on Northumberland, is such an example: it was added to the 1607 edition after he toured the northern counties of England with Robert Cotton, and with guidance from a local schoolmaster, Reginald Bainbrigg. The basic method of the book was topographical, beginning with the general geography of the British Isles, then proceeding to the history of its early settlement, and its administrative divisions. The bulk of the book was then taken up with descriptions of the individual counties, arranged in groups according to their original occupation by British tribes. Specifically he described antiquities, so that there was in fact little observation of the landscape or its beauty or intrinsic interest.

In this latter respect Camden's work may be compared with that of John Leland, his only recent predecessor in attempting to describe the whole nation. *Britannia* was systematic where Leland's *Itinerary*, really no more than a collection of notes, had been left in a state of chaos, but Camden's details of particular places, apart from features of historical or antiquarian interest, were in most cases less comprehensive and less engaging. It is not unexpected that the author of a pioneering work of such scope should have drawn upon numerous sources. Because Leland's work was so useful yet so disorganised, Camden made extensive use of it, but in such a way that it was possible for certain of his critics to level a charge of plagiarism. In a departure from the tradition of English antiquarianism of the time, Camden was sceptical about the 'Brut', preferring to base historical knowledge upon that for which there was substantial and corroborated evidence. In a work which came to command such a degree of authority as did *Britannia*, this was a significant step. It was not surprising that one so cognisant with scholarship across Europe should be prepared to compare impartially the views of Polydore Vergil and the beliefs of antiquaries following an essentially medieval scenario. And it is equally unsurprising that he should have drawn the ire of many English lovers of the old stories of Trojan kings, giants, and King Arthur.

Coinciding with this potential for academic debate, Camden was offered an appointment as Clarenceux Herald, evoking acrimony within the College of Heralds and especially from the York Herald, Ralph Brooke, who had himself been eyeing the post and who saw Camden as an imposter who was insufficiently skilled in the business of heraldry. Camden accepted, relinquishing his teaching at Westminster. Thereupon Brooke published a book of the errors to be found in *Britannia*, accusing its author of plagiarism, sloppy genealogy, and expressing offence at his dismissal of the medieval British History. To these criticisms Camden made reply, and the upshot was that he had indeed made errors in certain details, for example in the interpretation of heraldic devices on certain tombs. The most interesting aspect of this dispute is that the points of difference had to be resolved in the field: by visiting the tomb in question and observing it. This was indicative of a new method in antiquarian research; a readily apparent example in *Britannia* is the careful letter-by-letter recording of Latin inscriptions found on stones in places of Roman occupation. That which seems obvious now was an innovation in the late sixteenth century.

In describing Northumberland, Camden was concerned with both Roman and medieval history, and he sought his data archaeologically as well as from archives. The section resulted from a trip made with the young Robert Cotton, whose great library, accumulated in later years, was to be of such benefit to English scholarship in the seventeenth century and thereafter. Camden's field trip was the sort of innovative work which was to change the way the past was studied, even though it was a change which was slow in coming. For the most part, the landscape is overlooked: Camden writes about historical families and their great houses, battles, and Roman inscriptions. In the following short extract the landscape emerges as a mere background to the history, yet its brooding desolation and the hardiness of its inhabitants are inescapably evident. It is the opening of his chapter on Northumberland, beginning with general remarks about the county, then, using the chorographical strategy which became standard after Camden, more details are developed as the antiquary follows the courses of the main rivers. There were Roman vestiges in many places in Britain, but the remains of Hadrian's Wall must have been the greatest in extent of all.

The wall when it was built had a ditch along its Scottish side and a *vallum*, or ditch with a large bank on each side, along the southern side. Mostly it was built of local stone but in some areas, where stone was not readily available, it was built of turf blocks. At each Roman mile along the wall was a 'milecastle', or small fort, and between these were turrets, which were watchtowers. In some places there were camps at which up to a thousand personnel were stationed. These posts were occupied by the Romans over a period of three hundred years, so it not surprising that stone tablets bearing memorial and religious inscriptions might be found. The wall was the northernmost border of the Roman Empire and was also the most heavily fortified border. In *Britannia*, the section on Northumberland is immediately preceded by a section dealing with the history of the wall, which in Camden's time was more popularly known as the Picts' Wall. As the section from which the extract is taken continues, Camden reports on the finding of more inscribed stones and uses these to try to locate Roman leaders and events of which he had read in Roman accounts which had been written in contemporary times.

North-humber-land

From *Britannia*, translated by Philemon Holland, 1610, pp.799–800

North-humber-land, which the English Saxons called Noꝛþan-Ƕumbeꝛ-lonð, lieth after a sort enclosed in fashion of a Triangle, but not with equall sides. The Southside is shut in with *Derwent* running into *Tine*, and with *Tine* it selfe, where it butteth upon the Bishopricke of Durham. The Eastside the German sea lieth & beateth upon it. But the West side which reacheth out from South-west to North-east, is first parted from Cumber-land afterward with Cheviot and hills linked one to another, & lastly with the river *Twede*, it affronteth Scotland, and so was the limit of both kingdoms: over which were set in this County two governors: one called L. Warden of the Midle Marches, the other of the East marches. The ground it selfe for the most part rough, & hard to be manured,[2] seemeth to have hardened the inhabitants, whom the Scots their neighbours also made more feirce and hardy, while sometimes they keepe them exercised in warres, and other whiles in time of peace intermingle their manners among them, so that by these meanes they are a most warlike nation, & excellent good light horsemen. And wheras they addicted themselves as it were wholy to *Mars* and Armes, there is not a man among them of the better sort, that hath not his little towre or pile: and so it was divided it was into a number of *Baronies*: the Lords whereof in times past before King Edward the First his daies went commonly under the name Barons, although some of them were of no great living. But a wise and politicke devise this was of out Ancestours, to cherish and maintaine martiall proesse among them in the marches of the kingdome, if it were nothing else, but with an honorable bare title. Howbeit this title came to nothing among them, what time as under King Edward the First, those onely beganne to enjoie the name and honor of *Barons*, whom the Kings summoned unto the high Court of Parliament by speciall summons. Towards the sea and *Tine*, by diligence and good husbandry, it becommeth very fruitfull; but else where it is more barraine, rough and as it were un-manurable. And in many places, those stones *Lithanthraces*, which wee call *Sea coles*,[3] are digged up in great plenty to the greater gaine of the inhabitants, and commodity of others.

The hithermore part bending toward the South-west, and called *Hexam shire*, acknowledged a long time the Archbishop of Yorke for the Lord thereof, and chalenged unto it selfe, by what right I know not, the priviledge of a County Palatine: But after it became of late annexed unto the crowne land, upon an exchange made with Robert the Archbishop, by authority of Parliament it was laied[4] unto the County of Northumberland, that it should bee subject to the same jurisdiction, and in all causes have recourse to the high Sherife thereof.

South Tine (a river so called if wee may beleeve our Britans, for that by reason of his narrow bankes hee is streight pent in, for so signifieth *Tin*, as they say, (in the British tongue) having his spring-head in Cumberland neere unto *Alsten-more*, where there was an ancient coper mine, holding on his course by *Lambley*, sometime a Nunnerie built by the *Lucies*, and now with flouds for the most part undermined and fallen downe: also by *Fetherston-Haugh* the seat of the ancient and wel-descended family of *Fetherston*, when hee is come as farre as *Bellister Castle*, turning Eastward runneth directly forward with the WALL, which is no place three miles distant from it toward the North.

For, the *Wall* having left Cumberland behind it, and crossed over the *Irthing*, passed likewise with an arch over the swift riveret *Polrosse*, where I saw within the wall high mounts of earth cast up, as it were, to over looke and discover the country.[5] Nere this standeth *Thirl-wale Castle*, which is not great but strongly built,[6] yet it gave both habitation and surname, to the ancient and noble familie, which was first called *Wade*: where the Picts and Scottish made their passage into the Province betweene *Irthing* and *Tine* (and that verily upon good forecast) in that place where they had free entrance by reason of no river in their way, into the in more partes of England. But you shall better understand this; and the name of the place out of John *Forden* the Scottish Historian, whose words it will not bee amisse, as I thinke, to set downe here, because the booke is not every where to bee had.[7] *The Scottes* (saith hee) *when by conquest they had gotten the possession of those Countries, which are on this side of the Wall, toward Scotland, beganne to inhabite them; and having of a sodaine raised a fort of the Country people, with their mattockes, pickaxes, rakes, three tined forkes and spades, make wide gappes and a number of holes in it, by which breaches they might passe in and out readilie at their pleasure. Of those holes therefore, this mound of the wall afterward tooke the name* Thirlwall, *which is as much as a wall pierced through.* Then sawe we *Blenkensop*, which gave name unto a generous family, as also their habitation in a right pleasant country Southward: which was part of the *Baronie* of Sir Nicholas of *Bolteby*, a Baron of renowne in the time of King Edward the First.

When you are past *Thirlwall*, the said wall openeth it selfe unto the raging river *Tippall*, where in the descent of an hill, a little within the wall, is to bee seene the ground worke of a castle of the Romans in forme foure square, every side whereof taketh an hundred and fortie paces. The very foundations likewise of houses and trackes of streetes appeere still most evidently to the beholders. The *Rank-riders, or taking men* of the borders doe report, that a great port-way paved with flint and bigge stone led from hence through wastes unto *Maiden Castle in Stanemore*: Certes, it passed directly to *Kirkby Thor*, whereof I spake.[8] A poore old woman that dwelt in a little poore cottage hard by, shewed unto us an ancient little altar-stone in testimonie of some vow, with this inscription unto VITIRINEVS, a tutelar God, as it seemed of this place.

DEO
VITI
RINE___
___LIMEO
ROV
*P. L. M

This place is now named *Caer Vorran*: what it was in old time, it passeth my wit to finde out, seeing that amongst all the stations mentioned along the range of the *Wall*, there is not one commeth neere to it in name; neither have wee any light out of inscriptions to lead us thereunto.[9] What ever it was, sure the wall thereby was both strongest and highest by farre: for, scarce a furlong or two from hence, upon a good high hill, there remaineth as yet some of it to bee seene fifteene foot high and nine foote thicke, built on both sides with foure square ashler stone, although *Bede* reporteth it was not above twelve foot in higth.

1. *Britannia* had seven Latin editions from 1586 to 1607. The first English edition, translated by Philemon Holland, appeared in 1610. The *Annales* was written at the behest of Lord Burghley, who had been Elizabeth's chief minister. He gave Camden access to his personal papers and many state papers. The first part was published in 1615 and the second in 1625, after Camden's death.
2. *Manured*, tilled, cultivated.
3. *Sea coal*, coal, probably so called because a major source of coal was at the edge of the sea on the Northumberland coast.
4. In 1571 by Act of Parliament Hexham was incorporated into the County of Northumberland and became an ecclesiastical peculiar of, that is, under the jurisdiction of, the Diocese of York.
5. This was probably Poltross Burn Milecastle, still one of the best preserved milecastles of Hadrian's Wall.
6. Thirlwall Castle was built with stone taken from Hadrian's Wall in the 13th century.
7. *John Fordon,* John of Fordun, author with Walter Bower of *Scotichronicon,* a fourteenth century history.
8. Kirkby Thore is the location of the Roman camp Bravoniacum, which guarded Stainmore and was on the Roman road called Maiden Way. This sentence is misleading, because Camden is referring to a different place: Kirkby Thore is near Appleby in Westmorland and Stainmore is south-east of there, almost in the south-west corner of County Durham. The reference to Maiden Castle is confusing, for the site now known as Maiden Castle in the north of England is just out of the city of Durham.
9. *Caer Vorran* was identified by the antiquary Thomas Cox, in *The Magna Britannica et Hibernia* (1731), with Walwick, the site of Chesters Fort on Hadrian's Wall.

AFTER ANTIQUARIANISM

XXII
Newcastle and Cumberland: Celia Fiennes (1662–1741)

In marked contrast to all the foregoing authors, Celia Fiennes wrote place descriptions in which the antiquarian inclination was completely absent. While she might be regarded as an author coming 'after the antiquaries', she was nevertheless very much their contemporary, recording her observations of the countryside at the same time that Henry Chauncy was compiling his study of Hertfordshire. Her place in this collection is as a contrast: she was an adventurous traveller rather than a researcher of archives; she was an amateur writer rather than a scholar; she was a radical innovator rather than an adherer to tradition; she was a witness to the present rather than a preserver of the past. Her travel account is a stream of observations recorded just as they were encountered, making an excited, immediate, vivid narrative which apparently had little subsequent reordering and editing.

Celia Fiennes was born into an aristocratic Puritan family on 7 June 1662 at Newton Toney, near Salisbury.[1] Her father was Colonel Nathaniel Fiennes, second son of Lord Saye and Sele, who was one of the most influential of the leaders of the parliamentary opposition to King Charles I. Together with the dissenters John Pym, John Hampden, Oliver St John, Lord Warwick, Lord Brooke, and Henry Vane, Saye and Sele and his son had met secretly at his country seat, Broughton Castle, using the so-called Council Chamber, which they described as 'the room that hath no ears', to plan the parliamentary strategy. Their meetings took place between 1629 and 1641, the period when the king ruled the nation personally and absolutely. Eventually the king was forced to call a parliament, and what followed is well known. Lord Saye and Sele made a significant contribution to the main political outcomes of the conflict: parliamentary government and the abolition of the monarchy. He was, however, not a regicide; he hoped instead for the Civil War to end in a negotiated settlement, and he chose to retire from politics after the execution of the monarch in 1649. He eventually became a supporter of the restored monarchy after the interregnum. His son Nathaniel was a member of the

Long Parliament and a colonel in the parliamentary army, and his wife was active in the cause of nonconformist religion and was fined in 1671 for holding an illicit conventicle in her house.[2]

As might be expected, Celia Fiennes's background gave her an outlook which was not conservative: she was more interested in progress than tradition and appreciated modern buildings, which she judged to be convenient and commodious. At Cambridge she wrote dismissively of the older colleges: '... the Buildings are old and indifferent ...'; in comparing the library with the Bodleian she observed '... the Library farre exceeds that of Oxford, the Staires are wanscoted and very large and easye ascent all of Cedar wood, the room spacious and lofty paved with black and white marble ...'; of particular colleges she remarked that '... Queens College is old but a stately and lofty building; Claire Hall is very little but most exactly neate ...'[3] She was interested in manufacturing, mining, drainage projects and harbours. She lived in a time when social barriers between aristocrats and commoners were being maintained less rigorously and many of her own relatives, descendants of a viscount, married people from families in business. As a person, nothing is known of Fiennes except that there is a legal document, of 1706, which shows that she held a mortgage on a piece of land in Cheshire. It was an investment in keeping with her progressive outlook, for the land had a significant deposit of rock salt, the first ever found and subsequently mined in England.[4] Apart from her diaries, the only surviving piece of her writing is her will.

It must be supposed that her travel ventures were quite unusual, although Christopher Morris makes the pertinent point that we do not have evidence of just how 'adventurous' her exploits were.[5] She began her earlier, shorter travels (in the south of England) when in her twenties; undertook her longest journeys in her mid-thirties; and continued with shorter ventures, again in the south, up to the age of fifty. Being unmarried and obviously having some financial means she was an independent woman, and she exercised this independence in a very individual way. She travelled on horseback, alone except for a couple of servants, and she did not hesitate to take roads and paths which were rough and isolated. She reported her horse stumbling so badly that she came off on a couple of occasions, although in neither case was she seriously injured. There must always have been some risk of being accosted or attacked but only once, between Beeston and Whitchurch in Cheshire, was she actually approached by highwaymen. They were on foot and followed her along, and she suspected they were armed, but she and her servants soon came across men working in the adjacent fields, and the anticipated robbery was thwarted. In her diary she made little of the incident, and elsewhere gave no hint of any fear of such encounters. She was more concerned with problems of accommodation and food in lonely places, and reported plenty of experiences of dirty rooms and uncomfortable nights. Whenever possible she sought to stay at the houses of gentry people with whom she was related or acquainted, and she particularly enjoyed visiting great country houses, of whose interiors and gardens there are many descriptions in her narrative.

Naturally Celia Fiennes's interests reflect those that were popular in her times, and one of the most evident is the enthusiasm for the supposed health-giving properties of mineral springs or 'spaws'. Indeed, this seems to have been one of her main concerns when travelling, for she sought out the local springs wherever they were available and commented on the type of natural waters available, the facilities provided, and their efficacy in curing ailments. It is evident from her comments, moreover, that she had visited many of the spas more frequently than is recorded directly in her diaries. Indeed it was a growing fashion, with different places providing particularly for different ranks of society. In some cases the natural water was taken as a health drink, in others cases the visitors bathed in it, or perhaps they did both. The baths now most famous, at Bath, had not been much developed in Fiennes's time and had a reputation for being smelly, but she did bathe there, being particularly pleased with the garments provided for the baths, which covered her in such a way that the shape of her body was hidden. This last observation was in keeping with her sense of propriety, which also became evident when she commented on works of art in country houses. Her taste in art was simple and straightforward, and while she could admire the workmanship in paintings her appreciation was much diminished by immodest subjects, as at Lord Sandwich's house at Huntingdon, where she noted: '… over one of the Chimneys is a fine picture of Venus were it not too much uncloth'd …'[6]

When visiting houses, Fiennes usually reported in some detail on the interior decorations and the gardens. Considering that she must have written up her diary entry at the end of the day and not on the spot, it seems that she had quite remarkable acuity of observation. Here is her description of a hall, just part of her account of the interior of the house of Lord Orford, in Cambridgeshire:

> … the hall is very nobly paved with freestone a squaire of black marble at each corner of the freestone; there are two fine white marble tables veined with blew, its wanscoted with Wallnut tree the pannells and rims round with Mulbery tree that is a lemon coullour and the moldings beyond it round are of a sweete outlandish wood not much differing from Cedar but of a finer graine, the chairs are all the same; its hung with pictures att full proportion of the Royal family; the whole house is finely furnish'd with differing coulloured damask and velvets some figured and others plaine, at least 6 or 7 in all richly made up after a new mode …[7]

In gardens, she was especially interested in the application of hydraulic engineering to achieve special and surprising effects. At Chatsworth she was very impressed:

> ... there is another green walk and about the middle of it by the Grove stands a fine Willow tree, the leaves barke and all looks very naturall, the roote is full of rubbish or great stones to appearance, and all on a sudden by turning a sluce it raines from each leafe and from the branches like a shower, it being made of brass and pipes to each leafe but in appearance is exactly like any Willow; beyond this is a bason in which are the branches of two Hartichokes Leaves which weeps at the end of each leafe into the bason which is placed at the foote of lead steps 30 in number; on a little banck stands blew balls 10 on a side, and between each ball are 4 pipes which by a sluce spouts out water across the stepps to each other like an arbour or arch; while you are thus amused suddenly there runs down a torrent of water out of 2 pitchers in the hands of two large Nimphs cut in stone that lyes in the upper step, which makes a pleaseing prospect, this is designed to be enlarged and steps made up to the top of the hill which is a vast ascent, but from the top of it now they are supply'd with water for all the pipes so it will be easyer to have such a fall of water even from the top which will add to the Curiositye ...[8]

In her observation of buildings and devices she noticed the practical, the functional, and the useful; she was no romantic, and while she was nevertheless sensitive to the beauty of wild places, orderly gardens were her delight and she examined them carefully. Here she is walking through the grove of trees in Patshull Park, between Shrewsbury and Penkridge:

> ... the grove is the finest I ever saw, there are six walks thro' it and just in the middle you look twelve ways which discovers as many severall prospects either to the house or entrance or fountains or gardens or fields: the Grove it self is peculiar, being composed of all sorts of greens that hold their verdure and beauty all the yeare, and flourishes most in the winter season, when all other garden beautys fades, for Firrs (both Silver Scots Noroway) Cyprus Yew Bays, etc., the severall squares being set full of these like a Maze; they are compassed round each square with a hedge of Lawrell about a yard high cut exactly smooth and even, there are also Box trees in the middle ...[9]

She loved visiting cities, where she took in all the local attractions, examined public works, appraised the buildings and streets, and sought out nonconformist church meetings which she could attend. On the other hand, she had little time for rustic communities whose members had not put effort into self-improvement: her visits to Scotland and Wales she cut short because she found the backward standards of living depressing. Encountering the 'villages of sad little hutts' past Windermere, she imagined at first that the dwellings were only for the cattle, and attributed the occupants' poor conditions to their 'lazyness'. She was angered by bad service at inns and lodging-houses and expected fair value for her money, something she did not receive at Carlisle:

> … [Carlisle] is well supply'd as I am inform'd with provision at easye rates, but my Landlady notwithstanding ran me up the largest reckoning for allmost nothing; it was the dearest lodging I met with and she pretended she could get me nothing else, so for 2 joynts of mutton and a pinte of wine and bread and beer I had a 12 shilling reckoning; but since, I find tho' I was in the biggest house in town I was in the worst accomodation, and so found it, and a young giddy Landlady that could only dress fine and entertain the soldiers …[10]

In all, her diaries are a most valuable record of the England of her day, for they were written with no particular political agenda and for no particular patron. As well, they are remarkably comprehensive, telling us not only about towns, cities, public buildings and houses but also about markets, transport, food, clothing, and recreations. Her text was first transcribed and published in 1888 by Emily Griffiths, a daughter of the sixteenth Lord Saye and Sele, under the title *Through England on a Side Saddle in the time of William and Mary*. The manuscript was written with virtually no punctuation and a very arbitrary, very copious, use of capitalisation. In using the 1888 transcription in this instance, the punctuation used by Emily Griffiths has been reproduced, but, for easier reading, the capital letter usage has been confined to modern conventions. The first of the following extracts is the description of Newcastle, a city which Fiennes admired and in which she found much on which to report. It is a passage which reveals many of her own particular interests. In contrast, the second extract deals with a remote area, the country around Windermere, where she recounts her experiences of country cooking and a wild and lonely landscape.

Newcastle

From *Through England on a Side Saddle in the time of William and Mary*, edited by Emily Griffiths, 1888

Just at my entrance into Northumberland I ascended a very steep hill of which there are many, but one about 2 mile forward was exceeding steep full of great rocks and stone, some of it along on a row the remainder of the Picts walls or fortification[11] at the bottom of which was an old castle[12] the walls and towers of which was mostly standing. Its a sort of black moorish ground and so wet I observ'd as my man rode up that sort of precipice or steep his horses heeles cast up water every step, and their feete cut deepe in, even quite up to the top. Such up and down hills and sort of boggy ground it was and the night drawing fast on, the miles so long, that I tooke a guide to direct me to avoid those ill places.[13]

This Hartwhistle[14] is a little town; there was one inn but they had noe hay nor would get none, and when my servants had got some else where they were angry and would not entertaine me, so I was forced to take up in a poor cottage which was open to the thatch and no partitions but hurdles plaister'd.[15] Indeed the loft as they called it which was over the other roomes was shelter'd but with a hurdle; here I was forced to take up my abode and the Landlady brought me out her best sheetes which serv'd to secure my own sheetes from her dirty blanckets, and indeed I had her fine sheete to spread over the top of the clothes, but noe sleepe could I get, they burning turff and their chimneys are sort of flews or open tunnills, that the smoake does annoy the roomes. This is but 12 miles from another part of Scotland, the houses are but a little better built, its tru the inside of them are kept a little better. Not far from this a mile or two is a greate hill from which rises 3 rivers: the Teese which is the border between Durham and York, the Ouse that runs to Yorke, and the River Tyne which runs to NewCastle and is the divider of Northumberland and Durham. This river Tyne runs 7 miles and then joyns with the other river Tyne that comes out of Northumberland and so they run on to NewCastle. From Hartwhistle I went pretty much up hill and down and had the River Tyne much in view for 6 miles, then I cross'd over it on a large stone bridge and so rode by its bank or pretty much in sight of it on the other side to Hexholme[16] 6 mile more. This is one of the best towns in Northumberland except Newcastle, which is one place the sessions are kept for the shire,[17] its built of stone and looks very well, there are 2 gates to it, many streetes, some are pretty broad, all well pitch'd,[18] with a spacious Market place with a Town Hall on the Market Crosse. Thence I went through the Lord Darentwaters parke[19] just by his house which is an old building not very large, for 3 mile in all, to a little village where I cross'd over the Tyne on a long bridge of stone with many arches. The river is in some places broader than in others, its true at this tyme of the yeare being midsumer the springs are the lowest and the rivers shallow and where there is any rocks or stones left quite bare of water.

Thence I went 4 mile along by the Tyne, the road was good hard gravelly way for the most part but very steep up hills and down; on one of these I rode a pretty while with a great precipice on the right hand down to the river, it looked hazardous but the way was very broad. The river looked very reffreshing and the cattle coming to its sides and into it where shallow to coole themselves in the heate, for hitherto as I met with noe raines, notwithstanding the great raines that fell the 2 dayes before I left Woolsley, and the little showers I Had when I went to Holywell I was not annoy'd with wet nor extream heate, the clouds being a shade to me by day and Gods good providence and protection all wayes. This after noon was the hottest day I met with but it was seasonable being in July. As I drew nearer and nearer to NewCastle I met with and saw abundance of little carriages with a yoke of oxen and a pair of horses together, which is to convey the coales from the pitts to the barges on the river. There is little sort of dung-potts. I suppose they hold not above 2 or three chaudron.[20] This is the Sea-coale which is pretty much small coale tho' some is round coales, yet none like the cleft coales[21] and this is what the smiths use and it cakes in the fire and makes a great heate, but it burns not up light unless you put most round coales which will burn light, but then its soone gone and that part of the coale never cakes, there fore the small sort is as good as any—if its black and shining, that shows its goodness. This country all about is full of this coale the sulpher of it taints the aire and it smells strongly to strangers, upon a high hill 2 mile from NewCastle I could see all about the country which was full of coale pitts.

New-Castle lies in a bottom very low, it appears from this hill a greate flat. I saw all by the river Tyne which runns along to Tinmouth[22] 5 or 6 miles off, which could see very plaine and the Scheld[23] which is the key or fort at the mouth of the river which disembogues itself into the sea; all this was in view on this high hill which I descended—5 mile more, all in nine from that place.

NewCastle is a town and county of itself standing part in Northumberland part in the Bishoprick of Durham, the River Tyne being the division. Its a noble town tho' in a bottom, it most resembles London of any place in England, its buildings lofty and large, of brick mostly or stone. The streetes are very broad and handsome and very well pitch'd, and many of them with very fine cunduits of water in each allwayes running into a large stone cistern for every bodyes use. There is one great streete where in the Market Crosse, there was one great cunduit with two spouts which falls into a large fountaine paved with stone which held at least 2 or 3 hodsheads[24] for the inhabitants. There are 4 gates which are all double gates with a sort of bridge between each. The West gate which I entred I came by a large building of bricke within bricke walls which is the hall for the assizes and sessions for the shire of Northumberland. This is NewCastle on the Tyne and is a town and county. There is a noble building in the middle of the town all of stone for an Exchange on stone pillars severall rows. On the top is a building of a very large hall for the judges to keep the assizes for the town; there is another roome for the major and councill[25] and another for the jury out of the large room which is the hall, and opens into a balcony which looks out on the river and the key. Its a lofty good building of stone, very uniforme on all sides with stone pillars in the fronts both to the streete and market place and to the waterside. There is a fine clock on the top just as the Royal Exchange has. The Key is a very fine place and lookes itself like an exchange being very broad and soe full of merchants walking to and againe, and it runs off a great length with a great many steps down to the water for the conveniency of landing or boateing their goods, and is full of cellars or ware houses. The harbour is full of shipps but none that is above 2 or 300 tun can come up quite to the key, its a town of greate trade. There is one large Church built of stone with a very high tower finely carv'd full of spires and severall devises in the carving—all stone. The quire is neate as is the whole Church and curious carving in wood on each side of the quire, and over the font is a greate piramidy of wood finely carv'd full of spires.[26] There was a Castle in this town but now there is noe remaines of it but some of the walls which are built up in houses and soe only appears as a great hill or ascent, which in some places is 30 or 40 steps advance to the streetes that are built on higher ground where the castle was. There was one place soe like Snow Hill in London with a fine conduite. Their shops are good and are of distinct trades, not selling many things in one shop as is the custom in most country towns and cittys; here is one market for corne another for hay besides all other things which takes up two or three streetes; Satturday was their biggest market day which was the day I was there, and by reason of the extreame heate resolved to stay till the sun was low ere I proceeded farther, so had the opportunity of seeing most of the market which is like a faire for all sorts of provision, and good and very cheape. I saw one buy a quarter of lamb for 8*d* and 2*d* a piece: good large poultry. Here is leather, woollen and linnen and all sorts of stands for baubles. They have a very indifferent sort of cheese—little things, looks black on the outside. There is a very pleasant bowling-green, a little walke out of the town with a large gravel walke round it with two rows of trees on each side makeing it very shady: there is a fine entertaineing house that makes up the fourth side, before which is a paved walke and epyasses[27] of bricke. There is a pretty garden, by the side a shady walk, its a sort of spring garden where the gentlemen and ladyes walke in the evening—there is a green house in the garden, its a pleasant walke to the town by the walls. There is one broad walke by the side of the town runns a good length made with coale ashes and so well trodden, and the raines makes it firm. There is a walke all round the walls of the town. There is a good free school and 5 churches. I went to see the Barber Surgeons Hall which was within a pretty garden walled in, full of flowers and greens in potts and in the borders; its a good neate building of brick. There I saw the roome with a round table in it, railed round with seates or benches for the conveniency in their disecting and anatomiseing a body, and reading lectures on all parts. There was two bodyes that had been anatomised, one the bones were fastned with wires the other had had the flesh boyled off and so some of the ligeament remained and dryed with it, and so the parts were held together by its own muscles and sinews that were dryed with it. Over this was another roome in which was the skin of a man that was taken off after he was dead, and dressed, and so was stuff'd—the body and limbs. It look'd and felt like a sort of parchment. In this roome I could take a view of the whole town, it standing on high ground and a pretty lofty building.

Windermere

From *Through England on a Side Saddle in the time of William and Mary*, edited by Emily Griffiths, 1888

... Kendall is the biggest town and much in the heart of Westmorland, but Appleby 10 mile off is the shire town where the session and assizes are held and is 7 miles to this great Lake Wiandermer or great standing water, which is 10 mile long and near halfe a mile over in some places. It has many little hills or isles in it, one of a great bigness of 30 acres of ground on which is a house, the gentleman that is Lord of the Manour lives in it—Sir Christopher Phillips;[28] he has a great command of the water and of the villages thereabout and many priviledges, he makes a major or bailiff of the place during life; its but a small mean place, Mr Majors was the best entertaining house where I was. The isle did not looke to be so bigg at the shore but takeing boate I went on it and found it as large and very good barley and oates and grass. The water is very cleer and full of good fish, but the charr fish[29] being out of season could not easily be taken, so I saw none alive but of other fish I had a very good supper. The season of the charr fish is between Michaelmas and Christmas; at that tyme I have had of them, which they pott with sweete spices. They are as big as a small trout, rather slenderer and the skinn full of spotts, some red like the finns of a perch, and the inside flesh looks as red as any salmon if they are in season; their taste is very rich and fatt tho' not so strong or clogging as the lamprys are, but its as fatt and rich a food. This great water seemes to flow and wane about with the wind or in one motion but it does not ebb and flow like the sea with the tyde, neither does it run so as to be perceivable, tho' at the end of it a little rivulet trills from it into the sea, but it seemes to be a standing lake encompass'd with vast high hills that are perfect rocks and barren ground of a vast height from which many little springs out of the rock does bubble up and descend down and fall into this water. Notwithstanding great raines the water does not seem much encreas'd tho' it must be so, then it does draine off more at the end of the Lake. These hills which they call Furness Fells a long row continued some miles, and some of them are call'd Donum Fells and soe from the places they adjoyne to are named, but they hold the whole length of the water which is 10 mile; they have some parts of them that has wayes that they can by degrees in a compass ascend them and so they go onward. In the countrys, they are ferried over the Lake when they go to market. On the other side over those fells there is a sort of stones like rubbish or broken pieces of stones, which lies about a quarry, that lies all in the bottom of the water; where its so shallow as at the shores it is and very cleer you see the bottom; between these stones are weeds which grows up, that I had some taken up, just like samfyer and I have a fancy its a sort of sampire[30] that indeed is gather'd in the rocks by the sea and water, and this grows in the water but it resembles it in coullour, figure and the taste not much unlike—it was somewhat waterish; there was also fine moss growing in the bottom of the water. Here it was I saw the oat clap bread made. They mix their flour with water, so soft as to rowle it in their hands into a ball, and then they have a board made round and something hollow in the middle riseing by degrees all round to the edge a little higher, but so little as one would take it to be only a board warp'd, this is to cast out the cake thinn and so they clap it round and drive it to the edge in a due proportion till drove as thinn as a paper, and still they clap it and drive it round, and then they have a plaite of iron same size with their clap board, and so shove off the cake on it and so set it on coales and bake it; when enough on one side they slide it off and put the other side; if their iron plaite is smooth and they take care their coales or embers are not too hot but just to make it looke yellow, it will bake and be as crisp and pleasant to eate as any thing you can imagine, but as we say of all sorts of bread there is a vast deale of difference in what is housewifely made and what is ill made, so this if its well mixed and rowled up and but a little flour on the outside which will drye on and make it mealy is a very good sort of food. This is the sort of bread they use in all these countrys, and in Scotland they breake into their milk or broth or else sup that up and bite off their bread between while they spread butter on it and eate it with their meate. They have no other sort of bread unless at market towns and that is scarce to be had unless the market dayes, soe they make their cake and eate it presently, for its not so good if 2 or 3 dayes old. It made me reflect on the description made in scripture of this kneeding cakes and bakeing them on the hearth when ever they had company come to their houses, and I cannot but thinke it was after this manner they made their bread in the old tymes. Especially those Eastern Countryes where their bread might be soone dry'd and spoil'd. Their little carts I was speakeing of they use hereabout, the wheeles are fastned to the axletree and so turn altogether, they hold not above what 5 wheelbarrows would carry at three or four tymes, which the girles and boys and women does go about with drawn by one horse to carry any thing they want. Here is a great deal of good grass and summer corn and pastures, its rich land in the bottoms as one may call them considering the vast hills above them on all sides, yet they contain a number of lesser hills one below another, so that tho' at one looke you think it but a little land every body has, yet it being so full of hills its many acres which if at length in a plain would extend a vast way. I was about a quarter of an hour in the boate before I reach'd the island which is in the midst of the water so by that you may guesse at the breadth of the water in the whole, they ferry man and horse over it; its sometymes perfectly calme. Thence I rode almost all the waye in sight of this great water; some tymes I lost it by reason of the great hills interposeing and so a continu'd up hill and down hill and that pretty steep even when I was in that they called bottoms which are very rich good grounds, and so I gained by degrees from lower to higher hills which I allwayes went up and down before I came to another hill. At last I attained to the side of one of these hills or fells of rocks, which I passed on the side much about the middle, for looking down to the bottom it was at least a mile all full of those lesser hills and inclosures, so looking upward I was as farre from the top which was all rocks, and something more barren tho' there was some trees and woods growing in the rocks and hanging over all down the brow of some of the hills. From these great fells there are severall springs out of the rock that trickle down their sides, and as they meete with stones and rocks in the way, when something obstructs their passage and so they come with more violence, that gives a pleaseing sound and murmuring noise. These descend by degrees at last fall into the low grounds and fructifye it which makes the land soe fruit full in the valleys; and upon those very high fells or rocky hills its (tho') soe high yet a moorish sort off ground whence they digg abundance of peat which they use for their fewell, being in many places a barren ground yielding noe wood, &c. I rode in sight of this Winander Water up and down above 7 mile; afterwards as I was ascending another of those barren fells which tho' I at last was not halfe way up, yet was an hour going it up and down on the other side, going only on the side of it about the middle of it, but it was of such a height as to shew one a great deale of the country when it happens to be between those hills, else those interposeing hinders any sight but of the clouds. I see a good way behind me another of those waters or mers but not very bigge. These great hills are so full of loose stones and shelves of rocks that its very unsafe to ride them down.

There is good marble amongst those rocks: as I walked down at this place I was walled on both sides by those inaccessible high rocky barren hills which hangs over ones head in some places and appears very terrible, and from them springs many little currents of water from the sides and clefts, which trickle down to some lower part where it runs swiftly over the stones and shelves in the way, which makes a pleasant rush and murmuring noise, and like a snowball is encreased by each spring trickling down on either side of those hills, and so descends into the bottoms which are a moorish ground in which in many places the waters stand, and so forme some of those Lakes as it did here. The confluence of all these little springs being gathered together in this Lake, which was soe deep as the current of water that passed through it was scarce to be perceived till one came to the farther end from whence it run a good little river and pretty quick, over which many bridges are laid. Here I came to villages of sad little hutts made up of drye walls, only stones piled together and the roofs of same slatt; there seemed to be little or noe tunnells for their chimneys and have no morter or plaister within or without. For the most part I tooke them at first sight for a sort of houses or barns to fodder cattle in, not thinking them to be dwelling houses, they being scattering houses, here one, there another, in some places they may be 20 or 30 together, and the churches the same; it must needs be very cold dwellings but it shews some thing of the lazyness of the people; indeed here and there there was a house plaister'd, but there is sad entertainment—that sort of clap bread and butter and cheese and a cup of beer all one can have, they are 8 mile from a market town and their miles are tedious to go both for illness of way and length of the miles.

They reckon it but 8 mile from the place I was at the night before but I was 3 or 4 hours at least going it; here I found a very good smith to shoe the horses, for these stony hills and wayes pulls off a shoe presently and wears them as thinn that it was a constant charge to shoe my horses every 2 or 3 days, but this smith did shoe them so well and so good shoes that they held some of the shooes 6 weekes. The stonyness of the wayes all here about teaches them the art of makeing good shooes and setting them on fast.

1. For an excellent account of the life and writings of Celia Fiennes see Christopher Morris's introduction to his annotated edition of her work: *The Illustrated Journeys of Celia Fiennes, 1685–c.1712*, London; Sydney: Macdonald and Co., Exeter: Webb & Bower, 1982 (First Edition 1947), pp.10–31.
2. A *conventicle* was a meeting held for religious worship not conforming to the rites, sacraments, and prayers of the established Anglican Church. The Clarendon Code of 1662, a set of Parliamentary Acts whose purpose was to diminish nonconformity, included the Conventicle Act, which forbade the assembly of conventicles of more than five people who were not members of the same household.
3. Morris, *Celia Fiennes*, pp.78–80. Fiennes used the word 'neat' more than any other adjective of approval, and indeed it was a word which could be used in many ways. In late seventeenth-century dictionaries (Elisha Coles, 1676, and John Kersey the younger,

1702), its given meanings included: *spruce, cleanly, comly*; and it was listed as one of the meanings of the following words: *accurate, clean, curious, delicate, elegant, fine, gallant, genteel, handsome, polite, quaint, sightly, smug, spruce, terse, tidy, tight,* and *trim.*

4. Morris, *Celia Fiennes*, p.15.
5. *Ibid.*, p.23.
6. *Ibid.*, p.82.
7. *Ibid.*, p.140.
8. *Ibid.*, p.105.
9. *Ibid.*, p.187.
10. *Ibid.*, p.172.
11. This was the Roman Wall constructed by Hadrian. It was commonly referred to in the seventeenth century, notable by Camden, as the 'Picts' Wall'.
12. Morris notes that this was Thirlwall Castle.
13. There is no explanation of how, in so remote a place, a guide was procured; it must be supposed that it was not a difficult thing to do.
14. Haltwhistle.
15. *Hurdles*, supporting frames, wattles.
16. Hexham.
17. *Sessions*, court sittings.
18. *Pitched*, paved with stones set on end.
19. Lord Derwentwater.
20. *Dung-pot*, a container for carrying manure; *chaudron*, a dry measure of volume usually used for coals (equal to 36 bushels).
21. *Sea-coal*, coal washed up from the sea, found in abundance in early modern times on the coast of Northumberland.
22. Tynemouth.
23. South Shields.
24. *Hodshead*, hogshead, and imperial unit of measure equivalent to fifty-two gallons.
25. *Major*, mayor.
26. *Piramidy*, pyramid.
27. *Epyass*, perhaps piazza.
28. Morris notes this as Philipson.
29. *Char fish*, the char is a lake-dwelling fish regarded as a delicacy.
30. *Samphire*, a succulent herb growing amongst rocks near the sea.

XXIII
Cambridgeshire: Daniel Defoe (1660–1731)

As soon as we start to read from Daniel Defoe's description of his country, it is clear that, with the possible exception of Carew's *Cornwall*, it is quite unlike the preceding antiquarian examples. This author is no detached observer or collector, he is living in what he sees, enjoying it, appraising it, challenging it. It is a type of observation which grew out of his multifarious career, during which he engaged energetically and exuberantly with England, not so much as a place but as a modern and dynamic society. Best known as the author of *Robinson Crusoe* and *Moll Flanders*, Defoe was a prolific journalist and pamphleteer; a constant agitator for political, social and religious reform; a rebel against James II and a friend to William III; servant to ministers of state; government spy; merchant and somewhat imprudent investor; family man; and astute observer of human aspirations and follies. *A Tour thro' the Whole Island of Great Britain* was written in the last decade of his life, and is a lively portrait of the place and its people in the early eighteenth century. As a successor to the antiquarian survey, it is a description of the present, and is a world away from the memorial preservation of the past which underlies the genealogically-oriented works of the previous century, examples of which genre were nevertheless still being produced. Like all of his major works, the *Tour* is informed by the various experiences of its author's extraordinary life, and it is the voice of one who saw everything, tried everything and commented on everything that was going on in the tumultuous years from James II to George I. Yet little is known of his personal life: of his upbringing and his long and rewarding marriage he wrote nothing.

Daniel Defoe was born into a Puritan family in London in the year of the Restoration, 1660. The set of acts which were together called the Clarendon Code[1] were devised to ensure conformity to the beliefs and practices of the Anglican Church, outlawing religious meetings of people, such as the Defoes, who were described as Nonconformists, or Dissenters, and even forbidding the teaching of their beliefs within the family. There was some relief from these strictures with the Declaration of Indulgence of 1672,[2] so that it became possible for the young Daniel to be educated at a non-conformist school rather than at Oxford or Cambridge. He attended Charles Morton's Academy at Newington Green, which was not only nonconformist but also unorthodox in its educational methods. It was one of the best of the Dissenting Academies, offering more than the rhetoric and grammar of the university curricula, so here Defoe learned about philosophy, politics, history, economics, and science; Morton himself had been educated in the company of such luminaries as Robert Boyle and Christopher Wren.

In a life crowded with ventures, Defoe's simultaneous affairs followed diverse paths. Most prominent was his political guise, in which he pursued his opposition to mandatory adherence to the established church. Moreover, he was concerned at the prospect of the succession of the king's Catholic brother, the Duke of York, and supported instead the Protestant contender, Charles II's illegitimate son, the Duke of Monmouth. After the Duke of York did succeed as James II, Defoe was amongst those who fought, unsuccessfully, on Monmouth's side against the new king at the Battle of Sedgemoor. He avoided being caught, while many of Monmouth's supporters suffered before the 'Bloody Assizes' of Judge Jeffreys, and survived to see the eventual overthrow of the Catholic regime and the accession of William III and Mary II in 1688. He came to be on friendly terms with the new monarchs, and enjoyed a period of developing influence on public affairs. This was largely achieved through his prolific production of pamphlets on a wide range of subjects. Early in the reign of Queen Anne his work became so inflammatory that he was indicted by the House of Commons, sentenced to two days in the pillory, and confined for three months in Newgate Prison.

Undaunted, he embarked in 1704 on another career as a journalist, launching a journal of current affairs, the *Review*, which was soon appearing three times a week. It continued for nearly ten years, its emphasis being to analyse and comment on the news rather than simply to report it. In particular he used the *Review* to make comments about tensions with France, against whom a campaign was anticipated in the summer of 1704. Robert Harley, who had been Speaker of the House of Commons and by now had become Secretary of State, gave Defoe employment as both journalist and observer of interests, opinions and intrigues around the country. He was in effect a spy, travelling sometimes under an assumed name. In 1706, Harley agreed to send Defoe to Scotland, where he acted as a propagandist for the Union of England and Scotland, which was achieved by the Act of Union in 1707. He continued to write prolifically, and by 1719, when *Robinson Crusoe* was published, he was also producing eight periodicals.

At the same time Defoe was constantly pursuing mercantile ventures, starting with a hosiery business when he first came to London in 1681. By the reign of William and Mary, he had ventured into the uncertainties of overseas trading in various goods: beer, wine, spirits, tobacco and textiles. In 1692 Defoe's borrowing and risk-taking with his money (his more bizarre failures including the purchase of seventy civet cats for perfume manufacture, and a diving bell for the raising of sunken treasure) made him bankrupt, and he had to endure some months of confinement first in the Fleet Prison, then in the King's Bench Prison. He was nevertheless able to retain some land which he owned at Tilbury, and later established a brick and tile factory there. His creditors continued to pursue him until he was able to escape to Scotland, on a project for his supporter and employer Robert Harley, but even there, confident in his business acumen, he entered into new ventures which brought him new losses.

Defoe took to the writing of fiction later in life: his first extended work, *The Life and Strange Surprising Adventures of Robinson Crusoe*, first appeared in 1719 and was an instant success. Although he had not ever travelled overseas, he was well familiar with matters of foreign trade and the dangers of shipping, and had always been an avid reader of adventures of exploration, shipwreck and marooning on distant and lonely islands. His other works of fiction which were presented as memoirs—*Captain Singleton* and *Colonel Jack*—also exploited the themes of trade and adventures in the Americas and Africa. Other fiction included *The Memoirs of a Cavalier* and the vivid rendering of the horrors of the calamity which he had witnessed as a five-year-old, *A Journal of the Plague Year*. His interest in courtship, marriage, and sexual relations, matters on which he wrote extensively, were the themes of *Moll Flanders* and *Roxana*, the former a picaresque, like some of his earlier works of fiction, and the latter his first book with the elements and construction of a novel. Following these came *A Tour thro' the Whole Island of Great Britain*, which, while purportedly a factual narrative, also includes fictional elements, for it is not in fact a record of a real journey, but is constructed from memories of travels and imagination. A common feature of all this writing is the blurring of distinction between fact and fiction: narratives which seem to be factual reports are fictitious, narratives which are presented as fiction include material which is factual.

The *Tour* was published anonymously in three volumes between 1724 and 1726. It followed a series of books and pamphlets on England's social problems, both lamenting the lack of moral quality and advocating reforms for improvement. The *Tour*, however, takes a positive view, indeed the author of a recent study of Defoe calls it 'a panegyric on English wealth, power, and potential for growth'.[3] Defoe was especially keen to demonstrate change in the nation, suggesting in the introduction to the Second Volume that, if the description were rewritten annually, there would always be something new to report: new buildings, new roads, new projects, new trades. The descriptive material relating to East Anglia, from which the following passage is taken, constitutes the first of the thirteen journeys contained in the book, and there is evidence that it was indeed a record of an actual journey, in that it includes some specific dates. The relish with which he conducts his readers through the alleys of the Stourbridge Fair is a reflection of his enthusiasm for society, commerce, economic improvement, and quality of life.

Stourbridge Fair is reputed to have been the largest medieval fair in England, if not in Europe. Its beginnings were associated with a leper hospital, which in 1211 was granted a charter by King John to hold an annual three-day fair to supplement the lepers' income.[4] By the early seventeenth century the fair had become much larger and was held for several weeks, and Defoe remarks on the great number of hackney coaches that were engaged to bring visitors from London. With the opening up of trade through the development of safer roads across the country, its effectiveness as a market had diminished, and by the second half of the eighteenth century the fair's offerings were limited mainly to entertainment, drink, and food. It had by this time acquired a notorious reputation for its brothels and was popularly referred to as 'Stir-Bitch Fair'.[5] Edward Ward, in the 1700 pamphlet *A Step to Stir-Bitch-Fair*, wrote that London men came only to 'drink, smoke and whore.'[6] In 1811 the fields upon which the fair had always been held were enclosed, and much of the area was put to other uses. The fair went into a significant decline and was finally abolished in 1933.[7]

Defoe was observing the fair at the time when its commerce and entertainment were at their most profuse, yet he chose not to highlight the bawdy offerings that concerned some commentators. His reaction is one of delight: he embraces the excitement, the variety, the expansiveness, the liveliness; the word 'prodigious' is frequently called upon as the scene is described. It would seem that Defoe's description is not exaggerated: his remark, for example, that the section of the fair called the Duddery had sold 'one hundred thousand pounds worth of woollen manufactures' in less than a week is corroborated by the comments of other writers of the same time.

Sturbridge-fair

From *A Tour thro' the Whole Island of Great Britain*, edited by Samuel Richardson, London, 1742, Vol. I, pp.83–90

It is kept in a large Corn-field, near *Casterton*, extending from the Side of the River *Cam*, towards the Road, for about half a Mile square.[8]

If the Field be not cleared of the Corn before a certain Day in *August*, the Fair-keepers may trample it under-foot, to build their Booths or Tents.[9] On the other hand, to balance that Severity, if the Fair-keepers have not cleared the Field by another certain Day in *September*, the Plowmen may re-enter with Plow and Cart, and overthrow all into the Dirt; and as for the Filth, Dung, Straw, *&c.* left behind by the Fair-keepers, which is very considerable, these become the Farmers Fees, and make them full Amends for the trampling, riding, carting upon, and hardening the Ground.

It is impossible to describe all the Parts and Circumstances of this Fair exactly; the Shops are placed in Rows like Streets, whereof one is called *Cheapside*; and here, as in several other Streets, are all Sorts of Traders, who sell by Retale, and come chiefly from *London.* Here may be seen Goldsmiths, Toymen, Brasiers, Turners, Milaners, Haberdashers, Hatters, Mercers, Drapers, Pewterers, China-warehouses, and, in a Word, all Trades that can be found in *London*; with Coffee-houses, Taverns, and Eating-houses in great Numbers and all kept in Tents and Booths.

This great Street reaches from the Road, which, as I said, goes from *Cambridge* to *Newmarket*, turning short out of it to the Right towards the River, and holds in a Line near half a Mile quite down to the River-side. In another Street parallel with the Road are the like Rows of Booths, but somewhat larger, and more intermingled with Wholesale Dealers; and one Side, passing out of this last Street to the Left-hand, is a great Square, formed of the largest Booths, called the *Duddery*;[10] but whence so called, I could not learn. The Area of this Square is from 80 to 100 Yards, where the Dealers have room before every Booth to take down and open their Packs, and to bring in Waggons to load and unload.

This Place being peculiar to the Wholesale Dealers in the Woollen Manufacture, the Booths, or Tents are of a vast Extent, have different Apartments, and the Quantities of Goods they bring are so great, that the Insides of them look like so many *Blackwell-halls*,[11] and are vast Warehouses piled up with Goods to the Top. In this *Duddery*, as I have been informed, have been sold 100,000 Pounds-worth of Woollen Manufactures in less than a Week's time; besides the prodigious Trade carried on here by Wholesale-men from *London*, and all Parts of *England*, who transact their Business wholly in their Pocket-books, and meeting their Chapmen from all Parts, make up their Accounts, receive Money chiefly in Bills, and take Orders. These, they say, exceed by far the Sales of Goods actually brought to the Fair, and delivered in Kind; it being frequent for the *London* Wholesale-men to carry back Orders from their Dealers, for 10,000 Pounds-worth of Goods a Man, and some much more. This especially respects those People, who deal in heavy Goods, as Wholesale Grocers, Salters, Brasiers, Iron-merchants, Wine-merchants, and the like; but does not exclude the Dealers in Woollen Manufactures, and especially in Mercery Goods of all sorts, who generally manage their Business in this manner.

Here are Clothiers from *Halifax*, *Leeds*, *Wakefield* and *Huthersfield* in *Yorkshire*, and from *Rochdale*, *Bury*, &c., in *Lancashire*, with vast Quantities of *Yorkshire* Cloths, Kerseys,[12] Pennistons,[13] Cottons, *&c.*, with all sorts of *Manchester* Ware, Fustians,[14] and Things made of Cotton Wooll; of which the Quantity is so great, that they told me there were near 1000 Horse-packs of such Goods from that Side of the Country, and these took up a Side and Half of the *Duddery* at least; also a Part of a Street of Booths were taken up with Upholsterers Ware; such as Tickens,[15] Sackens,[16] *Kidderminster* Stuffs, Blankets, Rugs, Quilts, *&c.*

In the *Duddery* I saw one warehouse, or Booth, consisting of six Apartments all belonging to a Dealer in *Norwich* Stuffs only, who, they said, had there above 20,000 *l.* Value in those Goods.

Western Goods had their Share here also, and several Booths were filled with Serges,[17] Duroys,[18] Druggets,[19] Shalloons,[20] Cantaloons,[21] *Devonshire* Kersies, &*c.*, from *Exeter*, *Taunton*, *Bristol*, and other Parts West, and some from *London* also.

But all this is still out-done, at least in Appearance, by two Articles, which are the Peculiars of this Fair, and are not exhibited till the other Part of the Fair, *for the Woollen Manufacture,* begins to close up: These are the WOOLL and the HOPS. There is scarce any Price fixed for Hops in *England*, till they know how they sell at *Sturbridge-fair*; the Quantity that appears in the Fair is indeed prodigious, and they take up a large Part of the Field, on which the Fair is kept, to themselves; they are brought directly from *Chelmsford* in *Essex*, from *Canterbury* and *Maidstone* in *Kent*, and from *Farnham* in *Surrey*, besides what are brought from *London*, of the Growth of those and other Places ...[22]

The Article of Wooll is of several Sorts; but principally Fleece Wooll, out of *Lincolnshire*, where the longest Staple is found, the Sheep of those Parts being of the largest Breed.

The Buyers are chiefly the Manufacturers of *Norfolk*, *Suffolk,* and *Essex*, and it is a prodigious Quantity they buy.

Here I saw what I have not observed in any other County of *England*, a *Pocket* of Wooll,[23] which seems to have been at first called so in Mockery, this *Pocket* being so big, that it loads a whole Waggon, and reaches beyond the most extreme Parts of it, hanging over both before and behind; and these ordinarily weigh a Ton or 2500 lb. Weight of Wooll, all in one Bag.

The Quantity of Wooll only, which has been sold at this Place at one Fair, has been said to amount to 50 or 60,000 *l.* in Value; some say, a great deal more.

By these Articles a Stranger may make some Guess at the immense Trade which is carried on at this Place; what prodigious Quantities of Goods are bought and sold, and what a Concourse of People are seen here from all Parts of *England.*

I might proceed to speak of several other Sorts of *English* Manufactures, which are brought hither to be sold; as all Sorts of wrought Iron, and Brass Ware from *Birmingham*; edged Tools, Knives, *&c.*, from *Sheffield*; Glass Wares, and Stockens[24] from *Nottingham* and *Leicester*; and unaccountable Quantities of other Things of smaller Value every Morning.

To attend this Fair, and the prodigious Crouds of People which resort to it, there are sometimes no less than 50 Hackney Coaches, which come from *London*, and ply Night and Morning to carry the People to and from *Cambridge*; for there the Gross of them lodge; nay, which is still more strange, there are Wherries[25] brought from *London* on Waggons, to ply upon the little River *Cam*, and to row People up and down, from the Town, and from the Fair, as Occasion presents.

It is not to be wondered at, if the Town of *Cambridge* cannot receive or entertain the Numbers of People that come to this Fair; for not *Cambridge* only, but all the Towns round are full; nay, the very Barns and Stables are turned into Inns, to lodge the meaner Sort of People: As for the Fair People, they all eat, drink, and sleep in their Booths, which are so intermingled with Taverns, Coffee-houses, Drinking-houses, Eating-houses, Cooks Shops, *&c.* and so many Butchers and Higglers[26] from all the neighbouring Counties come in every Morning with Beef, Mutton, Fowls, Butter, Bread, Cheese, Eggs, and such Things, and go with them from Tent to Tent, from Door to Door, that there's no Want of Provisions of any Kind, either dressed, or undressed.

In a Word, the Fair is like a well-governed City, and there is the least Disorder and Confusion (I believe) that can be seen any-where, with so great a Concourse of People.

Towards the latter End of the Fair, and when the great Hurry of Wholesale Business begins to be over, the Gentry come in, from all Parts of the County round; and tho' they come for their Diversion, yet 'tis not a little Money they lay out, which generally falls to the Share of the Retalers; such as Toy-shops, Goldsmiths, Brasiers, Ironmongers, Turners, Milaners, Mercers, &*c.*, and some loose Corns[27] they reserve for the Puppet-shews, Drolls,[28] Rope-dancers, and such-like; of which there is no Want. The last Day of the Fair is the *Horse-fair*, where the Whole is closed both with Horse and Foot-races, to divert the meaner Sort of People only; for nothing considerable is offered of that Kind, and the late Act, I presume, must have put an End to the former.[29] Thus ends the whole Fair, and in less than a Week more, scarce any Sign is left, that such a thing has been there, except by the Heaps of Dung and Straw, and other Rubbish which is left behind, trod into the Earth, and is as good as a Summer's Fallow for the Land; and as I have said above, pays the Husbandman well for the Use of it.

1. The Municipal Corporations Act required that all municipal office-holders be communicant members of the Church of England; the Act of Uniformity required all ministers in the church to subscribe to the Thirty-Nine Articles and the *Book of Common Prayer*; the Conventicle Act outlawed religious meetings outside an Anglican church if more than five members of a family were present; the Five Mile Act forbade a cleric who had refused to take the oath of Uniformity from going within five miles of a parish where he had previously officiated.
2. Issued by Charles II, this declaration suspended penal laws against Catholics and Dissenters.
3. Maximillian E. Novak, *Daniel Defoe: Master of Fictions*, Oxford University Press, paperback edition, 2003, (first edition 2001), p.630.
4. The chapel of the hospital, built in 1125, still stands. It is probably the oldest complete building in Cambridge.
5. It is said that the fair was the model for John Bunyan's 'Vanity Fair'.
6. Edward Ward's 16-page publication was entitled *A Step to Stir-Bitch-Fair: with remarks upon the University of Cambridge*, and it appeared in 1700. Under the name 'Ned' Ward, he had been the author of *The London Spy*, an innovative monthly periodical which continued for eighteen months between 1698 and 1700. Written as if it were a collection of eye-witness accounts from visitors to the city, it depicted all aspects of London characters and institutions, highlighting especially the strange and unsavoury.
7. Since 2004, the Friends of the Leper Chapel have staged a re-creation of the medieval Stourbridge Fair in the grounds of the Chapel.
8. Defoe mentions that the fair is held off the road from Newmarket to Cambridge.
9. At the time Defoe was writing, the fair began on 24 August, St Bartholomew's Day.
10. The name went back a long time: it was mentioned in connection with Stourbridge by Leland in the mid-sixteenth century.
11. *Blackwell Hall*, near the Guildhall, London, was the site of a market for woollen cloths from the fifteenth to the seventeenth centuries.
12. *Kerseys*, a kersey was a coarse cloth of a slightly smaller size than those set by statute for cloths and broadcloths.
13. *Penniston*, a coarse woollen cloth.
14. *Fustian*, a coarse cloth made of cotton and flax.
15. *Ticken*, ticking, the strong linen material used to make *ticks*, that is, covers for mattresses or pillows.
16. *Sacken*, sacking, closely woven material used to make sacks and bags.
17. *Serge*, a woollen fabric used in earlier times for hangings and bed-covers but by Defoe's time often worn by poorer people because of its durability.
18. *Duroy*, a coarse woollen fabric from the west of England.
19. *Drugget*, a kind of stuff made of wool, perhaps with silk or linen, used to make clothes.
20. *Shalloon*, a closely woven woollen material used for linings.
21. *Cantaloon*, another woollen stuff from the west of England.
22. At this point Defoe's description includes a digression on the distribution of hops in England and why it is sold at the Stourbridge Fair in such quantities.
23. *Pocket of wool*, a bag of wool of a certain size.
24. *Stockens*, stockings.
25. *Wherry*, a light rowing-boat to carry passengers.
26. *Higgler*, an itinerant dealer, usually in poultry and dairy produce.
27. Probably *coins* was intended.
28. *Droll*, jester.
29. The reference is presumably to an act introduced by Parliament in 1740 to impose controls and restraints on horse racing.

XXIV

Cumberland and Westmorland: William Gilpin (1724–1804)

William Gilpin was a clergyman and schoolmaster who is remembered as one of the leading exponents of the aesthetic movement known as the *picturesque*.[1] This was a theory of the perception of beauty, a system for describing natural scenery, and a methodology for landscape painting. It was relevant, therefore, to both artists and travellers, and was formulated in descriptions of tours to parts of Britain, as well as in essays. Gilpin was not an antiquary, but the genre of his writing was a descendant of that of the antiquarian survey. Like those earlier scholars, he was a collector, but, unlike them, the objects of his interest were quite different: they included neither the manifestations of nature, nor the artefacts of people, nor the tenancies of estates, nor the pedigrees of families, but views of the countryside, recorded systematically for the use of artists and tourists.

Gilpin, born in Cumberland, grew up in an environment congenial to aesthetic pursuits, for his father, a soldier, was an amateur artist, and his brother Sawrey became a painter by profession. William, however, studied at Oxford and pursued a career in the church. In the same year as he graduated, 1748, he published a guide-book, *A Dialogue upon the Gardens ... at Stow in Buckinghamshire*, which was his first exposition of his aesthetic ideas. He became a curate, then a master at Cheam School, then, in 1755, headmaster at that school, and in 1777, Vicar of Boldre in Hampshire. During the summers in the 1760s and 1770s he travelled extensively in Britain, sketching and making notes on landscapes. These manuscripts were circulated amongst friends who included Thomas Gray, Horace Walpole, and King George III. Another friend, the poet William Mason, encouraged Gilpin to begin publication of his work, and in 1782 the first of his 'tour journals' appeared: *Observations on the River Wye, and Several Parts of South Wales, etc. relative chiefly to Picturesque Beauty, made in the Summer of the Year 1770*. Other similarly titled books followed, dealing successive with observations in 1772 of the lakes and mountains of Cumberland and Westmorland (1786); in 1776 of the Scottish Highlands (1789); after his move to Boldre, of the New Forest (1791); and in 1769 and 1773, of East Anglia and North Wales respectively (1809).

The application of the term 'picturesque' to a scenic view meant, at the most basic level, being 'like a picture'. This is an oversimplification, but it is a truth which lies at the heart of Gilpin's theory. By the time he was writing his tour journals between 1769 and 1776 there was a well-established association between the viewing of scenery and the painting of landscapes. It had had its origins, at least in part, in the familiarisation in Britain with Italian landscape paintings which were being brought into the country by travellers returning from the Grand Tour. This development had helped to break down the neoclassical sense of such art being inferior to 'history painting', whose status might have been likened to that of epic poetry amongst other literary genres. The Italian imports became models for British painters to the extent that scenes in Britain were often rendered in an unmistakeably Italian light and even with the mellow sepia tints that were characteristic of the works of Claude Lorrain and Gaspard Dughet.[2] Likewise painters sought to achieve in their landscapes certain features of these masters, such as the division of the picture into three 'distances': the foreground, usually comparatively darkened; a middle distance, more brightly lit; and a far-distant background; together with a framing of the whole by the trees or other components making up the foreground.

These compositional devices were adopted as conventions by the picturesque artists, who developed a jargon in terms of which not only paintings but also landscape scenes were described and appraised. Gilpin refers in his descriptions to, for example, 'side-screens', alternatively 'off-skips', meaning the framing landscapes of the foreground; 'contracted' and 'open' valleys, suitable respectively for foregrounds or distances; 'grandeur' and 'variety' as qualities of particular views. With such prescriptive structural methodology, authors of travel guides, such as Thomas West in his *Guide to the Lakes* (1778), specified 'stations' from which the best views could be sketched, giving quite precise indications of the position in which the observer should stand and the direction in which he should gaze. With remarkable incongruity, Gilpin suggested that, in spite of the care with which the picturesque stations were defined, the artist was at liberty to 'improve' the landscape in order to realise a scene which would conform more closely to the aesthetic ideals.

> In the mean time, with all this magnificence and beauty, it cannot be supposed, that every scene, which these countries present, is *correctly picturesque*. In such immense bodies of rough-hewn matter, many irregularities, and even many deformities, must exist, which a practised eye would wish to correct. Mountains

> are sometimes crouded—their sides are often bare, when contrast requires them to be wooded—promontories form the water-boundary into acute angles—and bays are contracted into narrow points, instead of swelling into ample basons.
>
> In all these cases the imagination is apt to whisper, What glorious scenes might here be made, if these stubborn materials could yield to the judicious hand of art!—And, to say the truth, we are sometimes tempted to let the imagination loose among them.
>
> By the force of this creative power an intervening hill may be turned aside; and a distance introduced.—This ill-shaped mountain may be pared, and formed into a better line.—To that, on the opposite side, a lightness may be given by the addition of a higher summit.—Upon yon bald declivity, which stretches along the lake, may be reared a forest of noble oak; which thinly scatter'd over the top, will thicken as it descends; and throw it's vivid reflections on the water in full luxuriance.[3]

It is clear that William Gilpin was representative of people who were seeing England in quite a different way from anything which had gone before. And the legacy of the aesthetic movement of which he was a part is with us still. Tourists do travel to see beautiful scenes; maps are marked with scenic drives and favourable lookout points; and even many of his ideas on composing a picture guide us still in taking photographs. One of the most prolific products of the picturesque movement was the travel guide, for Gilpin was only one of many travellers who enjoined others to follow them, and this literary phenomenon coincided with both a growing willingness to travel and the effective closure, due to hostilites, of the European continent to British travellers in the 1790s, with a consequent increase in tourism on the British Isles.[4]

Two particular features of the picturesque are notable. Firstly, the element most highly desirable in a scene was a ruin, usually of either an abbey or a castle. While it had earlier been the case that ruins were valued for their poignant evocation of ideas of the vanity of human endeavours, the picturesque viewer was impressed less by moral considerations than by the roughness, variety, and disorderliness of the lines, colours, and textures offered by ancient and broken walls. Gilpin famously commented that the remains of Tintern Abbey might have been afforded even greater picturesque beauty by 'a mallet judiciously used'.[5] If ruins were a pleasing 'embellishment' made by man in the landscape, gardens and cultivated fields were not so. Firstly, they provided order and neatness which were not in keeping with the qualities of picturesque beauty, but also they represented the labour of man and so were liable to suggest social or moral comment. Picturesque art was not intended to make any such statements, and even the figures who frequently appeared, on a tiny scale, in the foregrounds of picturesque paintings, were not meant to be functional in any way, that is, they had no propensity to interfere with nature. As Gilpin put it,

> Moral, and picturesque ideas do not always coincide. In a moral light, cultivation, in all it's parts, is pleasing; the hedge, and the furrow; the waving corn field, and the ripening sheaf. But all these, the picturesque eye, in quest of scenes of grandeur, looks at with disgust. ... In a moral view, the industrious mechanic is a more pleasing object than the loitering peasant. But in a picturesque light, it is otherwise. The arts of industry are rejected; and even idleness, if I may so speak, adds dignity to a character.[6]

The following extracts are taken from William Gilpin's tour of Cumberland and Westmorland, which, of course, was primarily concerned with the lake and mountain scenery of the Lake District. The first, however, is a description of a less remarkable section of the tour, and it is particularly illustrative of the application of picturesque theory in the viewing of the landscape. It is also interesting in that Gilpin gives some description of the interior of a ruined building and, in so doing, does reflect briefly on the lives of those who occupied it in the past. A second castle is described in even more detail, followed by a footnoted apology to explain that this interest was due to the place having been his childhood home. As he describes these castles, Gilpin is writing more candidly than when he is making picturesque analyses of scenes, and the narrative seems to be in the voice not of the critic, but of the man.

The second extract is a general description of Derwentwater, which precedes more detailed descriptions as a route around the lake is followed. It was the most celebrated location in the Lake District for scenery, and here is Gilpin appraising it critically in picturesque terms. In doing so, he finds the place wanting in several respects, comparing it unfavourably with Windermere, a lake which he had visited a little earlier in this tour. So intent is Gilpin on seeing the landscape as pictures, that he seems almost to miss the landscape itself. The frequent use of the term 'screen' to refer to parts of the view is indicative of the degree to which the picturesque landscape description was formed in terms of the making of a picture. There is also a similarity in such terms with the components of a stage-set, and indeed there was a real association at the root of this. Several landscape painters did work for theatres and one of them, Philip de Loutherbourg, working at Drury Lane in the 1770s, was influential in having landscape settings replace architectural backgrounds on the stage.[7]

Gillsland

From *Observations, relative chiefly to Picturesque Beauty, Made in the Year 1772, On several Parts of England; particularly the Mountains, and Lakes of Cumberland, and Westmorland*, vol. II, pp.115–125

On crossing the river Irthing, about seven miles from Carlisle, the country, which was before unpleasing, becomes rich, and interesting. Here we enter the barony of Gillsland, an extensive district, which consists, in this part, of a great variety of hill, and dale. The hills are sandy, bleak, and unpleasant: but the vallies, which are commonly of the contracted kind, are beautiful.[8] They are generally woody, and each of them watered by some little busy stream.— From these vallies, or *gills*, (as the country-people call them,) with which the whole barony abounds, Campden[9] supposes it to have taken the name of Gillsland.

On a delightful knoll, gently gliding into a sinuous *gill*, surrounded with full-grown oak, and overlooking the vale of Lanercost, stands Naworth-castle. The house, which consists of two large square towers, united by a main body, is too regular to be beautiful, unless thrown into perspective. It was formerly one of those fortified places, in which the nobility and gentry of the borders were obliged to live, in those times of confusion, which preceded the union.[10] And indeed the whole internal contrivance of this castle appears calculated either to keep an enemy out; or to elude his search, if he should happen to get in. The idea of a comfortable dwelling has been totally excluded. The staterooms are few, and ordinary: but the little apartments, and hiding holes, accessible only by dark passages, and blind stair-cases, are innumerable. Many of the close recesses, which it contains, are probably at this time, unknown. Nothing indeed can mark in stronger colours the fears, and jealousies, and caution of those times, than the internal structure of one of these castles. …[11]

… As we left this old fortress, and descended the hill towards the ruins of the abbey of Lanercost, which lie about two miles farther, the whole vale, in which they are seated, opened before us. It is esteemed one of the sweetest scenes in this country; and indeed we found it such. It's area is about half a mile in breadth, and two or three miles in length, consisting of one ample sweep.[12] The sides, which are gentle declivities, are covered thick with wood, in which larger depredations have been lately made, than are consistent with picturesque beauty.—At the distant end of the vale, where the woods appear to unite, the river Irthing enters; which is considerable enough, tho divided into two channels, to be fully adequate to the scene.—The banks of the river, and indeed the whole area of the vale, are sprinkled with clumps, and single trees; which have a good effect in breaking the lines, and regular continuity of the side-screens; and in hiding, here and there, the course of the river; and especially the bridges, which would otherwise be too bare and formal.

Near that extremity of the vale, which is opposite to Naworth-castle, lies the abbey. At a distance it forms a good object, rising among the woods. As you approach, it begins to raise a disappointment: and on the spot, it is but an unpleasing ruin. The whole is a heavy, Saxon, pile; compressed together without any of that airy lightness, which accompanies the Gothic.[13] Scarce one *detached* fragment appears in any point of view. The tower is low, and without either form, or ornament; and one of the great ailes is modernised into an awkward parish-church. The only beautiful part of the whole is the east end. It is composed of four broken ailes; every wall of which consists of two tiers of arches, affording, a very unusual appearance; and at the same time a very amusing confusion, from the uncommon multiplication of so many arches, and pillars.—This part of the abbey seems to have been a separate chapel; or perhaps an oratory belonging to the noble family of Dacre, which had once possessions in these parts. Here lie the remains of several ancient chiefs of that house; whose sepulchral honours are now almost intirely obliterated. Their blazoned arms, and Gothic tombs, many of which are sumptuous, are so matted with briars, and thistles, that even the foot of curiosity is kept at a distance.

Except these remains of the abbey-church no other parts of this ancient monastery are now left; except an old gateway; and a square building, patched into a farm-house, which has no beauty.

In returning to Carlisle we passed through the valley of Cambeck, which contains some pleasing scenery; and a very considerable Roman station, on a high bank at *Castlesteeds*.

Rivers often present us with very moral analogies; their characters greatly resembling those of men. The violent, the restless, the fretful, the active, the sluggish, the gentle, the bounteous, and many other epithets, belong equally to both. The little stream, which divides the valley of Cambeck, suggested the analogy. It's whole course is marked with acts of violence. In every part you see heaps of barren sand, and gravel, which in it's furious moods it has thrown up, sometimes on one side, sometimes on another; destroying every where the little scenes of beauty, and plots of cultivation.

About three miles further stand the ruins of Scaleby-castle. This was another of those fortified houses, which are so frequent in this country.

It stands, as castles rarely do, on a flat; and yet, tho it's site be ill-adapted to any modes of defence, it has been a place of more than ordinary strength. Rocks, knolls, and bold, projecting promontories, on which castles usually stand, suggest various advantages of situation; and generally determine the kind of structure. On a flat, the engineer was at liberty to choose his own. Every part was alike open to assault.

He first drew two circular motes round the spot he designed to fortify: the circumference of the outward circle was about a mile. The earth, thrown out of these two motes, which were broad and deep, seems to have been heaped up at the centre, where there is a considerable rise. On this was built the castle, which was entered by two drawbridges; and defended by a high tower, and a very lofty wall.

At present, one of the motes only remains. The other is filled up; but may still be traced. The castle is more perfect, than such buildings commonly are. The walls are very intire; and a great part of the tower, which is square, is still left. It preserved it's perfect form, till the civil wars of the last century; when the castle, in too much confidence of it's strength, shut it's gates against Cromwell, then marching into Scotland; who made it a monument of his vengeance.

What share of picturesque genius Cromwell might have, I know not.[14] Certain however it is, that no man, since Henry the eighth, has contributed more to adorn this country with picturesque ruins. The difference between these two masters lay chiefly in the style of ruins, in which they composed. Henry adorned his landscapes with the ruins of abbeys; Cromwell, with those of castles. I have seen many pieces by this master, executed in a very grand style; but seldom a finer monument of his masterly hand than this. He has rent the tower, and demolished two of it's sides; the edges of the other two he has shattered into broken lines. The chasm discovers the whole plan of the internal structure—the vestiges of the several stories—the insertion of the arches, which supported them—the windows for speculation; and the breastwork for assault.

The walls of this castle are uncommonly magnificent. They are not only of great height, but of great thickness; and defended by a large bastion; which appears to be of more modern workmanship. The greatest part of them is chambered within, and wrought in secret recesses. A massy portcullis gate leads to the ruins of what was once the habitable part of the castle, in which a large vaulted hall is the most remarkable apartment; and under it, are dark, and capacious dungeons.

The area within the mote, which consists of several acres, was originally intended to support the cattle, which should be driven thither in times of alarm. When the house was inhabited, (whose chearful and better days are still remembered,)[15] this area was the garden; and all around, on the outside of the mote stood noble trees irregularly planted, the growth of a century. Beneath the trees ran a walk around the castle; to which the situation naturally gave that pleasing curve, which in modern days hath been so much the object of art. This walk might admit of great embellishment.[16] On one hand, it commands the ruins of the castle in every point of view; on the other, a country, which, tho flat, is not unpleasing; consisting of extensive meadows, (which a little planting would turn into beautiful lawns,) bounded by lofty mountains.

This venerable pile has now undergone a second ruin. The old oaks and elms, the ancient natives of the scene, are felled. Weeds, and spiry grass have taken possession of the courts, and obliterated the very plan of the garden: while the house itself, (whose hospitable roof deserved a better fate,) is now a scene of desolation. Two wretched families, the only inhabitants of the place, occupy the two ends of the vaulted hall; the fragment of a tattered curtain, reaching half way to the top, being the simple boundary of their respective limits. All the rest is waste: no other part of the house is habitable. The chambers unwindowed, and almost unroofed, fluttering with rags of ancient tapestry, are the haunt of daws, and pigeons; which burst out in clouds of dust, when the doors are opened: while the floors, yielding to the tread, make curiosity dangerous. A few pictures, heir-looms of the wall, which have long deserved oblivion, by I know not what fate, are the only appendages of this dissolving pile, which have triumphed over the injuries of time.

Shakespear's castle of Macbeth could not be more the haunt of swallows and martins, than this. You see them every where about the ruins; either twittering on broken coins; threading some fractured arch; or pursuing each other, in screaming circles, round the walls of the castle.[17]

Derwentwater

From *Cumberland and Westmorland*, Vol. I, pp.179-185

On the 9th of July we set out on *horseback* (which I mention, as it is the only conveyance the road will admit) on an expedition to Borrodale; a wild country south-west of Keswick. Our road led along the lake of *Derwent*, which was the first object we surveyed.

But before we examined the particulars of this grand scene, we took a general view of the whole, from it's northern shore; which is the only part unblockaded by mountains. This is the isthmian part, which joins the valley of Derwent-water with that of Bassenthwait. It was easy from the higher grounds of this isthmus to obtain the station we desired.

The *lake of Derwent*, or *Keswick-lake*, as it is generally called, is contained within a circumference of about ten miles; presenting itself in a circular form, tho in fact it is rather oblong. It's area is interspersed with four or five islands:

three of which only are of consequence, *Lord's island*, *Vicar's island*, and *St Herbert's island*: but none of them is comparable to the island on Windermere, in point either of size, or beauty.

If a painter were desirous of studying the whole circumference of the lake from one station, St Herbert's island is the spot he should choose; from whence, as from a centre, he might see it in rotation. I have seen a set of drawings taken from this stand; which were hung round a circular room, and intended to give a general idea of the boundaries of the lake. But as no representation could be given of the lake itself; the idea was lost, and the drawings made but an awkward appearance.

Lord's island had it's name from being the place, where once stood a pleasure-house, belonging to the unfortunate family of Derwent-water, which took it's title from this lake.[18] The ancient manor-house stood on Castle-hill above Keswick; where the antiquarian traces also the vestiges of a Roman fort. But an heiress of Derwent-water marrying into the family of the Ratcliffs; the family-seat was removed from Keswick to Dilston in Northumberland.

As the boundaries of this lake are more mountainous than those of Windermere; they, of course, afford more *romantic scenery*. But tho the whole shore, except the spot where we stood, is incircled with mountains; they rarely fall abruptly into the water; which is girt almost round by a margin of meadow—on the western shores especially. On the eastern, the mountains approach nearer the water; and in some parts fall perpendicularly into it. But as we stood viewing the lake from it's northern shores, all these marginal parts were lost; and the mountains (tho in fact they describe a circle of twenty miles, which is double the circumference of the lake) appeared universally to rise from the water's edge.

Along it's western shores on the right, they rise smooth and uniform; and are therefore rather lumpish.[19] The more removed part of this mountain-line is elegant: but, in some parts, it is disagreeably broken.

On the eastern side, the mountains are both grander, and more picturesque. The line is pleasing; and is filled with that variety of objects, broken-ground,[20]—rocks,—and wood, which being well combined, take from the heaviness of a mountain; and give it an airy lightness.

The *front*-screen, (if we may so call a portion of circular form,) is more formidable, than either of the sides. But it's line is less elegant, than that of the eastern-screen. The fall of Lodoar,[21] which adorns that part of the lake, is an object of no consequence at the distance we now stood. But in our intended ride we proposed to take a nearer view of it.

Of all the lakes in these romantic regions, the lake we are now examining, seems to be the most generally admired. It was one admirably characterised by an ingenious person,[22] who, on his first seeing it, cryed out, *Here is beauty indeed—Beauty lying in the lap of Horrour!* We do not often find a happier illustration. Nothing conveys an idea of *beauty* more strongly, than the lake; nor of *horrour*, than the mountains; and the former *lying in the lap* of the latter, expresses in a strong manner the mode of their combination. The late Dr. Brown, who was a man of taste, and had seen every part of this country, singled out the scenery of this lake for it's peculiar beauty.[23] And unquestionably it is, in many places, very sweetly romantic; particularly along it's eastern, and southern shores: but to give it *pre-eminence* may be paying it perhaps as much too high a compliment; as it would be too rigorous to make any but a few comparative objections.

In the first place, it's form, which in appearance is circular, is less interesting, I think, than the winding sweep of Windermere, and some other lakes; which losing themselves in vast reaches, behind some cape or promontory, add to their other beauties the varieties of distance, and perspective. Some people object to this, as touching rather on the character of the river. But does that injure it's beauty? And yet I believe there are very few rivers, which form such reaches, as the lake of Windermere.

To the formality of it's shores may be added the formality of it's islands. They are round, regular, and similar spots, as they appear from most points of view; formal in their situation, as well as in their shape; and of little advantage to the scene. The islands of Windermere are in themselves better shaped; more varied; and uniting together, add a beauty, and contrast to the whole.

But among the greatest objections to this lake is the abrupt, and broken line in several of the mountains, which compose it's screens, (especially on the western, and on part of the southern shore) which is more remarkable, than on any of the other lakes. We have little of the easy sweep of a mountain-line: at least the eye is hurt with too many tops of mountains, which injure the ideas of simplicity, and grandeur. Great care therefore should be taken in selecting views of this lake. If there is a littleness even amidst the grand ideas of the original, what can we expect from representations on paper, or canvas? I have seen some views of this lake, injudiciously chosen, or taken on too extensive a scale, in which the mountains appear like hay-cocks.—I would be understood however to speak chiefly of the appearance, which the lines of these mountains *occasionally* make. When we change our point of view, the mountain-line changes also, and may be beautiful in one point, tho it is displeasing in another.

1. For an excellent introduction to the picturesque movement, see Malcolm Andrews, *The Search for the Picturesque: Landscape Aesthetics and Tourism in Britain, 1760-1800*, Scolar Press, 1989.
2. See the note on these artists in the Introduction.
3. *Cumberland and Westmorland*, I, pp.119-120.
4. At the time of hostilities with Napoleonic armies.
5. This much-quoted remark is from Gilpin's *Observations on the River Wye.* See for example, the edition of Sutherland Lyall, Richmond: The Richmond Publishing Co. Ltd, 1973, p.33.
6. *Cumberland and Westmorland*, II, p.44.
7. Malcolm Andrews, *The Search for the Picturesque*, p.30.
8. In an earlier section of *Cumberland and Westmorland* Gilpin offers some analysis of the components of a picturesque scene (vol I, pp.81-132). A *valley* is taken to be the diminutive of a *vale*. The *contracted* valley is contrasted with an *open* valley, which can only appear as an object of distant scenery (*ibid.*, pp.112-116). A contracted valley has sides of varying composition, and appears in the foreground, but may lead to the distance. A *gill*, otherwise known as a *dell*, is a type of contracted valley which is 'a narrow cleft, winding between two rocky precipices'.
9. William Camden.
10. The reference is to the union of England and Scotland.
11. Gilpin here gives some historical information about William Howard, once lord of the castle.
12. Gilpin consistently wrote the possessive form of the pronoun *it* with an apostrophe.
13. Saxon and Gothic are compared earlier (I, pp.13-17). Saxon ruins are 'coarse' and 'heavy', they are characterised by 'barbarism', while the Gothic, which Gilpin divides into three distinct periods, is 'beautiful' and 'elegant'.
14. The conscious irony of this paragraph serves to highlight the esteem in which ruins were held by the picturesque critic.
15. This remark is explained by a footnote inserted by Gilpin a little further on, at the end of this extract.
16. That is to say, it is a place where a garden (an 'embellished' landscape) could suitably be developed. Gilpin comments earlier (I, pp.9–10) that gardens in which 'the model of nature is adopted' are uniquely English. He continues:
    This is a mode of scenery intirely of the sylvan kind. As we seek among the wild works of nature for the sublime, we seek here for the beautiful: and where there is a variety of lawn, wood, and water; these are naturally combined; and not too much decorated with buildings, nor disgraced with fantastic ornaments; we find a species of landscape, which no other country, but England, can display in such perfection ...
17. Gilpin has a footnote at this point:
    In this old castle the author of this tour was born, and spent his early youth; which must be his apology for dwelling so long upon it.—Since this description was written, it has, in some degree, been repaired.
18. James Radcliffe, 3rd Earl of Derwentwater (1689-1716), was a leading figure in the 1715 Jacobite Rising. After surrendering at Preston, he was attainted and executed at Tower Hill.
19. In Volume I of this work, Gilpin describes some mountain shapes and their qualities. 'The beauty of a distant mountain in a great measure, depends on the line it traces along the sky ... Such forms also as suggest the idea of lumpish *heaviness* are disgusting—round, swelling forms, without any break to disincumber them of their weight.' [pp.82-83]
20. Gilpin explains 'broken-ground' as being rugged surfaces, rocks, ground littered with cut timber or branches (I, pp.105-106).

21. This waterfall was one of the most celebrated attractions of the Lakes tour, both for its appearance and its sound, amplified by the mountain echoes. (Andrews, *The Search for the Picturesque*, pp.191-192). In his account of the route around the shores of the lake, Gilpin recorded his impressions on taking a 'nearer view' (p.191):
    This water-fall is a noble object, both in itself, and as an ornament of the lake. It appears more as an object *connected with the lake*, as we approach by water. By land, we see it over a promontory of low ground, which, in some degree, hides it's grandeur. At the distance of a mile, it begins to appear with dignity.
    But of whatever advantage the fall of Lodoar may be as a piece of *distant* scenery, it's effect is very noble, when examined *on the spot*. As a single object, it wants no accompaniments of offskip; which would rather injure, than assist it. They would disturb it's simplicity, and repose. The greatness of it's parts affords scenery enough. Some instruments please in concert: others you wish to hear alone.
22. Gilpin's footnote:
    The late Mr. Avison, organist of St Nicholas at Newcastle upon Tyne.
23. Gilpin's footnote:
    In a letter to Lord Lyttleton, quoted above.

XXV
Cornwall: William Borlase (1695–1772)

William Borlase, a dutiful and contented village clergyman who dwelt in the westernmost part of Cornwall, was a scholarly antiquary whose work was so detailed and thorough that he might justifiably be regarded as one of the earliest English archaeologists.[1] Throughout his life he engaged, in his spare time, in the observation and collection of remains of the past in his native county, and in studies of its early history, the Cornish language, and mineralogy. Only in his fifty-fourth year did he submit his work for publication, producing a number of learned papers and three books before his death in 1772 at the age of seventy-six.[2] His was a very particular view of England, at first noticed by few, but which has continued to fascinate people ever since.

Born in 1695 on the family estate at Pendeen, William Borlase was a descendant of a Cornish gentry family whose lineage was thought to go back to the Normans. He studied at Oxford, graduating with the degrees of BA in 1716 and MA in 1719. In 1720 he was ordained as a priest and in 1722 became rector of Ludgvan, less than ten miles from Pendeen, a living which he retained for the rest of his life. In 1732 he also obtained the vicarage of his home parish, St Just, to which he appointed a curate. In later life he became a Fellow of the Royal Society and an Honorary Doctor of Laws of Oxford University. He married and raised a family, and his private life was happy and fulfilled, except that he suffered from rheumatism, for which he was treated by his friend Dr William Oliver, at Bath. His other important friend was Sir John St Aubyn, baronet, owner of St Michael's Mount, and M.P. for West Cornwall. These two, together with Edward Collins, vicar at nearby St Erth, did much to encourage Borlase in his pursuit of materials concerning the antiquities and history of Cornwall.

The western peninsula of Cornwall is rich in antiquities: standing stones, dolmens, stone circles, barrows, rock basins, and caves;[3] which, although lacking in 'striking beauty or magnificence', as Borlase remarked in a letter to

William Stukeley,[4] aroused his curiosity and provoked his desire to discover more about their nature and their origins. In the absence of a substantial library in Cornwall, he felt isolated from current scholarship, and so tended to rely primarily on his own fieldwork. He explained this in the same correspondence:

> Upon examining frequently those monuments and authors concerning them, I thought something might be added to the accounts I met with from a faithfull measurement and observation of the structure, shape, situation and some other peculiarities of these monuments, although at the distance I have allways lived from libraries my conceptions must needs be rude and new to those who have every book at their command.[5]

In the preface to the *Antiquities of Cornwall* the limitation of his studies to his native county has become a matter of pride: he makes the observation that it is often remarked that English travellers know little of their own country, and know more of Greece and Italy. Those aware of the Grecian and Roman antiquities, 'have seldom any relish for the ruder products of Ancient Britain'. Finding that his 'situation in life' restricted him to local monuments, he studied these, and advocated that no-one should confine his experiences to 'the superior flavour and beauty of what comes from abroad'.[6] Borlase was aware, moreover, that little research had been undertaken on Cornwall's ancient sites. Carew, he wrote, was the first to survey the county, but he only 'faintly touched' on history and monuments. Norden's work was a 'meer transcript' of Carew's, and those writers who included Cornwall as part of the whole country (Leland, Camden and Speed) made only incomplete studies.[7]

Because Borlase was one of the first antiquaries to practise systematic fieldwork, it is tempting to account him an archaeologist, but the scope of his investigations went well beyond the usual limits of that discipline, embracing all phenomena that became evident in his collecting. The best appraisal of his work can be made not in his publications but in his field notebooks, the majority of which have been preserved.[8] In these, a contemporary archaeologist might find a greater kinship with Borlase, for they reveal more of his methods and of his observations as he made them. The *Antiquities of Cornwall*, on the other hand, while making use of the field observations, has as its goal a narrative explanation of the history of man, from ancient times, in Cornwall. In the book, then, we are not seeing Borlase seeing Cornwall, rather it is Borlase reflecting on having seen Cornwall. At the same time, the explanations of the field observations apply contemporary theories, and many can be dismissed as mistaken. One of his most striking misconceptions, for example, was that the 'Rock-Basons' which he found on the upper surfaces of rocks, and which in fact are natural phenomena, were made by ancient inhabitants. In his chapter on this subject[9] he contemplates their shapes and sizes and their possible uses: to extract salt from water, to crush tin ore, or in religious ceremonies. His conclusion is that they were used in rites of purification by water, based both on his observations of the nature of the basins and his knowledge of the use of water in the ceremonies of other religions and cultures, including the Jews, the Egyptians, the Greeks and the Romans. But he was a pioneer, and it is only to be expected that his reasoning should be positioned in the prevailing concepts of his time. That this led to erroneous conclusions does not in any way detract from his great achievement. Moreover, the significance of ancient monuments is not fully known still: the archaeological discovery of a place such as Cornwall, to which he was an early contributor, continues in our own time, and the elucidation of the distant past is still incomplete.

That said, it must be acknowledged that the speculative element in Borlase's narratives is conspicuous and it is sometimes difficult to subtract it from his descriptions of what he observed. The whole of Book II of the *Antiquities of Cornwall*, more than a hundred pages, is devoted to customs, religion, and ceremonies of Druids, the priestly order whose history had been revived in England in the later seventeenth century. Druids had been discussed in Hellenistic times, had been reported in Britain by Roman invaders, and had been rediscovered by Renaissance scholars of classical texts. Aylett Sammes proposed the ancient colonisation of Britain by Phoenicians, with whom the priestly order was mysteriously associated, as early as 1676, and Aubrey suggested the link between Druids and Stonehenge, but it was the antiquary William Stukeley (1687–1765) who did most to establish the Druidic tradition and its association with stone circles and megalithic monuments.[10] The supposed regime was thereafter frequently brought into speculative history as the purposes and uses of monuments were considered. One of the more vivid scenarios imagined by Borlase was postulated for a group of stone circles at Botallack, in the parish of St Just:

> ... some of these Circles include, and intersect one another, as in the curious cluster of Circles at Botallek ... in the seeming confusion of which, I cannot but think that there was some mystical meaning, or, at least, distinct allotment to particular uses. Some of these might be employed for the Sacrifice, and to prepare, kill, examine, and burn the Victim, others allotted to Prayer, others to the Feasting of the Priests, others for the station of those who devoted the Victims: whilst one Druid was preparing the Victim in one place, another was adoring in another, and describing the limits of his Temple: a third was going his round at the extremity of another Circle of Stones; and, likely, many

> Druids were to follow one the other in these mysterious Rounds: others were busy in the Rights of Augury, that so all the Rites, each in its proper place, might proceed at one and the same time, and under the inspection of the High-Priests; who, by comparing and observing the indications of the whole, might judge of the Will of the Gods with the greater certainty: lastly, that these Circles intersected each other in so remarkable a manner as we find them in this Monument, might be, to intimate that each of these Holy Rites, though exercised in different Circles, and their own proper compartments, were but so many Rings, or Links, of one and the same chain; and that there was a constant dependance and connexion betwixt Sacrifice, Prayer, Holy-Feasting, and all the several parts of their Worship.[11]

On the page facing this passage is Borlase's observation: a meticulous plan, to scale, of the monument, providing a restrained counterpoise to the lurid scene of druidical ritual which he proposed as its function. Here are brought together the scientific and the speculative, the two complementary aspects of antiquarian research, as if we are on a balancing point between superstition and empirical analysis. Indeed it is a balance so fine that Borlase himself in his preface takes account of the unease it may engender:

> In treating of the Superstition and *Rock-Monuments* of the *Druids*, I may seem too conjectural to those who will make no allowances for the deficiencies of History, nor be satisfied with any thing but evident Truths; but, where there is no Certainty to be obtained, Probabilities must suffice; and Conjectures are no faults, but when they are either advanced as real Truths, or too copiously pursued, or peremptorily insisted upon as decisive.—In Subjects of such distant Ages, where History will so often withdraw her taper, Conjecture may sometimes strike a new light, and the truths of Antiquity be more effectually pursued than where people will not venture to guess at all. One Conjecture may move the veil, another partly remove it, and a third, happier still, borrowing light and strength from what went before, may wholly disclose what we want to know.[12]

Who can see a mysterious landscape and not wonder about its past? For Borlase, the observations demanded explanations, and the sources of these were ancient wisdom and imagination. Yet his tempering of conjecture with caution shows the beginnings of empirical thinking coming to maturity, and the realization that certainty cannot be achieved by speculative reasoning. The passage which follows, dealing with caves, one of them just outside the village of his childhood, and with which he must long have been familiar, while being far more circumspect than the explanation of the Botallack stone circles, shows the antiquarian process of research: observation, followed by speculation and testing of hypotheses, leading necessarily to an explanation, without which the description could not be thought complete.

Of the Caves of the Ancient Cornish Britans

From *Antiquities Historical and Monumental of the County of Cornwall*, pp.292–297

Of these Caves I shall only describe three, nothing either of introduction, or pleasure, resulting from a multiplicity of measurements, where things are not materially distinct.

In the Tenement of Bolleit[13] in the parish of St Berian,[14] in the Western part of Cornwall, at the end of a little inclosure, is a Cave called the Fogou;[15] its entrance is about four feet high, and wide. The Cave goes straight forward, nearly of the same width as the entrance, seven feet high, and 36 from end to end. About five feet from the entrance, there is on the left hand a hole two feet wide, and one foot six inches high, within which there is a Cave four feet wide, and four feet six inches high; it goes nearly East about 13 feet, then to the South five feet more; the sides and end faced with Stone, and the roof covered with large flat stones. At the end fronting the entrance, there is another square hole, within which there was also a further vault now stopt up with stones, through which you see the light; and therefore I doubt not but here was a passage for light and air, if not a back way of conveying things into and out of these Cells; a property, which other Caves have as well as this. This Cave is not in the village of Bolleit, but about a furlong[16] distant, and indeed, but for the entrance (the ground is so level above, and on each side of it), no one would suspect that there was a Cave below. There is a cave of the same name in the parish of St Eval near Padstow.

In the tenement of Bodinar, in the parish of Sancred,[17] some what higher than the present village, is a spot of ground amounting to no more than half an acre of land (formerly much larger), full of irregular heaps of stone overgrown with heath and brambles. It is of no regular shape, neither has it any vestiges of Fortification. In the Southern part of this plot, you may with some difficulty enter into a hole, faced on each side with a stone-wall, and covered with flat stones. Great parts of the walls as well as covering are fallen into the Cave, which does not run in a straight line, but turns to the left hand at a small distance from the place where I entered, and seems to have branched itself out much farther than I could then trace it, which did not exceed twenty feet. It is about five feet high, and as much in width, called the Giant's Holt, and has no other use at present than to frighten and appease froward children. As the hedges round are very thick, and near one the other, and the inclosures within them extremely small, I imagine these ruins were formerly of much greater extent, and have been removed into the hedges; the stones of which, appearing sizeable, and as if they had been used in Masonry, seem to confirm the conjecture. Possibly here might be a large British town (as I have been informed the late Mr. Tonkin thought), and this Cave might be a private way to get into or sally out of it; but the walls are every where crushed or fallen, and nothing regular to be seen; I will only add, that this Cave, or under-ground passage, was so well concealed, that though I had been in it in the year 1738, yet, when I came again to examine it in the year 1752, I was a long while before I could find it.

Of all the artificial Caves I have seen in Cornwall, that called Pendeen Vau[18] (by the Welsh pronounced Fau) is the most entire, and curious. It consists of three Caves or galleries; the entrance is four feet six inches wide, and as many high; walled on each side with large Stones, with a rude arch on the top. From the entrance you descend six steps, and advance to the N. N. E. the floor dipping all the way as in the section.[19]

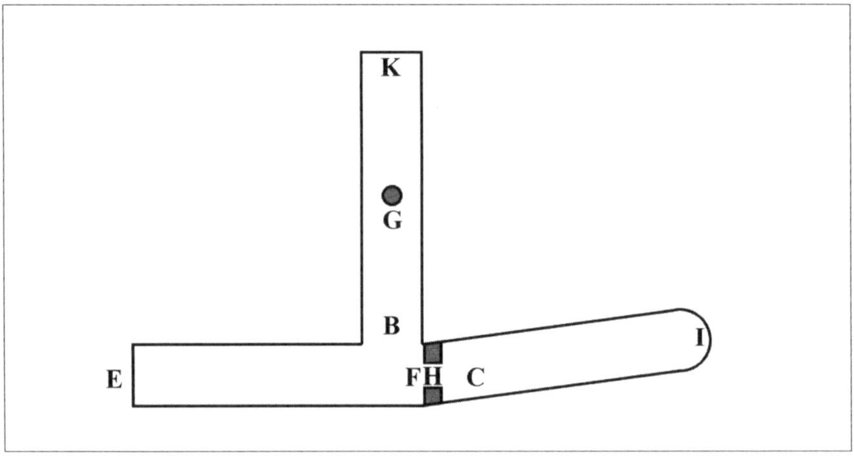

The sides built of Stone draw nearer together, as they rise, the better to receive the flat Stones DD, which form the covering, and are full six feet high from the ground; this first cave is 28 feet long from E to F. Before you come to F, at right angles, turns off to the left hand the second Cave B, its sides the same distance, and roof formed only five feet six inches high. In the middle of this second Cave, observing a low place, I caused the floor to be dug, and found there a round pit, G, three feet diameter, and two feet deep, but nothing in it remarkable; in other parts, I afterwards tried the floor, and found the natural ground, as left when the work was finished: at the end K, it has a hole in the roof through which a man may climb up into the field. This is all I found worth noteing in the second Cave. At H, fronting the entrance, there is a square hole, two feet wide, and two feet six inches high, through which you creep into a third Cave C, six feet wide, and six feet high, neither sides nor roof faced with stone, but the whole dug out of the natural ground; the sides formed regularly and straight, and the arch of the roof a semi-circle. The plan also ends in a semi-circle of the same dimensions at I, at the distance of twenty-six feet six inches. I caused the floor of this Cave to be dug in two places, but found neither Cell nor Grave, but the natural ground only, without any appearances of its having been moved. You see nothing of this Cave, either in the field or garden, 'till you come to the mouth of it, as much privacy as possible being consulted.

Norden, in his Survey of Cornwall, p.40. tells us 'that the tide flows into this Cave, at high water, very far under the earth,' but the sea is in truth more than a quarter of a mile from any part of it.

The common people also thereabout tell many idle stories of like kind, not worth the reader's notice, neglecting the structure, which is really commodious, and well executed.

There are many other Caves still to be seen in these parts, and some have been rifled and destroyed by converting the Stones to other uses, but none have come to my notice, different enough from the foregoing to merit a particular description. I shall now proceed therefore to enquire into the use and design of those caves.[20]

In most countries the ancients thought themselves under a necessity of providing themselves with such private receptacles; and when their country did not afford them natural ones, they made to themselves, as here in Cornwall, artificial ones. They had more reasons than one, for betaking themselves to these retired places. In cold countries they retired into their Caves to avoid the severity of Winter, says Tacitus of the Germans;[21] and Xenophon, concerning the cold country of the Armenians, tells us that their houses were under ground, the mouth or entrance of them like that of a well, but underneath wide and spreading; there are ways for cattle to enter, but the men go down by stairs.[22] This they did, doubtless, because, when the ground was frozen, or covered with snow, for any long time, their cattle as well as themselves, might go into the Caves where the ground was not affected by either, and the air less piercing. But the Winters are not so so [*sic*] severe in Cornwall, as that they can be reasonably supposed to have given occasion for the making of those Caves.

The Druids taught in Caves, and in Caves people were initiated into the mysteries of Mithras; but for both these purposes the Ancients generally made use of natural not artificial caves.

It was a very ancient way of Sepulture (if not the first manner that obtained) to bury in Caves: thus Abraham buried Sarah his wife in the field of Mackpelah (Gen. xxi. 19.), in which chapter the sacred historian gives us at length the treaty for purchasing this Cave, shewing how sollicitous the Patriarch was to have the property of it secured to him for a family burial-place: this whole passage intimates, that it was then the custom of the greatest princes to have sepulchres (see ver. 6.) peculiar to their families, either more ornamented, or more spacious, than the burying places of the vulgar, and that these sepulchres were Caves: but notwithstanding the Cell which I found in Cave the second (B) of Pendeen Vau, I do not take that work to have been sepulchral. It may be suggested that there was an urn buried in this place (for in such Cells we often find them), and might be taken away by persons who had searched here before. This is possible; but that a work of so much labour, and of three apartments, should be made for burying, and only one Pit, and one supposed urn, is not at all probable. If this Cave had been designed for the dead, many Cells would offer with their Urns, or many Graves. For there is yet another reason why the ancients made these underground structures, a reason which prevails in all countries; and that is, to hide and secure what they possessed and valued in times of war and danger. Plutarch says,[23] that the Characitanians in any danger of war descended into their Caves, carrying in their booty with them, free from all apprehensions when they were thus concealed: and of the Germans, Tacitus relates the same custom.[24] 'In such places as these Caves, says he, they endeavour to soften the rigour of the season, and if at any time an enemy approaches, he will lay waste and carry off all that he can readily lay his hand on; but these secret subterraneous retreats are either not known, or not thought of in a hurry, or escape notice fir this reason, because they must take up time in searching for.' In several parts of Britain, Caves of this nature must occur. 'In the Island of Skie there are several little stone houses built under ground, called Earth-houses, which serve to hide a few people, and their goods in the time of war.'[25] The same author tells us, 'that in the isle of Ila there is a large Cave called Vâh-Vearnag, or Man's Cave, which will hold 200 men.' There is a remarkable one published and planned in the Louthiana, (Lib. III. Pl. X. 16.) imagined by the author, with good reason, to have been 'intended originally for a sort of granary to conceal corn, and, perhaps, other effects of value, from mountain-robbers. All this part of Ireland, continues he, abounds with such Caves, not only under Mounts, Forts, and Castles; but under plain fields, some winding into little hills and risings, like a volute, or ram's horn; others running zig-zag, like a serpent; others, again right forward, connecting Cell with Cell; the common Irish think they are skulking-holes of the Danes, after they had lost their superiority in that island.'[26] Upon which I cannot but observe, that they would have judged more rightly if they had attributed these hiding-places to the natives than to foreigners, the latter having but little reason to flatter themselves with any hope of concealment from the former; but the former, born and bred upon the spot, a great deal of reason to conclude, that many private places might be retired to, which strangers and temporary invaders might never discover.

The true intent then of these Caves in Cornwall was, as I apprehend, to secure their provisions, and moveable goods, in times of danger;[27] and the reason that they are many in number, because Cornwall has been the seat of much war; and, therefore, few countries have had more occasion for such private store-houses than the Cornish. That Cornwall has been the Theatre of much war, appears by the multitude of entrenchments on the shores, particularly in the Western parts, where every promontory has its fortification, every neck of land its ditch and *vallum* reaching from sea to sea, and not a hill of any eminence without what we call a castle. Some ruined towns are also still to be seen, testifying the desolations of war. It was during these troublesome times that I imagine the several Caves I have now mentioned, and others of like kind, were made by the natives, to secure their effects, and, perhaps, to keep the field, from the piratical invasions of the Saxons and Danes. Exposed to the sea on every side, as Cornwall is, what is now looked upon as their greatest security by the inhabitants, proved at that time the perpetual instrument of their misery. As soon as the Saxons came to understand their trade of piracy, they found it more for their advantage to attack the British nation in its extream parts, than at the heart and centre of the island; consequently Cornwall had its share of their visits, in proportion to its remoteness from the seat of protection and power, and the opportunities which its numerous creeks gave these sons of plunder to land and pillage. The Danes were still more troublesome and cruel, as they were more constant visitors, and continued many ages to waste, burn, and destroy, whatever fell in their way; so that the poor Cornish Britans because of these rapacious enemies, as 'the children of Israel because of the Midianites, made them the Dens which are in the Mountains, and Caves, and strong Holds.'[28]

1. On the life and work of William Borlase, see the introductory material in William Borlase, *Antiquities Historical and Monumental of the County of Cornwall*, Second Edition (originally published in London, 1769), reprinted with an introduction by P. A. S. Pool and Charles Thomas, Wakefield, Yorkshire: EP Publishing Limited, 1973, pp.v–xxii. Hereafter this work will be referred to as *Antiquities of Cornwall*.
2. His books were: *Antiquities of Cornwall* (1754), *Observations on the Ancient and Present State of the Islands of Scilly* (1756), and *Natural History of Cornwall* (1757). He brought out the second, revised and enlarged, edition of the *Antiquities* in 1769 (which is the one from which the extract given here is taken). Works which were unpublished in his lifetime were a second edition of the *Natural History* and an unused introduction to the *Natural History*, recast in 1771 as *Private Thoughts of the Creation and the Deluge, by a Country Clergyman*.

3. Of these, the rock basins were natural formations, but Borlase attributed them to the Druids.
4. Written 10 November, 1749. Cited by P. A. S. Pool, *ibid.*, p.vii. The source of Borlase's letters is the William Borlase Correspondence, Penzance Library, Morrab Gardens, Penzance, Cornwall.
5. *Ibid.*
6. The Preface, 'To the Reader', *Antiquities of Cornwall*, pp.v-vi.
7. *Ibid.*
8. At the Penzance Library and the Royal Institution of Cornwall.
9. *Antiquities of Cornwall*, pp.240-258.
10. Aylett Sammes (1636–1679), antiquary, published his idiosyncratic British history in 1675. Stukeley, a physician and medical researcher with scholarly interests in natural philosophy, astronomy, and many other emerging fields, as well as antiquarian studies, was a friend of Isaac Newton and Edmund Halley, and became a member of the Royal Society. His major contribution was in the archaeological description of Stonehenge and Avebury, for he undertook meticulous field work and made extensive measurements and surveys, but his imaginative and misleading interpretations of the monuments remained influential right through to the twentieth century.
11. *Antiquities of Cornwall*, p.199.
12. *Antiquities of Cornwall*, Preface, p.ix.
13. Boleigh.
14. St Buryan.
15. In the Cornish-English vocabulary included by Borlase, 'fogou' is listed as the Cornish word for 'cave'.
16. 220 yards.
17. Sancreed.
18. In the Cornish-English vocabulary included by Borlase, the word 'ffau', equivalent to the Cornish 'vau' is listed as meaning 'den'.
19. The cave entrance is at E on the accompanying plan. The stones DD, shown by Borlase on a small sketch, form the exterior wall running from E to F on the right hand side, that is, the lower side on the plan.
20. The purposes for which the caves were built have not been ascertained.
21. Borlase's footnote: 'Solent et subterraneos specus aperire, eosque multo insuper simo onerant, suffugium hyemi, et receptaculum frugibus.' De M. G. cap. xvi.
22. Borlase's footnote: De Exped. Cyri, Lib. IV.
23. Borlase's footnote: In vita Sertorii.
24. Borlase's footnote: Ibid. ut supra.
25. Borlase's footnote: Martin of the Isles, p.154.
26. Borlase's footnote: Ireland.
27. Borlase's footnote: Since writing these papers, an ingenious modern author has given us an account of the same means used in time of distress in the Island of Minorca. 'Their Caves, which they call Covas, have with incredible labour been scooped out of the rock; they are so numerous and spatious, as to contain all the inhabitants of the country in time of danger, and were used long after the erection of houses, as places of security for women, children, and the most valuable moveables upon any sudden alarm.' Armstrong's History of Minorca.
28. Borlase's footnote: Judges vi. 2.

XXVI

Selborne, Hampshire: Gilbert White (1720–1793)

Gilbert White's account of his parish of Selborne is in several ways unlike most of the descriptions which have been included in previous pages. Its most noticeable similarity is with Richard Carew's description of Cornwall, sharing an engaging personal quality, coloured by the author's sheer delight in writing of his home surroundings. It also quite clearly shares with the work of John Aubrey a scientific approach and an inquiring purpose. But its remarkable difference from all the others is its extraordinary popularity: since it first appeared in 1789 it has had over two hundred editions, a number exceeded by few other books of any genre.[1] Far from being an antiquarian curiosity, it has, over more than two centuries, struck an harmonious chord with the sentiments of English readers, and probably of others as well. White's biographer, Paul Foster, claims for the book a place in English national consciousness.[2] Such an enduring evocation of nostalgia surely owes much to the ingenuousness and immediacy of White's record of his observations especially of birds, and also of other animals and plants in his garden and neighbourhood.

The author, who has come to be regarded as England's first ecologist, was born in Selborne, Hampshire, in 1720 and lived there for most of his life. He gained admittance to Oxford University in 1739 and took his MA in 1746. He remained in Oxford for several more years, becoming Dean of his college (Oriel) and a Junior Proctor of the University in the 1750s. He pursued a career as a clergyman, and after his ordination in 1749 he became a deacon of Oxford Cathedral and curate in two villages near Selborne. During this time he also sojourned with friends in other counties, finally settling in Selborne itself in 1755. Several years later, he inherited the family estate, The Wakes, where he lived as a bachelor, cultivated his garden, and made his studies of the natural world.[3]

The observation of nature seems to have delighted White since his childhood, but his specific and sustained record-keeping began on the encouragement of his brother-in-law, Thomas Barker, with whom he had stayed in Rutland in 1751. His first diary, which he kept for twenty years, was the *Garden Kalendar*, recording his sowing and planting in his garden, and noting the results of his efforts. On some days the entries were short and in a telegraphic style, but on others he recorded some particular initiative or observation with such purpose and spontaneity that it is as if he had just walked in from his grounds. On 8 October 1759, for example, he wrote:[4]

> Now perfect summer weather again after one wet day. The Grapes in the bags unusually fine; & both bunches, & single grapes are as large again as usual. It is to be observed that as this new Culture swells the berries so much; they are apt in this Cluster-sort to press too hard on each other, & prevent ripening, & occasion mouldiness: therefore if the grapes were thinn'd out the beginning of the summer with the points of a pair of scissars, it would certainly prove an advantage.

He grew most of the flowers listed in contemporary gardening manuals,[5] taking particular interest in the cultivation of annuals in hotbeds. A greater interest was in fruits and vegetables, especially potatoes, the growing of which White encouraged amongst the people of the district, in order to improve diet and public health. The much shorter *Flora Selborniensis*, a diary kept during the year 1766, took a more comprehensive view, recording weather conditions and natural phenomena both wild and in the garden. In such a work White was becoming more conscious of the contribution he might make to the improvement of country life and the agrarian economy. While he did not maintain this particular record in subsequent years, his continuing *Garden Kalendar* henceforth included more meteorological details.

When in 1767 he met the published naturalist Thomas Pennant and began providing him with information about the flora and fauna of central southern England, it was his first opportunity to share his interests with someone with greater experience in the same field.[6] Thus began the correspondence upon which the first part of *The Natural History of Selborne* was based. In 1767 Pennant introduced White as a correspondent to Daines Barrington, who had devised a publication, *The Naturalist's Journal*, to be used in making records of natural occurrences, in order to aid the improvement of agriculture.[7] Barrington sent a copy to White, who began to use it on 1 January 1768, and continued to do so, completing an annual volume in each year till his death in 1793. The ensuing correspondence with Barrington formed the basis of the second part of White's book on Selborne, and it was Barrington who encouraged both the writing of detailed descriptions of local birds and animals and the plan to publish all the letters as a local study. There is some additional material, presented in the form of letters, but the whole preserves the enthusiasm and freshness of letters written to capture the immediate experience of a naturalist who has just returned from the field.

Gilbert White's observations were careful and systematic, but it was his special gift to be able to present ordinary natural events as wonders. The vividness of his narrative consists in conveying not only the observed but the experience of observing, as in this account of the grasshopper-warbler:[8]

> The *grasshopper-lark* began his sibilous note in my fields last *Saturday*. Nothing can be more amusing than the whisper of this little bird, which seems to be close by though at an hundred yards distance; and, when close to your ear, is scarce louder than when a great way off. Had I not been a little acquainted with insects, and known that the grasshopper kind is not yet hatched, I should have hardly believed but that it had been a *locusta* whispering in the bushes. The country people laugh when you tell them that it is the note of a bird. It is a most artful creature, sculking in the thickest part of a bush; and will sing at a yard distance, provided it be concealed. I was obliged to get a person to go on the other side of the hedge where it haunted; and then it would run, creeping like a mouse, before us for a hundred yards together, through the bottom of the thorns; yet it would not come into fair sight: but in a morning, early, and when undisturbed, it sings on the top of a twig, gaping and shivering with it's wings.

With White we are seeing England close up; we catch the details of feathers and claws, we hear quiet, close songs and distant calls, we feel the keenness of the snow and the warmth of the chimney. Perhaps this explains the enduring appeal of his book, which so clearly brings to its reader the feel and look of a place long ago; a beautiful place observed with unbounded love and constant surprise. There is a mythology about White which represents him as well-meaning but naive and childlike. This has perhaps developed because he has been appreciated more as a writer than as a scientist. Ted Dadswell in a recent critique of White's work argues that the value of his scientific contribution was his recognition of the significance of animal *behaviour* at a time when most naturalists were concerned only with classification.[9] In White's own words, 'True naturalists will thank you more for the life & conversation of a few animals well studyed & investigated; than for a long barren list of half the Fauna of the globe'.[10]

The first of the following extracts is White's general description of Selborne, from the first letter to Thomas Pennant, although this was not a real letter: the first letters were clearly contrived to create the setting for what follows. White presents Selborne basically in the formula which had been used in many county surveys, specifying the boundaries, the soil, the rivers, and the farm produce. But this is a miniature, encompassing not the sweep of a whole county but a parish only, and so it is brought into unusually sharp focus, and we are at once engaged in an intimate tour extending no further than White's neighbourhood. The description is informed by the aesthetic sensitivities of the later eighteenth century, and White responds to the landscape not only as a naturalist but also as viewer of a scene: it is a romantic description far removed from the seventeenth century, when the landscape was a matter mostly of indifference and merely provided a backdrop to past events and great estates.

The second extract is one of White's ornithological studies, in which he presents an account of the sand-martin, one of the several hirundine birds to which he accorded considerable attention. It is a good example of the results of the observation of animal behaviour: for all that the sand-martin is a reclusive bird, seldom seen, the careful naturalist has discovered much about it. The study demonstrates also the restraint and circumspection of White's methodology, assuming no more than can be substantiated by observation, and acknowledging the limitations of the naturalist in the field. The third extract is a description of a particularly severe period in the winter of 1776, and is a combination of the naturalist's recording of measured observations and his delight in the experience of those observations. The short scientific essay on the sand-martin is nicely complemented by the final extract, an example of White's poetry, in which the naturalist is humbled by the mysteries of the world he seeks to examine; 'man's prying pride' is baffled by the secrets even of his neighbourhood environment. The poem in its style and references also brings White the naturalist into conjunction with White the classical scholar.

Selborne Parish

From *The Natural History of Selborne*, pp.1–4

From *Letter I to Thomas Pennant, Esq.*

The parish of SELBORNE lies in the extreme eastern corner of the county of *Hampshire*, bordering on the county of *Sussex*, and not far from the county of *Surrey*; is about fifty miles south-west of *London*, in latitude 51, and near midway between the towns of *Alton* and *Petersfield*. Being very large and extensive it abuts on twelve parishes, two of which are in *Sussex*, viz., *Trotton* and *Rogate*. If you begin from the south and proceed westward, the adjacent parishes are *Emshot*, *Newton Valance*, *Faringdon*, *Harteley Mauduit*, *Great Ward le ham*,[11] *Kingsley*, *Hedleigh*,[12] *Bramshot*, *Trotton*, *Rogate*, *Lysse*,[13] and *Greatham*. The soils of this district are almost as various and diversified as the views and aspects. The high part of the south-west consists of a vast hill of chalk, rising three hundred feet above the village; and is divided into a sheep down, the high wood, and a long hanging wood called *The Hanger*. The covert of this eminence is altogether beech, the most lovely of all forest trees, whether we consider it's smooth rind or bark, it's glossy foliage, or graceful pendulous boughs. The down, or sheep-walk, is a pleasing park-like spot, of about one mile by half that space, jutting out on the verge of the hill-country, where it begins to break down into the plains, and commanding a very engaging view, being an assemblage of hill, dale, wood-lands, heath, and water. The prospect is bounded to the south-east and east by the vast range of mountains called *The Sussex Downs*, by *Guild-down* near *Guildford*, and by the *Downs* round *Dorking*, and *Ryegate*[14] in *Surrey*, to the north-east, which altogether, with the country beyond *Alton* and *Farnham*, form a noble and extensive outline.

At the foot of this hill, one stage or step from the uplands, lies the village, which consists of one single straggling street, three quarters of a mile in length, in a sheltered vale, and running parallel with *The Hanger*. The houses are divided from the hill by a vein of stiff clay (good wheat-land), yet stand on a rock of white stone, little in appearance removed from chalk; but seems so far from being calcarious,[15] that it endures extreme heat. Yet that the freestone still preserves somewhat that is analogous to chalk, is plain from the beeches which descend as low as those rocks extend, and no further, and thrive as well on them, where the ground is steep, as on the chalks.

The cart-way of the village divides, in a remarkable manner, two very incongruous soils. To the south-west is a rank clay, that requires the labour of years to render it mellow; while the gardens to the north-east, and small enclosures behind, consist of a warm, forward, crumbling mould, called *black malm*, which seems highly saturated with vegetable and animal manure; and these may perhaps have been the original site of the town; while the woods and coverts might extend down to the opposite bank.

At each end of the village, which runs from south-east to north-west, arises a small rivulet: that at the north-west end frequently fails; but the other is a fine perennial spring, little influenced by drought or wet seasons, called *Well-head*.[16] This breaks out of some high grounds joining to *Nore Hill*, a noble chalk promontory, remarkable for sending forth two streams into two different seas. The one to the south becomes a branch of the *Arun*, running to *Arundel*, and so falling into the *British* channel: the other to the north.[17] The *Selborne* stream makes one branch of the *Wey*; and, meeting the *Black-down* stream at *Hedleigh*, and the *Alton* and *Farnham* stream at *Tilford-bridge*, swells into a considerable river, navigable at *Godalming*; from whence it passes to *Guildford*, and so into the *Thames* at *Weybridge*; and thus at the *Nore* into the *German* ocean.

Our wells, at an average, run to about sixty-three feet, and when sunk to that depth seldom fail; but produce a fine limpid water, soft to the taste, and much commended by those who drink the pure element, but which does not lather well with soap.[18]

To the north-west, north and east of the village, is a range of fair enclosures, consisting of what is called *white malm*, a sort of rotten or rubble stone, which, when turned up to the frost and rain, moulders to pieces, and becomes manure to itself.[19]

Still on to the north-east, and a step lower, is a kind of white land, neither chalk nor clay, neither fit for pasture nor for the plough, yet kindly for hops, which root deep into the freestone, and have their poles and wood for charcoal growing just at hand. This white soil produces the brightest hops.

As the parish still inclines down towards *Wolmer-forest*, at the juncture of the clays and sand the soil becomes a wet, sandy loam, remarkable for timber, and infamous for roads. The oaks of *Temple* and *Blackmoor* stand high in the estimation of purveyors, and have furnished much naval timber; while the trees on the freestone grow large, but are what workmen call *shakey*, and so brittle as often to fall to pieces in sawing. Beyond the sandy loam the soil becomes an hungry lean sand, till it mingles with the forest; and will produce little without the assistance of lime and turnips.

The sand-martin

From *The Natural History of Selborne*, pp.175–179

From *Letter XX to the Hon. Daines Barrington*

The sand-martin, or bank-martin, is by much the least of any of the *British hirundines*;[20] and, as far as we have ever seen, the smallest known hirundo: though *Brisson* asserts that there is one much smaller, and that is the *hirundo esculenta*.[21]

But it is much to be regretted that it is scarce possible for any observer to be so full and exact as he could wish in reciting the circumstances attending the life and conversation of this little bird, since it is *fera naturâ*,[22] at least in this part of the kingdom, disclaiming all domestic attachments, and haunting wild heaths and commons where there are large lakes: while the other species, especially the swallow and house-martin, are remarkably gentle and domesticated, and never seem to think themselves safe but under the protection of man.

Here are in this parish, in the sand-pits and banks of lakes of *Woolmer-forest*, several colonies of these birds; and yet they are never seen in the village; nor do they at all frequent the cottages that are scattered about in that wild district. The only instance I ever remember where this species haunts any building is at the town of *Bishop's Waltham*, in this county, where many sand-martins nestle and breed in the scaffold-holes of the back wall of *William* of *Wykeham*'s stables: but then this wall stands in a very sequestered and retired enclosure, and faces upon a large and beautiful lake. And indeed this species seems so to delight in large waters, that no instance occurs of their abounding, but near vast pools or rivers: and in particular it has been remarked that they swarm in the banks of the *Thames* in some places below *London-bridge*.

It is curious to observe with what different degrees of architectonic skill Providence has endowed birds of the same genus, and so nearly correspondent in their general mode of life! for while the swallow and the house-martin discover the greatest address in raising and securely fixing crusts or shells of loam as cunabula[23] for their young, the bank-martin terebrates[24] a round and regular hole in the sand or earth, which is serpentine, horizontal, and about two feet deep. At the inner end of this burrow does this bird deposit, in a good degree of safety, her rude nest, consisting of fine grasses and feathers, usually goose-feathers, very inartificially laid together.

Perseverance will accomplish any thing: though at first one would be disinclined to believe that this weak bird, with her soft and tender bill and claws, should ever be able to bore the stubborn sandbank without entirely disabling herself: yet with these feeble instruments have I seen a pair of them make great dispatch, and could remark how much they had scooped that day by the fresh sand which ran down the bank, and was of a different colour from that which lay loose and bleached in the sun.

In what space of time these little artists are able to mine and finish these cavities I have never been able to discover, for reasons given above; but it would be a matter worthy of observation, where it falls in the way of any naturalist to make his remarks. This I have often taken notice of, that several holes of different depths are left unfinished at the end of summer. To imagine that these beginnings were intentionally made in order to be in the greater forwardness for next spring, is allowing perhaps too much foresight and *rerum prudentia*[25] to a simple bird. May not the cause of these *latebræ*[26] being left unfinished arise from their meeting in those places with strata too harsh, hard, and solid, for their purpose, which they relinquish, and go to a fresh spot that works more freely? Or may they not in other places fall in with a soil as much too loose and mouldering, liable to flounder, and threatening to overwhelm them and their labours?

One thing is remarkable—that, after some years, the old holes are forsaken and new ones bored; perhaps because the old habitations grow foul and fetid from long use, or because they may so abound with fleas as to become untenantable. This species of swallow moreover is strangely annoyed with fleas: and we have seen fleas, bed-fleas (*pulex irritans*), swarming at the mouths of these holes, like bees on the stools of their hives.

The following circumstance should by no means be omitted—that these birds do *not* make use of their caverns by way of hibernacula,[27] as might be expected; since banks so perforated have been dug out with care in the winter, when nothing was found but empty nests.

The sand-martin arrives much about the same time with the swallow, and lays, as she does, from four to six white eggs. But as this species is *cryptogame*, carrying on the business of nidification, incubation, and the support of it's young in the dark, it would not be so easy to ascertain the time of breeding, were it not for the coming forth of the broods, which appear much about the time, or rather somewhat earlier than those of the swallow. The nestlings are supported in common like those of their congeners,[28] with gnats and other small insects; and sometimes they are fed with *libellulæ* (dragonflies) almost as long as themselves. In the last week in *June* we have seen a row of these sitting on a rail near a great pool as *perchers*; and so young and helpless, as easily to be taken by hand: but whether the dams ever feed them on the wing, as swallows and house-martins do, we have never yet been able to determine; nor do we know whether they pursue and attack birds of prey.

When they happen to breed near hedges and enclosures, they are dispossessed of their breeding-holes by the house-sparrow, which is on the same account a fell adversary to house-martins.

These *hirundines* are no songsters, but rather mute, making only a little harsh noise when a person approaches their nests. They seem not to be of a sociable turn, never with us congregating with their congeners in the autumn. Undoubtedly they breed a second time, like the house-martin and swallow; and withdraw about *Michaelmas*.[29]

Though in some particular districts they may happen to abound, yet on the whole, in the south of *England* at least, is this much the rarest species. For there are few towns or large villages but what abound with house-martins; few churches, towers, or steeples, but what are haunted by some swifts; scarce a hamlet or single cottage chimney that has not it's swallow; while the bank-martins, scattered here and there, live a sequestered life among some abrupt sand-hills, and in the banks of some few rivers.

These birds have a peculiar manner of flying; flitting about with odd jerks, and vacillations, not unlike the motions of a butterfly. Doubtless the flight of all *hirundines* is influenced by, and adapted to, the peculiar sort of insects which furnish their food. Hence it would be worth inquiry to examine what particular genus of insects affords the principal food of each respective species of swallow.

Notwithstanding what has been advanced above, some few sand-martins, I see, haunt the skirts of *London*, frequenting the dirty pools in *Saint George's-Fields*, and about *White-Chapel*. The question is where these build, since there are no banks or bold shores in that neighbourhood: perhaps they nestle in the scaffold-holes of some old or new deserted building. They dip and wash as they fly sometimes, like the house-martin and swallow.

Sand-martins differ from their congeners in the diminutiveness of their size, and in their colour, which is what is usually called a mouse-colour. Near *Valencia*, in *Spain*, they are taken, says *Willlughby*,[30] and sold in the markets for the table; and are called by the country people, probably from their desultory jerking manner of flight, *Papilion de Montagna*.

The frost of January 1776

From *The Natural History of Selborne*, pp.291–295

From *Letter LXI to the Hon. Daines Barrington*

There were some circumstances attending the remarkable frost in *January* 1776 so singular and striking, that a short detail of them may not be unacceptable.

The most certain way to be exact will be to copy the passages from my journal, which were taken from time to time as things occurred. But it may be proper previously to remark that the first week of *January* was uncommonly wet, and drowned with vast rains from every quarter: from whence may be inferred, as there is great reason to believe is the case, that intense frosts seldom take place till the earth is perfectly glutted and chilled with water;[31] and hence dry autumns are seldom followed by rigorous winters.

January 7th.—Snow driving all the day, which was followed by frost, sleet, and some snow, till the 12th, when a prodigious mass overwhelmed all the works of men, drifting over the tops of the gates and filling the hollow lanes.

On the 14th the writer was obliged to be much abroad; and thinks he never before or since has encountered such rugged *Siberian* weather. Many of the narrow roads were now filled above the tops of the hedges; through which the snow was driven into most romantic and grotesque shapes, so striking to the imagination as not to be seen without wonder and pleasure. The poultry dared not to stir out of their roosting places; for cocks and hens are so dazzled and confounded by the glare of snow that they would soon perish without our assistance. The hares also lay sullenly in their seats, and would not move till compelled by hunger; being conscious, poor animals, that the drifts and heaps treacherously betray their footsteps, and prove fatal to numbers of them.

From the 14th the snow continued to increase, and began to stop the road wagons and coaches, which could no longer keep on their regular stages; and especially on the western roads, where the fall appears to have been deeper than in the south. The company at *Bath*, that wanted to attend the *Queen's birth-day*, were strangely incommoded: many carriages of persons who got in their way to town from *Bath* as far as *Marlborough*, after strange embarrassments, here met with the *ne plus ultra*. The ladies fretted, and offered large rewards to labourers if they would shovel them a track to *London*: but the relentless heaps of snow were too bulky to be removed; and so the 18th passed over, leaving the company in very uncomfortable circumstances at the *Castle* and other inns.

On the 20th the sun shone out for the first time since the frost began; a circumstance that has been remarked before much in favour of vegetation. All this time the cold was not very intense, for the thermometer stood at 29, 28, 25, and thereabout; but on the 21st it descended to 20. The birds now began to be in a very pitiable and starving condition. Tamed by the season, skylarks settled in the streets of towns, because they saw the ground was bare; rooks frequented dunghills close to houses; and crows watched horses as they passed, and greedily devoured what dropped from them; hares now came into men's gardens, and, scraping away the snow, devoured such plants as they could find.

On the 22nd the author had occasion to go to *London* through a sort of *Laplandian-scene*, very wild and grotesque indeed. But the metropolis itself exhibited a still more singular appearance than the country; for being bedded deep in snow, the pavement of the streets could not be touched by the wheels or the horses' feet, so that the carriages ran about without the least noise. Such an exemption from din and clatter was strange, but not pleasant; it seemed to convey an uncomfortable idea of desolation:

'-- -- -- -- -- -- -- ipsa silentia terrent.'[32]

On the 27th much snow fell all day, and in the evening the frost became very intense. At *South Lambeth*, for the four following nights, the thermometer fell to 11, 7, 6, 6; and at *Selborne* to 7, 6, 10; and on the 31st of *January*, just before sunrise, with rime on the trees and on the tube of the glass, the quicksilver sunk exactly to zero, being 32 degrees below the freezing point; but by eleven in the morning, though in the shade, it sprang up to 16½.—a most unusual degree of cold this for the south of *England*! During these four nights the cold was so penetrating that it occasioned ice in warm chambers and under beds; and in the day the wind was so keen that persons of robust constitutions could scarcely endure to face it. The *Thames* was at once so frozen over both above and below bridge that crowds ran about on the ice. The streets were now strangely encumbered with snow, which crumbled and trod dusty; and, turning grey, resembled bay-salt: what had fallen on the roofs was so perfectly dry that, from first to last, it lay twenty-six days on the houses in the city; a longer time than had been remembered by the oldest housekeepers living. According to all appearances we might now have expected the continuance of this rigorous weather for weeks to come, since every night increased in severity; but, behold, without any apparent cause, on the 1st of *February* a thaw took place, and some rain followed before night; making good the observation above, that frosts often go off as it were at once, without any gradual declension of the cold. On the 2nd of *February* the thaw persisted; and on the 3rd swarms of little insects were frisking and sporting in a court-yard at *South Lambeth*, as if they felt no frost. Why the juices in the small bodies and smaller limbs of such minute beings are not frozen is a matter of curious inquiry.

Severe frosts seem to be partial, or to run in currents; for, at the same juncture, as the author was informed by accurate correspondents, at *Lyndon*, in the county of *Rutland*, the thermometer stood at 19; at *Blackburn*, in *Lancashire*, at 19; and at *Manchester* at 21, 20, and 18. Thus does some unknown circumstance strangely overbalance latitude, and render the cold sometimes much greater in the southern than the northern parts of this kingdom.

The consequences of this severity were, that in *Hampshire*, at the melting of the snow, the wheat looked well, and the turnips came forth little injured. The laurels and laurustines were somewhat damaged, but only in *hot aspects*. No evergreens were quite destroyed; and not half the damage sustained that befell in *January* 1768. Those laurels that were a little scorched on the south-sides were perfectly untouched on their north-sides. The care taken to shake the snow day by day from the branches seemed greatly to avail the author's evergreens. A neighbour's laurel-hedge, in a high situation, and facing the north, was perfectly green and vigorous; and the *Portugal laurels* remained unhurt.

As to the birds, the thrushes and blackbirds were mostly destroyed; and the partridges, by the weather and poachers, were so thinned that few remained to breed the following year.

The Naturalist's Summer-Evening Walk
To Thomas Pennant, Esquire.

… equidem credo, quia sit divinitus illis Ingenium.[33] Virg., *Georg.*

When day declining sheds a milder gleam,
What time the may-fly haunts the pool or stream;
When the still owl skims round the grassy mead,
What time the timorous hare limps forth to feed;
Then be the time to steal adown the vale,
And listen to the vagrant cuckoo's tale;
To hear the clamorous curlew call his mate,
Or the soft quail his tender pain relate;
To see the swallow sweep the dark'ning plain
Belated, to support her infant train;
To mark the swift in rapid giddy ring
Dash round the steeple, unsubdu'd of wing:
Amusive[34] birds!—say where your hid retreat
When the frost rages and the tempests beat;
Whence your return, by such nice instinct led,
When spring, soft season, lifts her bloomy head?
Such baffled searches mock man's prying pride,
The God of Nature is your secret guide!
While deep'ning shades obscure the face of day
To yonder bench leaf-shelter'd let us stray,
'Till blended objects fail the swimming sight,
And all the fading landscape sinks in night;
To hear the drowsy dorr[35] come brushing by
With buzzing wing, or the shrill cricket cry;
To see the feeding bat glance through the wood;
To catch the distant falling of the flood;
While o'er the cliff th'awakened churn-owl[36] hung
Through the still gloom protracts his chattering song;"
While high in air, and pois'd upon his wings,
Unseen, the soft, enamour'd woodlark sings:
These, Nature's works, the curious mind employ,
Inspire a soothing melancholy joy:
As fancy warms, a pleasing kind of pain
Steals o'er the cheek, and thrills the creeping vein!
Each rural sight, each sound, each smell, combine;

The tinkling sheep-bell, or the breath of kine;
The new-mown hay that scents the swelling breeze,
Or cottage-chimney smoking through the trees.
The chilling night-dews fall: away, retire;
For see, the glow-worm lights her amorous fire!
Thus, ere night's veil had half obscur'd the sky,
Th'impatient damsel hung her lamp on high:
True to the signal, by love's meteor led,
Leander hasten'd to his Hero's bed.[37]
I am, &c.

1. It has been claimed that only the Bible, Shakespeare's plays, and John Bunyan's *Pilgrim's Progress* have been published more frequently. See John Clegg's Introduction to Gilbert White's *Garden Kalendar*, London: The Scolar Press, 1975, p.xv. Grant Allen says in his 1900 edition that the greatest appeal of *The Natural History of Selborne* is historical, for it illuminates early scientific method: 'we are admitted to see science in the making' (p.xiii). Allen was writing at a time when scientific progress was very apparent and there was a complacent sense that most knowledge was already discovered. Indeed he says this of English biology: 'At the present day, unless one devotes oneself to the minuter forms of life, one has little chance of discovering anything new in Britain.' His comments serve to shed some light on the popularity of the book in an earlier period.
2. Paul G.M. Foster, *Gilbert White, Naturalist, Poet, Priest and Scholar (1720-93): a Brief Biography*, Selborne Paper Number One, Selborne: Gilbert White's House & The Oates Museum, 2000.
3. Gilbert White's house and garden at The Wakes, in the High Street of Selborne, have been restored according to his descriptions, and are now open to the public, attracting many visitors throughout the year.
4. Gilbert White, *Garden Kalendar 1751–1771*, facsimile edition with an introduction by John Clegg, London: The Scolar Press, 1975, p.217v.
5. For example, Philip Miller, *The Gardeners Dictionary,* (1731 and many subsequent editions); John Abercrombie, *Every Man his own Gardener* (1767).
6. Pennant had published the several volumes of his *British Zoology* in 1761-1766.
7. Barrington was a lawyer and the author, in 1781, of a book of antiquarian essays, *Miscellanies*. He was a friend of Dr Johnson and Boswell. Both Barrington and White were motivated by Stillingfleet's proposal for the discovery of a natural calendar. Benjamin Stillingfleet (1702–1771), studied and wrote on botany, especially the work on classification by Linnaeus.
8. *Selborne*, pp.60–61. White called the bird a 'grasshopper-lark'. Grant Allen, who edited White's work in 1900, reported that it was in his time known as a grasshopper-warbler.
9. Ted Dadswell, *The Selborne Pioneer: Gilbert White as naturalist and scientist: a re-examination*, Aldershot, Hampshire: Ashgate, 2003.
10. Cited by Dadswell, *op.cit.*, Preface, p.xiv., from Paul G. M. Foster, 'The Gibraltar Correspondence of Gilbert White', *Notes and Queries*, vol. 32 (1985), p.492.
11. Worldham.
12. Headley.
13. Liss.
14. Reigate.

15. Now usually *calcareous*, like or containing calcium carbonate.
16. White's footnote: This spring produced, September 10, 1781, after a severe hot summer, and a preceding dry spring and winter, nine gallons of water in a minute, which is 540 in an hour, and 12,960, or 216 hogsheads, in twenty-four hours, or one natural day. at this time many of the wells failed, and all the ponds in the vales were dry.
17. It is suggested by Grant Allen that this punctuation, which is as given in the first and subsequent editions of White's book, is erroneous: he inserts a comma after 'other', replaces the comma after 'north' with a full stop, and inserts a comma after 'Selborne stream'.
18. White's footnote: The water is hard, being strongly impregnated with lime from the chalk.
19. White's footnote: This soil produces good wheat and clover.
20. *Hirundines*, swallows and similar birds.
21. Mathurin Jacques Brisson, French naturalist, 1723–1806, published his *Ornithologie* in 1760.
22. *Fera naturâ*, belonging to a species accepted as wild even though particular birds may be tame.
23. *Cunabula*, cradle, hence, first abode.
24. *Terebrates*, bores.
25. *Rerum prudentia*, having a prudent nature.
26. *Latebra*, a small spherical mass of white yolk in the centre of the yellow yolk of an egg. White is presumably writing metaphorically in this sentence.
27. *Hybernaculum*, a place where an animal hibernates.
28. *Congeners*, species of the same genus.
29. 29 September.
30. Francis Willughby (1635–1672) was a naturalist and the patron of John Ray (1628–1705), who is regarded as the father of natural history in Britain. Ray sought to develop a natural system of classification of plants and animals based on overall morphology rather than, as in the system of Linnaeus, a single characteristic. Willughby travelled with Ray to Europe to observe and collect specimens and his own (Latin) posthumous book on birds was translated into English by Ray in 1678 as *The Ornithology of Francis Willughby*.
31. White's footnote: The autumn preceding January 1768 was very wet, and particularly the month of September, during which there fell at Lyndon, in the county of Rutland, six inches and a half of rain. And the terrible long frost in 1739–40 set in after a rainy season, and when the springs were very high.
32. Quoted from Virgil, *Aeneid*, II, 755: 'even the silence is frightening'.
33. From the *Georgics I*, line 415. Translation by J. W. MacKail (in Publius Virgilius Maro, *Georgics of Virgil*, Boston & New York: Houghton Mifflin & Co, 1904) is '… to my thinking … their instinct is divine …' L. P. Wilkinson in his *Virgil, The Georgics* (Penguin Books, 1982) renders it '… I believe, that heaven has granted them/ Intelligence, and fate especial foresight'. Renaissance and later writers on gardening and agriculture often looked to the *Georgics*, whose subject-matter is agricultural, for inspiration and even advice. The theme, developed by Virgil, of rural retirement and peaceful toil, free from worries of money and politics, was clearly an ideal important to Gilbert White.
34. *Amusive*, obsolete meanings include deceptive, beguiling, as well as interesting, intriguing.
35. *Dorr*, bumble-bee.
36. *Churn-owl*, night-jar.
37. Hero and Leander, a pair of lovers in Greek mythology, dwelling on opposite sides of the Hellespont. Leander swam each night from Abydos to be with Hero, a priestess of Aphrodite, guided by a light which she placed in her tower at Sestos. One night the light was extinguished in a storm and Leander was drowned, whereupon Hero killed herself by leaping from her tower. The light of the female, wingless, glow-worm (which is in fact a beetle, *Lampyris noctiluca*) attracts the flying male prior to mating.

Imagining England

> I am sensible there be some who slight and despise this sort of learning, and represent it to be a dry, barren, monkish study. I leave such to their dear enjoyments of ignorance and ease. But I dare assure any wise and sober man, that historical antiquities, especially a search into the notices of our own nation, do deserve and will reward the pains of any English student; will make him understand the state of former ages, the constitution of governments, the fundamental reasons of equity and law, the rise and succession of doctrines and opinions, the original of ancient, and the composition of modern tongues, the tenures of property, the maxims of policy, the rites of religion, the characters of virtue and vice, and indeed the nature of mankind.[1]

This proposition was made by White Kennett in 1695, in the introduction to his meticulous annals of the history of the Oxfordshire parish of Ambrosden; it is probably one of the most concise statements of the seventeenth-century antiquarian agenda. It was an agenda which had been motivated all along by the desire to know history: the history of the world; of the nation; of the county; of the parish; of the family. The knowing of these histories might confer a range of benefits: from the satisfaction, for all time, of the knowledge that the nation had been part of the original civilization of the ancient world; down to the possession of particular evidence that, in the immediacy, might prove title to a measure of land, a venerable name, or a traditional privilege. But the knowing of history also offered, as White Kennett succinctly stated, understanding of people and of the fabric of the society and the politics in which they participate. Thus history *per se* had begun to diverge from the mere collecting of historical data, which was the business of the antiquarian.

Yet antiquarianism in England was more than the desire to know and to understand the past: it was a manifestation of an affinity with the past, characterised variously by nostalgia, tradition, custom, and even a degree of identification with the past. Of course this was not an attitude confined to the English, but it had come, probably in the sixteenth century, with both the sense of nationhood under the Tudors and the renaissance awareness of the classical world, to be a particularly keen quality of the English consciousness. It has emerged prominently at intervals: in the post-civil war yearning for the flourishing ages of medieval centuries; in the romanticism of the picturesque and other aesthetic movements of the eighteenth century; in the pre-Raphaelite and the Arts and Crafts movements of the nineteenth century; and in the popular views of rural and village England sought out by tourists in our own times. Each of these was an invented England, but they are all indicative of the place of the past and the landscape of the past in the idea of England.

The elements of the landscape are the natural and built environments and it is in the latter that the past can be seen as well as sensed historically. From standing stones to Roman roads and walls, from half-timbered cottages to Norman cathedrals, the buildings of England are the antiquities which were so assiduously described in the books from which the preceding extracts have been taken. Those antiquaries who investigated the natural world—John Aubrey and Robert Plot, for example—were scientific in their Baconian methodology: they observed, measured, recorded, and thereby, like the genealogical collectors of names and titles amassing historical data, they collected raw material for the understanding of England's plants and animals and its fossils and ancient monuments. And they, too, showed a consciousness of belonging to the countryside which has ever since been part of that popular idea of England as being imbued not only with history but also with outstanding pastoral beauty. The trees, flowers, grasses, and animals; the rivers and lakes, the valleys and mountains; all these are more than biological and geological specimens, but are the components of a whole fabric which has called forth sentiments romantic, bucolic, and nostalgic.

The fascination of the past finds expression in studies of such disciplines as archaeology, local history, and genealogy, which are also means of seeking empathy with people of the past: their popularity is the ongoing counterpart of the fascination with antiquities. At the same time, the scholarly antiquarian agenda has continued, testament to which is the publication of the Victoria County Histories, which began in 1899 and has continued ever since, with over 240 volumes in print so far. The appreciation of the idea of England is altogether informed by England's landscape and England's past. While seeing England now is not the same as seeing England three or four hundred years ago, there is an England which may be imagined still which is perhaps like that distant seventeenth-century vision, and its origins may be discerned in the observations, usually staid and formal, but sometimes spontaneous and lively, made in those times by antiquaries, naturalists, and travellers.

1. White Kennett, Parochial Antiquities attempted in the History of Ambrosden, Burcester, and other adjacent parts in the counties of Oxford and Bucks, Oxford, 1695, Preface, p.xvii. Kennett (1660-1728) studied at Oxford under Anthony Wood, amongst others. He became vicar of the small parish of Ambrosden in 1685, a living which allowed him time for his scholarly and antiquarian pursuits. His clerical career led eventually to his becoming Bishop of Peterborough.

Bibliography

1. SOURCES OF READINGS

Ashmole, Elias, *The Antiquities of Berkshire,* London, E. Curll, 1719

Aubrey, John, *The Natural History of Wiltshire*, edited by John Britton, London: J. B. Nichols and Son for the Wiltshire Topographical Society, 1847, reprinted as *Aubrey's Natural History of Wiltshire*, with an Introduction by K. G. Ponting, Newton Abbot, Devon: David & Charles (Publishers) Limited, 1969

Aubrey, John, *Monumenta Britannica, or A Miscellany of British Antiquities*, edited by John Fowles and annotated by Rodney Legg, Sherborne, Dorset: Dorset Publishing Company, 1980

Aubrey, John, *Remaines of Gentilisme and Judaisme*, edited by John Britten, 1881, reprinted by Kraus Reprint Limited, Liechtenstein, 1967

Borlase, William, *Antiquities Historical and Monumental of the County of Cornwall*, second edition, London, 1769, reprinted with an introduction by P. A. S. Pool and Charles Thomas, Wakefield, West Yorkshire: EP Publishing Limited, 1973

(Bray, William) Anonymous, *A Sketch of a Tour in Derbyshire and Yorkshire*, London: B. White, 1778

Browne, Thomas, *The Works of Sir Thomas Browne*, 5 vols., ed. by Geoffrey Keynes, London: Faber & Faber Limited, 1928

Butcher, Richard, *The survey and antiquitie of the towne of Stamford in the county of Lincolne*, London, 1660, in Francis Peck, *Academia Tertia Anglicana, or, The Antiquarian Annals of Stanford*, London, 1727, reprinted with an introduction by A. Rogers and J. S. Hartley, Wakefield, West Yorkshire: EP Publishing Limited, 1979

Camden, William, *Britannia*, translated by Philemon Holland, London, 1610

Carew, Richard, *The Svrvey of Cornwall,* London, 1602, reprinted as No. 100 of *The English Experience, its record in early printed books published in facsimile*, Amsterdam: Theatrum Orbis Terrarum; New York: Da Capo Press, 1969

Chauncy, Henry, *The Historical Antiquities of Hertfordshire*, second edition, Bishop's Stortford: J. M. Mullinger, 1826; reprinted with an introduction by Carola Oman, Dorking: Kohler and Coombes, 1975. (Original edition, London, 1700)

Defoe, Daniel, *A Tour thro' the Whole Island of Great Britain*, edited by Samuel Richardson, London, 1742, 4 vols., third edition, reprinted New York and London: Garland Publishing, Inc., 1975 (also *A Tour through the Whole Island of Great Britain*, introduced by G. D. H. Cole and D. C. Browning, London: J. M. Dent & Sons Ltd, 1962, 2 vols.)

Drake, Francis, *Eboracum: or, the History and Antiquities of the City of York*, London: W. Bowyer, 1736, reprinted with an Introduction by K. J. Allison, Wakefield, West Yorkshire: EP Publishing, 1978

Drayton, Michael, *The Works of Michael Drayton*, 4 vols., edited by J. William Hebel, Kathleen Tillotson, B. H. Newdigate, and B. E. Juel-Jensen, Oxford: Basil Blackwell, 1931-1941

Dugdale, William, *The Antiquities of Warwickshire Illustrated,* London, 1656

Dugdale, William, *The Antiquities of Warwickshire Illustrated*, edited by William Thomas, London, 1730, reprinted Didsbury, Manchester: E. J. Morten, 1973

Fiennes, Celia, *Through England on a Side Saddle in the time of William and Mary*, edited by Emily Griffiths, 1888, http://www.visionofbritain.org.uk/travellers/index.jsp (accessed May 2007)

Gilpin, William, *Observations, relative chiefly to Picturesque Beauty, Made in the Year 1772, On several Parts of England; particularly the Mountains, and Lakes of Cumberland, and Westmorland*, London: R. Blamire, 1786 (2 vols), reprinted as one volume, *Observations on the Mountains and Lakes of Cumberland and Westmorland* with an introduction by Sutherland Lyall, Richmond, Surrey: Richmond Publishing Co, Ltd., 1973

Gough, Richard, *Human Nature Displayed in the History of Myddle*, with an Introduction by W. G. Hoskins, Fontwell, Sussex: Centaur Press Ltd., 1968

Kennett, White, *Parochial Antiquities attempted in the History of Ambrosden, Burcester, and other adjacent parts in the counties of Oxford and Bucks*, edited by B. Bandinel, Oxford: the Clarendon Press, 1818. (Original edition 1695)

Lambarde, William, *A Perambulation of Kent conteining the description, hystorie, and customes of that shyre* , second edition, London, 1596. (Original edition 1576)

Plot, Robert, *The Natural History of Oxford-Shire*, second edition, Oxford, 1705, facsimile reproduction, Menston, Yorkshire: Scolar Press, 1972. (Original edition, 1677)

Somner, William, *The Antiquities of Canterbury, or, a Survey of that Ancient City, with the Suburbs and the Cathedral*, Second Edition, revised and enlarged by Nicolas Battely, London, 1703, reprinted with an introduction by William Urry, Wakefield, West Yorkshire: EP Publishing Limited, 1977

Smith, William, *Particular Description of* Cheshire, in *The Vale-Royal of England or, The County Palatine of Chester Illustrated*, edited by Daniel King, 1656, reprinted as No. 20 of *The Printed Sources of Western Art*, Portland, Oregon: United Academic, 1972

Stow, John, *A Survay of London*, London, 1598

Tradescant, John, *Musæum Tradescantianum: Or, A Collection of Rarities Preserved at South-Lambeth neer London by John Tradescant,* 1656

Webb, William, *A Description of the City and County Palatine of Chester*, in *The Vale-Royal of England or, The County Palatine of Chester Illustrated*, edited by Daniel King, 1656

Westcote, Thomas , *A View of Devonshire in MDCXXX; with a Pedigree of most of its Gentry*, edited by George Oliver and Pitman Jones, Exeter, 1845

White, Gilbert, *The Natural History and Antiquities of Selborne in the County of Southampton*, London: B. White and Son, 1789, reprinted Menston: Scolar Press, 1972

2. REFERENCE

Early English Books Online (http://eebo.chadwyck.com/home, accessed 2007))

Oxford English Dictionary (http://www.oed.com, accessed 2007)

Oxford Dictionary of National Biography (http://www.oxforddnb.com, accessed 2007)

3. FURTHER READING

Ackroyd, Peter, *Albion: the Origins of the English Imagination*, London: Chatto & Windus, 2002

Andrews, Malcolm, *The Search for the Picturesque: Landscape Aesthetics and Tourism in Britain, 1760-1800*, Aldershot: Scolar Press, 1989

Churton, Tobias, *Magus: The Invisible Life of Elias Ashmole*, Lichfield: Signal Publishing, 2004

Dadswell, Ted, *The Selborne Pioneer: Gilbert White as naturalist and scientist: a re-examination*, Aldershot, Hampshire: Ashgate, 2003

Fiennes, Celia, *The Illustrated Journeys of Celia Fiennes, 1685–c.1712*, edited by Christopher Morris, London & Sydney: Macdonald & Co., 1982 (First Edition 1947)

Foster, Paul G. M., *Gilbert White, Naturalist, Poet, Priest and Scholar (1720–93): a Brief Biography*, Selborne Paper Number One, Selborne: Gilbert White's House & The Oates Museum, 2000

Fussner, Frank: *The Historical Revolution: English Historical Writing and Thought, 1580-1640* , Westport, Connecticut: Greenwood Press, 1976

Hardin, Richard F., *Michael Drayton and the Passing of Elizabethan England*, The University of Kansas Press, 1973

Kendrick, Thomas, *British Antiquity*, London: Methuen, 1950

MacGregor, Arthur (editor), *Tradescant's Rarities: Essays on the Foundation of the Ashmolean Museum, 1683, with a catalogue of the Surviving Early Collections*, Oxford: Clarendon Press, 1983

Mayer, Robert, *History and the Early English Novel*, Cambridge University Press, 1997

McKisack, May, *Medieval History in the Tudor Age*, Oxford: Clarendon Press, 1971

Mendyk, Stan A. E., *'Speculum Britanniae': Regional Study, Antiquarianism, and Science in Britain to 1700*, University of Toronto Press, 1989

Novak, Maximillian E., *Daniel Defoe: Master of Fictions*, Oxford University Press, (first edition 2001)

Parry, Graham, *The Seventeenth Century: the Intellectual and Cultural Context of English Literature,* London, New York: Longman, 1989

Parry, Graham, *The Trophies of Time: English Antiquarians of the Seventeenth Century*, Oxford University Press, 1995

Piggott, Stuart, *Ancient Britons and the Antiquarian Imagination*, London: Thames and Hudson, 1989

Post, Jonathan F. S., *Sir Thomas Browne*, Boston: Twayne, 1987

Shapiro, Barbara, *Probability and Certainty in Seventeenth-Century England*, Princeton University Press, 1983

Sharpe, Kevin, *Sir Robert Cotton, 1586–1631: History and Politics in Early Modern England*, Oxford University Press, 1979

Simmons, Jack, *English County Historians,* Wakefield, West Yorkshire, EP Publishing, 1978

Sweet, Rosemary, *Antiquaries: the Discovery of the Past in Eighteenth-Century Britain*, London: Hambledon & London, 2004

Warnicke, Retha M., *William Lambarde: Elizabethan Antiquary 1536-1601,* London and Chichester: Phillimore, 1973

Woodman, Francis, *The Architectural History of Canterbury Cathedral*, London & Boston: Routledge & Kegan Paul, 1981

Index